A THEORY OF
ACHIEVEMENT MOTIVATION

Edited by

JOHN W. ATKINSON

Professor of Psychology and Research Associate
Survey Research Center
The University of Michigan

NORMAN T. FEATHER

Associate Professor of Psychology
The University of New England
Australia

 ROBERT E. KRIEGER PUBLISHING COMPANY
HUNTINGTON, NEW YORK

ORIGINAL EDITION 1966
REPRINT 1974

Printed and Published by
ROBERT E. KRIEGER PUBLISHING CO., INC.
BOX 542, HUNTINGTON, NEW YORK, 11973

Library of Congress Card Number 00-00000
ISBN 0-88275-166-2

Printed in the United States of America

Library of Congress Cataloging in Publication Data

Atkinson, John William, 1923-   ed.
   A theory of achievement motivation.

   Reprint of the ed. published by Wiley, New York.
   Bibliography: p.
   1. Achievement motivation.   I. Feather, Norman T.,
joint ed. II. Title.
[BF683.A88 1974]   152.5   74-7064
ISBN 0-88275-166-2

Preface

In this book we present a theory of achievement motivation and the studies which so far provide the main body of evidence concerning the validity of its behavioral implications. The theory identifies the mainsprings of action as an individual is confronted with the challenge to achieve and the threat of failure that are both present whenever his ability is put to the test and when there is some degree of uncertainty about whether he will succeed or fail. The theory asserts that a person's motive to achieve (n Achievement), his motive to avoid failure, and his expectation of success in some venture strongly influence the character of his motivation as it is expressed in level of aspiration, preference for risk, willingness to put forth effort and to persist in an activity.

The core of the book is a set of studies accomplished by interacting members of a research seminar at The University of Michigan between 1956 and 1962. Their common effort was supported by a grant from the Ford Foundation for research on personality dynamics. Among the chapters included are the results of six doctoral theses and one senior honors thesis completed between 1958 and 1961. These interrelated studies are supplemented by further work of the same investigators and other contributors who have applied the theory to analysis of the determinative role of achievement motivation in vocational aspiration, social mobility, economic behavior, and the effects of ability grouping of children in schools.

Our intention is to make accessible an orderly arrangement of a number of interrelated studies that are otherwise scattered among scientific journals since 1957 and some new contributions, which comprise one third of the book. We hope to provide an opportunity for more thorough review of evidence and evaluation of the method of study and the adequacy of theory than is possible from shorter, summary reviews of some of the findings that have appeared elsewhere (McClelland, 1961, Chapter 6; Atkinson, 1964, Chapter 9; Atkinson, 1965).

Our focus of interest throughout is on the *contemporaneous* determinants of achievement-oriented activities—the *dynamics* of achievement motivation. This is one important aspect of the broad program of research on achievement motivation that was initiated almost twenty years ago by McClelland and coworkers and was first summarized in *The Achievement Motive* (McClelland, Atkinson, Clark, and Lowell, 1953). More recent books have focused on other problems: the method employed to assess and study individual differences in motivation (Atkinson, 1958a), and the social origins and consequences for society of achievement motivation (McClelland, 1961). The present book is not intended to be an up-to-date summary of all of this work, nor does it purport to review other contemporary viewpoints concerning striving for achievement. Our limited objective is to present for review and appraisal a theory that evolved in the trials and checks of an earlier exploratory phase of research, when the matter of central interest was summarized by a simple question: How are individual differences in strength of *n* Achievement, as assessed by content analysis of imaginative stories, related to overt behavior?

The reader familiar with the earlier works on achievement motivation may find it useful to scan the table of contents for the new and previously unpublished work (Chapters 1, 7, 11, 15, 18, 19) and then to begin with the restatement of theory, review, and critical appraisal of evidence that is presented in the final chapter (Chapter 20). In it he will find discussion in depth of unresolved methodological and theoretical issues and our views concerning new directions suggested in the work to date.

The reader who is less familiar with this work may find it profitable to follow his reading of the introductory chapter (Chapter 1), which outlines the contents of the book, with a perusal of the last major section of the final chapter, "The study of personality and process." In this last section, we construct a more complete picture of the achievement-oriented personality and the failure-threatened personality than will be found in the many detailed empirical findings presented separately in the intervening chapters. Here we present the fruit of our effort to bridge the gap in theory and research between what Cronbach (1957) has called "the two disciplines of scientific psychology"—the one concerned with measurement of individual differences, the other with experimental analysis of basic behavioral process.

Appropriate acknowledgement of financial support for continuations and extensions of the work encouraged by the grant from the Ford Foundation (1956-1962) is made at the beginning of each of the chapters. We are indeed grateful for this support, and also for research grants from the University of New England.

We want to acknowledge with thanks the guidance and criticism provided by members of one or more of six doctoral dissertation committees at the University of Michigan: David Birch, Edward S. Bordin, Dorwin Cartwright, Clyde C. Coombs, John R. French, Jr., Gerald Gurin, William L. Hays, Roger W. Heyns, Daniel Katz, John B. Lansing, Gerhard E. Lenski,

Wilbert J. McKeachie, Warren E. Miller, James N. Morgan, Theodore Newcomb, Warren T. Norman, Max S. Schoeffler, Stanley J. Segal, Joseph Veroff, Seymour Yellin.

The early guidance of Duncan Howie of the University of New England is also gratefully acknowledged.

For help in the clerical and secretarial tasks associated with preparation of the manuscript, we thank Frances (Holland) Ferguson, Camille Buda, Gay Clark, and Bryan Burke.

Permission to reprint selections from books or journals was kindly granted by the following publishers: American Psychological Association, Inc.; American Sociological Association; Duke University Press; The University of Chicago Press; Harper and Row, Publishers, Inc.

JOHN W. ATKINSON
NORMAN T. FEATHER

Ann Arbor and Armidale
January, 1966

Contents

Part I: The Basic Concepts

1 Introduction and Overview   3
by the Editors

2 Motivational Determinants of Risk-Taking Behavior   11
by John W. Atkinson

3 Subjective Probability and Decision under Uncertainty   31
by Norman T. Feather

4 The Study of Persistence   49
by Norman T. Feather

Part II: Aspiration and Persistence

5 Achievement Motive and Test Anxiety Conceived as Motive to Approach Success and Motive to Avoid Failure   75
by John W. Atkinson and George H. Litwin

6 Motivational Correlates of Probability Preferences   93
by Lawrence W. Littig

7 Achievement Motivation, Expectancy of Success, and Risk-Taking Behavior   103
by George H. Litwin

8 The Relationship of Persistence at a Task to Expectation of Success and Achievement-Related Motives   117
by Norman T. Feather

9 Persistence at a Difficult Task with Alternative Task of Intermediate Difficulty   135
by Norman T. Feather

10 Effects of Success and Failure on Level of Aspiration as Related to Achievement Motives   147
by Robert W. Moulton

Part III: Applications and Social Implications

 11   Notes Concerning the Generality of the Theory of Achieve-
      ment Motivation   163
        by John W. Atkinson

 12   Fear of Failure and Unrealistic Vocational Aspiration   169
        by Charles H. Mahone

 13   The Achievement Motive and Differential Occupational
      Mobility in the United States   185
        by Harry J. Crockett, Jr.

 14   The Achievement Motive and Economic Behavior   205
        by James N. Morgan

 15   Motivational Implications of Ability Grouping in Schools   231
        *by Patricia O'Connor, John W. Atkinson, and
        Matina Horner*

Part IV: Critical Problems

 16   Achievement Motive, Test Anxiety, and Subjective Prob-
      ability of Success in Risk-Taking Behavior   251
        by Nathan Brody

 17   The Relationship of Expectation of Success to *n* Achieve-
      ment and Test Anxiety   261
        by Norman T. Feather

 18   The Influence of Testing Conditions on Need for Achieve-
      ment Scores and Their Relationship to Performance Scores   277
        by Charles P. Smith

 19   Neglected Factors in Studies of Achievement-Oriented
      Performance: Social Approval as an Incentive and Per-
      formance Decrement   299
        by John W. Atkinson and Patricia O'Connor

 20   Review and Appraisal   327
        by the Editors

      References   371

      Author Index   383

      Subject Index   387

A THEORY OF ACHIEVEMENT MOTIVATION

PART I

The Basic Concepts

1.

THE EDITORS

Introduction and Overview

This book is a report of research growing out of a project on personality dynamics, sponsored by the Ford Foundation at the University of Michigan from 1956 to 1962. It is also a progress report of a program studying achievement motivation, which was initiated in experiments on projective expression of needs by McClelland and coworkers (McClelland and Atkinson, 1948).

A summary of the initial exploratory phase of research on the effects of individual differences in strength of achievement motivation (or n Achievement, as it is usually called) is presented in *The Achievement Motive* (McClelland, Atkinson, Clark, and Lowell, 1953).

The second phase of work, in which the projective method of assessing human motivation is critically examined and extended to experimental analysis of the effects of other important social motives and their social origins and consequences, is surveyed in *Motives in Fantasy, Action, and Society* (Atkinson, Ed., 1958a). That book, essentially a research handbook, made the method for assessment of motivation readily available for research workers. It ends where this book begins.

Since 1958 research on achievement motivation has taken two important directions; one is primarily concerned with the social origins and molar social consequences of the need for achievement. This direction of inquiry has been guided by David McClelland's elaboration of a hypothesis that the achievement motive is the mainspring of entrepreneurial activity fostering the economic development of a society. He has produced a persuasive collation of relationships between societal indices of n Achievement and economic indices that mark the rise and fall of societies. As systematically elaborated in *The Achieving Society* (McClelland, 1961), this concern with the implications of the psychology of achievement motivation for the social issues of our time constitutes a harbinger of things to come in behavioral science; it begins to define what is expected of a psychology of human motivation, and provides incentive to improve the methods of assessment and study. This concern also spurs us to get on with the basic scientific task of

3

sharpening the psychological theory of motivation, of testing and refining it, and working it into a more useful conceptual tool for solution of significant motivational problems than it is at present. This task requires a continuous, self-corrective dialogue between theoretical concepts born in creative speculation and empirical facts ground out in systematic experimental inquiry; it defines the other important direction of contemporary research on achievement motivation, which is the topic of this book.

The evolution and refinement of a scientific theory involves a seemingly endless series of small steps in experimentation that are highlighted by an occasional giant step. We consider it something of a giant step in the research on achievement motivation to have recovered some basic ideas about striving for success that were advanced in an earlier analysis of the determinants of an individual's level of aspiration (Escalona, 1940; Festinger, 1942b; Lewin, Dembo, Festinger, Sears, 1944). These ideas are discussed in two initial theoretical statements developed quite independently by the editors (Atkinson, 1957 and Feather, 1959a) and are presented as Chapters 2 and 3—the basic concepts of a theory of achievement motivation. The studies which follow all have a common focus. They explore and test implications of the theory, often uncovering stubborn and as yet unsolved problems, often initiating some new method of study, but always throwing some new light on the determinants of an individual's achievement-oriented actions, that is, actions undertaken with full knowledge that skill and competence will be evaluated in relation to some standard of excellence.

The theoretical model of achievement motivation presented in Chapter 2 is similar in general conceptual approach to the resultant valence theory of level of aspiration (Lewin, et al., 1944) and especially in the assumption of an inverse relationship between the incentive value of success at a particular activity and the strength of an individual's expectancy of success (or subjective probability of success) at the activity. Yet the model discussed in Chapter 2 differs from the traditional model of level of aspiration in the precision of its assumptions, and in its emphasis on the role of both relatively general and stable individual differences in personality (motives), and more specific and transient environmental factors (expectations and incentive values) that determine achievement-oriented activities. In this latter respect, the theory of achievement motivation, which focuses on the interaction of personality and immediate environment—as summarized in Lewin's famous programmatic equation $B = (P,E)$—also differs from several other contemporary conceptions of motivation in which the determinative role of an individual's expectations of the consequences of his actions is of paramount importance (Chapter 3).

In its elaboration of the nature of the interaction between stable motives that characterize the personality and immediate situational influences, the theory of achievement motivation represents a step toward conceptual integration of "the two disciplines of scientific psychology" (Cronbach, 1957): one concerned with assessment of individual differences, the other with basic behavioral processes. The potentials of an approach dealing explicitly with the interaction of personality and environmental influences in its analysis of the process of motivation may be appraised by contrasting its treatment of the problem of persistence—the hallmark of purposive behavior—with that of the traditional disciplines of psychology (Chapter 4).

The theory of achievement motivation is a miniature system applied to a specific context, the domain of achievement-oriented activities, which is characterized by the fact that the individual is responsible for the outcome (success or failure), he anticipates unambiguous knowledge of results, and there is some degree of uncertainty or risk (McClelland, 1961). Yet it is our belief that the type of theory that views the strength of an individual's goal-directed tendency as jointly determined by his *motives,* by his *expectations* about the consequences of his actions, and by the *incentive values* of expected consequences will have wider utility when these concepts are applied to analysis of behavior in other kinds of situations directed toward other goals.

Our selection and organization of material was guided by several considerations. First, we sought to identify the central thread of work contributing to the evolution of this theory of achievement motivation by bringing together the reports of research, which, although previously unpublished or scattered among a number of scientific journals of different years, were with several notable exceptions all conceived and executed by interacting members of a research seminar during the Ford Foundation project. The exceptions are the chapters contributed by James N. Morgan and Robert W. Moulton. Second, we sought to approximate chronological order in the presentation of studies so as to convey the evolution of our own understanding of the theory's implications as it was initially stated. Third, we wished to present several explicit applications of the theory to social problems and to place these close to the experimental studies to accentuate the theoretical justification for making the jump from laboratory experiment to the analogous problem in society. Fourth, we aimed at preserving each investigator's interpretive discussion of his intentions and the meaning of his results, for it would be the height of folly to bury any possible clue to one of the many unsettled problems. Finally, we have attempted to allow unsettled problems and potential inadequacies in our methodology to have center stage, even when the data creating the disturbance is relatively weak. We realize that we have already formed the habit of thinking about achievement motivation in a particular way, and conceptual habits are particularly difficult to break. Kenneth Boulding has delicately phrased the problem: "In the scientific ethic the scientist is supposed to be delighted if his own theory is proved wrong. In practice this delight is often moderate." (1964, p. 45.)

The book is organized into four parts. In Part I the basic concepts are introduced. A theory of achievement motivation (originally called "motivational determinants of risk-taking behavior") is presented by Atkinson (Chapter 2). It is treated as an instance of a class of similar theories of motivation (Chapter 3), and is contrasted with traditional approaches to the problem of persistence (Chapter 4) by Feather. These chapters thus serve to introduce the theory and relate it to similar theoretical formulations that have arisen in such different domains as decision making (Edwards, 1954b), clinical psychology and social behavior (Rotter, 1954), and in earlier years in level of aspiration (Lewin, Dembo, Festinger, and Sears, 1944) and maze performance of animals (Tolman, 1932, 1955).

The reader should be as interested as we were in our own initial misreading of the implications of the theory concerning the effect of the tendency to avoid failure on achievement-oriented performance (Chapter 2). Since the mistake was noted and corrected in formulating hypotheses for some of the studies constituting subsequent chapters, we call attention to it and correct it with appropriately labeled comments on the spot.

One of the more novel implications of a consistently applied expectancy $\times$ value-type of theory of motivation is the notion that the anticipation of a *negative* consequence should *always* produce *negative* motivation, that is, a tendency to inhibit activity that is expected to produce the negative consequence. This concept, treated at length in the final chapter, was missed in the initial theoretical statement (Atkinson, 1957), only barely discernible in a somewhat muddled restatement of the theory (Atkinson, 1960, p. 265), but finally expounded fully (Atkinson, 1964, Chapter 9). Science would be something less than a human enterprise if there were not occasions when an investigator failed to understand what a theory is trying to say. This is most likely to happen when an implication of a theory runs counter to an expectation based on intuition or one that is firmly anchored in the habitual scientific mode of thought. The conventional notion that "anxiety about failure" should instigate achievement-oriented actions literally blocked appreciation of the new idea generated by the inherent logic of the theory. This episode provided us with a lesson in learning to heed the implications of a theory, and particularly those that are not especially obvious.

In Part II some of the major hypotheses of the theory are examined in studies of the effects of individual differences in *n* Achievement and anxiety on aspiration, performance, and persistence in achievement-oriented activity. In Chapter 5, Atkinson and Litwin examine the construct validity of both projective and self-report tests of achievement motive and also the Test Anxiety Questionnaire within the context of a study which provides measures of achievement-oriented risk preference (or level of aspiration), level of performance, and persistence in achievement-oriented activity for the same individuals. Littig (Chapter 6) then investigates the influence of achievement-related motivation on gambling preferences more thoroughly than did an earlier exploration by Atkinson, Bastian, Earl, and Litwin (1960). And in Chapter 7 Litwin develops several different measures of preference for intermediate degree of risk, and, in addition, presents evidence concerning a basic assumption of the theory that incentive value of success is a linear inverse function of the subjective probability of success.

In Chapters 8 and 9 Feather extends the method of study to demonstrate differences in the degree to which persons highly motivated to achieve and those anxious about failure persist at an insoluble achievement task in the face of continual failure, as a function of whether they initially believed the task to be easy or very difficult. And in Chapter 10 Moulton presents solid evidence confirming implications of the theory concerning what are traditionally called "typical" and "atypical" shifts in aspiration following success and failure. These studies, perhaps more dramatically than the others, illustrate what it means to assert that motivation is the result of *interaction* between characteristics of personality and immediate environmental influences.

Part III presents some applications and social implications of the theory of achievement motivation. Four studies dealing with the effects of achievement motivation on aspiration, performance, and persistence in the achievement-oriented activities of everyday life are preceded by some comments by Atkinson (Chapter 11) that were originally distributed informally as mimeographed notes in the spring of 1959. These notes concern the applicability of the basic concepts of the theory of achievement motivation to social behavior and to the question of child-rearing practices. In Chapter 12, Mahone investigates the relationships between an individual's need to achieve and his anxiety about failure and the realism of his vocational aspiration. Crockett (Chapter 13), using extensive national survey data, which included—for the first time—a thematic apperceptive test of motivation (Veroff, Atkinson, Gurin, and Feld, 1960), examines differential occupational mobility in the United States in relation to the measure of achievement motivation. In Chapter 14, Morgan, also using survey data, considers economic behavior of individuals in relation to a novel measure of achievement motive suggested by the theory. And finally, O'Connor, Atkinson, and Horner (Chapter 15) consider implications of the theory of achievement motivation for the educational problem of whether children should be grouped in classes that are homogeneous or heterogeneous in ability.

Part III, in brief, extends interest to everyday behavioral issues: attempting to motivate school children; setting one's sight on a career goal; working hard and persistently to move up the occupational ladder, which conventionally defines success in life; working for more income, saving it, and planning for the education of children. We attempt to show how the theory of achievement motivation may aid in conceptual analysis and study of these and other important social problems.

Part IV, the concluding section, includes studies that are addressed to one or another critical aspect of the theory or the methods employed in studies of achievement motivation. Brody, in Chapter 16, and Feather, in Chapter 17, investigate the possibility that an individual's expectation of success (one of the determinants of motivation) may not be independent of his motives (another of the determinants of motivation). Each presents a different theoretical interpretation of results bearing on this question. In Chapter 18 Smith considers the influence of testing conditions on the relationship between n Achievement and achievement-oriented performance, once more confronting the problem of the confounding influence of other motives and incentives on achievement-oriented performance that was raised in studies by Atkinson and Reitman (1956) and by Reitman (1960). He also critically examines assumptions made in thematic apperceptive assessment of achievement motivation. Atkinson and O'Connor (Chapter 19) are disappointed to find that an achievement risk-preference scale that appears promising does not work as a substitute measure of achievement motivation; but, more important, they are led by unanticipated results to consideration of some neglected factors in the study of achievement-oriented performance: social approval as an incentive and the possibility of performance decrement when motivation to perform well becomes very intense. Other results obtained by Smith (1963) also suggest the need for caution concerning presumptions about the range of conditions to which implications of the theory (stated for the ideal case) directly apply and the need for systematic study of confounding variables.

Each of these studies is open-ended and a reminder that our present conceptual scheme, while a more heuristic guide to analysis of the problems of achievement motivation than any before, should not be taken as a settled creed. In Chapter 20 we elaborate on this general appraisal of the contemporary theory of achievement motivation, identify the implications of this work for a theory of motivation, and underscore some directions for future research. This final chapter contains a summary restatement of the theory and an illustration of how one may derive from it a descriptive picture of an *achievement-oriented* personality and a *failure-threatened* personality.

2.

JOHN W. ATKINSON

Motivational Determinants
of Risk-Taking Behavior

There are two problems of behavior which any theory of motivation must come to grips with. They may finally reduce to one; but it will simplify the exposition which follows to maintain the distinction in this paper. The first problem is to account for an individual's selection of one path of action among a set of possible alternatives. The second problem is to account for the amplitude or vigor of the action tendency once it is initiated, and for its tendency to persist for a time in a given direction. This paper will deal with these questions in a conceptual framework suggested by research which has used thematic apperception to assess individual differences in strength of achievement motivation (Atkinson, 1954; McClelland, 1955; McClelland, Atkinson, Clark, and Lowell, 1953).

The problem of selection arises in experiments which allow the individual to choose a task among alternatives that differ in difficulty (level of aspiration). The problem of accounting for the vigor of response arises in studies which seek to relate individual differences in strength of motivation to the level of performance when response output at a particular task is the dependent variable. In treating these two problems, the discussion will be constantly focused on the relationship of achievement motivation to risk-taking behavior, an important association uncovered by McClelland (1955, 1961) in the investigation of the role of achievement motivation in entrepreneurship and economic development.

Earlier studies have searched for a theoretical principle which would explain the relationship of strength of motive, as inferred from thematic apperception, to overt goal-directed performance. The effect of situation cues (e.g., of particular instructions) on this relationship was

Reprinted and abridged by permission of the author and the American Psychological Association from the *Psychological Review*, 1957, **64**, 359–372.

detected quite early (Atkinson, 1950, 1953), and subsequent experiments have suggested a theoretical formulation similar to that presented by Tolman (1955) and Rotter (1954). It has been proposed that *n* Achievement scores obtained from thematic apperception are indices of individual differences in the strength of achievement motive, conceived as a relatively stable disposition to strive for achievement or success. This motive-disposition is presumed to be latent until aroused by situation cues which indicate that some performance will be instrumental to achievement. The strength of *aroused* motivation to achieve as manifested in performance has been viewed as a function of both the strength of motive and the *expectancy* of goal-attainment aroused by situation cues. This conception has provided a fairly adequate explanation of experimental results to date, and several of its implications have been tested (Atkinson, 1954; Atkinson and Reitman, 1956).

The similarity of this conception to the expectancy principle of performance developed by Tolman, which also takes account of the effects of a third variable, *incentive,* suggested the need for experiments to isolate the effects on motivation of variations in strength of expectancy of success and variations in the incentive value of particular accomplishments. The discussion which follows was prompted by the results of several exploratory experiments. It represents an attempt to state explicitly how individual differences in the strength of achievement-related motives influence behavior in competitive achievement situations. . . .

Three variables require definition and, ultimately, independent measurement. The three variables are *motive, expectancy,* and *incentive*. Two of these—expectancy and incentive—are similar to variables presented by Tolman (1955) and Rotter (1954). An expectancy is a cognitive anticipation, usually aroused by cues in a situation, that performance of some act will be followed by a particular consequence. The strength of an expectancy can be represented as the subjective probability of the consequence, given the act.

The incentive variable has been relatively ignored, or at best crudely defined, in most research. It represents the relative attractiveness of a specific goal that is offered in a situation, or the relative unattractiveness of an event that might occur as a consequence of some act. Incentives may be manipulated experimentally as, for example, when amount of food (reward) or amount of shock (punishment) is varied in research with animals.

The third variable in this triumvirate—motive—is here conceived differently than, for example, in the common conception of motivation as nondirective but energizing *drive* (Brown, 1953, 1961). A motive is conceived as a disposition to strive for a certain kind of satisfaction, as a capacity for satisfaction in the attainment of a certain class of incentives. The names given motives—such as achievement, affiliation, power—are really names of classes of incentives which produce essentially the same kind of experience of satisfaction: pride in accomplishment, or the sense of belonging and being warmly received by others, or the feeling of being in control and influential. (See Atkinson, 1958c.) McClelland (1951, pp. 341–352 and 441–458; McClelland, Atkinson, Clark, and Lowell, 1953) has presented arguments to support the conception of motives as relatively general and stable characteristics of the personality which have their origins in early childhood experience. The idea that a motive may be considered a *capacity for satisfaction* is suggested by Winterbottom's finding that children who are strong in achievement motive are rated by teachers as deriving more pleasure from success than children who are weak in achievement motive. (McClelland, Atkinson, Clark, and Lowell, 1953; Winterbottom, 1953, 1958.)

The general aim of one class of motives, usually referred to as appetites or approach tendencies, is to maximize satisfaction of some kind. The achievement motive is considered a disposition to approach success.

The aim of another class of motives is to minimize pain. These have been called aversions, or avoidant tendencies. An avoidance motive represents the individual's capacity to experience pain in connection with certain kinds of negative consequences of acts. The motive to avoid failure is considered a disposition to avoid failure and/or a capacity for experiencing shame and humiliation as a consequence of failure.

The Principle of Motivation. The strength of motivation to perform some act is assumed to be a multiplicative function of the strength of the motive, the expectancy (subjective probability) that the act will have as a consequence the attainment of an incentive, and the value of the incentive: Motivation $= f$ (Motive $\times$ Expectancy $\times$ Incentive). This formulation corresponds to Tolman's (1955) analysis of performance except, perhaps, in the conception of a motive as a relatively stable disposition. When both motivation to approach and motivation to avoid are simultaneously aroused, the resultant motivation is the algebraic summation of approach and avoidance. The act which is performed among a set of alternatives is the act for which the resultant motivation is most positive. The magnitude of response and the persistence of behavior are functions of the strength of motivation to perform the act relative to the strength of motivation to perform competing acts.

Recent experiments (Atkinson and Reitman, 1956) have helped to clarify one problem concerning the relationship between measures of the strength of a particular motive (*n* Achievement) and performance. Performance is positively related to the strength of a particular motive only when an expectancy of satisfying that motive through performance has been aroused, and when expectancies of satisfying other motives through the same action have not been sufficiently aroused to confound the simple relationship. This is to say that when expectancies of attaining several different kinds of incentives are equally *salient* in a situation, the determination of motivation to perform an act is very complex. Performance is then overdetermined in the sense that its strength is now a function of the several different kinds of motivation which have been aroused. The *ideal situation* for showing the relationship between the strength of a particular motive and behavior is one in which the only *reason* for acting is to satisfy that motive.

The theoretical formulation which follows pertains to such an *ideal achievement-related situation,* which is at best only approximated in actual experimentation or in the normal course of everyday life. The discussion will deal only with the effects of the two motives, to achieve and to avoid failure, normally aroused whenever performance is likely to be evaluated against some standard of excellence.

Behavior Directed Toward Achievement and Away from Failure. The problem of selection is confronted in the level-of-aspiration situation where the individual must choose among tasks which differ in degree of difficulty. The problem of accounting for the vigor of performance arises in the situation which will be referred to as *constrained performance.* Here there is no opportunity for the individual to choose his own task. He is simply given a task to perform. He must, of course, decide to perform the task rather than to leave the situation. There *is* a problem of selection. In referring to this situation as constrained performance, it is the writer's intention to deal only with those instances of behavior in which motivation for the alternative of leaving the situation is less positive or more negative than for performance of the task that is presented. Hence, the individual does perform the task that is given. The level of performance is the question of interest.

Elaboration of the implications of the multiplicative combination of motive, expectancy, and incentive, as proposed to account for strength of motivation, will be instructive if we can find some reasonable basis for assigning numbers to the different variables. The strength of expectancy can be represented as a subjective probability ranging from 0 to 1.00. But the problem of defining the positive incentive value of a particular accomplishment and the negative incentive value of a particular failure is a real stickler.

In past discussions of level of aspiration, Escalona (1940) and Festinger (1942b; see Lewin, Dembo, Festinger, and Sears, 1944) have assumed that, within limits, the attractiveness of success is a positive function of the difficulty of the task, and that the unattractiveness of failure is a negative function of difficulty, when the type of activity is held constant. The author will go a few steps farther with these ideas, and assume that degree of difficulty can be inferred from the subjective probability of success P_s. The task an individual finds difficult is one for which his subjective probability of success P_s is very low. The task an individual finds easy is one for which his subjective probability of success P_s is very high. Now we are in a position to make simple assumptions about the incentive values of success or failure at a particular task. Let us assume that the incentive value of success I_s is a positive linear function of difficulty. If so, the value $1 - P_s$ can represent I_s, the incentive value of success. When P_s is high (e.g., .90), an easy task, I_s is low (e.g., .10). When P_s is low (e.g., .10), a difficult task, I_s is high (e.g., .90). The negative incentive value of failure I_f can be taken as $-P_s$. When P_s is high (e.g., .90), as in confronting a very easy task, the sense of humiliation accompanying failure is also very great (e.g., $-.90$). However, when P_s is low (e.g., .10), as in confronting a very difficult task, there is little embarrassment in failing (e.g., $-.10$). We assume, in other words, that the (negative) incentive value of failure I_f is a negative linear function of difficulty.

It is of some importance to recognize the dependence of incentive values intrinsic to achievement and failure upon the subjective probability of success. One cannot anticipate the thrill of a great accomplishment if, as a matter of fact, one faces what seems a very easy task. Nor does an individual experience only a minor sense of pride after some extraordinary feat against what seemed to him overwhelming odds. The implications of the scheme which follows rest heavily upon the assumption of such a dependence.

In Table 1, values of 1 have been arbitrarily assigned to the achievement motive M_S and the motive to avoid failure M_{AF}. Table 1 contains the strength of motivation to approach success $(M_S \times P_s \times I_s)$ and motivation to avoid failure $(M_{AF} \times P_f \times I_f)$ through performance of nine different tasks labeled A through I. The tasks differ in degree of difficulty as inferred from the subjective probability of success (P_s). The incentive values of success and failure at each of the tasks have been calculated directly from the assumptions that incentive value of success equals $1 - P_s$ and that incentive value of failure equals $- P_s$; and P_s and P_f are assumed to add to 1.00.

Table 1

Aroused motivation to achieve (approach) and to avoid failure (avoidance) as a joint function of motive (M), expectancy (P), and incentive (I), where $I_s = (1 - P_s)$ and $I_f = (-P_s)$

	Motivation to Achieve				Motivation to Avoid Failure				Resultant Motivation
	$M_s \times$	$P_s \times$	$I_s =$	Ap-proach	$M_{AF} \times$	$P_f \times$	$I_f =$	Avoid-ance	(Approach—Avoidance)
Task A	1	.10	.90	.09	1	.90	−.10	−.09	0
Task B	1	.20	.80	.16	1	.80	−.20	−.16	0
Task C	1	.30	.70	.21	1	.70	−.30	−.21	0
Task D	1	.40	.60	.24	1	.60	−.40	−.24	0
Task E	1	.50	.50	.25	1	.50	−.50	−.25	0
Task F	1	.60	.40	.24	1	.40	−.60	−.24	0
Task G	1	.70	.30	.21	1	.30	−.70	−.21	0
Task H	1	.80	.20	.16	1	.20	−.80	−.16	0
Task I	1	.90	.10	.09	1	.10	−.90	−.09	0

Table 1 may be considered an extension of ideas presented in the *resultant valence* theory of level of aspiration by Escalona and Festinger (see Lewin, Dembo, Festinger, and Sears, 1944). The present formulation goes beyond their earlier proposals (*a*) in making specific assumptions regarding the incentive values of success and failure, and (*b*) in stating explicitly how individual differences in strength of achievement motive and motive to avoid failure influence motivation.[1]

When the Achievement Motive Is Stronger $(M_S > M_{AF})$. The right-hand column of Table 1 shows the resultant motivation for each of the tasks

[1] In the resultant valence theory of level of aspiration, the resultant force (f^*) for a particular level of difficulty equals probability of success (P_s) times valence of success (Va_s) minus probability of failure (P_f) times valence of failure (Va_f). It is assumed that the valence of a goal $[Va(G)]$ depends partly on the properties of the activity and specific goal (G) and partly on the state of need $[t(G)]$ of the person, $[Va(G) = F(G,t \ (G)]$ (Lewin, 1951, p. 273). In the present conception, the relative rewarding or punishing properties of specific goals (i.e., incentive) and the more general disposition of the person toward a class of incentives (i.e., his motive) are given independent status.

in this special case where achievement motive and motive to avoid failure are equal in strength. In every case there is an approach-avoidance conflict with resultant motivation equal to 0. This means that if the achievement motive were stronger than the motive to avoid failure—for example, if we assigned M_S a value of 2—the resultant motivation would become positive for each of the tasks and its magnitude would be the same as in the column labeled *Approach*. Let us therefore consider only the strength of approach motivation for each of the tasks, to see the implications of the model for the person in whom the need for achievement is stronger than his disposition to avoid failure.

One thing is immediately apparent. Motivation to achieve is strongest when uncertainty regarding the outcome is greatest, i.e., when P_s equals .50. If the individual were confronted with all of these tasks and were free to set his own goal, he should choose Task E where P_s is .50, for this is the point of maximum approach motivation. The strength of motivation to approach decreases as P_s increases from .50 to near certainty of success $(P_s = .90)$, and it also decreases as P_s decreases from .50 to near certainty of failure $(P_s = .10)$.

If this person were to be confronted with a single task in what is here called the constrained performance situation, we should expect him to manifest strongest motivation in the performance of a task of intermediate difficulty where P_s equals .50. If presented either more difficult tasks or easier tasks, the strength of motivation manifested in performance should be lower. The relationship between strength of motivation as expressed in performance level and expectancy of success at the task, in other words, should be described by a bell-shaped curve.

When the Motive to Avoid Failure Is Stronger ($M_{AF} > M_S$). Let us now ignore the strength of approach motivation and tentatively assign it a value of 0, in order to examine the implications of the model for any case in which the motive to avoid failure is the stronger motive. The resultant motivation for each task would then correspond to the values listed in the column labeled *Avoidance*.

What should we expect of the person in whom the disposition to avoid failure is stronger than the motive to achieve? It is apparent at once that the resultant motivation for every task would be negative for him. This person should want to avoid all of the tasks. Competitive achievement situations are unattractive to him. If, however, he is constrained (e.g., by social pressures) and asked to set his level of aspiration, he should *avoid* tasks of intermediate difficulty $(P_s = .50)$ where the arousal of anxiety about failure is greatest. He should choose either the easiest $(P_s = .90)$ or the most difficult task $(P_s = .10)$. The strength of avoidant motivation is weakest at these two points.

In summary, the person in whom the achievement motive is stronger should set his level of aspiration in the intermediate zone where there is moderate risk. To the extent that he has any motive to avoid failure, this means that he will voluntarily choose activities that *maximize* his own anxiety about failure! On the other hand, the person in whom the motive to avoid failure is stronger should select either the easiest of the alternatives or should be extremely speculative and set his goal where there is virtually no chance for success. These are activities which *minimize* his anxiety about failure.

How does the more fearful person behave when offered only a specific task to perform? He can either perform the task or leave the field. If he chooses to leave the field, there is no problem. But if he is constrained, as he must be to remain in any competitive achievement situation, he will stay at the task and presumably work at it. But how hard will he work at it? He is motivated to avoid failure, and when constrained, there is only one path open to him to avoid failure—success at the task he is presented. So we expect him to manifest the strength of his motivation to avoid failure in performance of the task. He, too, in other words, should *try hardest*[2] when P_s is .50 and less hard when the chance of winning is either greater or less. The 50–50 alternative is the last he would choose if allowed to set his own goal, but once constrained he must try hard to avoid the failure which threatens him. Not working at all will guarantee failure of the task. Hence, the thought of not working at all should produce even stronger avoidant motivation than that aroused by the task itself.

In other words, irrespective of whether the stronger motive is to achieve or to avoid failure, the strength of motivation to perform a task when no alternatives are offered and when the individual is constrained should be greatest when P_s is .50. This is the condition of greatest uncertainty regarding the outcome. But when there are alternatives which differ in difficulty, the choice of level of aspiration by persons more disposed to avoid failure is diametrically opposite to that of persons more disposed to seek success. The person more motivated to achieve should prefer a moderate risk. His level of aspiration will fall at the point where his positive motivation is strongest, at the point

[2] I do not mean to exclude the possibility that the very anxious person may suffer a performance decrement due to the arousal of some "task-irrelevant" avoidant responses, as proposed in the interpretation of research which has employed the Mandler-Sarason Measure of Test Anxiety (Mandler and Sarason, 1952).

where the odds seem to be 50–50. The fearful person, on the other hand, must select a task even though all the alternatives are threatening to him. He prefers the least threatening of the available alternatives: either the task which is so easy he cannot fail, or the task which is so difficult that failure would be no cause for self-blame and embarrassment.

(*Editors' Note:* The two preceding paragraphs and other sections of this 1957 statement of theory contain several grossly misleading conjectures about the effect of motivation to avoid failure on the level of performance. The misleading ideas, which clearly depart from the inherent logic of the theory as stated, were soon discovered in the course of designing some of the experiments reported in later chapters. The basic error was in supposing that motivation to avoid failure ($M_{AF} \times P_f \times I_f$) might sometimes function to instigate (or excite) achievement-oriented performance. We wish to call the reader's attention to this misleading departure from what the theory actually implies. We shall anticipate, in other words, the clarification of the theory brought about by several of the studies designed to test it (see, particularly, Chapters 4, 5, 8).

The *positive* product of $M_s \times P_s \times I_s$, which is called motivation to achieve or motivation to approach success, is interpreted as a tendency to undertake an activity that is expected to lead to success. The *negative* product of $M_{AF} \times P_f \times I_f$, called motivation to avoid failure, must therefore be consistently interpreted as a tendency to *avoid* undertaking an activity that is expected to lead to failure. Motivation to avoid failure should *always* be conceived as inhibitory in character. It specifies what activities a person is not likely to undertake, not what activities he is likely to undertake. This avoidant tendency *always* opposes, resists, or dampens the influence of motivation to achieve success and extrinsic positive motivational tendencies to undertake some task. This function is clearly apparent in the conception of Resultant Motivation as the algebraic sum of Approach and Avoidance tendencies as shown in Table 1. It is also clearly apparent when one asserts that an individual in whom $M_{AF} > M_s$ will not undertake an achievement-oriented activity at all unless constrained by some other extrinsic source of positive motivation (e.g., the need for social approval).

Given this concept of a tendency to inhibit (i.e., to avoid) performance of actions that are expected to lead to failure, it follows that the person in whom $M_{AF} > M_s$ should *always* resist achievement-oriented activity and that his resistance will be greatest when P_s is .50. The theory does not imply, as was erroneously concluded in 1957 in the preceding paragraphs, that such a person would "try hardest" when P_s is .50, perhaps only to suffer a performance decrement because he is anxious; quite the contrary. The theory implies that the person in whom $M_{AF} > M_S$ should *always* suffer a decrement in the final strength of achievement-oriented tendencies and the greatest decrement when P_s is .50, because extrinsic motivation to undertake the task is opposed by the greatest inhibitory tendency when P_s is .50. This weakening of the total motivation to undertake an achievement-oriented activity should normally produce a decrement in the level of performance (but see Chapter 19 for a possible exception). Achievement-oriented activity should be completely depressed (i.e., not undertaken at all, when motivation to avoid failure is stronger than the positive motivation to undertake an activity. The latter is attributable to motivation to achieve plus extrinsic sources of positive motivation. This initially elusive conception of how motivation to avoid failure influences behavior is developed fully in Atkinson (1964) and in a contemporary restatement of the theory given in the concluding chapter.)

The tendency for anxious persons to set either extremely high or very low aspirations has been noted over and over again in the literature on level of aspiration (Lewin, Dembo, Festinger, and Sears, 1944). Typically, *groups* of persons for whom the inference of greater anxiety about failure seems justified on the basis of some personality assessment show a much greater variance in level of aspiration than persons whose motivation is inferred to be more normal or less anxious. When the details of behavior are examined, it turns out that they are setting their aspiration level either *defensively* high or *defensively* low.

Without further assumptions, the theory of motivation, which has been presented when applied to competitive-achievement activity, implies that the relationship of constrained performance to expectancy of goal-attainment should take the bell-shaped form shown in Figure 1, whether the predominant motive is to achieve or to avoid failure (see Editors' Note, p. 19). Further, the theory leads to the prediction of exactly opposite patterns for setting the level of aspiration when the predominant motivation is approach and when it is avoidant, as shown in Figure 2.

Both of these hypotheses have been supported in recent experiments. The writer (Atkinson, 1958b) offered female college students a modest monetary prize for good performance at two 20-minute tasks. The probability of success was varied by instructions which informed the subject of the number of persons with whom she was in competition

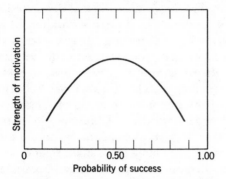

Figure 1   Strength of motivation to achieve
or to avoid failure as a function of the subjective probability of success (i.e., the difficulty of the task).

and the number of monetary prizes to be given. The stated probabilities were 1/20, 1/3, 1/2, and 3/4. The level of performance was higher
at the intermediate probabilities than at the extremes for subjects having high thematic apperceptive *n* Achievement scores, and also for
subjects who had low *n* Achievement scores, presumably a more
fearful group.[3]

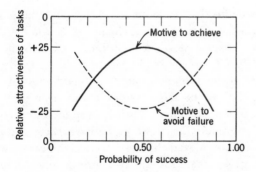

Figure 2   Relative attractiveness of tasks which
differ in subjective probability of success (i.e., in
difficulty). The avoidance curve has been inverted
to show that very difficult and very easy tasks
arouse less fear of failure and hence are less unattractive than moderately difficult tasks.

[3] New evidence has been presented by French and Lesser (1964) and Lesser, Krawitz,
and Packard (1963) concerning the circumscribed conditions under which TAT *n*

McClelland (1958b) has shown the diametrically opposite tendencies in choice of level of aspiration in studies of children in kindergarten and in the third grade. One of the original level-of-aspiration experiments, the ring-toss experiment, was repeated with five-year-olds, and a nonverbal index of the strength of achievement motive was employed. Children who were high in *n* Achievement more frequently set their level of aspiration in the intermediate range of difficulty. They took more shots from a modest distance. Children who were low in *n* Achievement showed a greater preponderance of choices at the extreme levels of difficulty. They more often stood right on top of the peg or stood so far away that success was virtually impossible. The same difference between high and low *n* Achievement groups was observed on another task with children in the third grade. McClelland views these results as consistent with his theoretical argument concerning the role of achievement motivation in entrepreneurship and economic development (1955). He has called attention to the relationship between achievement motivation and an interest in enterprise which requires moderate or calculated risks, rather than very safe or highly speculative undertakings.

In an experiment designed for another purpose, Clark, Teevan, and Ricciuti (1956) have presented results with college students comparable to those of McClelland. Immediately before a final examination in a college course, students were asked a series of questions pertaining to grade expectations, affective reactions to grades, and the grades they would *settle for* if excused from taking the exam. A number of indices were derived from responses to these questions, by which the students were classified as: *hopeful of success*, i.e., if the *settle-for* grade was near the maximum grade the student thought he could possibly achieve; *fearful of failure*, i.e., if the *settle-for* grade was near the minimum grade the student thought he might possibly drop to; and *intermediate*, i.e., if the *settle-for* grade fell somewhere between these two extremes. Previously obtained *n* Achievement scores were significantly higher for the *intermediate* group than for the two groups who set either extremely high or low levels of aspiration.

In terms of the model presented in Table 1, the two extreme pat-

---

Achievement scores yield valid indication of the strength of motivation in female college students. The earlier assumption of the validity of the scores of the females *S*s now seems unwarranted. The average level of performance of all female *S*s was highest when P_s was .50. This result is consistent with the theory if it can be assumed that on the average M_S is stronger than M_{AF} in a representative sample of college women. (The Editors.)

terns of aspirant behavior which were designated *hope of success* and *fear of failure* by Clark, et al., are to be considered two *phenotypically* dissimilar alternatives that are *genotypically* similar. That is, they both function to avoid or reduce anxiety for the person in whom the motive to avoid failure is stronger than the motive to achieve.

A question may arise concerning the legitimacy of inferring relatively stronger motive to avoid failure from a low *n* Achievement score in thematic apperception. The inference seems justified on several counts. First, the kind of learning experience which is thought to contribute to the development of a positive motive to achieve (McClelland, 1951; Winterbottom, 1958) seems incompatible with the kind of experience which would contribute to the development of an avoidant motive. . . . Second, even if it is assumed that high and low *n* Achievement groups may be equal in the disposition to be fearful of failure, the fact that one group does not show evidence of a strong motive to achieve (the group with low *n* Achievement scores) suggests that fear of failure should be *relatively* stronger in that group than in the group which does show evidence of strong *n* Achievement (high *n* Achievement scores). Finally, Raphelson (1956) has presented evidence that *n* Achievement, as measured in thematic apperception, is *negatively* related to both scores on the Mandler-Sarason Scale of Test Anxiety and a psychogalvanic index of manifest anxiety obtained in a test situation. Test anxiety scores and the psychogalvanic index of manifest anxiety were *positively* correlated, as they should be if each is an effective measure of fear aroused in a competitive situation.[4] . . .

The details of the exploratory experiments suggest that one further assumption be made. In both experiments, the high *n* Achievement groups showed evidence of maximum motivation when the observed or stated probability of success was approximately .33. At this point, the high *n* Achievement group showed the highest level of constrained performance. And this point was most favored by the high *n* Achievement group in setting level of aspiration in the McClelland experiment. The assumption to be made seems a reasonable one: the relative strength of a motive influences the subjective probability of the consequence consistent with that motive, i.e., biases it upwards. In other words, the stronger the achievement motive relative to the motive to avoid failure, the higher the subjective probability of success, given

[4] More recent evidence, presented in subsequent chapters, suggests that the two motives are uncorrelated among college men. This means that resultant achievement motivation, and hence also preference for intermediate risk, will be weaker when *n* Achievement is low, even though a low *n* Achievement score may not imply that $M_{AF} > M_S$. (The Editors.)

stated odds. The stronger the motive to avoid failure relative to the achievement motive, the higher the subjective probability of failure, given stated odds or any other objective basis for inferring the strength of expectancy. Some evidence from two earlier studies is pertinent. When subjects stated the score that they *expected* to make on a test with very ambiguous or conflicting cues from past performance (Mc-Clelland, Atkinson, Clark, and Lowell, 1953, p. 247) or when faced with a novel task at which they had no experience (Pottharst, 1955), the stated level of *expectation* was positively related to *n* Achievement. The biasing effect of the motive on subjective probability should diminish with repeated learning experience in the specific situation.

When this assumption is made, the point of maximum motivation to achieve now occurs where the stated (objective) odds are somewhat *lower* than .50; and the point of maximum motivation to avoid failure occurs at a point somewhat higher than stated odds of .50, as shown in Figure 3. The implications of this assumption for constrained performance in somewhat novel situations are evident in the figure. When the achievement motive is stronger than the motive to avoid failure, there should be a tendency for stronger motivation to be expressed in performance when the objective odds are long, i.e., below .50. When the motive to avoid failure is stronger than the achievement motive, there should be greater motivation expressed when the objective odds are short, i.e., above .50 (see Editors' Note, p. 19).

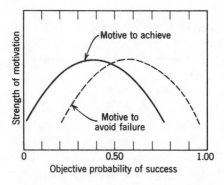

Figure 3   Strength of motivation to achieve and to avoid failure as a function of the *objective* probability of success. It is assumed that the subjective probability of the consequence consistent with the stronger motive is biased upwards.

The Effects of Success and Failure. Let us return to the model and ask, "What are the effects of success and failure on the level of motivation?" We may refer back to Table 1 to answer this question. First, let us consider the effects of success or failure on the level of motivation in a person whose motive to achieve is stronger than his motive to avoid failure. In the usual level-of-aspiration situation, he should initially set his goal where P_s equals .50. In Table 1, this is Task E. If he succeeds at the task, P_s should increase. And, assuming that the effects of success and failure generalize to similar tasks, the P_s at Task D, which was initially .40, should increase toward .50. On the next trial, P_s at Task E is now greater than .50, and P_s at Task D now approaches .50. The result of this change in P_s is diminished motivation to achieve at the old task, E, and increased motivation to achieve at Task D, *an objectively more difficult task*. The observed level of aspiration should increase in a step-like manner following success, because there has been a change in motivation.

A further implication of the change in strength of motivation produced by the experience of success is of great consequence: given a single, very difficult task (e.g., $P_s = .10$), the effect of continued success in repeated trials is first a gradual increase in motivation as P_s increases to .50, followed by a gradual decrease in motivation as P_s increases further to the point of certainty ($P_s = 1.00$). Ultimately, as P_s approaches 1.00, satiation or loss of interest should occur. The task no longer arouses any motivation at all. Why? Because the subjective probability of success is so high that the incentive value is virtually zero. Here is the clue to understanding how the achievement motive can remain insatiable while satiation can occur for a particular line of activity. The strength of motive can remain unchanged, but interest in a particular task can diminish completely. Hence, when free to choose, the person who is stronger in achievement motive should always look for new and more difficult tasks as he masters old problems. If constrained, the person with a strong achievement motive should experience a gradual loss of interest in his work. If the task is of intermediate difficulty to start with ($P_s = .50$), or is definitely easy ($P_s > .50$), his interest should begin to wane after the initial experience of success.

But what of the effect of failure on the person who is more highly motivated to achieve than to avoid failure? Once more we look at the *Approach* column of Table 1. If he has chosen Task E ($P_s = .50$) to start with and fails at it, the P_s is reduced. Continued failure will mean that soon Task F (formerly $P_s = .60$) will have a P_s near .50. He should shift his interest to this task, which was *objectively less difficult* in the initial ordering of tasks. This constitutes what has been called a lowering of the level of aspiration. He has moved to the easier task as a consequence of failure.

What is the effect of continued failure at a single task? If the initial task is one that appeared relatively easy to the subject (e.g., $P_s = .80$) and he fails, his motivation should increase! The P_s will drop toward .70, but the incentive value or attractiveness of the task will increase. Another failure should increase his motivation even more. This will continue until the P_s has dropped to .50. Further failure should then lead to a gradual weakening of motivation as P_s decreases further. In other words, the tendency of persons who are relatively strong in achievement motive to persist at a task in the face of failure is probably attributable to the relatively high subjective probability of success, initially. Hence, failure has the effect of increasing the strength of their motivation, at least for a time. Ultimately, however, interest in the task will diminish if there is continued failure. If the initial task is perceived by the person as very difficult to start with ($P_s < .50$), motivation should begin to diminish with the first failure.

Let us turn now to the effect of success and failure on the motivation of the person who is more strongly disposed to be fearful of failure. If the person in whom the motive to avoid failure is stronger has chosen a very difficult task in setting his level of aspiration (e.g., Task A where $P_s = .10$) and succeeds, P_s increases and his motivation *to avoid* the task is paradoxically increased! It would almost make sense for him deliberately to fail, in order to keep from being faced with a stronger threat on the second trial. If there are more difficult alternatives, he should raise his level of aspiration to avoid anxiety! Fortunately for this person, his strategy (determined by the nature of his motivation) in choosing a very difficult task to start with protects him from this possibility, because P_s is so small that he will seldom face the paradoxical problem just described. If he fails at the most difficult task, as is likely, P_s decreases further, P_f increases further, and the aroused motivation to avoid failure is reduced. By continued failure he further reduces the amount of anxiety about failure that is aroused by this most difficult task. Hence, he should continue to set his level at this point. If he plays the game long enough and fails continuously, the probability of failure increases for all levels of difficulty. Sooner or later the minimal motivation to avoid failure at the most difficult task may be indistinguishable from the motivation to avoid failure at the next most difficult task. This may ultimately allow him to change his level of aspiration to a somewhat less difficult task without acting in gross contradiction to the proposed principle of motivation.

If our fearful subject has initially chosen the easiest task (Task I where $P_s = .90$) and if he fails, P_s decreases toward .80, and his motivation to avoid the task also increases. If there is no easier task, the most difficult task should now appear least *unattractive* to him, and he should jump from the easiest to the most difficult task. In other words, continued failure at a very easy task decreases P_s toward .50; and, as Table 1 shows, a change of this sort is accompanied by increased arousal of avoidant motivation. A wild and apparently irrational jump in level of aspiration from very easy to very difficult tasks, as a consequence of failure, might be mistakenly interpreted as a possible effort on the part of the subject to gain social approval by seeming to set high goals. The present model predicts this kind of activity without appealing to some extrinsic motive. It is part of the strategy of minimizing expected pain of failure after one has failed at the easiest task.

If our fear-disposed subject is successful at the most simple task, his P_s increases, his P_f decreases, and his motivation to avoid this task decreases. The task becomes less and less unpleasant. He should continue playing the game with less anxiety.

Table 1, when taken in its entirety, deals with the special case of the person in whom the two motives are exactly equal in strength. The implications are clear. In the constrained-performance situation, he should work hardest when the probability of success is .50, because motivation to achieve and motivation to avoid failure will summate in the constrained instrumental act which is at the same time the pathway toward success and away from failure. (This summation should also occur in the cases where one motive is stronger.)[5] But in the level-of-aspiration setting where there is an opportunity for choice among alternatives, the avoidance motivation exactly cancels out the approach motivation. Hence, the resultant motivation for each of the alternatives is zero. His choice of level of aspiration cannot be predicted from variables intrinsic to the achievement-related nature of the task. If there is any orderly pattern in this conflicted person's level of aspiration, the explanation of it must be sought in extrinsic factors, e.g., *the desire to gain social approval.* Such a desire can also be conceptualized in terms of motive, expectancy, and incentive, and the total motivation for a particular task can then be attributed to both achievement-related motives and other kinds of motives engaged by the particular features of the situation.

---

[5] Here again is the error discussed in the Editors' Note on page 19. The summation of approach and avoidance motivation will always reduce the resultant strength of the approach tendency. When M_s and M_{AF} are equal, resultant achievement motivation is zero. (The Editors.)

In recent years there has been something of a rebirth of interest in the problems of level of aspiration, particularly in pathological groups. The tendency for anxious groups to show much greater variability in level of aspiration, setting their goals either very high or very low relative to less anxious persons, was noted in early studies by P. Sears (1940), Rotter (1954), and others (Lewin, Dembo, Festinger, and Sears, 1944). Miller (1951), Himmelweit (1947), and Eysenck and Himmelweit (1946) have produced substantial evidence that persons with affective disorders (neurasthenia or dysthymia) typically set extremely high goals for themselves; hysterics, on the other hand, show a minimal level of aspiration, often setting their future goal even below the level of past performance. In all of these studies, normal control groups have fallen between these two extremes, as might be expected from the present model if *normals* are relatively more positive in their motivation in achievement-related situations.

In the work of Eysenck (1955) and his colleagues, both dysthymics and hysterics show greater *neuroticism* than normal subjects. Eysenck's interpretation of this factor as autonomic sensitivity is consistent with the implications of the present model, which attributes the setting of extremely high or low levels of aspiration to relatively strong motivation to avoid failure. A second factor, *extraversion-introversion*, discriminates the affective disorders and hysterics where the present model, dealing only with motives intrinsic to the competitive achievement situation, does not. An appeal to some other motivational difference, e.g., in strength of n Affiliation, might also predict the difference in pattern of level of aspiration.

PROBABILITY PREFERENCES

The present analysis is relevant to another domain of current research interest, that specifically concerned with the measurement of subjective probability and utility. Edwards (1953, 1954a), for example, has reported probability preferences among subjects offered alternative bets having the same expected value. We (Atkinson, Bastian, Earl, and Litwin, 1960) have repeated the Edwards type experiment (e.g., 6/6 of winning $.30 versus 1/6 of winning $1.80) with subjects having high and low n Achievement scores. The results show that persons high in n Achievement more often prefer intermediate probabilities (4/6, 3/6, 2/6) to extreme probabilities (6/6, 5/6, 1/6) than do persons low in n Achievement. What is more, the same differential preference for intermediate risk was shown by these *same* subjects when they were allowed to choose the distance from the target for their shots in a shuffleboard game. In other words, the incentive values of winning *qua* winning, and losing *qua* losing, presumably developed in achievement activities early in life, generalize to the gambling situation in which winning is really *not* contingent upon one's own skill and competence.

SOCIAL MOBILITY ASPIRATIONS

Finally, the present model may illuminate a number of interesting research possibilities having to do with social and occupational mobility. The ranking of occupations according to their prestige in Western societies clearly suggests that occupations accorded greater prestige are also more difficult to attain. A serious effort to measure the perceived probability of being able to attain certain levels on the occupational ladder should produce a high negative correlation with the usual ranking on prestige. If so, then the present model for level of aspiration, as well as its implications for persons who differ in achievement-related motives, can be applied to many of the sociological problems of mobility aspirations. A recent paper by Hyman (1953) has laid the groundwork for such an analysis.

3. N. T. FEATHER

Subjective Probability and
Decision under Uncertainty

In this paper it is intended to review generally five approaches which relate to the analysis of behavior in a choice situation where a decision is made between alternatives having different subjective probabilities of attainment. The present discussion is mainly concerned with the way in which the concept of subjective probability has been incorporated into each model.

The five contributions to be reviewed are: (a) the Lewin, Dembo, Festinger, and Sears (1944) analysis of level of aspiration behavior; (b) Tolman's (1955) discussion of the principles of performance; (c) Rotter's (1954) basic equation in his social learning theory; (d) Edwards' (1954b, 1955) discussion of the SEU model from decision theory; and (e) Atkinson's (1957) risk-taking model.

The remarkable fact about these five approaches is their similarity with respect to concepts employed and equations advanced. Recently Siegel (1957) has noted the close similarity between the level of aspiration analysis by Lewin, et al. (based on the earlier work of Escalona, 1940, and Festinger, 1942b) and the SEU decision model. The *first* main aim of this paper is to show that the parallel may be taken further to include the analyses by Tolman, Rotter, and Atkinson. This parallel is all the more interesting and significant in that these models have developed from different areas of research. Lewin, et al., are concerned with goal-setting in the level of aspiration situation; Tolman's analysis is related to animal experimentation; Rotter's social learning theory is applied to clinical problems; the Edwards SEU model relates to research in decision theory; and Atkinson is concerned with the effect on risk-taking behavior of individual differences in motive strength. It

Reprinted by permission of the author and the American Psychological Association from the *Psychological Review*, 1959, **66**, 150–164.

would appear, then, that interpretations of research from diverse areas are converging upon a similar type of model.

Despite this parallel, however, there is a discrepancy in the way in which subjective probability is included in the different analyses. The *second* main aim of this paper is to bring this discrepancy to light. The discrepancy concerns whether or not concepts which are akin to utility in the various models are taken to be *independent* of subjective probability. In other words, are utilities, valences, reinforcement values, and similar concepts related to subjective probability in these models, or are they assumed to be independent? It will be argued that this question can be approached experimentally, and an experimental study (Feather, 1959b) testing hypotheses, derived from assumptions about the effects of past learning on behavior in choice situations, will be outlined in an attempt to resolve some of the disagreement.

THE FIVE ANALYSES

Lewin, et al. The Lewin, et al. analysis[1] of level of aspiration behavior involves the concepts of force, valence, and subjective probability. The positive valence of future success Va $(Suc\ A^n)$ at Level n, as it appears to the subject when he sets his goal, is positively related to the expected difficulty of attaining that level. Further, the negative valence of future failure Va $(Fai\ A^n)$ at Level n is inversely related to the expected difficulty. However, since the subject is dealing with future success and failure, Lewin, et al. consider also the probabilities of occurrence of these events. In accordance with Lewin's (1943) general approach, these are subjective and two such probabilities are distinguished, the subjective probability of success $Prob.$ $(Suc\ A^n)$ at Level n, and the subjective probability of failure $Prob.$ $(Fai\ A^n)$ at Level n. The subjective probability of success is inversely related to difficulty, while the relationship of the subjective probability of failure to difficulty level is direct. Thus, in the model, the positive valence of future success decreases with increase in the subjective probability of success, and, likewise, the negative valence of future failure decreases with increase in the subjective probability of failure; i.e., valences and subjective probabilities are *inversely* related.

The choice of a particular level is assumed to be determined by a combination of these valences and subjective probabilities. Lewin, et

---

[1] This model is in some respects similar to Cartwright and Festinger's (1943) theoretical account of decision time, which involves the concept of restraining forces and random fluctuation of subjective magnitudes around a mean value.

al. postulate a weighted valence of success ^0Va $(Suc\ A^n)$ at Level n as a multiplicative function of the valence and subjective probability of success at that level.

$$^0Va\ (Suc\ A^n) = Va\ (Suc\ A^n) \cdot Prob.\ (Suc\ A^n)$$

Similarly, the weighted valence of failure ^0Va $(Fai\ A^n)$ at Level n is given by:

$$^0Va\ (Fai\ A^n) = Va\ (Fai\ A^n) \cdot Prob.\ (Fai\ A^n)$$

Driving forces are coordinated to each of these weighted valences, and it is assumed that Level n will be selected if the resultant weighted valence at that level is a maximum. This model is used to interpret many of the results from level of aspiration studies.

Tolman. Tolman (1955) discusses the question of how his assumed cognitive and motivational variables issue into actual behavior. He sets out principles which are concerned with molar acts identifiable by observing responses in more than one concrete test situation. Specifically, he discusses a hungry rat's performance of lever pressing in a Skinner box, in terms of the following variables: the need-push for food n_f, the positive valence of expected food v_f, the expectation of food exp_f, the need-push against work n_{-w}, the negative valence of the expected work v_{-w}, and the expectation of work exp_w.

These variables are related to the performance vector Pv in the following equation:

$$Pv = f_x\ (n_f,\ v_f,\ exp_f) - f_y\ (n_{-w},\ v_{-w},\ exp_w)$$

The functions f_x and f_y are left unspecified, but Tolman suggests that it is possible that they might be multiplicative. The equation is applied to discussion of some basic types of animal experimentation, including discrimination in a simple choice situation. Tolman does not consider in his paper the possibility that, in some situations, there may be relationships between valences and expectations.

Rotter. Rotter indicates that the emphasis in his social learning theory "... is on performance, on the selection of alternative behaviors, rather than on the acquisition of responses or on early conditioning of physiological reflex behavior." (1954, pp. 80–81.) His is an expectancy-reinforcement point of view involving the concepts of behavior potential, expectancy, and reinforcement value. The approach is essentially molar and shows the influence of Tolman and Lewin.

Behavior potential is determined from the behavior actually occurring when the individual makes a choice, and measures are relative so that in any situation where alternatives are present, it is possible to order behavior potentials according to their strength. Rotter's expectancy refers to a probability held by the individual, which can nevertheless be objectively measured (see, for example, Rotter, Fitzgerald, and Joyce, 1954). Reinforcement value is determined from a choice situation where expectancy is held constant for the alternatives present.

The three concepts are related in Rotter's fundamental equation,

$$B.P._{x, s_1, R_a} = f\left(E_{x, R_a, s_1} \text{ and } R.V._a\right)$$

which is read as follows: "The potential for behavior *x* to occur in situation 1 in relation to reinforcement *a* is a function of the occurrence of reinforcement *a* following behavior *x* in situation 1 and the value of reinforcement *a*." (1954, p. 108.) Rotter is careful to avoid any precise mathematical formulation, but it is clear from his discussion (1954, pp. 108–109) that he favors a multiplicative relationship. He extends his fundamental equation to cover sets of reinforcements, behaviors, and situations, but the essential relationship is maintained.

It should be noted that reinforcement value and expectancy are held, in general, to be *independent* and may be related only under specific conditions. This is in contrast to the inverse relationship between valence and subjective probability in the Lewin, et al. analysis.

Edwards' SEU Model. In recent years a considerable body of literature concerning the theory of decision has appeared, much of it influenced by von Neumann and Morgenstern's (1944) book, *Theory of Games and Economic Behavior*. Edwards (1954b) has reviewed this literature, and in a later article (1955) he argues on the basis of his research into probability preferences (1953) that a comprehensive model for risky choice would include both the concepts of utility and subjective probability.

Edwards discusses a model which asserts that people choose so as to maximize subjectively expected utility (SEU). This is expressed (1955, p. 201) in the following equation:

$$\text{SEU} = \Sigma p_i{}^* u_i$$

where $p_i{}^*$ refers to the subjective probability corresponding to the objective probability of the ith outcome, and u_i is the utility or subjective value. Similar models have been presented by Ramsey (1931), Savage (1954), and by Coombs and Beardslee (1954).

It should be noted that utility and subjective probability are generally considered to be independent in SEU models. Thus Edwards writes, "If utilities and subjective probabilities are not independent, then there is no hope of predicting risky decisions unless their law of combination is known, and it seems difficult to design an experiment to discover that law of combination" (1954b, p. 400). This line is also taken by Coombs and Beardslee (1954, p. 263) in their assumption that utility of prize and utility of stake are independent of psychological probability. In this respect these models appear to be closer to Rotter's approach, which, we have seen, provides a similar independence assumption concerning reinforcement value and expectancy.

Atkinson. Atkinson's (1957) analysis of risk-taking behavior (Chapter 2) may be considered as an extension of the Lewin, et al. resultant valence theory of level of aspiration. This model involves six variables: The subjective probability (i.e., expectancy) of success P_s, the subjective probability of failure P_f, the incentive value of success I_s, the negative incentive value of failure I_f, the achievement motive (M_S), and the motive to avoid failure (M_{AF}). The subjective probabilities refer to situationally aroused expectancies in the person concerning the probability of the consequences of instrumental acts. Positive incentives refer to potential rewards and goals, negative incentives to potential punishments and threats, both types of incentive being experimentally manipulable. Motives are conceived as dispositions within the person to approach certain classes of positive incentives or to avoid certain classes of negative incentives. The general method of inferring strength of motive is through content analysis of thematic apperception (Atkinson, 1958a).

It will be noted that the model differs from the Lewin, et al. theory in giving motives and incentive values independent status. However, Atkinson suggests that the valence or utility of an incentive may be considered as a function of strength of motive and incentive value (1958a, pp. 303–304).

Specific assumptions are made concerning the incentive values of success and failure. The incentive value of success I_s is taken as the complementary of the subjective probability of success P_s, that is, $I_s = 1 - P_s$. Further, the negative incentive value of failure I_f is taken as $-P_s$. In short, incentive values and subjective probabilities are inversely and linearly related.

The variables are combined multiplicatively in the following equation:

Resultant motivation $= (M_S \times P_s \times I_s) + (M_{AF} \times P_f \times -I_f)$

Predictions are made from this model concerning the effects of individual differences in the strength of achievement motive and motive to avoid failure on both level of performance and risk-taking. Atkinson (1957) reports experiments which are consistent with these predictions.

Summary and Discussion. It is apparent that the above five approaches are generally similar in the concepts they employ and the equations which they advance. In each of them a "resultant force" is related to a maximized combination of "valence" and "subjective probability" factors. The basic type of relationship for each is summarized in Table 1.

Table 1

Concepts in five theoretical statements related to the variables subjective probability, attainment attractiveness, and choice potential

Theorist	Concepts	Resultant
Lewin, et al.	Subjective probability × valence	Force (weighted valence)
Tolman	Expectation, need-push, valence	Performance vector
Rotter	Expectancy and reinforcement value	Behavior potential
Edwards	Subjective probability × utility	SEU
Atkinson	Expectancy × (motive × incentive value)	Resultant motivation

This table shows that similar types of equations are being advanced from five different areas and suggests that it might be possible to effect some integration, perhaps by combining the mathematical sophistication of decision theory with some of the experimental insights from the other areas.

It also seems, however, that there appears to be a discrepancy in the way subjective probability has been incorporated into these models. The basis of this discrepancy is expressed in the question, "Are valences, reinforcement values, and utilities independent of subjective probability?" If they are not independent, then the prediction of decision under uncertainty becomes a complex matter. As we have seen, Lewin, et al. assume an inverse relationship between valence and subjective probability; Atkinson likewise relates incentive value inversely to subjective probability; Tolman does not consider the question; Rotter argues that his concepts of reinforcement value and expectancy are in general independent, while Edwards, and Coombs and Beardslee, assume independence between utility and subjective probability.

It is, of course, quite feasible that, if utility type concepts are independent of subjective probability, this independence might be confined to particular types of situation and activity. Decision theorists usually begin by defining these concepts as independent and, in their experiments, attempt to deal with situations and activities where this assumption may be justified. We would argue, however, that a more comprehensive theory of decision would also consider situations and activities where this assumption might not be reasonable, and would in addition set out a theoretical basis for independence or otherwise. While it is quite legitimate to make the assumption of independence and to see where it leads in terms of prediction from the decision model, there is point to the question of *when* the assumption should be made, the clarification of the conditions under which it might or might not be reasonable, and the theoretical basis for the judgment.

An experimental approach to this problem has recently been made by Feather (1959b) in a study of the effect of varying subjective probability of attainment in a decision situation involving different goal objects. No attempt is made to provide a sophisticated mathematical analysis. Instead, the hypotheses are related to rather general assumptions which stress the effects of past learning experiences on the present decision, for different types of situation.

DEFINITIONS, ASSUMPTIONS, HYPOTHESES

Three concepts, *attainment attractiveness, choice potential,* and *success probability,* are defined as follows:

1. Given a number of goal objects A,B,C . . . the attainment attractiveness of A> attainment attractiveness of B> . . . if, in a situation in which S is required to express his wishes with respect to attainment, and in the absence of any commitment to the choice, he states that he would prefer to get A, rather than to get B. . . .

2. Given a number of goal objects A,B,C, . . . the choice potential associated with A> choice potential associated with B> . . . if, in a situation in which there is the implication that S is committed to his choice, he chooses to get A, rather than B. . . .

3. The success probability associated with a goal object refers to the probability held by S that a particular goal object may be obtained.

Thus attainment attractiveness is defined by a situation where S merely expresses wishes concerning which goal object he would *like to get*[2] the most, whereas the definition of choice potential involves a

---

[2] It should be noted that the definition refers to the attractiveness of *attaining* a goal object rather than to the attractiveness of a goal object. This is in contrast to the variable studied in many of the object preference studies (Filer, 1952; Irwin, Armitt, and Simon, 1943; Wright, 1937), but is clearly similar to the positive valence of success in the Lewin, et al. analysis.

situation where he decides which particular goal object he would *try for*. Success probability obviously corresponds to the subjective probabilities of Lewin, et al., Atkinson, Edwards, Coombs and Beardslee, and also to Tolman and Rotter's expectancy. Attainment attractiveness corresponds to the concepts of valence, reinforcement value, and utility; choice potential to the concepts of force, resultant motivation, performance vector, behavior potential, and SEU.

The following assumptions are involved in the hypotheses of the investigation:

1. It is assumed that the attainment attractiveness of a goal object may be related not only to its attractiveness *qua* object but also to the value which S places on its *achievement;* his wishes reflect both the attractiveness of the object for him and the extent to which he values achieving it.

2. It is assumed that, in general, S places greater value on the attainment of a goal object when it is difficult to get than when it is easy to get. In our culture it is common to praise the successful achievement of a difficult goal, while failure to attain an easy goal is often deprecated and is, in some cases, punished. With the relatively consistent occurrence of these rewards and punishments, one might expect that S will come to develop achievement values which vary with difficulty level as assumed.

3. It is assumed that the value placed on the attainment of a difficult goal object is *greater* in: *(a)* ego-related than in chance-related situations;[3] *(b)* achievement-oriented than in relaxed situations.[4] Again it is possible to consider general learning experiences in our culture. In some situations, achieving the difficult is praised more than in others, and, conversely, failing to achieve the easy is punished more in some situations than in others. Thus one might expect that S will come to learn to relate his achievement values to the situation. Specifically, he should tend to value achieving the difficult more in a situation in which he can obviously ascribe success to his own efforts or skill (ego-related) than in one where success may be seen as mainly due to chance factors beyond his control (chance-related); and more in a situation which is structured as a test, involving considerable pressure towards doing well (achievement-oriented), than in one which is structured as a game with little pressure towards high achievement (relaxed).

[3] This is in line with the distinction made by Filer (1952) between merit and nonmerit conditions in a study of factors affecting the attractiveness of goal objects, and a distinction made by Phares (1957) between skill and chance situations.
[4] This is in line with distinctions made by McClelland, Atkinson, Clark, and Lowell (1953) and Atkinson (1954) in investigations of the achievement motive.

4. It is assumed that the choice potential associated with a goal object may be related to those factors assumed to underlie its attainment attractiveness and, in addition, to the *constraining effect*[5] on choice in a commitment situation, of the success probability associated with the goal object. This assumption considers the effect of background learning experiences in past decision situations which differ in the way in which the choice is structured. In a decision situation which implies that S is committed to his choice and may have to act upon it, an important consideration in making the decision is the *possibility of failure and loss,*[6] a factor not present when a wishful choice is elicited. It may be argued that in the past the attempt to achieve the unlikely in these situations has often led to failure and consequent loss of the goal object, whereas choice of the easy has usually led to success. As a result of these experiences, one might expect the development of a tendency to choose the easy rather than the difficult in a commitment type of choice situation, i.e., low success probability should tend to constrain or oppose committed choice, channelling choice in the direction of the easy. But here also, it is necessary to consider the role of achievement values and their relation to situational context. It may happen, for example, that in situations which are highly achievement-oriented and ego-related, the value placed on the difficult achievement is the dominant factor in the decision, and hence committed choice is in line with S's wishes.

In terms of these assumptions the following two hypotheses are advanced:

HYPOTHESIS 1. The attainment attractiveness of a goal object should tend to vary *inversely* with the associated success probability. This assumed co-variation should tend to be *more* apparent in (a) ego-related than in chance-related situations and (b) achievement-oriented than in relaxed situations.

---

[5] This constraining effect of subjective probability is apparent in the models discussed. It is also apparent in an experiment conducted by Mosteller, Bush, and Goodnow and reported in Bush and Mosteller (1955, pp. 294–296). They contrasted a gambling situation in which losses were subtracted from the final score with one in which losses were overlooked and only wins were counted. They found that subjects in the former situation moved more rapidly and more completely to a concentration of choices on the more probable alternative.

[6] One might also include as a factor the negative value or repulsiveness of failure per se apart from loss of the goal (Lewin, et al., Atkinson). In situations where goal objects are low in value and have little interest for the subjects, one might expect this "failure repulsiveness" to affect the committed choice. It is assumed, however, that in the experimental situation to be discussed this is not a salient factor, the important thing being the possibility of loss of the goal object.

HYPOTHESIS 2. The choice potential associated with a goal object should tend to vary *directly* with the associated success probability. This assumed co-variation should tend to be *less* apparent in *(a)* ego-related than in chance-related situations and *(b)* achievement-oriented than in relaxed situations.

Hypothesis 1 proposes that as a goal object becomes *less* likely for *S*, he should tend to wish to get it *more* and that this increase in attainment attractiveness should be more apparent in ego-related and achievement-oriented situations where higher value is placed on the difficult achievement. It is apparent that the investigation of this hypothesis may help to elucidate the question of whether or not concepts of the utility type are related to subjective probability and, if so, under what conditions. There is no statement of independence in Hypothesis 1, but it should be noted that the inverse relationship between attainment attractiveness and success probability has limits imposed upon it according to situational conditions. Thus it is predicted that *S* should wish to get a difficult goal object more in a situation which is test-like in nature than in one which is structured as a game, and more in a situation where he can ascribe success to his own skill than in one in which success is obviously a chance phenomenon. It might in fact happen that where a situation is relaxed and success is chance-related, there may be little evidence of the presence of achievement values related to difficulty, and the inverse relationship might not occur. Here, then, an independence assumption would be justified. The general theoretical basis for Hypothesis 1 is contained in the first three assumptions.

Hypothesis 2 proposes that as a goal object becomes *less* likely for *S*, there should be *less* tendency for him to choose it even though achievement of it is more highly valued. It is, however, possible that the direct relationship may not be apparent under ego-related and achievement-oriented conditions because of the relatively higher value placed on achievement of the difficult in these situations. Here committed choice might mirror *S*'s wishes. All four assumptions are involved in this hypothesis.

AN EXPERIMENTAL STUDY

More detailed description of experimental procedure is presented in another report (Feather, 1959b). The variables were incorporated into a $2 \times 2 \times 2$ factorial design, and 24 boy *S*s sampled from New South Wales Primary Schools were randomly assigned to each of the eight groups. Testing was individual.

Five different candies were used as goal objects in the procedure. These were selected on the basis of pilot research so as to be similar in attractiveness and were presented to each S in a paired-comparison arrangement, the 10 different pairs being presented successively. One candy in each pair was easier to get than the other, the difference in subjective probability being related to different task requirements, T_1 and T_2.

Ss in the ego-related situation were first required to sort a deck of 36 cards into 3 trays for 6 trials, and for each trial a fictitious prearranged time score was reported. Similar sequences of times were used for all Ss in this situation in order to allow them the same opportunity of arriving at an estimate of their ability on what to them was a novel task. Following the 6 trials, the 10 pairs of candies were presented successively and for each pair the success probability associated with each candy was determined by implying that attainment would be contingent upon sorting the cards in a specified time. Thus, "Suppose you were actually trying to get one of these, and that you would get it only if you could sort the cards within a certain time. . . . If you decided to try for this one, you would get it only if you sorted the cards within 41 seconds (T_1). If you tried for this one, you would get it only if you sorted the cards within 46 seconds (T_2). So this packet is an *easy* one to get, this one is a *hard* one to get." This, then, is the sort of situation in which success can obviously be ascribed by S to his own skill.

The Ss tested under chance-related conditions were shown a lottery box containing 15 red marbles and 5 blue marbles. One of the marbles could be rolled through a gate at the bottom of the box. The 10 pairs of candies were presented successively and for each pair the success probability associated with each candy was determined by implying that attainment would depend upon rolling out a marble of a particular color. Thus, "If you decided to try for this one you would get it only if you rolled a blue marble out of the box (T_1). If you tried for this one you would get it only if you rolled a red marble out of the box (T_2)." In contrast to the preceding example, this is the sort of situation in which success can be seen by S as largely a matter of chance.

Under achievement-oriented conditions, card-sorting was introduced as a test of speed and the lottery box as a test of luck. In the relaxed situation, card-sorting was introduced as a game played with cards and the lottery box as a marble game.

The S was required to make his selection from each pair of candies in accordance with the dependent variable studied. For attainment attractiveness, the question was, "Now if you were to get one of these, which one would you feel most pleased about getting? Which one do you *wish* you could get the most?" For choice potential, the question was, "Which one would you actually *choose* to try to get . . . ?" The *S* was not, however, required to act upon his choice. The *S*s were also asked to give a reason for each selection made.

Using an extended χ^2 analysis (Sutcliffe, 1957), it was possible to compare the proportion of times a candy was selected when it was easy to get as against when it was difficult to get for each dependent variable over the different situational conditions.

Later all *S*s were tested individually under *actual* choice conditions with the same pair of candies being used throughout. Instructions were as follows: "I'm going to let you actually try to get one of these today. . . . Which one are you *actually* going to choose to try to get . . . ?" It was thus possible to compare an *S*'s selection from this pair in the first or verbal situation with his choice in the second or actual situation, other conditions remaining the same. A binomial test was used to evaluate the significance of changes.

Table 2

Frequencies of selection (+) and nonselection (−) of Candy C
for all experimental conditions (hypothesis 1)

Condition	Choices		Total
	Selected (+)	Not Selected (−)	
Ego, achievement, T_2 (easy)	5	43	48
Ego, achievement, T_1 (difficult)	42	6	48
Ego, relaxed, T_2 (easy)	16	32	48
Ego, relaxed, T_1 (difficult)	30	18	48
Chance, achievement, T_2 (easy)	9	39	48
Chance, achievement, T_1 (difficult)	31	17	48
Chance, relaxed, T_2 (easy)	25	23	48
Chance, relaxed, T_1 (difficult)	27	21	48
Totals	185	199	384

Note: Table 2 is to be read as follows: In the ego-related, achievement-oriented situation Candy C is selected 5 times and rejected 43 times in the 48 pairs in which its attainment depends upon satisfying the performance requirement T_2 (sorting the cards within 46 or 47 seconds) and when attainment attractiveness is the dependent variable.

Table 3

Frequencies of selection (+) and nonselection (−) of Candy C
for all experimental conditions (hypothesis 2)

| | Choices | | |
| | Selected | Not Selected | |
Condition	(+)	(−)	Total
Ego, achievement, T_2 (easy)	17	31	48
Ego, achievement, T_1 (difficult)	31	17	48
Ego, relaxed, T_2 (easy)	38	10	48
Ego, relaxed, T_1 (difficult)	12	36	48
Chance, achievement, T_2 (easy)	23	25	48
Chance, achievement, T_1 (difficult)	31	17	48
Chance, relaxed, T_2 (easy)	35	13	48
Chance, relaxed, T_1 (difficult)	9	39	48
Totals	196	188	384

Note: Table 3 is to be read as follows: In the ego-related, achievement-oriented situation Candy C is selected 17 times and rejected 31 times in the 48 pairs in which its attainment depends upon satisfying performance requirement T_2 (sorting the cards within 46 or 47 seconds) and when choice potential is the dependent variable.

RESULTS AND IMPLICATIONS

In general, the results, which are presented with the statistical analysis in detail elsewhere (Feather, 1959b), confirm both hypotheses. Tables 2 and 3 serve to indicate the basic type of data analyzed for Hypotheses 1 and 2. Table 2 presents results bearing upon Hypothesis 1 for Candy C.

Table 3 presents results bearing upon Hypothesis 2 for Candy C.

Subject to the scope of this investigation, the major results may be summarized.

1. Where attainment attractiveness is the dependent variable there is, for all situational conditions combined, a significant *decrease* in the proportion of + selections for each of the goal objects as success becomes subjectively more likely (i.e., less of a tendency to wish to get the candy, as it becomes easier to get). This supports Hypothesis 1.

2. Where choice potential is the dependent variable there is, for all situational conditions combined, a significant *increase* in the proportion of + selections for each of the goal objects as success becomes

subjectively more likely (i.e., more of a tendency to choose to get the candy, as it becomes easier to get). This supports Hypothesis 2.

3. These results are in turn related to situational context, differences in relationships between situations being generally in line with prediction. Thus, for example, the decrease in the proportion of + selections for each of the goal objects, with increase in success probability when attainment attractiveness is the dependent variable, is greater under achievement-oriented conditions than under relaxed conditions, and greater for the ego-related situation than for the chance-related situation. However, it is interesting to note that when the frequency data bearing on Hypothesis 1 are considered separately for the chance-related, relaxed situation alone, there is little evidence for an inverse relationship between attainment attractiveness and success probability; that is, it appears that the independence assumption might be justified here. Further, under achievement-oriented conditions, the relationship between choice potential and success probability swings to inverse; that is, there is an *increase* in the proportion of + choices of a candy with decrease in success probability. It appears that achievement values are particularly important factors for both wishful and committed choice under these testlike conditions.[7]

4. Subjects, in giving their reasons for selection, indicate the importance for them of the attractiveness of the object, achievement values, and the constraint of success probability as factors affecting their decisions in the different situations. The reasons given are in agreement with the assumptions involved in the hypotheses. For example, wishing to get the difficult is most often explained in terms of "wanting to do well," etc., that is, by reference to achievement values; while choosing to get the easy is generally explained in terms of the probability factor, e.g., "You've got more chance of getting it."

5. The constraining effect of success probability on choice behavior in a commitment situation becomes particularly apparent where the choice is *actual*, i.e., where the person is, in fact, required to act upon his choice. Situations can vary in the degree to which they imply commitment; an actual situation seems to show to best advantage the role of success probability as a constraint on choice behavior.

These results appear to have the following implications with respect to the role of subjective probability in decision under uncertainty.

---

[7] This particular result is of course subject to the goal objects used in this investigation. For goal objects of high value one might expect less of a tendency to choose the difficult under achievement-oriented conditions, since the loss attendant upon failure is greater.

1. It is suggested that it is important to define clearly the *meaning* of success for a person in a decision situation where alternatives of different subjective probabilities are presented. This study has indicated that achievement values related to difficulty level may have an effect on the decision, and the evidence supports a fairly general inverse relationship between attainment attractiveness and success probability. This is consistent with the inverse relationship assumed by Lewin, et al. between positive valence of success and subjective probability, and with Atkinson's assumption of an inverse relationship between incentive value of achievement and subjective probability. It does not agree, however, with the independence assumptions of Rotter, Edwards, and Coombs and Beardslee. It should be noted that both the Lewin, et al. and Atkinson models are related to the level-of-aspiration type of situation where achievement values might be expected to play an important role. In contrast, decision-theoretical models have, to date, been mainly concerned with chance-related situations which may be so structured as to make achievement values related to difficulty relatively unimportant, since personal endeavor cannot effect the external random event on which the outcome depends. Situations in which achievement or non-achievement of a goal may have personal relevance are, in the language of decision theory, cases of uncertainty rather than risk. These constitute an important class of situations which decision theory will ultimately have to consider; they pose complex and difficult issues requiring detailed analyses and research. It is to be hoped that in time it will be possible to relate decision in these situations to sophisticated and rigorous mathematical models. Recently Drèze (1958) has attempted to extend decision theory in this direction in a theoretical analysis of individual decision making under partially controllable uncertainty.

It should be pointed out, however, that the results of the present study suggest that the independence assumption may in fact be an oversimplification even for chance-related situations (cf. results in Table 2 for chance-related, achievement-oriented conditions), and Atkinson makes the same point when he argues (1957, pp. 370–371) that incentive values may generalize to gambling situations in which winning is really not contingent upon one's own skill and competence. It is also possible that some tasks used in decision studies, while objectively chance-related, may be seen by S as involving an element of skill (e.g., the pinball apparatus used by Edwards, 1953), and, further, that achievement values related to difficulty might generalize to them on the basis of past experience. We would therefore question the reasonableness of an independence assumption in some of these studies. As we have noted previously, it would be quite legitimate to assume independence between utility and subjective probability and then see where the decision model leads with respect to agreement of logical prediction and observation. But surely a more comprehensive model would carefully consider the conditions under which an independence assumption may or may not be justified and would present the theoretical rationale and criteria for arriving at the judgment of whether to make the assumption or not.

2. It is suggested that it is important to consider the way in which the decision is structured, particularly the degree to which it involves commitment. The results have shown important differences in relationships involving subjective probability, according to whether or not a committed choice or a wishful choice is studied. There is further support for this from level-of-aspiration studies (Festinger, 1942a; Irwin and Mintzer, 1942) which have indicated that the type of question asked can affect the response.

3. Finally, it is suggested that it is important to study decision for different situational contexts. The results have shown that there are differences for ego-related *versus* chance-related situations, and for achievement-oriented *versus* relaxed situations. Thus, for example, the results indicate that the direct relationship between choice potential and success probability, which occurs under relaxed conditions, swings to inverse in the achievement-oriented situation; that is, in this type of situation, committed choice tends to be in line with the S's wishes. We have considered these differences in terms of situational effects on achievement values, but there is a further possibility to consider here, namely, a possible situational effect on subjective probability which would affect the decision. Under achievement-oriented conditions, for example, there may be a tendency to overestimate probabilities. Lewin, et al. write as follows: ". . . the various parts of the life-space are an interdependent field . . . the expectancy or reality level of the psychological future is also affected by the wish and fear (irreality) level of the psychological future" (1944, p. 367). Related to this are investigations by Marks (1951), Irwin (1953), Crandall, Solomon and Kellaway (1955), and Worell (1956) which have studied whether stated expectations are influenced by the value of anticipated events. Atkinson (1957) discusses the possible biasing effect of achievement motive and motive to avoid failure on subjective probabilities.

Further, it is possible that a person's attitude towards probability might vary across ego-related and chance-related situations. It might happen, for example, that an individual tends to judge probability as more "dependable" in the former type of situation. Phares (1957) has found that a chance situation produces smaller expèctancy changes than a skill situation, since in a chance situation scores may provide little basis for generalization to future trials. Goodnow (1955) in her studies has shown that the task set is an important condition of probability matching, "all-or-none" behavior in predicting occurring more frequently in a gambling task than in a task presented as a problem to be solved. All of these studies indicate the importance of considering the relationship of decision to different situational contexts and suggest that the basis for these relationships may be complex.

The above discussion underlines the complexity of the decision process and is consistent with the general emphasis in this paper on the need to consider the context of past experience as an important influence. Decisions made now are to some extent continuous with those made previously, and the recognition and analysis of this background may lead to a better understanding of the role of subjective probability in decision under uncertainty.

SUMMARY

This paper is concerned with the way in which the concept of subjective probability has been incorporated into five approaches which relate to decision under uncertainty, namely, the analysis of level of aspiration behavior by Lewin, et al., Tolman's principles of performance, Rotter's fundamental equation in his social learning theory, the Edwards SEU model in decision theory, and Atkinson's risk-taking model. These approaches are shown to be similar with respect to the concepts employed and the equations advanced. A discrepancy is noted in the relationship of valence, reinforcement value, and utility to subjective probability.

In an attempt to clarify this relationship, the concepts of attainment attractiveness, choice potential, and success probability are defined. Attainment attractiveness is defined in terms of a wishful choice relating to attainment in a situation free from commitment; choice potential is defined by a choice in a situation where there is implied commitment. Success probability refers to the probability held by the person concerning successful attainment. In terms of these concepts, two hypotheses are advanced. Assumptions involved in these hypotheses emphasize the effect on decision of past learning experiences, particularly in wishful-choice and committed-choice situations, and the influence of relatively common cultural achievement values related to success probability, which are also in part a function of situational context.

It is predicted that attainment attractiveness should tend to be inversely related to success probability and that choice potential should tend to be directly related to success probability. The hypotheses also consider differences in these relationships for ego-related as against chance-related situations, and achievement-oriented as against relaxed situations. An experimental study is outlined whose results generally support these hypotheses.

Some implications of this study for decision under uncertainty are considered: (a) the importance of considering achievement values as possible factors in the decision, (b) the need to consider the way in which the decision is structured (whether it involves a statement of wishes in the absence of commitment or a choice where commitment is implied or actual), and (c) the importance of studying decision behavior in different types of situation, in line with the assumed variation in achievement values for different situations and the possible effect of situational contexts on judgments of probability.

The Study of Persistence

The present review of studies of persistence has two main aims:

1. Of primary importance, it will consider the different approaches which have been made in the literature to the investigation of persistence with humans.

2. As a more specialized aim, it will attempt to clarify the relationship of persistence at a task to motives and expectations by considering the following two questions: How does the initial ease or difficulty of a task influence the persistence displayed by a subject in his attempt to perform the task? How do individual differences in strength of motive to achieve success M_S and strength of motive to avoid failure M_{AF} influence persistence at a task?

The general paradigm of the persistence situation is that in which a person is confronted with a very difficult or insoluble task and is unrestricted in either the time or number of attempts he can work at it. He is unsuccessful at each of these attempts at the task, but can turn to an alternative activity whenever he wishes. Persistence may be measured by the total time or total trials which the person works at the task before he turns to the alternative activity. The former measure is sometimes referred to in the literature as temporal persistence; the latter measure is analogous to resistance to extinction.

Persistence may be distinguished from the performance level or effort involved in an activity and from the direction which an activity takes, but belongs with both of these as an important behavioral symptom of motivation. This distinguishing characteristic of motivated behavior has long been recognized in the literature. To cite a few examples of its widespread recognition, McDougall (1908), in his discussion of instinct, lists persistence as one of the objective features of purposive behavior; Tolman (1932), while rejecting the mentalistic teleology of McDougall's

Reprinted and abridged by permission of the author and the American Psychological Association from the *Psychological Bulletin*, 1962, 59, 94–115.

position, considers persistence-until-ends-are-attained as a basic criterion for molar, purposive behavior; Lewin (1935) discusses the persistence of tension within the regions of the person, a conception which has a crucial part in the interpretation of the research concerning rigidity, substitute activity, and interrupted tasks (cited in Lewin, 1946); and both Hull (1943) and Dollard and Miller (1950), within the context of drive theory, are concerned with the problem of continuing action. More recently Peak (1955) and Atkinson (1957) have emphasized that a theory of motivation has as one of its important aims the conceptualization of persistence in behavior; and Bindra (1959), arguing within the general framework of Hebb's concepts (1949), considers persistence as one of the defining characteristics of goal directed action. Thus, there is no lack of recognition of the importance of accounting for persistence in behavior despite diversity in conceptual approaches.

The background research falls into three fairly distinct classes. The *first* class comprises studies which are concerned with persistence as a trait or uniformity in behavior. Typically, these study—by correlational techniques—relationships between persistence scores (usually in terms of time) for a variety of different types of task. In more recent research, factor analytic methods have been used in an attempt to account for the obtained correlations. The overriding interest in these studies is in consistency in behavior. Will a subject who persists at one task also tend to persist at another? Consistency, where it occurs, is assumed to allow the inference of a relatively stable personality characteristic. The role of situational factors in determining behavior tends to be ignored, since the emphasis is on personality structures or traits which transcend the situation. To the extent that momentary situational influences are excluded from consideration, the trait approach commits the "organism error" (MacKinnon, 1944).

The *second* class of studies comprises those with humans which are concerned with the problem of resistance to extinction. Although they are not commonly discussed as persistence studies, the structure of the situation is to some extent similar to that employed in studies where persistence is conceived as a trait. In the trait studies a common technique is to measure the time for which the subject persists at a very difficult, effortful, or insoluble task *without success*, i.e., temporal persistence. In the extinction studies the subject typically performs a task *without reinforcement* after having been subjected to a particular type of reinforcement schedule during an acquisition series. Number of trials to extinction is taken as the measure. This similarity should not blind us to important differences between these situations. Extinction studies generally ignore the possible effect of relatively stable personality differences and focus more on the influence of situational variables, particularly differences in the pattern and amount of reinforcement in the acquisition series. In this respect they are in marked contrast to the personality oriented trait studies and, to the extent that they exclude personality differences from consideration, they commit the "situation error" (MacKinnon, 1944).

Finally, the *third* class of studies comprises those in which persistence is conceived as a motivational phenomenon. On the one hand, the theory may consider persistence mainly in terms of situational parameters leaving personality variables relatively unspecified. Lewinian field theory appears to come close to this approach in its detailed analysis of factors in the psychological environment, such as valences and barriers, and its relative lack of an explicit analysis of the individual. On the other hand, the approach may be more thoroughly interactive, as in the theory of achievement motivation (Atkinson, 1957, 1960), which conceives of stable personality dispositions or motives in interaction with expectations and incentive values which are both situationally defined. It is this latter approach that permits clarification of the question of how persistence might be related to differences in strength of achievement-related motives and initial expectation of success. Hence, more attention will be given to the experimental literature from this area, and only a partial sampling of studies from the other two classes of investigation will be presented.

The three classes of studies may be seen as falling on a continuum with personality oriented trait studies at one end, situation oriented extinction studies at the other end, and studies which consider the interaction of personality and situation between the two extremes.

PERSISTENCE CONCEIVED AS A TRAIT UNDERLYING BEHAVIOR

These investigations fall into two main groups:

1. Those which investigate correlations between persistence scores for a large number of different tasks or correlations between persistence scores and other variables such as age, intelligence, or academic success, but which do not proceed to a factor analysis. These, in general, are the early trait studies as exemplified by the classical research of Hartshorne, May, and Maller (1929). They will be designated "nonfactorial trait" investigations of persistence.

2. Those which do proceed to a factor analysis. These are designated "factorial trait" investigations of persistence.

The transition from 1 to 2 exemplifies the initial steps in the evolution towards a scientific explanation. There is progression from the concept of persistence as a property of persons, some possessing it more than others, to the attempt to classify different types of persistence. It will be argued, however, that classification is only a preliminary step, albeit a most important one, and that the factor analytic studies fail to provide an adequate conceptualization of why people differ in persistence between situations.

Nonfactorial Trait Studies. Many of these early investigations of persistence are reviewed by Ryans (1939). Perhaps the best illustration of a nonfactorial trait study is to be found in the monumental research of Hartshorne, May, and Maller (1929). In this investigation a wide variety of tasks were used, some of which were administered individually, others in a group setting. The eight persistence tests that were employed consisted of story resistance, puzzle mastery, paper and pencil puzzle solution, fatigue and boredom in mental work, hunting for hidden objects, continued standing on right foot, eating cracker and whistling, and solving a toy puzzle. The reliability coefficients were found to range from .40 to .85. Validity coefficients obtained by comparing test results with teachers' ratings of persistence were from zero to .33. The correlations between the various tests were generally low. There was low positive correlation between results of persistence tests and intelligence test scores. Some tendency was found for persistence to increase with age for the age range (9–16 years) investigated.

In common with the foregoing study, other early trait studies of persistence investigated an extensive and often bewildering variety of tasks which ranged from subjective ratings of persistence, through difficult or insoluble puzzle tasks, to measures of physical endurance. Persistence was usually measured by total time taken at the task. In addition to differences in the types of task employed, one would also expect differences in the test context in which these tasks were presented, e.g., the degree to which the situation was achievement oriented, whether or not the task was administered individually or to a group. In view of these differences it is not surprising that intercorrelations of persistence scores were often low. With the increasing use of factor analytic methodology it was natural for investigators to look for order in the concomitances and to go beyond the often puzzling examination of the correlation table to the statistical intricacies of factor extraction.

Factorial Trait Studies. One of the earliest factor analytic studies concerned with persistence was carried out by Webb (1915). Working within the context of a Spearman analysis, he correlated ratings and isolated a *W* factor, which was thought to comprise component traits such as reliability, tact, and persistence of motives. Crutcher (1934) in another early factorial investigation tested London school children (age range 7–16 years) on persistence tests including card-house building, mechanical puzzle solution, addition, picture copying, and canceling A's. He found a correlation of .30 between persistence and intelligence, and a tendency for more persistent children to be slightly inclined towards introversion. When the intercorrelations between time taken on each of the various persistence tasks by his subjects were analyzed by the Spearman tetrad method, Crutcher found some evidence for a general factor. Alexander (1935) identified an X factor, which ran through school subjects but not through ability measures, as involving persistence, and this was consistent with the generally obtained positive correlation between persistence measures and school success.

Later investigations by Ryans (1938), Thornton (1939), Rethling-schafer (1942), Kremer (1942), and MacArthur (1955) are reviewed by Eysenck (1953) in some detail. He considers MacArthur's study as methodologically the most satisfying. MacArthur, following preliminary investigation, selected a large number of individual and group tests for administration, including the traditional tests which had been used in the measurement of persistence, as well as measures of intelligence, school grades, age, self-ratings, peer ratings, and ratings by teachers. Subjects were 120 boys and the influence of ability on persistence was partialed out. A Thurstone analysis of intercorrelations yielded five factors as follows: (a) general persistence, with peer ratings (.603) and time spent on magic square (.584) having the highest saturations; this factor ran through both ideational and physical measures, word building had a saturation of .472 and maintained handgrip .432; (b) a bipolar factor contrasting individuality with prestige suggestibility; tests in which subject had no knowledge about performance of classmates were positively loaded; tests where this knowledge was available were negatively loaded; this factor resembled Kremer's "will to community" factor; (c) a bipolar factor contrasting measures of reputation for persistence with objective measures of time spent by subject at the task; this reputation factor resembled Kremer's "stability of character" factor; further, measures opposite in sign were very similar to those defining Thornton's "keeping at a task" factor running through ideational tests; (d) a factor running through the physical tests and closely resembling Thornton's "withstanding discomfort to achieve a goal" and Rethlingshafer's "willingness and/or ability to endure discomfort"; (e) a factor running through spatial and numerical tasks and interpreted as spatial-numerical persistence. MacArthur's results thus brought together in the one study many of the previous findings. A persistence score based on a combination of the eight tests with the highest communalities correlated .30 with school marks with intelligence partialed out, and had an index of reliability of .90. MacArthur found it best to avoid suggesting that persistence was desirable and provided activities to which the subject could turn when he had spent as long as he wished at the task.

Eysenck (1953) summarizes the general results of the foregoing studies as follows:

The evidence is fairly conclusive that persistence constitutes an important trait in our culture; that this trait is of relatively unitary nature and can be measured to the extent indicated by a validity of .9. In addition to this general factor of persistence, we find groups of activities which cluster together and define more specific types of persistence, such as persistence in physical tasks or persistence in ideational tasks. These smaller and less important factors also are subject to measurement with a degree of validity probably not much below general persistence itself. Persistence as measured by tests is fairly closely related to persistence as rated by others, and can be said to predict performance in life situations to a definitely significant extent. Persistence tends to show slight correlations with intelligence, more impressive ones with "w" or lack of neuroticism and with introversion (p. 290).

These latter results, involving neuroticism and extraversion-introversion, were discovered in research conducted in Eysenck's laboratory (1947, 1952). Persistence in these investigations was measured by a physical endurance test (holding leg above an adjacent chair). Recently, Eysenck (1957) has attempted to give a theoretical account of the relationship of persistence to personality dimensions using assumptions about the development of inhibitory and excitatory potentials, a conception which is related to Pavlov's (1927) theory of experimental neurosis. Extraverts are assumed to be individuals in whom excitatory potential is generated slowly and at a weak level, but in whom inhibitory potential develops quickly to a strong level and then dissipates slowly. In contrast, introverts are assumed to be individuals in whom excitatory potential is generated quickly and at strong level, but in whom inhibitory potential develops slowly to a weak level and then dissipates quickly. Differences between introverts and extraverts in persistence are related to the differential in inhibitory potential. The stronger inhibitory potential developed in extraverts would lead to the expectation that they should show relatively less persistence at a task than introverts. This expectation is supported in the investigations using the physical endurance test.

Evaluation of Trait Studies. Without question the factor analytic approach to the study of persistence marked an advance over the earlier simple correlation-type studies. While these latter investigations did contribute a rich variety of tasks, they often appear to have involved a rather uncritical lumping together of diverse activities without much attempt to account for similarities and differences in results. The factor analytic studies contributed to the *classification* of these tasks and thus assisted in bringing some order into a complex pattern of relationships. In this respect they represented a step in the direction of scientific progress. But, while it is of value to know, for example, that ideational persistence tasks separate in factor analytic research from physical persistence tasks, and that there are differences in persistence for tasks administered in a group setting and tasks administered individually, this information itself serves only as a starting point. The scientist typically goes beyond classification to explanation. He wants to know not only how phenomena may be grouped together, but also how they are uniformly related to other phenomena in terms of a conceptual framework which will provide both a scientific account of extant findings and a promising direction to new research. Factor analytic studies of persistence are theory oriented only insofar as they invoke the concept of trait, which carries with it the implication of a stable structure transcending the immediate situation. But it is argued that such a concept offers only an incomplete understanding. The discovery of the fine-grain of the observed phenomenon will involve not only knowledge of personality structures but also a thorough understanding of the role of the immediate situation in relation to behavior, and the interaction between such situational factors and personality dispositions. It should be possible to account both for differences between individuals in persistence in the one situation, and differences in persistence for the one individual in different situations.

The next set of studies to be discussed certainly does not satisfy this interactional requirement. In fact, these investigations appear to stand at the opposite extreme from the trait studies in that they examine the effect of variations in *situation* on persistence and tend to ignore relatively stable personality variables. Thus, like the trait studies, they are one-sided. They are, however, of interest in showing how persistence, in terms of resistance to extinction, varies with changes in an acquisition series. This type of study may be conceived as bearing more upon the relationship of persistence to expectation.

PERSISTENCE CONCEIVED AS RESISTANCE TO EXTINCTION

As indicated previously, studies with humans in which resistance to extinction is related to different types of reinforcement schedules are not commonly classified as persistence investigations. However, continuing an activity in the face of uniform nonreinforcement is similar to the familiar persistence situation in which the subject works at a task without success. The relevance of extinction studies to the present review is increased further by the fact that one common interpretation of the obtained results relates the number of responses to extinction to a concept of expectancy and its manner of change. The studies considered in the present section are restricted to those in which discussion of results involves some reference to a concept of expectancy. The reader is referred to reviews by Jenkins and Stanley (1950) and Lewis (1960) for comprehensive coverage of the partial reinforcement literature.

The general finding in these extinction studies is that

All other things equal, resistance to extinction after partial reinforcement is greater than after continuous reinforcement when behavior strength is measured in terms of single responses (Jenkins and Stanley, 1950, p. 222).

Jenkins and Stanley review a large number of studies which support this conclusion.

For example, Humphreys (1939b) in an early study of eyelid conditioning found that random alternation of reinforcement and nonreinforcement led not only to as much conditioning as reinforcement per trial but also to greater resistance to extinction. During extinction, responses for subjects who were partially reinforced first increased in frequency and then decreased. This result can be considered in terms of expectancy theory since the subject would presumably have a greater expectation of a reinforcement after one or two nonreinforcements, particularly since in the acquisition stage of the experiment there were never more than two successive nonreinforcements. Humphreys argued that the shift from intermittent reinforcement to uniform nonreinforcement must have led more slowly to the expectation of uniform nonreinforcement for subjects who were partially reinforced, while this change in expectation would occur more rapidly for subjects who were uniformly reinforced during acquisition.

In a subsequent experiment, Humphreys (1939a) used an apparatus in which two lights were arranged on a board. The subject had to guess when one of these lights was turned on, whether or not it would be followed by the other light. Half of the subjects were trained with the first light invariably following the second; for the other half the second light was turned on only in random alternation so that it appeared half of the time. Humphreys found that, under extinction conditions (i.e., the first light was never followed by the second), the uniform reinforcement group quickly developed the hypothesis of uniform non-reinforcement. The intermittent reinforcement group showed an initial rise in expectation followed by gradual acceptance of the hypothesis that there would be no second light.

More recently, Lewis and Duncan (1958) have studied the way in which variation in the frequency of reward during an acquisition stage and variation in the length of an acquisition stage affects the number of trials to extinction and stated expectation of reinforcement. An electronic slot machine was used in the experiment and was set to pay off according to a prearranged schedule when buttons were pushed and a lever was pulled. In a factorial design, a constant payoff occurred on 33%, 67%, and 100% of trials during acquisition, combined with 3, 6, 12, and 21 acquisition plays. Following the last acquisition play extinction began with no further payoffs. The subject could play the machine for as long as he liked. Lewis and Duncan found that the larger the number of acquisition trials, the less the plays to extinction. There was a tendency for smaller percentages of reinforcement to be associated with a greater number of plays to extinction, the usual partial reinforcement effect. Expectancies, measured before each trial by a rating technique, were found to increase differentially during acquisition as a direct function of the percentage of reinforcement. Expectancies decreased differentially during extinction as a direct function of the percentage of reinforcement, a result which is not inconsistent with the Humphreys' interpretation. Finally, there was no clearcut statistical evidence that number of acquisition trials had any effect upon expectancies. In an earlier study (Lewis and Duncan, 1957) using the same apparatus, it was found that when magnitude of reward was varied, larger amounts of reward were associated with more plays to extinction.

Lewis and Duncan (1958) maintain that their results are consistent with a discrimination hypothesis concerning extinction (Bitterman, Federson, and Tyler, 1953). Extinction is assumed to occur because it is clear to the subject that no more rewards will occur. He responds to the acquisition series as a whole. Under conditions where extinction conditions are similar to acquisition conditions, discrimination is difficult and extinction therefore prolonged. Where acquisition and extinction series are very dissimilar, discrimination is easier and extinction therefore more rapid. Percentage of reward is an important factor in similarity-dissimilarity of the two series. If the percentage of reward is low in the acquisition series, then the acquisition series is more similar to the extinction series; discrimination is difficult and thus extinction takes longer.

James and Rotter (1958), in an interesting methodological contribution to the literature, argue that studies of the partial reinforcement effect have failed to consider differences between those situations in which the subject is likely to see the occurrence of the reinforcements as *outside his control* and primarily contingent upon external conditions, and those situations in which the subject can relate the occurrence of the reinforcements to *his own skill.* They believe that the chance-skill dimension is an important one along which situations can be categorized. Thus, for example, Phares (1957) found significantly greater changes in expectancies for skill groups than for chance groups, although all subjects had the same number and pattern of reinforcements. In research by Feather (1959b) this dimension was found to be important with respect to the influence of variation in subjective probability of success on the attractiveness of attaining a goal and the tendency to choose it (See Chapter 3). Littig (1959) in discussing the results of his study of probability preferences and subjective probability proposes a similar distinction between skill and chance situations (See Chapter 6).

James and Rotter (1958) argue.that in an acquisition series involving uniform reinforcement the subject receives no cues of nonreinforcement. Hence, when the extinction series begins, he is able to utilize the first nonreinforcements as cues that the situation has changed. If he perceives control of the situation as *external,* a sudden decrease in expectancy should tend to occur and rapid extinction. But, under partial reinforcement conditions these cues of nonreinforcement are present in the training series. Hence, when the extinction series begins, the first nonreinforcement is not a new cue which can be used to discriminate a change in situation. Consequently, extinction should be more gradual, with more trials required before the subject recategorizes the situation. In a chance type of situation resistance to extinction is also increased by the subject's tendency to count and verbalize relationships. In the acquisition series he is likely to develop the hypothesis that a series of nonreinforced trials will probably be followed by a trial on which reinforcement is forthcoming. This "gambler's fallacy" may also occur during the extinction series. Thus increased resistance to extinction should result.

However, where the situation involves *skill,* the subject perceives reinforcements and cues as produced by factors controlled by himself. In the uniform reinforcement situation he is less likely (when the extinction series begins) to recategorize the situation as having changed. Under these conditions one would not expect sudden decreases in expectancy. Furthermore, when the subject is partially reinforced in the skill situation, the gambler's fallacy should not be operative, since non-reinforcement is attributed to lack of skill rather than to luck factors. James and Rotter (1958) maintain that this theoretical analysis would lead to the prediction that in skill situations a 100% reinforcement group would be more resistant to extinction than a partial reinforcement group. To test this prediction they contrasted 100% and 50% random reinforcement under conditions where subjects were instructed either that success at the task was determined by chance or by their own skill. Using a simple card guessing game, presented tachistoscopically with chance versus skill instructions, they found that under skill conditions the usual superiority of the partial reinforcement group did not occur. In fact, 100% reinforcement led to less rapid extinction than 50% reinforcement, although the difference was not statistically significant. The usual partial reinforcement effect was obtained in the chance situation. The 100% chance group extinguished significantly faster than the 50% chance group.

Evaluation of Extinction Studies. The above investigations by Humphreys and by Lewis and Duncan imply that a high expectation of reinforcement developed in an acquisition series of trials will tend to be associated with low behavioral persistence, as indicated in rapid extinction when rewards are no longer forthcoming. Conversely, low expectation of reinforcement will tend to be associated with high behavioral persistence, as indicated in a greater resistance to extinction. However, the study by James and Rotter suggests that it would be unwise to proceed to such a generalization for all situations. Usually partial reinforcement studies have been conducted with tasks in which the reinforcements, when they occur, appear to be externally controlled and independent of the skill of the subject. In contrast, as we saw in the preceding section, research in persistence in most cases has used tasks which are on the skill side of the continuum, where success and failure can be related to the subject's own efforts and not to conditions outside of his control.

Furthermore, persistence tasks of the insoluble puzzle variety usually provide a wide and relatively inexhaustible range of alternative responses following failure, whereas in the extinction study the response tends to be restricted to a particular action. Presumably, in the former case a number of different alternative responses have to extinguish while in the latter case only one.

Finally, it is worth noting again the situational emphasis in these extinction studies. The stress is on varying the way in which reinforcements occur in an acquisition series and tends to exclude consideration of the effect of relatively stable personality differences on resistance to extinction. As indicated, these studies may be conceived as more relevant to the relationship of persistence to situationally elicited expectations. Thus, neither the trait studies nor the studies discussed in this section take account of both personality and situation parameters in interaction, and their approach is to this extent limited. The studies to be discussed in the next section do attempt to recognize this interaction in their theoretical conceptualization although they vary in the degree to which the interaction is made explicit.

PERSISTENCE CONCEIVED AS A MOTIVATIONAL PHENOMENON

The studies in this section conceive of persistence in relation to a theory of motivation. Two theories are particularly relevant to this review: Lewinian field theory with its assumption of behavior determined by the psychological life space and all that it involves; the theory of achievement motivation (Atkinson, 1957, 1960) with its interactive assumption of motivation as a function of motives, expectations, and incentive values.

While both of these theories are interactional in the sense that each considers situational and personality parameters, it will be argued that the latter marks an advance over the former in the way in which persistence may be conceived, in that it offers a more explicit formulation both of individual differences in motive and the way in which motives, expectations, and incentives are combined. Therefore it is considered that the theory of achievement motivation offers greater potential for an explicit account of persistence in achievement contexts than Lewinian field theory. In this section, as in the discussion of trait studies, successive sets of studies exemplify an advance in the evolution of scientific explanation, in this case from fairly general field theory to a more explicit model concerned with behavior in the achievement situation.

Lewinian Field Theory. Lewinian field theory in its basic equation $B = f(P, E)$ has long recognized the necessity of considering behavior in terms of interacting personality and situational factors. It is of interest to examine the approach taken to the problem of persistence by this theory.

The typical situation employed in the investigation of persistence can probably be represented topologically and dynamically in Lewinian terms as a frustration situation in which a person in a state of tension is separated at some psychological distance from a goal (or region of positive valence) by a barrier. This barrier is the source of restraining forces which oppose the driving forces acting upon the person in the direction of the goal. The barrier may be objectively insurmountable, as when the subject is given an insoluble puzzle and asked to solve it, or the barrier may represent a very difficult task in which case the opposing restraining forces would be very strong but could possibly be surmounted. There may be other regions of positive valence in the psychological environment to which the subject may turn if he so desires.

It is true that there are some situations in the persistence literature which do not appear to conform to this paradigm. For example, the investigation of persistence against boredom and fatigue would appear to be more related to the Lewinian studies of satiation, and dynamically different from the frustration type of situation already mentioned. But Lewin (1946) himself appears to consider persistence in terms of the person-barrier-goal situation when he writes, "What is usually called persistence is an expression of how quickly goals change when the individual encounters obstacles" (p. 824). He discusses research by Fajans (cited in Lewin, 1946) as falling within this context. Fajans, in a study of success, persistence, and activity in infants and young children, investigated the effect of separating children from a goal object at different distances. She found that previous failure at a task decreased persistence when subjects were again confronted with the same type of difficulty and when persistence was measured by duration of approach. In contrast, success led to a relative increase in persistence. When the same task was repeated, a combination of success and praise was more effective in increasing persistence than success alone. Similar effects of success and failure were found by Wolf (1938). Persistence was also found to increase with decreasing distance from the goal. These results are relevant to the present review to the extent that previous success and failure may be considered important determinants of present expectations of success and failure. Considered in this light, the Fajans research implies that persistence is positively related to the subject's expectation of success and negatively related to his expectation of failure.

It is important to note that Fajans' research, and indeed the great bulk of Lewinian investigations, does not take account of individual differences in both nature and strength of motive. While the concept of tension is basic in Lewin's conceptualization of the person and influences the way in which the person sees the environment, it is not spelled out in any detail in the theory. It is a concept consistent with the field emphasis of a person in an environment each influencing the other, but it applies to an individual and differences between persons with respect to tension are not explicitly formulated. One might ask how many different types of tension there are, whether Individual X is stronger than Individual Y with respect to one type of tension, how these tensions develop, to what extent they are stable, what is their precise relationship to valence, etc. But perusal of Lewinian field theory does not provide definite answers to these questions. Perhaps this is a consequence of the emphasis on the individual case, and the protest against Aristotelian class concepts. In actual experiments it appears to lead to operations which are more concerned with manipulating the psychological environment of a person, and details of differences in personality structure tend to be left unspecified. Where the *P* is manipulated, the operations are directed to producing an *intraindividual* effect for the one person rather than studying the effect of variation *between* persons.

That personality differences are important is recognized by Henle (1955) in her research on substitute value within a Lewinian context. Thus she writes,

The relevant segment of behavior does not consist simply of activity directed to satisfy a quasi-need to complete a particular task, but must be thought of as activity to a more inclusive goal (p. 536).

Presumably then we need to consider not only transient situational factors but also the specific behavior of the person in relation to more general and inclusive life goals and motives. In this sense the theory of achievement motivation is more explicit than Lewinian field theory. It involves not only a conceptualization of the effects of momentary situation (in terms of the concepts of expectation and incentive value) but also provides for the influence of relatively stable dispositions (or motives) on behavior. The theory is more restricted than Lewinian field theory since it is specifically directed to the analysis of behavior in achievement contexts where performance may be related to standards of excellence. However, it is possible that the general "expectancy value" approach, of which the theory of achievement motivation is a particular example, may ultimately clarify our understanding of behavior in many other types of situation.

Theory of Achievement Motivation. Of the four studies of persistence to be considered in this section only the latter two studies by Atkinson and Litwin (Chapter 5) and by Feather (Chapter 8) are historically an outcome of the theory of achievement motivation. The other two investigations by Winterbottom (1958) and by French and Thomas (1958) preceded the theory and are more readily classified with earlier studies (McClelland, Atkinson, Clark, and Lowell, 1953), which were concerned initially with the development of a valid measure of the achievement motive. This validation was of two main kinds: experiments concerned with the effect of experimental arousal of motivation on imaginative thought, and experiments concerned with the effect of individual differences in motive strength on behavior. The initial approach adopted toward validating the measuring instrument had a common-sense basis. It was expected that the achievement motive would be more strongly elicited under achievement oriented or test conditions than in a relaxed situation, and that subjects with high achievement motive would demonstrate this in behavior, e.g., by working harder at a task than subjects with weaker achievement motive. The studies by Winterbottom, and by French and Thomas, fit into this class since they investigated the common-sense prediction that subjects with high achievement motive should have relatively higher motivation to succeed and hence should tend to show greater persistence.

Winterbottom (1958) as part of an investigation of the relationship of n Achievement to early childhood training experiences, observed 29 8-year-old boys in a puzzle solving situation. During the test each child was given the opportunity to ask for help whenever he wanted it, and was offered help and rest at intervals. Using the projective thematic apperception (TAT) method (McClelland, et al., 1953) of measuring the achievement motive, Winterbottom found that boys who were high in n Achievement on stories obtained immediately after the puzzle solution period (i.e., under achievement oriented conditions), less frequently requested help and more often refused an invitation to stop work and rest than boys low in n Achievement. Boys high in n Achievement under both relaxed and achievement oriented conditions more often refused help even when it was offered. Thus, she obtained evidence for greater persistence in the high n Achievement group in the sense of desire to continue with the task without external assistance or rest. In common with a great deal of research in achievement motivation, Winterbottom defined high and low n Achievement groups on the basis of a median split in the distribution of scores.

French and Thomas (1958) in a study involving 92 subjects from a United States Air Force base, found a clear positive relationship between time spent on a complicated mechanical problem and n Achievement assessed by the French Test of Insight, an apperceptive content device scored for n Achievement in the same way as the TAT (French, 1958). Again, high and low n Achievement groups were contrasted on the basis of a median split. The majority of the high motive group used most or all of the time available for the puzzle (35 minutes), while only a few of the low motive group continued with the puzzle to the end. Thomas (1956) had previously found that strength of achievement motive was related to the length of time a subject would work at a problem without objective knowledge of progress.

As we have indicated, these two studies were not conceived with any theoretical model in mind. However, it was natural that, with the accumulation of research concerning achievement motivation, attempts would be made to conceptualize results in terms of some systematic framework. McClelland and Clark (McClelland, et al., 1953, Chapter 2), in the course of a discussion of a more inclusive theory of motivation involving the concept of affective arousal, had made some suggestions about the status of the achievement motive with respect to this theory. In the *Nebraska Symposium on Motivation* Atkinson (1954), drawing on formalizations of expectancy theory by MacCorquodale and Meehl (1953) and Tolman and Postman (1954), analyzed the role of the situation in relation to behavior in achievement contexts in terms of the expectations which are elicited. This line of thinking was further elaborated in his later analysis of risk-taking behavior in terms of a theory of achievement motivation (Atkinson, Chapter 2). The general approach of which the theory of achievement motivation is a particular case, considers motivation[1] expressed in the direction, magnitude, and persistence of behavior, as a positive function of the strength of motive within the person, the strength of the expectancy of satisfying the motive through some action instrumental to the attainment of a goal or incentive, and the value of the specific goal or incentive that is presented in a given situation. As such, this approach belongs to a class of expectancy value theories which all involve somewhat similar concepts (Feather, Chapter 3). . . .

The theory assumes that the basic variables combine multiplicatively to determine positive achievement motivation ($M_s \times P_s \times I_s$) and negative failure avoidant motivation ($M_{AF} \times P_f \times I_f$). These two component motivations combine additively to generate resultant motivation.

The theory implies that this resultant motivation to perform the task is positive when the motive to achieve success is stronger than the motive to avoid failure (i.e., $M_s > M_{AF}$) and negative or task avoidant when $M_{AF} > M_s$. Hence, an individual in whom $M_s > M_{AF}$ should demonstrate positive interest in achievement-related tasks whereas an

---

[1] The theory draws a sharp distinction between motive and motivation. Strength of motive is one influence on strength of motivation. Others factors influencing strength of motivation are levels of expectation and magnitude of incentive value.

individual in whom $M_{AF} > M_S$ should tend to avoid achievement-related tasks unless he is constrained to perform them. Predictions can be made from the theory concerning the effects of individual differences in the strength of M_S and M_{AF} on level of task performance, risk taking, and persistence. . . .

Of particular interest to the present review is the study carried out by Atkinson and Litwin (Chapter 5). Using the theory of achievement motivation they predicted that, holding task constant, stronger M_S should be associated with greater persistence, and stronger M_{AF} should be associated with less tendency to persist. Actually the study had a much wider set of aims for it was designed to show the extent to which the resultant motivation as predicted from the theoretical model would be manifested in the defining characteristics of behavior *qua* motivated, namely, choice (direction), performance level, and persistence. In particular, Atkinson and Litwin were interested in providing evidence for the construct validity of the French Test of Insight (French, 1958) and the Mandler-Sarason Test Anxiety Questionnaire (Mandler and Sarason, 1952) as methods for assessing strength of M_S and M_{AF}, respectively. The construct validity of these tests would be strengthened by showing that, when they are used for assessing the corresponding motives, measures of risk taking, performance level, and persistence (holding task constant in a crude qualitative way) are all consistent with implications from the theory of achievement motivation. . . .

The study provided clear support for the construct validity of the Test of Insight and the Test Anxiety Questionnaire as methods of assessing M_S and M_{AF}, respectively. Predictions from the theory of achievement motivation were confirmed using each test separately and the two tests in combination. The three dependent variables of the investigation were positively correlated implying that individual differences in strength of motive tend to be stable from situation to situation.

It should be noted that the Atkinson-Litwin study was restricted to the investigation of persistence at a task in relation to differences in strength of achievement related motives. It made no attempt to vary systematically expectations of success and failure as related to situational cues or to specify clearly the level of initial P_s. Nor did it attempt to account for why an individual stops working at a task. (Italics added.) A recent study by Feather (1960; Chapter 8) focuses on these problems for the first time and investigates persistence in relation to the *interaction* of motives and situationally elicited expectations by varying both factors simultaneously. This study therefore helps to
. clarify the more specialized questions raised at the beginning of this

review concerning the relation of persistence at a task both to initial expectation of success and to individual differences in strength of motive to achieve success and motive to avoid failure. Hence the approach will be considered in some detail.

The theoretical analysis involved in the investigation is applied to the persistence situation where the subject works at an achievement task which is presented to him as part of an important test and which is in fact insoluble. He undergoes repeated failure in his attempts to perform the task but may turn to an alternative achievement task when he so desires. The analysis is based on the relationship of total motivation to perform the task to total motivation to perform the alternative. It is assumed that the subject will persist at the initial task as long as total motivation to perform it is stronger than total motivation to perform the alternative.

Total motivation to perform the initial achievement task is attributed to the following three components: motivation to achieve success at the task, motivation to avoid failure at the task, and extrinsic motivation to perform the task. Total motivation to perform the alternative activity is attributed to the same three component motivations since the alternative is also achievement related. Both motivation to achieve success and motivation to avoid failure are conceptualized in accordance with the theory of achievement motivation as multiplicative products of strength of motive, level of expectation, and magnitude of incentive value. Extrinsic motivation refers to motivation to perform the task attributable to motives other than those which are achievement related (i.e., motives other than M_S and M_{AF}). For example, the usual social constraints (e.g., desire for approval, fear of disapproval) provide an important source of motivation in any situation where a subject is required to work at a task.[2] Ultimately such extrinsic motivation may also be conceptualized as resulting from relatively stable personality dispositions (motives) in interaction with more transitory situational influences (expectations and incentive values). Extrinsic motivation to comply with instructions may, for example, vary with the strength of affiliation motive and the degree to which the subject expects that compliance will produce certain affiliation rewards in the situation, e.g., approval for being a cooperative subject. In the present analysis of persistence, extrinsic motivation to perform the initial achievement task is assumed to be stronger than extrinsic motivation to perform the alternative, since the initial task is presented by the experi-

---

[2] This is especially so for subjects in whom $M_{AF} > M_S$. If these subjects are to perform an achievement task at all, some stronger positive motivation must exist to oppose their tendency to avoid the task.

menter as the first in a defined sequence of achievement tasks. Furthermore, both sets of extrinsic motivation are assumed to be constant across the different experimental conditions.

It is assumed in the theoretical analysis that *the subject will turn to the alternative achievement activity whenever total motivation to perform the initial task becomes weaker than total motivation to perform the alternative.* (Italics added.) The problem then becomes that of specifying the basis for a *decrease* in total motivation to perform the initial task as the subject works at it unsuccessfully. This decrease is assumed to be mediated by changes in both the motivation to achieve success at the initial task and the motivation to avoid failure at the task. These changes are in turn assumed to be determined by a successive decrease in subjective probability of success P_s as the subject repeatedly fails at the initial achievement task. Hence, *decrease in expectation of success with repeated failure becomes the basis dynamic principle.* When this principle is used in conjunction with the theory of achievement motivation and certain additional assumptions,[3] it becomes possible to derive the following four hypotheses:

HYPOTHESIS 1 states that subjects in whom the motive to achieve success is stronger than the motive to avoid failure ($M_S > M_{AF}$) should persist longer at a task for which the initial subjective probability of success is high ($P_s > .50$) than similar subjects for whom the initial P_s is low ($P_s < .50$).

HYPOTHESIS 2 states that subjects in whom $M_{AF} > M_S$ should persist longer at a task for which the initial P_s is low ($P_s < .50$) than similar subjects for whom the initial P_s is high ($P_s > .50$).

HYPOTHESIS 3 states that when initial P_s is high ($P_s > .50$), subjects in whom $M_S > M_{AF}$ should persist longer at a task than subjects in whom $M_{AF} > M_S$.

HYPOTHESIS 4 states that when initial P_s is low ($P_s < .50$), subjects in whom $M_{AF} > M_S$ should persist longer at a task than subjects in whom $M_S > M_{AF}$. . . .

Evaluation of Motivational Approach. The type of approach adopted in derivation of the hypotheses of the foregoing investigation raises a number of issues that are relevant for the future study of persistence:

[3] It is assumed that P_s for the alternative task is constant across the experimental conditions, that reduction in P_s for the initial task to a particular value will require more unsuccessful attempts at the task when P_s is initially high than when it is initially low, and that rate of decrease in P_s is not systematically related to strength of M_S or M_{AF}.

1. The theoretical analysis suggests the importance of specifying the components of both total motivation to perform the task with which the subject is presented and total motivation to perform the alternative to which he may turn, when attempting to predict degree of persistence. The persistence situation is similar to a complex problem in decision where the subject is continually confronted with the choice of continuing with the unsolved task or turning to the alternative. From this point of view the basic theoretical problem is that of specifying precisely all of the component motivations involved in the decision, the way in which they combine to determine a resultant, and the manner in which they change as the subject works unsuccessfully at the task.

2. The theoretical analysis also suggests the possibility of conceptualizing each of the component motivations as a function of strength of motive, level of expectation, and magnitude of incentive value. Such a conceptualization would necessitate the precise specification and measurement of the particular motive, expectation, and incentive value assumed to determine any component motivation, together with assumptions about how these three factors combine to determine the strength of the component motivation. It is of interest to note that most expectancy value theories have employed a multiplicative rule of combination (Feather, Chapter 3).

3. The theoretical analysis focuses attention on change in expectation as the basic dynamic principle mediating change in motivation. The task used in the investigation was one in which expectation of success could be assumed to decrease with experience since the subject failed at every attempt. But there are tasks, involving some degree of partial success, where expectation of success might be expected to rise initially before falling. Furthermore, it appears important to consider the degree to which the task involves skill. It is a basic assumption in the investigation that it should take more unsuccessful attempts at a task to reduce an expectancy to a particular level from a high initial expectation of success than from a low initial expectation of success. The results from the investigation and from the earlier study by James and Rotter (1958) suggest that this assumption is tenable in situations where the subject can relate success to his own efforts or skill, and failure to his own inadequacy rather than to the influence of external agencies beyond his control. However, when the subject considers success and failure beyond his control (as in chance-type situations), expectancy may decrease more rapidly in extinction when initial expectation of success is high than when it is low, an assumption which is consistent with the usual partial reinforcement effect obtained under external control conditions. Clearly then, predictions about persistence

using the dynamic principle of expectation change require explicit assumptions about the *manner* in which expectation changes with experience at the activity and assumptions about conditions affecting the *rate* of change in expectation.

4. Finally, the theoretical analysis suggests by contrast a number of persistence situations which differ in important respects from the one investigated. In particular the following persistence situations appear worthy of study:

(a) Situations where performance of the alternative activity involves motives which are not involved in performance of the initial task. In the present investigation both initial task and alternative task belong to the same class of activity. Both tasks are achievement related and total motivation to perform each is attributable to the same component motivations. But one can conceive of situations where performance of the alternative involves different component motivations. For example, in the study of persistence by Atkinson and Litwin (Chapter 5), the activity in which the subject engaged when he left the examination room may have been quite unrelated to achievement, involving a different set of component motivations.

(b) Situations where component motivations involve the influence of incentive values which are independent of expectations. In the specific achievement context dependencies are assumed between incentive values and expectations, e.g., $I_s = 1 - P_s$. But *in most other situations it would be assumed that incentive values and expectations are independent. This means that, in the more general case, motivation to perform the activity would be expected to decrease continuously with decrease in the expectation of goal attainment.* (Italics added.) This decrease is in contrast to changes assumed to occur in the achievement situation where both motivation to achieve success and motivation to avoid failure show an initial increase in strength as the expectation of success falls to $P_s = .50$.

(c) Situations where the incentive is objectively present, e.g., a young child trying to overcome a barrier in order to get some candy. In the present investigation and also in extinction studies, the incentive is not in view and the experimenter has to take special precautions to insure that the subject does not develop the expectation that there is in fact no incentive, e.g., that there is no solution to the problem or that the apparatus has been "fixed" to prevent the occurrence of further reinforcements. Should this happen the situation would become one in which the subject sees success and failure as beyond his control.

(d) Situations involving different assumptions about extrinsic motivation. In the present study it was assumed that extrinsic motivation to perform the initial achievement task is stronger than extrinsic motivation to perform the alternative. This assumption is a reasonable one when tasks are presented in a defined sequence with the implication that one has to be performed before the other. However, one can conceive of situations where different assumptions about extrinsic motivation could be made. For example, extrinsic motivation may be assumed constant across tasks in the type of situation where the subject has free choice among various alternatives. The typical level of aspiration situation falls into this class. Thus, in a ring toss game the subject can select any one of a number of different lines from which to throw the ring. The only constraint is that he make a choice. There is no suggestion that he should follow a definite sequence in selecting some lines before others. There may also be situations in which extrinsic motivation to perform the alternative activity is stronger than extrinsic motivation to perform the initial task. For example, the experimenter might present the first task as a practice item and attach little importance to it. In contrast, the alternative might be introduced as the test item and the experimenter might suggest that this is the task in which he is really interested. Thus, the theoretical approach suggests a wide array of different classes of persistence situation. It is believed that the kind of interactional approach discussed above, based on a motivational analysis, will help to elucidate the investigation of persistence in these other types of situation.

SUMMARY AND CONCLUSIONS

The present review has attempted to distinguish between different approaches made in the literature to the study of persistence. As a more specialized aim, it has examined the relationship of persistence at an achievement task to the subject's initial expectation of success and to the strength of his achievement related motives. The survey of the literature suggests the following main conclusions:

1. Studies of persistence may be classified into three main classes in terms of the extent to which the approach adopted is personality oriented, situation oriented, or considers both personality and situation parameters.

2. Trait studies of persistence are personality oriented and concentrate on stable characteristics of the person which are assumed to transcend the immediate situation and to determine some consistency in behavior. This type of approach has difficulty in accounting for variations in persistence from situation to situation.

3. Studies of persistence conceived as resistance to extinction are situation oriented and concentrate on properties of the immediate situation, particularly the characteristics of the acquisition series. This type of approach has difficulty in accounting for variations in persistence from person to person. Extinction studies of the partial reinforcement type offer suggestive evidence concerning the relationship of persistence to expectation, but there are problems in generalizing these results which are related to important differences between the typical partial reinforcement and persistence situations.

4. Studies which conceive of persistence as a motivational phenomenon in general take both person and situation parameters into account. This type of approach is thus unlike the two preceding ones for it has the potential of being able to account both for variations in persistence from situation to situation and for variations from person to person. In addition, it allows for the study of both in interaction. Lewinian field theory, while recognizing the interaction of person and psychological environment in its basic equation, appears to deal mainly with variations in the latter in its actual experimentation. The theory of achievement motivation, developed by Atkinson, is more explicit in recognizing the interaction of stable aspects of the personality (motives) and more transitory situationally determined influences (expectations and incentive values) in determining motivation.

5. A recent experimental study of persistence in an achievement context (Feather, Chapter 8) is based on a detailed analysis of the different motivational components involved in performance of the initial achievement task and performance of the alternative achievement task. A dynamic principle of decrease in expectation of success as the subject works at the initial task unsuccessfully is used in conjunction with the theory of achievement motivation to generate differential predictions about persistence for subjects differing in the relative strength of achievement related motives and in initial expectation of success. Results are in agreement with predictions. . . .

6. The study indicates the possibility of considering persistence as a motivational phenomenon, where the theory of motivation considers the interaction of both personality characteristics and situationally determined influences. The theoretical analysis involved in the investigation shows: the importance of a detailed analysis of the component motivations involved in performance of both initial task and alternative, the possibility of conceptualizing each component motivation in "expectancy value" terms, and the importance of change in expectation as a dynamic principle mediating change in motivation. The theoretical analysis also suggests a number of different types of persistence situation worthy of further investigation.

PART II

Aspiration and Persistence

5.

JOHN W. ATKINSON AND GEORGE H. LITWIN

Achievement Motive and Test Anxiety
Conceived as Motive to Approach Success
and Motive to Avoid Failure

Since 1950 there have been an increasing number of studies using thematic apperceptive (or equivalent) measures of *n* Achievement (McClelland, Atkinson, Clark, and Lowell, 1953; Atkinson, 1958a; French, 1958) and the Mandler-Sarason Test Anxiety Questionnaire (TAQ) (Mandler and Sarason, 1952; Sarason, Mandler, and Craighill, 1952; Mandler and Cowen, 1958), which amply demonstrate that knowledge of motivational differences enhances prediction of achievement related performances. The reader who is familiar with this literature will have noted that studies of *n* Achievement show it to be a motive that generally enhances performance in achievement situations while studies of Test Anxiety show it to be a motive that normally produces decrements in achievement test performance. Interpretations of the results of studies that have employed only a measure of *n* Achievement have often included some reference to Ss having low *n* Achievement scores as apparently more fearful of failure (Atkinson, 1953; Brown, 1953; Moulton, Raphelson, Kristofferson, and Atkinson, 1958). On the other hand, studies that have employed only the measure of Test Anxiety (Mandler and Sarason, 1952; Sarason and Mandler, 1952; Sarason, et al., 1952) have viewed the behavior of Ss having low Test Anxiety scores as less conflicted and more task oriented. One might be tempted to think that these two sets of research findings overlap completely and that the measures employed merely tap opposite ends of a single motivational variable. This would seem a plausible inference in light of the correlation of —.43 between the two measures reported by Raphelson (1957) in a study that also showed

Reprinted by permission of the authors and the American Psychological Association from the *Journal of Abnormal and Social Psychology*, 1960, **60**, 52–63.

each to be related in the expected direction to a physiological index of manifest anxiety in a stressful test situation.

The position taken here, however, is that the measure of n Achievement obtained from thematic apperception (McClelland, et al., 1953; Atkinson, 1958a) or the French Test of Insight (French, 1955, 1958; French and Thomas, 1958), a very similar projective instrument, and the measure of Test Anxiety obtained from the self-knowledge scale developed by Mandler and Sarason are not measures of the same variable. Rather, it is assumed that these particular measures of n Achievement indicate the strength of a motive to approach success, while Mandler-Sarason Test Anxiety scores indicate the strength of a motive to avoid failure.

A theoretical model explaining how these two motives influence risk taking (i.e., selection) and level of performance in achievement test situations has been presented (see Chapter 2). It provides a basis for testing assumptions about what is being measured by the two instruments. According to the theory, when a person's motive to achieve success is stronger than his motive to avoid failure, the resultant of the conflict is always positive; i.e., approach motivation, no matter what the level of difficulty of the task. An individual so motivated is most attracted to tasks of intermediate difficulty where the subjective probability of success is .50. Here the resultant positive motivation is strongest. However, if the motive to avoid failure (which is presumed to be a disposition to become anxious about failure under achievement stress) is stronger, then the resultant of the approach-avoidance conflict is avoidant motivation for all levels of difficulty. The maximum strength of avoidant motivation, i.e., the strongest anxiety about failure, occurs when tasks are of intermediate difficulty. Hence, according to the theory, a person so motivated finds all achievement tasks unattractive, particularly ones of intermediate difficulty. He performs them only when constrained by social pressures (otherwise he would "leave the field"),[1] and he performs them inefficiently; i.e., he suffers a performance decrement as a consequence of conflict engendered by competing avoidant tendencies, to the extent that his anxiety is aroused (Sarason, et al., 1952).

The present study tests several hypotheses derived from the theoretical model and simultaneously, the assumptions that *(a)* n Achievement, as measured by thematic apperception or a similar projective instrument, is a positive disposition to approach success and that *(b)* what has

---

[1] "Social pressures" reduce to other kinds of motivation, extrinsic to achievement, for performing the tasks (e.g., desire for social approval), which are not normally measured in experiments of this sort.

been called Test Anxiety is a disposition to avoid failure. The dependent variables are: goal setting (level of aspiration) when individuals are confronted with tasks which differ in difficulty (ring toss from distances ranging from 1 to 15 ft.); persistence at an achievement task when it is not clear that success has been attained (length of time spent working on a final examination); and efficiency of performance, or level of accomplishment (score on the final examination).

The hypotheses are as follows: Persons in whom the motive to achieve success is stronger than the motive to avoid failure (a) more often select tasks of intermediate difficulty, (b) work for a longer time on the final examination, and (c) get higher scores on the final examination than persons in whom the motive to avoid failure is the stronger motive. Hence, given the previously stated assumptions about the meaning of measures derived from the two tests, it is expected that *n* Achievement scores obtained from the French Test of Insight should be positively related to preference for intermediate risk, persistence, and efficiency of performance, and that scores from the TAQ should be negatively related to these same variables. Predictions should be enhanced when *S*s are simultaneously classified as high or low on both measures.

A secondary interest is to explore the behavioral correlates of another measure called *n* Achievement which is obtained from the Edwards Personal Preference Schedule (1954). To date, there have been strong indications that direct (i.e., assent or preference) and indirect (i.e., imaginative or projective) methods of measuring achievement motivation do not yield comparable results. DeCharms, Morrison, Reitman, and McClelland (1955) have found this to be true when a direct and indirect method of measuring *n* Achievement were compared in terms of predictions to behavior. Birney (see McClelland, 1958a) has found that measures of *n* Achievement obtained from thematic apperception and the Personal Preference Schedule (PPS) are uncorrelated ($r = -.002$, $N = 300$). This absence of relationship between the two measures is also reported by Marlowe (1959) who found, in addition, that the thematic apperceptive measure of *n* Achievement was positively related to peer group ratings of achievement related behavior, while the measure obtained from the PPS was not.

In summary, the purpose of this investigation is to examine the construct validity (see Cronbach and Meehl, 1955) of three contemporary measures of achievement related motives. Predictions concerning the behavioral correlates of the measures employed are generated by a theory that conceives the achievement motive and the motive to avoid failure as independent, latent, directional dispositions and states the conditions *under* which and the degree *to* which they are aroused and manifested in overt action.

METHOD

Subjects. The Ss were male students enrolled in a sophomore-junior level psychology course at the University of Michigan in the fall of 1957. The data were collected in the laboratory sections of the course. The instructors served as Es.[2] There were 49 Ss on whom both the measures of *n* Achievement and Test Anxiety were available. Not all of these Ss, however, appeared for all of the later data collection sessions. In all comparisons, the largest possible number of Ss is used, even though this results in slight fluctuations in the size of samples among the various comparisons.

Measure of *n* Achievement and Test Anxiety. Early in the semester Ss were administered, under neutral classroom conditions, a Test of Insight developed by Elizabeth French (1958). The test consists of 10 short verbal statements about people which Ss are asked to analyze. Both Forms I and II of the Test of Insight were used, half of the Ss getting each form. The interpretations of behavior, which are very similar to TAT stories, were scored for *n* Achievement (according to the method of content analysis described by McClelland, et al. 1953; Atkinson, 1958a) by a scorer whose reliability had been established above .90 on training materials.[3] The distribution of *n* Achievement scores for each form was broken at the median. Ss above the median were classified as high in *n* Achievement and those below as low in *n* Achievement.

Test Anxiety scores were obtained from the Mandler-Sarason TAQ (see Mandler and Cowen, 1958). The TAQ were distributed in class and Ss were asked to complete them outside of class and to return them the following week. The questionnaires were scored by dividing each scale into intervals, assigning a score of 1–4 for each scale, and summing the scale scores to obtain the Test Anxiety score. This scoring method correlates very highly with that originally described by Mandler and Sarason ($r = .94$, $N = 50$), and differs from that recently described by Mandler and Cowen only in that it uses 4 intervals instead of 10. The distribution of Test Anxiety scores was dichotomized at the median. The PPS developed by Edwards (1954) was administered to Ss in class. The distribution of PPS *n* Achievement scores was also dichotomized at the median.

Goal Setting in Modified Ring Toss Game. Several weeks after the individual difference measures had been obtained, Ss played a ring toss game. Four games

---

[2] We wish to acknowledge the assistance of Joseph Veroff and Lawrence Littig.

[3] We wish to acknowledge the assistance of Lois Hendrickson, who scored the protocols. Because many of the interpretations had no achievement imagery, the Unrelated Imagery category (UI) was scored 0 instead of −1.

were set up in the room when they entered, one on each side, one in the front, and one in the back of the room. Each game consisted of a wooden peg 2 in. in diameter and 12½ in. high mounted on a round wooden base, a ring 10 in. in diameter, and 15 lines marked on the floor at 1-ft. intervals. A number was marked on the floor next to each line. The closest line was 1 ft. from the target and numbered 1; the farthest line was 15 ft. from the target and numbered 15.

The Ss were told: "Today you are going to play a ring toss game. You will have an opportunity to take 10 shots at the target from any line you wish. You may move after each shot or shoot from the same line. Someone will record your shots and get your code number when you finish. We want to see how good you are at this." The instructor then kept track of the shots and hits of the first few Ss, and these Ss then kept score for the rest of the class. Two of the ring toss games were used by men and two by women. There was a good deal of informal banter during the session. No attempt was made to interfere with or to control the lifelike situation. Only the results for men are considered here since there remain unresolved questions concerning the validity of measures of *n* Achievement and Test Anxiety when applied to women.

Data from Final Examination. The final examination in the course from which the Ss were drawn was a multiple choice and short answer test held several months later. It was scheduled to last from 9:00 to 12:00 AM. Most of the students did not take the full three hours. As each student left the examination room after turning in his exam, and when he was out of sight of students still working on the exam, he was handed a card with the time written on it and asked to write his code number on it. The code number made it possible to relate the amount of time spent working on the exam to the individual difference measures, to goal setting behavior in the ring toss game, and to the final examination scores. The data were transcribed into a score for each S which represented the number of minutes spent working on the final examination.[4]

RESULTS

Descriptive Analysis of Goal-Setting Data. The Ss were classified simultaneously as high or low *n* Achievement and Test Anxiety. It follows from our assumptions about the two measures that the group classified High *n* Achievement-Low Test Anxiety should be more strongly motivated to approach success than to avoid failure. The Low *n* Achievement-High Test Anxiety group, on the other hand, should be more strongly motivated to avoid failure than any other group. The other two groups, the High *n* Achievement-High Test Anxiety group and the

---

[4] Because of overflow in the main examination room, 20 to 30 students took the examination in a different room. A constant of 5 minutes was subtracted from the score of these students since they began the examination about 5 minutes later.

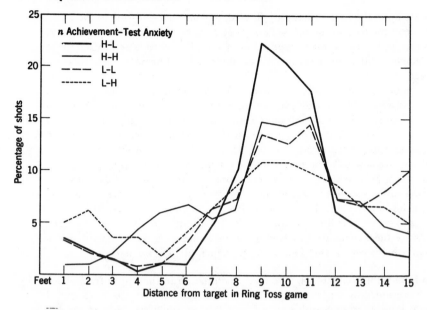

Figure 1 Percentage of shots taken from each line. Graph is smoothed according to the method of running averages, for Ss classified as High or Low simultaneously in *n* Achievement and Test Anxiety, H–L (*N* = 13), H–H (*N* = 10), L–L (*N* = 9), L–H (*N* = 13).

Low *n* Achievement-Low Test Anxiety group should be more conflicted or intermediate in resultant motivation.

Figure 1 presents a smoothed curve for each of the four groups describing the percentage of shots taken from each distance. The curves are smoothed by the method of running averages. From Figure 1 it can be seen that all four groups show some preference for the distances around 9–11 feet. However, Ss high in *n* Achievement and low in Test Anxiety prefer this region most strongly, while the Low *n* Achievement-High Test Anxiety group shows the weakest preference for it. The other two groups are between these two as predicted. At both the closest and farthest distances, the Low *n* Achievement Test Anxiety group takes more shots than the High *n* Achievement-Low Test Anxiety group. The curves indicate a relative difference between the motivation groups in preference for intermediate difficulty.

In Table 1, various ways of analyzing the data into easy, intermediate, and difficult regions are explored. The first method (I) is to divide the range of distances into equal geographic thirds. This is the method employed by Atkinson, Bastian, Earl, and Litwin (1960) in an earlier study. The second method (II) is to use the obtained distribution of shots to determine the easy, intermediate, and difficult regions. Use of the obtained distribution of shots to define degrees of difficulty was suggested by McClelland (1958b) in an investigation of risk-taking in children. The obtained distribution was first broken into approximate thirds (II-A) and then into the approximate interquartile range and

Table 1

Percentage of ten ring toss shots taken by Ss simultaneously classified high and low in *n* Achievement and in Test Anxiety using alternative criteria for definition of degree of difficulty (or risk)

Basis for Definition of Three Degrees of Difficulty (or Risk)	Distance in Feet	Motivation (*n* Achievement-Test Anxiety)			
		High-Low N = 13	High High- N = 10	Low- Low N = 9	Low- High N = 13
I. Using geographic distance: equal thirds	1–5	8%	15%	9%	21%
	6–10	70	55	49	43
	11–15	22	30	42	36
II. Using obtained distribution of shots: A. approximate thirds	1–8	22	31	28	39
	9–10	55	39	30	25
	11–15	22	30	42	36
B. approximate interquartile range versus extreme quarters	1–7	11	26	18	32
	8–11	73	48	48	41
	12–15	16	26	34	28
III. Using both obtained distribution of shots and geographic distance: middle third of distance about the obtained median shot (9.8 ft.)	1–7	11	26	18	32
	8–12	82	60	58	48
	13–15	7	14	24	20

extreme quarters (II-B) to show the effect of widening the region of intermediate difficulty. The third method (III) takes the middle third of distance around the obtained median of 9.8 feet.

Examination of Table 1 shows that all of the methods yield comparable results. The High *n* Achievement-Low Test Anxiety group consistently takes the greatest percentage of shots from the intermediate region and the Low *n* Achievement-High Test Anxiety group consistently takes the least number of shots from the intermediate region. The difference between the percentage of shots taken by these two groups from the intermediate distances ranges from 27% to 34%. The High *n* Achievement-High Test Anxiety group and the Low *n* Achievement-Low Test Anxiety groups fall between the two extreme groups as expected.

Effects of *n* Achievement and Test Anxiety. It is desirable to express the goal setting tendency of each person as a single score in statistical tests.

An Average Deviation score, which was found by Litwin (Chapter 7) to be the most consistent measure across tasks of the tendency of persons to prefer intermediate risk, was used. An Average Deviation score was computed for each shot as follows: Distance of shot—median distance of all shots/Average Deviation of all shots. The Average Deviation score for each *S* was the mean of his scores (irrespective of sign) on the 10 shots. A low Average Deviation score means that shots were taken from intermediate distances; a large score means that shots were taken from very close or very far back in relation to the median of all shots.

Table 2

Median score on three dependent variables for *S*s classified high
or low in *n* Achievement and percentage of *S*s above
or below the combined group median

Variable	Item	*n* Achievement High	*n* Achievement Low	High versus Low*
Risk-taking: average deviation score in ring toss game	N	23	22	$U = 177.5$
	Median	.63	.91	$p = .04$
	% below combined group median	61	36	
Persistence: minutes spent working on final exam.	N	25	19	$U = 156.5$
	Median	164.9	154.0	$p = .03$
	% above combined group median	60	32	
Efficiency: final exam score	N	25	19	$U = 152.5$
	Median	101	85	$p = .02$
	% above combined group median	64	32	

Note: The slight fluctuation in *N* is explained in the Method section.
* Mann-Whitney *U* Test. All tests of significance are one-tailed tests.

In Table 2 the performance of *S*s high and low in *n* Achievement is summarized for the three dependent variables: ring toss Average Deviation score, minutes spent working on the final exam, and the score on the final exam. From Table 2 it can be seen that the High *n* Achievement group tends to have lower Average Deviation scores, i.e., to show a greater preference for intermediate risk, to spend more time working on the final exam, and to have higher final examination scores than the low *n* Achievement group. The differences between the two groups were tested by the Mann-Whitney U test. Since the direction of differences was predicted in each case, one-tailed tests were made. The differences between the High and Low *n* Achievement groups are all statistically significant. Table 2 also shows the percentage of *S*s falling above or below the combined group median in each case; 60–64% of the

High *n* Achievement group fall in the predicted cell, and 64–68% of the Low *n* Achievement group fall in the predicted cell.

Table 3

Median score on three dependent variables for Ss classified high or low in Test Anxiety and percentage of Ss above or below the combined group median

Variable	Item	Test Anxiety		High versus Low*
		High	Low	
Risk-taking: average deviation score in ring toss game	N	23	22	$U = 177$
	Median	1.00	.63	$p = .04$
	% below combined group median	35	64	
Persistence: minutes spent working on final exam	N	22	22	$U = 176$
	Median	154.8	165.2	$p = .06$
	% above combined group median	32	64	
Efficiency: final exam score	N	22	22	$U = 177$
	Median	91.0	101.5	$p = .06$
	% above combined group median	41	59	

Note: The slight fluctuation in *N* is explained in the Method section.
* Mann-Whitney *U* Test. All tests of significance are one-tailed tests.

Table 3 presents the same information for the High and Low Test Anxiety groups. Again, all the results are as predicted. The High Test Anxiety group tends to have higher Average Deviation scores, i.e., to show greater avoidance of intermediate risk, to leave the final exam sooner, and to have lower final examination scores than the Low Test Anxiety group. Mann-Whitney *U* tests were computed on the differences between the motivation groups; one-tailed tests were made. The groups differ significantly in Average Deviation scores ($p = .04$). For both the number of minutes spent working on the final exam and final examination scores, the probability of the difference in the predicted direction is .06. It can be seen that 59–64% of the Low Test Anxiety group, and 59–68% of the High Test Anxiety group fall in the predicted cells in relation to the combined group median.[5]

[6] When only the extreme quartiles are compared, as is common in research using the Test Anxiety Questionnaire, the percentage of groups ($N = 11$) falling into predicted cells is increased somewhat to 63–72%. The median split is used here both because the *N* is relatively small to begin with and also to call attention to the relative sensitivities of the various measures of achievement related motivation when applied to the same dependent variables.

Table 4

Median score on three dependent variables for Ss simultaneously classified
high or low in n Achievement and Test Anxiety and percentage
of Ss above or below the combined group median

Variable	Item	High-Low	High-High	Low-Low	Low-High	High-Low versus Low-High
		n Achievement-Test Anxiety				
Risk-taking: average deviation score in ring toss game	N	13	10	9	13	*U* = 42.5
	Median	.48	1.03	.88	.93	*p* < .025
	% below combined group median	77	40	44	31	
Persistence: minutes spent working on final exam	N	15	10	7	12	*U* = 40.5
	Median	165.3	157.5	148.3	154.5	*p* < .01
	% above combined group median	73	40	43	25	
Efficiency: final exam score	N	15	10	7	12	*U* = 47.5
	Median	102.3	96.5	91	82.5	*p* < .025
	% above combined group median	67	60	43	25	

Note: The slight fluctuation in N is explained in the Method section.
* Mann-Whitney U Test. All tests of significance are one-tailed tests.

In Table 4, Ss are again simultaneously classified on n Achievement and Test Anxiety. The High n Achievement-Low Test Anxiety group is seen to have the lowest Average Deviation score (i.e., the greatest preference for intermediate risk), to spend the most time working on the final exam, and to have the highest final examination scores. The Low n Achievement-High Test Anxiety group tends to have the highest Average Deviation scores, (i.e., the weakest preference for intermediate risk), to leave the final exam the earliest, and to have the lowest final examination scores. The High n Achievement-High Test Anxiety group and the Low n Achievement-Low Test Anxiety group generally fall between the two extreme groups as predicted. Mann-Whitney U tests of the differences between the High n Achievement-Low Test Anxiety group and the Low n Achievement-High Test Anxiety group employing one-tailed alternative hypotheses are all statistically significant. When the percentage of Ss in each of the motivation groups falling above or below the combined group median is computed, 67–77% of the High n Achievement-Low Test Anxiety group are correctly placed, and 69–75% of the Low n Achievement-High Test Anxiety group are correctly placed. Simultaneous classification on both approach and avoidance motives clearly improves the prediction.

The examinations were graded A+ (excellent) to E (failure) before this analysis was even begun. It is of interest to note that the median final examination score for the High *n* Achievement-Low Test Anxiety group (102.3) was a B— grade on the final exam, and that 67% of this group received B— or better on the exam, while only 7% received a grade of D or E. On the other hand, the median final examination score for the Low *n* Achievement-High Test Anxiety group (82.5) was a D grade; 58% of this group received a D or an E on the final exam and only 25% received a grade of B— or better.[6]

Table 5

Median score on three dependent variables for *S*s classified high or low in PPS *n* Achievement and percentage of *S*s above or below the combined group median

Variable	Item	PPS *n* Achievement High	PPS *n* Achievement Low	High versus Low*
Risk-taking: average deviation score in ring toss game	*N*	22	21	$U = 137.5$
	Median	.97	.50	$p = .02$
	% below combined group median	36	62	
Persistence: minutes spent working on final exam	*N*	24	20	$U = 223.5$
	Median	157.5	163.0	$p = .70$
	% above combined group median	42	55	
Efficiency: final exam score	*N*	24	20	$U = 181.5$
	Median	100.0	89.5	$p = .17$
	% above combined group median	58	40	

Note: The slight fluctuation in *N* is described in the Method section.
* Mann-Whitney *U* Test. All tests of significance are two-tailed tests.

The Measure Called *n* Achievement on the PPS. Table 5 presents the results for *S*s classified as High or Low on PPS *n* Achievement. The

[6] These results are viewed as consistent with the idea that highly anxious individuals suffer a performance decrement on achievement tests (Sarason, et al., 1952). It may be argued that unmeasured differences in ability and not differential anxiety are responsible for the result. Perhaps *S*s score high on Test Anxiety because they have performed badly in the past (also as a consequence of low ability). The argument is plausible, but so also is the alternative. Accordingly, finding that *S*s who score high on Test Anxiety also score low on some independent test of academic ability would be expected since ability is always measured under the very kind of stressful test conditions that produce performance decrements in anxious *S*s. Experimental evidence (e.g., Sarason, et al., 1952) which shows that anxious *S*s perform as well or better than nonanxious *S*s under nontest conditions, but more poorly under achievement test conditions, makes the motivational interpretation plausible pending the discovery by someone of a method of isolating the motivational and aptitudinal influences on the usual so-called test of ability.

only statistically significant result is for the ring toss Average Deviation scores, and here it is directly opposite to what would be expected if the test measured the strength of motive to achieve success as conceived in the risk taking theory. The High PPS n Achievement group have significantly higher Average Deviation scores, (i.e., greater avoidance of intermediate risk) than the Low PPS n Achievement group ($p = .02$). Two-tailed alternative hypotheses were used here since there is little evidence in previous research to support any assumptions about what this test measures. For neither time spent working on the final examination nor final examination scores are the differences between the two PPS n Achievement groups statistically significant. The trends are inconsistent. If anything, Ss having high PPS n Achievement scores do not work as long on the exam but get better grades than those having low scores.

Since the PPS n Achievement measure behaves as if it were a measure of the motive to avoid failure (at least in the risk-taking game), the PPS n Achievement measure was substituted for the Test Anxiety measure in a simultaneous classification with n Achievement (French Test of Insight). The High n Achievement–Low PPS n Achievement group ($N = 11$) had 82% of its Ss below the combined group median for Average Deviation score; the Low n Achievement–High PPS n Achievement group ($N = 10$) had 30% of its Ss below the combined group median. The difference between these two extreme groups was very significant ($U = 16$, $p = .01$ in this direction), larger than the comparable difference shown in Table 4 when Test Anxiety is used to assess the tendency to avoid failure!

When Ss were classified on all three of the measures, n Achievement, Test Anxiety, and PPS n Achievement, striking differences were noted. The High n Achievement–Low Test Anxiety–Low PPS n Achievement group ($N = 7$) had 100% of its Ss below the combined group median for Average Deviation score while the Low n Achievement–High Test Anxiety–High PPS n Achievement group ($N = 8$) had only 25% of its members below the combined group median. The difference between these two groups was highly significant ($p = .001$).

Intercorrelation of Variables. Spearman rank order correlations were used to ascertain the degree of intercorrelation among the independent and dependent variables. The three measures of achievement-related motives were not significantly related. The correlations between the several measures were as follows: Test Anxiety and PPS n Achievement, .11 ($N = 47$); PPS n Achievement and n Achievement, $-.05$ ($N = 47$); Test Anxiety and n Achievement, $-.15$ ($N = 47$).

The three dependent behavioral variables, however, tended to be positively related to one another. The index of risk-taking preference, Average Deviation score (low scores given high ranks), and the measure of persistence, time spent working on the final exam, were correlated .34 ($N = 40$, $p < .05$); number of minutes spent working on the final exam and final examination score were correlated .27 ($N = 40$, $p < .10$); the Average Deviation score (low scores given high ranks) and final examination scores were correlated .19 ($N = 40$, $p < .25$). A more substantial relationship is evident between the two behavioral indices of motivation, risk-taking and persistence, that are not strongly influenced by academic ability, than between either of these measures and exam performance which is strongly influenced by ability.

DISCUSSION

Construct Validity of Three Tests. These results yield support for the assumptions stated earlier regarding the nature of the variables being measured by the French Test of Insight and the Mandler-Sarason TAQ. Since Litwin (Chapter 7) reports directly comparable risk-taking results when using thematic apperception to assess achievement motivation, it can be concluded that n Achievement scores obtained from thematic apperception or the Test of Insight indicate the strength of a motive to approach success. Test Anxiety scores yield results consistent with the assumption that the variable involved is a disposition to avoid failure. This assumption is not at variance with Mandler and Sarason's (1952; Sarason, et al., 1952) explanation of the performance decrement shown by anxious persons under achievement stress: the anxious person's performance suffers when task-irrelevant (avoidant) responses interfere with task-relevant (approach) responses.

The results concerning efficiency of performance, or level of accomplishment, under achievement-oriented conditions replicate earlier findings concerning n Achievement (Atkinson and Reitman, 1956; French, 1955) and Test Anxiety (Mandler and Sarason, 1952; Sarason, et al., 1952). The positive relationship between n Achievement and persistence at a task replicates an earlier finding by French and Thomas (1958) and is further evidence of the tendency also noted in recall of interrupted tasks (Atkinson, 1953). To our knowledge, this is the first study to relate Test Anxiety to a measure of persistence. The relationship of Test Anxiety to risk-taking or goal setting behavior was first noted by Vitz (1957), and Litwin (1958) has recently replicated the present risk-taking findings using several different tasks.

The results concerning the measure of *n* Achievement obtained from the Edwards PPS are nebulous. This is the third occasion on which no relationship has been found between this direct preference measure and an indirect or projective measure of *n* Achievement. The observed tendency of persons having high PPS *n* Achievement scores to avoid intermediate risk, as if they were in fact more strongly motivated to avoid failure than to achieve, dramatically reinforces the statement that *different methods of assessing human motives do not yield comparable results* (see McClelland, 1958a). The inconsistency and lack of statistical significance of the other results pertaining to the PPS measure of *n* Achievement make it very difficult to understand just what is being measured by this test. One suggestive lead is provided by some unpublished results obtained by Charles Seashore.[7] He had Ss judge the social desirability of all the statements on the PPS on a seven-point scale about three months after taking the test and found a correlation of .47 ($N = 50$) between PPS *n* Achievement score and judged social desirability of the achievement statements. One might conclude from this that although the paired items are equated for *average* social desirability, individual differences in scores obtained from this test can be considered measures of individual differences in what is deemed socially desirable. This conclusion is supported by a recent study by Corah, Feldman, Cohen, Gruen, Meadow, and Ringwall (1958) in which judged social desirability of items within pairs on the PPS correlated highly with the item selected. Arguing in a similar vein, McClelland (1958a) has suggested designating measures obtained by direct preference or assent methods as "values," e.g., *v* Achievement (see also de Charms, et al., 1955), in order to avoid the inevitable confusion that arises in trying to reconcile research findings involving variables assessed by different methods but gratuitously called by the same name.

In terms of the theoretical conception of risk-taking and achievement-related behavior presented in Chapter 2 and the assumptions regarding the variables measured here, the present findings provide considerable evidence of construct validity for the *n* Achievement scores obtained from the French Test of Insight and for Test Anxiety scores interpreted as measures of the strength of a disposition to be anxious about, and hence motivated to avoid, failure. However, until national norms are available for each of these measures, the crude designations as "high" and "low" of groups who stand above or below the median score in a college population are at best crude estimates of relative strength.

[7] Personal communication, Sept., 1958.

The Relationship of *n* Achievement and Test Anxiety. The zero-order correlation between *n* Achievement and Test Anxiety reported here is at variance with Raphelson's (1957) earlier report of a negative correlation. Yet the results may not, in fact, be inconsistent. In the present study the projective measure of *n* Achievement was presented under *neutral* classroom conditions, and the results show that persons having high *n* Achievement scores are as likely as not also to have high Test Anxiety scores. In Raphelson's study, the *n* Achievement scores were obtained from thematic apperceptive stories written by Ss under *achievement orientation* during a rest period in the middle of a rather stressful test situation. The results of Martire (1956) and Scott (1956) clearly point to the possibility that persons who are strong in *both* achievement motive and motive to avoid failure may inhibit or distort the expression of achievement related imagery when anxiety about failure has been actively aroused in them by threatening situational cues. If so, it would be expected that persons classified High in *n* Achievement (on the basis of *neutral* thematic apperceptive or Test of Insight scores) and also high in Test Anxiety should express less achievement-related imagery when anxiety about failure is aroused. This state of affairs would induce the negative correlation between the measures reported by Raphelson.

Given only high (above the median) *n* Achievement scores, one can assume that the achievement motive is relatively strong in relation to an unmeasured motive to avoid failure; given low *n* Achievement scores, one can assume that the motive to achieve success is relatively weak in relation to an unmeasured motive to avoid failure. When the motive to avoid failure is also measured, using the Test Anxiety Questionnaire, and Ss having high *n* Achievement scores but also having high Test Anxiety scores are segregated, we then have more reason to be confident that our inference of relatively stronger motive to achieve success in the remaining High *n* Achievement-Low Test Anxiety group is correct, as the present results indicate. Similarly, segregating Ss who have low scores on both *n* Achievement and Test Anxiety leaves a group low in *n* Achievement and high in Test Anxiety in whom we have more reason to be confident that the motive to avoid failure is relatively stronger. Yet in a group of college students it is unlikely that these are all persons in whom the absolute strength of motive to avoid failure is greater than the absolute strength of achievement motive. We find that this group does not actually *avoid* intermediate risk, as would be expected if the avoidance motive were stronger than the approach motive. Instead we find only a relatively weak preference for intermediate risk, in comparison with other groups. Presumably, most persons in whom the avoidant motive is actually stronger in an absolute sense are eliminated long before they reach college. The findings of Miller (1951), Eysenck (1955), and Eysenck and Himmelweit (1946) concerning extremely high levels of aspiration set by persons diagnosed as neurasthenic and extremely low levels of aspiration among persons diagnosed as hysteric represent the pathological extremes in avoidant motivation which may appear very rarely in college groups. The present research used all available Ss and made its cutting point in the distributions at the median. Perhaps the choice of more extreme groups of Ss, as has been common in research with the Mandler-Sarason test, would produce such avoidant groups even in a college population. The small number of Ss in the present investigation precluded this possibility.

The Measure of Subjective Probability of Success. An issue of fundamental importance that is treated rather inadequately here is the measurement of subjective probability of success. Strong assumptions are made concerning how the chances of success must appear to Ss as they approach the ring toss game. It is implicitly assumed here, as in an immediately preceding study (Atkinson, et al., 1960), which made the point explicit that the probability of success must have appeared closer to 1.00 than to .50 at 1 foot and closer to 0 than to .50 at 15 feet. The zone of intermediate risk or intermediate difficulty, i.e., where probability of success approximates .50, must therefore fall somewhere in between.

The actual probabilities of success obtained from the shots taken by Ss in this experiment, while not altogether relevant since it is probability of success as it appears to Ss at the beginning of the game that is required to test hypotheses from the risk-taking theory, do nevertheless provide some support for the assumptions made. At 1 foot, the actual probability of success was 1.00. At 15 feet, it was 0. And at 7 feet, the actual probability of success was .52. However, the average observed probability of success was only .23 between 8 and 12 feet where most shots were taken by the High *n* Achievement-Low Test Anxiety group.

Some data collected by Litwin (Chapter 7) in a follow-up study illuminate the problem somewhat. Litwin found that when Ss were asked to estimate their chances of hitting from each line in an 18-foot game before performing, the average reported probability of success was nearest to .50 at 11–12 feet. This was two-thirds of the distance from the easiest to the most difficult line. In the present experiment, the modal point of shots by the High *n* Achievement-Low Test Anxiety group was 9–10 feet, two thirds of the distance from 1 foot to 15 feet. The Ss in Litwin's study approached the game with overly optimistic expectancies of success. In all likelihood the same thing occurred in the present experiment, though no evidence can be presented to support the claim.

SUMMARY

It is assumed that measures of n Achievement obtained from the French Test of Insight (and thematic apperception) indicate the strength of a motive to achieve success and Mandler-Sarason Test Anxiety scores indicate the strength of a motive to avoid failure. Given these assumptions and a theory of motivational determinants of risk-taking behavior, the following hypotheses are investigated: persons in whom the motive to achieve success is stronger than the motive to avoid failure (a) should prefer tasks of intermediate difficulty, (b) should show greater persistence in working at an achievement related task, and (c) should show more efficiency, or a higher level of accomplishment, than persons in whom the motive to avoid failure is stronger than the motive to achieve success.

Results on 49 college men regarding distance of shots in a ring toss game, time spent working on a final examination, and score on the final examination support the hypotheses and hence the construct validity of the two measures of motive strength.

Relationships between these behavioral variables and the variable called n Achievement on the PPS do not support the inference that strength of motive to achieve success is being measured by this test.

The three measures of achievement related motives are not correlated. These results highlight the importance of discovering why different methods of measuring apparently the same human motive do not yield comparable results.

6.

LAWRENCE W. LITTIG

Motivational Correlates
of Probability Preferences

Atkinson, in an analysis of risk-taking behavior (Chapter 2), proposed that preferences for different probabilities of achieving success or avoiding failure are related to individual differences in motivation and developed a model to explain certain motive-related level of aspiration phenomena. This model has implications for such decision-making experiments as those conducted by Edwards (1953, 1954a) and Mosteller and Nogee (1951). The present study examined experimentally certain hypotheses developed from Atkinson's model in a game of chance. . . .

This paper reports an experimental attempt to determine more precisely the relationships between n Achievement, fear of failure, and probability preferences in chance situations in the context of hypotheses derived from theory. The specific hypotheses tested were:

1. Individuals in whom $M_S > M_{AF}$ will prefer a probability of success of .50 in a game of chance.
2. Individuals in whom $M_{AF} > M_S$ will avoid a probability of success of .50 in a game of chance.

Of further interest was the stability of probability preferences associated with individual differences in motivation. It seemed reasonable to assume that experience with probabilities would reduce the effect of motivation on probability preferences. Hence, the experiment was conducted over an extended series of trials in an attempt to discover if any effects present on early trials would be changed or eliminated.

The literature has recently been complicated by evidence that probability preferences found by some investigators (Atkinson et al., 1960; Edwards, 1953; Edwards, 1954a) may in fact reflect preferences for variance (Coombs and Pruitt, 1960), i.e., preferences for different

Adapted and developed from L. W. Littig, "Effects of Motivation on Probability Preferences," *Journal of Personality*, 1963, **31**, 417–427 by permission of author and publisher.

amounts which may be won or lost. To avoid this ambiguity, variance was controlled, and the hypothesis-testing aspects of the research were combined with an exploratory investigation of motive-related variance preferences.

METHOD

Subjects. Fifty undergraduate men enrolled in introductory psychology at the University of Michigan served as an initial pool of Ss from which 16 Ss were selected for the experiment. The motive to achieve success (M_S) was measured using the thematic apperceptive (TAT) method to provide n Achievement scores (McClelland, Atkinson, Clark and Lowell, 1953); the motive to avoid failure (M_{AF}) was assessed with the test anxiety questionnaire (TAQ) of Mandler and Sarason (1952). The fifty TAT protocols were scored for n Achievement by two experienced scorers, both of whom had obtained reliability correlations above .90 with pretested practice materials prepared by Smith and Feld (1958). The interscorer reliability correlation was .80 (rho). Eight of the original 50 Ss who received high TAT scores from both scorers and low TAQ scores, and 8 who were given low TAT scores by both scorers and received high TAQ scores, were selected as Ss for the experiment on the assumption that the former were stronger in M_S than in M_{AF} ($M_S > M_{AF}$) and the latter stronger in M_{AF} than in M_S ($M_{AF} > M_S$). The usefulness of this assumption has been demonstrated by Atkinson, et al. (1960). The mean TAT and TAQ scores for the $M_S > M_{AF}$ group were 8.0 and 76.25, respectively, and for the $M_{AF} > M_S$ group they were −0.5 and 112.5, respectively. The 16 Ss were organized into three groups of six, six, and four Ss, with Ss in whom $M_S > M_{AF}$ and Ss in whom $M_{AF} > M_S$ equally proportioned among the groups. Each group met with E for eight experimental sessions on consecutive days during which they played a competitive game of chance.

Procedure. Ss played a game of poker dice following a procedure previously used by Preston and Baratta (1948) in a study of subjective probability. In this game, players roll five dice in an attempt to make a combination of numbers which is "higher" than a five number "poker hand." The game was constructed as follows: Five poker dice hands were found, 55541, 55441, 66431, 33642, 11432, which had, respectively, the following mathematical probabilities of being beaten: .10, .30, .50, .70, .90. Each of these five probabilities was paired with four levels of variance: 500, 1000, 2500, and 5000. For each of the 20 resulting probability-variance combinations, a value was computed which represented the prize, or number of points, that S could win by beating a hand. The computed prize values often ended in numbers other than zero. To simplify Ss' task, the nearest zero-ending number to the computed prize was used. This introduced a negligible lack of equivalence among hands classified as having the same variance. It was Ss' task to competitively bid for an opportunity to attempt to win these prizes.

Table 1 summarizes the game. Column 1 shows the five poker dice hands, column 2 their objective probabilities of being beaten, and columns 3 through 6 the prize values (*a*) and zero expected value bids (*b*) for each of the 20 probability-variance combinations.[1] The number in parenthesis following each prize is the exact variance of that probability-prize combination.

Table 1

The game matrix: five poker dice hands with associated probabilities of winning, prize values (*a*), and zero expected value bids (*b*), for four levels of variance.

		Variance			
Hand	Probability	500	1000	2500	5000
55541	.10	*a* 80(576) *b* 8	100(900) 10	170(2601) 17	240(5184) 24
55441	.30	*a* 50(525) *b* 15	70(1029) 21	110(2541) 33	150(4725) 45
66431	.50	*a* 50(625) *b* 25	60(900) 30	100(2500) 50	140(4900) 70
33642	.70	*a* 50(525) *b* 35	70(1029) 49	110(2541) 77	150(4725) 105
11432	.90	*a* 80(576) *b* 72	100(900) 90	170(2601) 153	240(5184) 216

Note: Exact variances are in parentheses.

The probability-variance combinations were presented to the groups of *Ss* serially in random sequence on separate 5″ × 8″ note cards. Three sets of 20 cards were used and each card carried the following information: a poker dice hand made of five numbers; the objective probability of beating that hand; and the number of points to be won by beating the hand. The cards had the appearance of this example:

Hand: 55441

Probability of beating: 3/10

Points to be won: 100

An experimental session consisted of the presentation of the 60 cards to *Ss* and the collection of their bids for each card. During a session *Ss* were seated around a large table and *E* presented the cards one at a time. At each presentation of a card *Ss* wrote privately on a piece of paper from a 3″ × 5″ pad the number of points they bid for the hand on that card. After each *S* had written

---

[1] Prize values are obtained from the following formula for variance: $v = a^2 \, p(1-p)$, in which v = variance, p = probability of winning, and a = amount to be won. Zero expected value bids (*b*) = *pa*.

his bid, the bids were passed to *E* and were recorded. The group setting was deliberately used to emphasize the competitive nature of the game and to stimulate *S*s to bid high for the hands they especially wanted, since a hand went to the highest bidder. Payoff plays by *S*s did not occur at the time of bidding, however. Rather, following the collection of bids for a hand, *E* selected five dice from a pool of 15 dice (to reduce bias which might be inherent in any repeatedly used set of five dice) and made a "practice roll" to "see if the hand would have been beaten." Following each practice roll, *E* announced whether or not the hand would have been beaten to call *S*s' attention to the verification of the stated objective probabilities by the dice. After bids had been made for all 60 probability-variance combinations, the highest bidders for each were given an opportunity blindly to draw three hands to play from among the hands they had acquired from their bidding.

Two considerations dictated this mode of play. First, it was believed that if *S*s knew that only a sample of the hands they had acquired through their bidding would actually be played they would be more careful in bidding to acquire only those hands they preferred. Second, it was considered desirable to eliminate immediate payoffs so that strategy over the course of bidding would not be determined by momentary fluctuations in the wins and losses of the players.

After receiving three hands, each *S* was given the dice and allowed to roll them against the probability-variance combinations represented by the three hands. On these payoff plays *S* paid the number of points he bid to acquire the hand. If he won with a successful roll, he was given the number of points represented by the prize value for the hand. The *S* in each experimental group who won the largest number of points was given a monetary reward of 50 cents. An additional monetary prize of five dollars was awarded the *S* who had the highest total score at the end of the experiment. The *S*s were paid at the rate of one dollar per hour for eight two-hour sessions.

The experiment was carried out for 480 trials broken into these eight sessions. In all, 7,680 individual bids were collected.

Treatment of Data. During the 60 trials of each experimental session each of the 20 probability-variance combinations was presented three times. Consequently, each *S* made three bids for each probability-variance combination during each session. The mean of these three bids was computed on the assumption that the mean of the three bids was the best estimate of the number of points *S* was willing to offer for a particular combination of probability and variance during a given session. Thus, the original 7,680 bids were reduced to 2,560 mean bids.

A second conversion of the data was made to provide a baseline for making comparisons among bids for the 20 different hands. This conversion was made by dividing each mean bid by the appropriate zero expected value bid. These ratios were used to analyze the relationships among motivation, probability, and variance. Henceforth, "bid" will refer to these computed mean ratios of the zero expected value bids.

RESULTS

The eight experimental sessions were divided into two sets of four sessions each. Set I consists of data obtained during sessions 1 through 4 and was used to test the hypotheses. Set II consists of data obtained during sessions 5 through 8 and was used to evaluate the effects of experience.

Hypotheses 1 and 2. Results relevant to Hypothesis 1 are presented in Table 2. There is a tendency when $M_S > M_{AF}$ to bid relatively more as the objective probability of winning increases; however, differences in bidding are not statistically significant ($F = 1.28$, $df = 4$ and 28, $p > .20$; Table 3) and Hypothesis 1 is not supported.

Table 2

Mean bids for five probabilities of winning when $M_S > M_{AF}$ and when $M_{AF} > M_S$ during sessions 1–4 (Set I) and sessions 5–8 (Set II)

($N = 8$ for each motive group)

Motive	Set I Probability					Set II Probability				
	.10	.30	.50	.70	.90	.10	.30	.50	.70	.90
$M_S > M_{AF}$	.75	.73	.86	1.03	.94	.43	.56	.64	.85	.89
$M_{AF} > M_S$	1.23	.81	.80	.86	.78	.82	.74	.80	.82	.76

Results relevant to Hypothesis 2 also appear in Table 2 where the mean bids obtained in the case of $M_{AF} > M_S$ during Set I are reported. The most striking feature of these bids is that the mean bid for the .10 probability of success is nearly 25 per cent greater than the zero expected value bid. A negative expected value is being created to obtain this probability and the difference among the bids for the five probabilities is statistically significant ($F = 2.71$, $df = 4$ and 28, $p < .05$; Table 3).

The high bid for the .10 probability and low bids for the other probabilities obtained when $M_{AF} > M_S$ are consistent with the assumption upon which Hypothesis 2 is based, though the bidding pattern does not conform directly with the hypothesis. The minimum motivation to avoid failure will be associated with either the highest or the lowest probability of winning if the maximum motivation to avoid failure occurs at the probability of success of .50. The bidding pattern obtained is consistent with the prediction of Hypothesis 2 that the .50 probability of success would be avoided.

Table 3

Analyses of variance of Set I and Set II bids when $M_S > M_{AF}$ and $M_{AF} > M_S$ for five probabilities of winning

| | | Set I | | | | Set II | | | |
| | | $M_S > M_{AF}$ | | $M_{AF} > M_S$ | | $M_S > M_{AF}$ | | $M_{AF} > M_S$ | |
Source	df	MS	F	MS	F	MS	F	MS	F
Probability (P)	4	2.01	1.28	4.65	2.71*	4.77	4.49†	.15	
Sessions (S)	3	.43		.95		1.97	3.58*	.57	
$P \times S$	12	.13		.46		.21	1.62	.21	
Ss	7	4.32		4.38		5.39		3.13	
$P \times Ss$ (error)	28	1.58		1.72		1.08		1.28	
$S \times Ss$ (error)	21	.57		.90		.55		.55	
$P \times S \times Ss$ (error)	84	.17		.54		.13		.29	
Total	159								

* $p < .05$.
† $p < .01$.

The effects of experience on probability preferences may be seen in Table 2, which also contains the Set II mean bids for $M_S > M_{AF}$ and $M_{AF} > M_S$. A systematic difference in amounts bid for the five objective probabilities occurs when $M_S > M_{AF}$, in the form of an orderly increase in amount bid as objective probability of winning increases. The ordering is regular and without reversals (.90 > .70 > .50 > .30 > .10). The difference among these mean bids is statistically significant ($F = 4.49$, $df = 4$ and 28, $p < .01$; Table 3.)

On the other hand, when $M_{AF} > M_S$ the mean bids almost describe a horizontal line (Table 2), and the bidding may be characterized as expressing indifference to the five probabilities.

Variance. The analysis of the effect of variance on bidding is based upon all data collected in all experimental sessions. Table 4 presents the mean bids for the 20 probability-variance combinations of both motive groups. When $M_S > M_{AF}$ there is a tendency to bid relatively more as variance increases, but this tendency is not statistically signifi-

Table 4

Mean bids for 20 probability-variance combinations for Ss
in whom $M_S > M_{AF}$ and in whom $M_{AF} > M_S$

	$M_S > M_{AF}$				$M_{AF} > M_S$			
Probability	500	1000	2500	5000	500	1000	2500	5000
.10	.57	.53	.61	.65	.88	.90	1.05	1.26
.30	.64	.69	.64	.61	.62	.83	.86	.80
.50	.73	.75	.75	.78	.76	.78	.80	.86
.70	.89	.95	.94	.97	.79	.83	.86	.86
.90	.89	.91	.93	.93	.73	.75	.78	.81

Note: Each mean bid is based upon 24 bids made by each of 8 Ss.

cant and variance does not interact with probability at a statistically
significant level (Table 5). Variance has a strikingly different effect
when $M_{AF} > M_S$. Within all probability categories these Ss bid rela-

Table 5

Analyses of variance of bids of Ss in whom $M_S > M_{AF}$ and in
whom $M_{AF} > M_S$ for 20 probability-variance combinations.

Variable	df	$M_S > M_{AF}$		$M_{AF} > M_S$	
		MS	F	MS	F
Probability (P)	4	6.19	2.58	2.84	1.25
Variance (V)	3	.12		1.61	7.31†
P × V	12	.07	1.40	.36	2.40*
Ss	7	4.35		5.01	
P × Ss (error)	28	2.40		2.28	
V × Ss (error)	21	.21		.22	
P × V × Ss (error)	84	.05		.15	
Total	159				

* $p < .025$.
† $p. < .005$.

tively more for the higher variance options, and this is especially true
when high variance is paired with the .10 objective probability of
winning. Both variance alone ($F = 7.31$, $df = 3$ and 21, $p < .005$) and

in interaction with probability ($F = 2.40$, $df = 12$ and 84, $p < .025$) produce highly significant results (Table 5). Ss in whom $M_{AF} > M_S$ show evidence of preferring high variance to low variance and especially prefer a long shot (a .10 objective probability of winning) when it is offered with an opportunity to win a large prize, i.e., when variance is great.

DISCUSSION

Probability Preferences and the Motive to Avoid Failure. The bids obtained for the five objective probabilities of winning from Ss in whom $M_{AF} > M_S$ were consistent with the risk-taking implications of Atkinson's (Chapter 2) model which places the point of strongest motivation to avoid failure at the probability of success of .50 and, consequently, the least resultant motivation to avoid failure at the extreme probabilities of success. Relatively higher bids would, therefore, be expected to occur for either the least or greatest probabilities of winning. It would seem that the competitive cues created by the experimental setting and by the instructions given to Ss aroused motive to avoid failure and produced motive-related behavior consistent with the theory.

With experience these Ss moved to a bidding pattern which can be interpreted as reflecting indifference to the five probabilities used in the game. If it is assumed that the motive to avoid failure is not aroused during the later experimental sessions, indifference to probability is to be expected in the context of this experiment. The median time spent by Ss in the experimental situation for these Set II data was 12 hours. Twelve hours is sufficient time to learn the game thoroughly as well as to become well acquainted with E and the other Ss in the experimental group. It may be argued that those cues assumed to be the achievement-related cues which, during the early sessions, aroused a motive to avoid failure are no longer sufficient to maintain this motive in an aroused state.

Probability Preferences and the Motive to Achieve Success. Hypothesis 1, which predicted probability preferences when $M_S > M_{AF}$, received no support. However, a pattern of bidding developed as the experiment progressed which indicated a preference for the higher probabilities of success used in the experiment.

The conservative style of play which is reflected by the bidding of these Ss would seem to indicate that they are attempting to exert some control over the outcome of the game by obtaining, through their bids, those objective probabilities which most insure winning *qua* winning even though the prize to be won when playing a high probability is very small. A new finding seems to be presented by these data, viz., individuals with strong achievement motivation and weak motivation to avoid failure prefer to minimize risk in situations they cannot influence directly through the application of their skills. Atkinson's model does not generalize to chance situations, at least in the case of $M_S >$ M_{AF}. . . .

It may be argued that the minimal achievement cues of the game were sufficient to arouse both motive to achieve success and motive to avoid failure. Atkinson has stated that his model of risk-taking ". . . pertains to . . . an *ideal achievement-related situation* (his italics). . . ." (Chapter 2, p. 14), and that motive to achieve success and motive to avoid failure are ". . . normally aroused whenever performance is likely to be evaluated against some standard of excellence. . . ." (Chapter 2, p. 14). It appears that the first statement is correct but that the second needs modification. These motives are not as situation-dependent for their arousal as Atkinson's writings suggest. Rather, a minimal achievement situation, such as a game of chance, seems sufficient to arouse them. However, when the motives are aroused in less than "ideal achievement-related situations" they lead to behavior which is not predicted by the model when M_S is assumed to be stronger than M_{AF}. When the selection of a probability is made by an S in whom $M_S > M_{AF}$, the total situation must be considered to understand his selection. The present data indicate that the aspect of the situation which must be considered when applying Atkinson's model to risk-taking behavior is that which is represented by the incentive component of the model. This component represents the reward value of successful achievement which is inherent in the situation. The model relates the mathematical value of incentive directly to the value assigned to the probability of success. In the case of incentive of success, $I_s = 1 - P_s$. The present data indicate that this assumption is incorrect.

For example, if it is assumed that the incentive value of winning in a game of chance, such as the one used in this experiment, is minimal *vis-à-vis* achieving in a skill situation, it would be more appropriate to assign some constant value to the incentive of winning (I_w) rather than assigning the arbitrary $1 - P_s$ value. Some minimal value may be used irrespective of the stated probability of winning, for example, .10. If the suggested substitute values are manipulated as in Atkinson's model, resultant motivation when $M_S > M_{AF}$ is strongest when the probability of winning is greatest.

Unfortunately, if it is necessary to fit the model to new data as they are obtained, it loses much of its general usefulness. It is valuable to do so only to focus attention upon a weak assumption in the model, that $I_s = 1 - P_s$. The present results indicate that this is a limited assumption which is not valid for all situations involving risk, especially for those which do not have some standard of excellence against which performance may be evaluated by individuals in whom the motive to achieve success is stronger than the motive to avoid failure.

Motivation and Variance Preferences. The finding of variance preferences among Ss in whom $M_{AF} > M_S$ supports the contention of Coombs and Pruitt (1960) that variance should be controlled in studies of probability preferences. It also indicates that the issue of variance preferences may be further complicated by the presence of unmeasured individual differences in motivation in studies of the effect of variance on risk taking.

SUMMARY

Certain theoretical relationships, proposed by Atkinson, among achievement-related motives and probability preferences were examined experimentally in a game of chance. It was hypothesized that: (1) when motive to achieve success (M_S) is stronger than motive to avoid failure (M_{AF}), intermediate probabilities of success will be preferred; (2) when $M_{AF} > M_S$, intermediate probabilities of success will be avoided.

M_S was inferred from content analysis of TAT stories for n Achievement, and M_{AF} from the Mandler and Sarason Test Anxiety Questionnaire. Probability preferences were assessed in a game of poker dice in which points were bid to play against poker dice hands having, respectively, .10, .30, .50, .70, and .90 probabilities of being beaten (i.e., probabilities of success for the bidder).

The results supported Hypothesis 2 but did not support Hypothesis 1.

7.

GEORGE H. LITWIN

Achievement Motivation, Expectancy of Success, and Risk-Taking Behavior

A model for risk-taking behavior was proposed by Atkinson (Chapter 2) to predict from the assessment of an individual's achievement motivation *(a)* which of a set of tasks varying in difficulty he will prefer, and *(b)* how much effort he will expend trying to succeed at a task. The present investigation deals with (1) the applicability of the model to a number of different situations, that is, with its generality; (2) tests of two assumptions made in the use of the model; and (3) the comparison of several different measures of moderate risk-taking. . . .

The hypotheses for this study are as follows:

HYPOTHESIS 1. *Ss* motivated to achieve success will take moderate risks, and *Ss* motivated to avoid failure will take more extreme (or less moderate) risks in a number of different games.

HYPOTHESIS 2. *Ss* will report expectancies of success that are "biased" in a direction consistent with their motivation. Specifically, *Ss* motivated to achieve success will report higher expectancies of success than *Ss* motivated to avoid failure.

HYPOTHESIS 3. *Ss* in a Ring Toss Game will assign monetary values to success at the various levels of difficulty that are a negative linear function of the expectancies of success assigned to the same levels of difficulty by *Ss* of similar motivation. In all of these, group differences rather than relation to an absolute standard are emphasized because our classification of motivation is based on the distribution of test scores and describes only the relative strength of competing motives. In a college population, one might expect that most individuals are more

This is a revised version of an unpublished honors thesis submitted to the Department of Psychology, University of Michigan, in 1958.

motivated to achieve success than to avoid failure, though relative differences should still be important.

METHOD

The subjects were 78 men enrolled in an introductory psychology course at the University of Michigan. Serving as an *S* in an experiment was a course requirement. Several weeks prior to the experimental session, *S*s were brought together to write stories in response to four thematic apperception pictures (B, H, A, and G). The method of collecting stories is described in McClelland, et al. (1953). At the same time, *S*s completed a short form of the TAQ. This short form was the first of the three parts of the TAQ, the one dealing with group intelligence or aptitude tests. The first section was selected because of the three, it was found to correlate best with the total questionnaire score ($r = .88$, $N = 50$). The method of scoring was the same as that described by Mandler and Cowen (1958) except that five intervals instead of ten were used.

The thematic apperception stories were scored for *n* Achievement according to the manual by McClelland, et al. (1953). The scoring was done independently by two scorers who had previously established high correlations with materials scored by experts. The rank-order correlation of the *n* Achievement scores obtained by the two scorers was .85 ($N = 78$). Twenty-four scores on which the scorers disagreed as to the presence of achievement imagery were scored by an expert scorer.[1] For the stories scored by three people, scores were obtained which were based on agreement of two of the three scorers. On all other stories the *n* Achievement score was the mean of the scores obtained by the two original scorers. The rank-order correlation of *n* Achievement and Test Anxiety was $-.005$ ($N = 78$). Both tests were administered under neutral conditions.

For the experimental session, only *S*s showing clear-cut dispositions to achieve or to avoid failure were used. Twenty *S*s were selected with *n* Achievement scores above the group median and Test Anxiety scores below the group median. For these *S*s, the motive to achieve is thought to be relatively stronger than the motive to avoid failure. These are the achievement-oriented subjects. Another 20 *S*s were selected with *n* Achievement scores below the group median and Test Anxiety scores above the group median. For these *S*s, the motive to avoid failure is relatively stronger than the motive to achieve. These are the failure-oriented *S*s.

The Experimental Session. In order to obtain estimates of expectancy based on the appearance of the games, and spontaneous risk-taking behavior from *S*s who had not been forced to make systematic appraisals of risk, the *S*s were divided into two experimental conditions: an *Assessment Condition* and a *Behavior Condition*. The intuition that asking for estimates of difficulty would

[1] The author wishes to acknowledge the assistance of Professor John W. Atkinson, who served as expert scorer and C. Ann Litwin, who served as scorer.

change the Ss' approach to the games was supported by spontaneous remarks made by faculty members and advanced graduate students in a seminar demonstration of the experiment. Given a chance to play the game after first assessing their chances, these sophisticated Ss reported being much more concerned in testing the validity of their estimates by sampling different levels of difficulty than in "playing the game." Half the Ss in each condition were achievement-oriented and half were failure-oriented. There was a total of four experimental sessions, two for each condition.

Behavior Condition Procedure. After Ss had assembled they were given the following instructions: "Today we are going to play a series of four games; some of them will be games of skill; others will be games of chance. What we are interested in is how well you can do at these games. . . . Naturally we want you all to try to do as well as you can." The Ss were then shown the Ring Toss and told they could take ten shots from any of eighteen lines varying in distance from the target. The closest line was 10 inches from the target and the subsequent lines were 10 inches apart. A placard designating the number of the line was placed at lines 3, 6, 9, 12, 15, and 18. Line 1 was the closest line. The target was a round wooden peg; the ring was made of wire covered with black tape and was 10 inches in diameter. Two of the Ring Toss games were set up in the experimental room. An assistant, who recorded the line from which the S shot, sat 6 feet from the game, approximately opposite line 6. Just before the Ss began to play they were told, "Go ahead and shoot and see how good you are at this." Two Ss were asked to volunteer to begin the game.

After all Ss had completed the Ring Toss, the Penny Pitch was introduced. "This is a game we call Penny Pitch. There are nine targets, each with a different size hole. The idea is to pitch the penny into one of the boxes." The boxes were gray cardboard, $2\frac{3}{4}$ inches high, by $12\frac{3}{4}$ inches long, by $10\frac{5}{8}$ inches wide. The targets were numbered from 1 to 9 and were designated by placards. The diameters of the holes were (in inches): 10, $8\frac{11}{16}$, $7\frac{5}{8}$, $6\frac{5}{8}$, $5\frac{11}{16}$, $4\frac{11}{16}$, $3\frac{11}{16}$, $2\frac{5}{16}$, $2\frac{1}{8}$. Box 1 had the largest hole. The Ss stood 5 feet from the targets. The assistant sat near box 1. There were two Penny Pitch games set up in the experimental room.

After all Ss had completed the Penny Pitch, they were seated in a group and the Horse Race Game was described. This game consisted of turning over a deck of cards—each card representing a horse—one at a time; the order in which the cards came up was the order of finish. Each S drew the name of one horse and was allowed to bet only on this horse. Ss could place bets varying in probability of winning from 1/10 to 9/10 (i.e., they could bet on the horse to finish first, first or second, etc.). The E attempted to arouse and maintain interest by acting as track announcer while he shuffled the cards and turned them over. All bets had equal positive expected values, that is, Ss would win an average of 10 points in each race no matter which odds they picked. The points had only symbolic meaning; accumulating a large number was not emphasized nor were the scores made public. Ten races were conducted; after each race the betting forms were collected and new ones distributed.

Following the Horse Race Game, Ss in the Behavior Condition were introduced to an ESP game: "Some of you may know of the research being done on extrasensory perception. It has been reported that certain people who are called good receivers can guess what another person is thinking with remarkable accuracy. We are going to try this with a slightly different twist. I have here a deck of special cards. Of these I am going to designate a certain number as 'winning cards.' We want you to try and guess when these winning cards will turn up. Before I turn up each card I will say, 'Ready . . . now!' I will concentrate hard on the number and I want you to try to do the same. . . . Each time I draw a card and attempt to 'transmit the message,' you are to concentrate hard and then circle either the word 'win' or the word 'lose.' " The Ss guessed "win" or "lose" on 30 trials. Nothing was actually won or lost by the S. The purpose of this game was to attempt to measure subjective probability of success in a situation where no cues about objective probabilities are available.

After the ESP game, the Pencil Maze booklets were distributed. These booklets contained a series of 9 mazes, varying in complexity and difficulty. The easiest was about 1-inch square and contained only three choice points, while the most complex covered most of an $8\frac{1}{2}$ x 11-inch sheet and contained more than 30 choice points. The Ss read the instructions, looked briefly over the puzzles, and then selected 1 puzzle to work on. They were allowed 1 minute to try to complete it. After each trial the booklets were collected and new booklets distributed.

Estimate of the Subjective Value of Success. The Ss in the Behavior Condition were given the following instructions after they had finished playing all the games: "We are thinking of running the Ring Toss again at a later date and of paying money for each hit. I would like you to designate what value in money should be assigned from each one of these lines. Values may run anywhere from 0 to $1.00." Most of the Ss walked around the Ring Toss while recording their judgments as to what prize should be awarded to a hit from each line.

Assessment Condition Procedure. The Ss in the Assessment Condition played the Ring Toss, Penny Pitch, Horse Race Game, and Pencil Maze. They did not play the ESP game or estimate the value of hitting in the Ring Toss. However, before playing each game they were asked to estimate the probability of success at each level of difficulty. No estimates of probability of success were collected for the Horse Race Game, since objective probabilities were clearly stated.

RESULTS

Estimated Probability of Success. Ss in the Assessment Condition estimated the difficulty of each alternative in each game, using only the task's appearance. The mean estimated probabilities for the achievement-oriented Ss ($N = 10$) and the failure-oriented Ss ($N = 10$) are

Table 1

Mean estimated probabilities of success assigned to each of the alternatives
in three games by the ten achievement-oriented Ss and the
ten failure-oriented Ss in the Assessment Condition

| | Ring Toss* | | | Penny Pitch* | | | Puzzle† | |
| | Achievement-Oriented | Failure-Oriented | Box | Achievement-Oriented | Failure-Oriented | N | Achievement-Oriented | Failure-Oriented |
Line								
1	.99	1.00	1	.88	.92	1	.95	.97
2	.99	1.00						
3	.98	.99	2	.85	.84	2	.89	.86
4	.92	.92						
5	.89	.88	3	.77	.77	3	.78	.70
6	.82	.82						
7	.76	.75	4	.66	.67	4	.67	.54
8	.70	.69						
9	.63	.65	5	.54	.57	5	.57	.41
10	.59	.59						
11	.56	.54	6	.46	.43	6	.46	.32
12	.47	.50						
13	.39	.47	7	.29	.32	7	.33	.19
14	.34	.42						
15	.28	.36	8	.22	.23	8	.25	.10
16	.26	.30						
17	.24	.27	9	.14	.16	9	.21	.08
18	.23	.25						
Mean Ps:	.61	.63		.53	.55		.57	.46

* Analysis of variance shows no significant effects other than the very significant effect for alternatives (rows).
† Analysis of variance shows a weak effect for motivation ($F = 1.93$, $df = 1/18$, $p < .20$) and a statistically significant motivation $\times$ alternatives interaction ($F = 9.02$, $df = 8/144$, $p < .001$) along with the very significant effect for alternatives (rows).

presented in Table 1. Examination of the data indicates that the two
groups of subjects assigned almost identical estimated probabilities to
the alternatives in the Ring Toss and Penny Pitch games. The Pencil
Maze was the only game in which a fairly large difference between the
groups was found. The data were subjected to Type I analyses of variance, described by Lindquist (1956). The significant effects are summarized in the footnotes to Table 1. As expected, all three games
showed highly significant effects for level of difficulty. In the Ring Toss
and Penny Pitch no other significant effects appeared. In the Pencil
Maze the effect of motivation approached statistical significance ($F =
1.93$, $df = 1/18$, $p < .20$), and the interaction of motivation and level
of difficulty was significant ($F = 9.02$, $df = 8/144$, $p < .001$). The

hypothesis that the achievement-oriented Ss would assign higher probabilities than the failure-oriented Ss in all games is not supported. In the Pencil Maze, however, the achievement-oriented Ss did assign higher probabilities than the failure-oriented Ss to all but the easiest mazes.

The guesses of "win" or "lose" in the ESP game demonstrated a difference among subjects in what might be called "strictly subjective probability of success." Thirty trials were run. The mean number of "wins" chosen by the achievement-oriented Ss was 16.4 or 55%, and by the failure-oriented Ss, 14.0 or 47%; this difference is statistically significant ($t = 2.73$, $df = 18$, $p < .02$). Thus, achievement-oriented Ss seem to think they will win more often than do failure-oriented Ss, and this finding supports the hypothesis that achievement-related motivation is associated with strength of expectancy of success.

Risk-Taking Behavior. Three measures of the degree of risk-taking were developed. For the Estimated Probability Index, the task selected was first assigned an expectancy, which was the average probability estimate made by Assessment Condition Ss of similar motivation (shown in Table 1); the index is the difference between this expectancy and .50.

The Distribution Index is the discrepancy of a given choice from the median of the distribution of all task choices for that game. The difference between the task chosen (x) and the median $(Md.)$ is divided by the average deviation (AD) from the median task choice for that game. The units of measurement are the tasks themselves:

$$DI = \frac{|x - Md|}{AD}$$

Separate Distribution Indices were computed for the Assessment and Behavior conditions.

The Geographic Index is simply the number of tasks between the selected task and the middle of the geographic range. Since the object of all of these indices is to show an individual's tendency to select tasks that are "close to" or "far from" the middle, directionality was ignored. For each of the three indices, the Ss score for a game is the mean of his index scores on each trial.

The mean scores for the two orientations on each of these risk-taking indices are shown in Table 2. Low scores uniformly represent a preference for tasks of intermediate difficulty. The mean index scores for the achievement-oriented Ss tend to be smaller, as anticipated, than the scores for the failure-oriented Ss. Summaries of Type 1 analyses of variance described by Lindquist (1956) are shown in Table 3.

Table 2

Mean scores on the three indices of risk-taking preference
for the ten achievement-oriented Ss and the ten
failure-oriented Ss in the Behavior Condition

Game	Motivation	Estimated Probability Index	Average Deviation Index	Geographic Index
Ring Toss	Achievement-oriented	.15	.77	2.05
	Failure-oriented	.14	1.23	2.18
Penny Pitch	Achievement-oriented	.12	.86	1.46
	Failure-oriented	.19	1.14	1.86
Horse Race	Achievement-oriented	—	.84	1.84
	Failure-oriented	—	1.17	1.77
Puzzle	Achievement-oriented	.21	.93	2.06
	Failure-oriented	.32	1.11	2.59
Grand mean	Achievement-oriented	.16	.85	1.85
	Failure-oriented	.22	1.16	2.10

Note: Low scores represent preference for intermediate level of difficulty.

Table 3

Summaries of analysis of variance for each of the indices of risk-taking
preference for the Behavior Condition (data presented in Table 2)

Index	Source	df	Mean Square	F
Estimated Probability Index	Motivation	1	.06	10.91‡
	Error (b)	18	.0055	
	Games	2	.08	15.09‡
	Interaction	2	.02	3.58†
	Error (w)	18	.0053	
Distribution Index	Motivation	1	2.00	7.41†
	Error (b)	18	.27	
	Games	3	.003	.01
	Interaction	3	.14	.50
	Error (w)	54	.28	
Geographic Index	Motivation	1	1.22	3.39*
	Error (b)	18	.36	
	Games	3	1.80	3.67†
	Interaction	3	.37	.76
	Error (w)	54	.49	

* $p < .10$
† $p < .05$
‡ $p < .005$

The Estimated Probability Index demonstrates the anticipated overall difference between the two motivation groups. But as Table 3 shows, there is a significant interaction effect. T-tests described by Cochran and Cox (1957) show that the achievement-oriented Ss have a significantly lower score than the failure-oriented Ss on the Penny Pitch $(t = 2.12, p < .05)$ and the Pencil Maze $(t = 3.33, p < .01)$, but that the scores of the two do not differ for the Ring Toss. The achievement-oriented Ss have consistently lower Distribution Index scores showing their tendency to prefer intermediate risks $(F = 7.41, df = 1/18, p < .05)$. Results using the Geographic Index are in the expected direction for all games, but the overall difference between the motivation groups only approaches significance $(F = 3.39, df = 1/18, p < .10)$. Thus, the predicted tendency of achievement-oriented Ss to prefer intermediate risks more often than failure-oriented Ss is evident. This relationship is clear when the Distribution Index is used, is observed in two out of three games when the Estimated Probability Index is used, and is consistent though weak when the Geographic Index is used.

CORRELATION OF INDICES. Within each game an attempt was made to determine the similarity of scores on the three indices, using Kendall's coefficient of concordance. For the Ring Toss, the three indices were not significantly related: $W = .41$ $(\chi^2 = 23.37, df = 19, p < .25)$. For the Penny Pitch and Pencil Maze, the three indices were very highly related and were, respectively, $W = .93$ $(\chi^2 = 53.02, df = 19, p < .001)$; $W = .87$ $(\chi^2 = 49.59, df = 19, p < .001)$.

ASSESSMENT CONDITION RESULTS. Table 4 contains the risk-taking data for the Assessment Condition Ss: it is comparable in all respects to Table 2. Analyses of variance of these data were conducted exactly as described for the Behavior Condition data. Since so few of the effects were significant, the results of the analyses are summarized in the footnotes to Table 4. The two motivation groups showed no tendency to vary in the preference for tasks of intermediate difficulty after having been asked to estimate the chances of success. The Horse Race Game is the only one in which the results for the two conditions look similar; in terms of the Assessment Condition, it is the only game showing results in the predicted direction. The Horse Race Game is the one game for which no prior estimates of difficulty were required.

Estimated Value of Success. Subjects in the Behavior Condition estimated the monetary value of succeeding from each line in the Ring Toss. This was an attempt to measure the incentive value of success, which, according to the theoretical model developed by Atkinson, is a

Table 4

Mean scores on the three indices of risk-taking preference
for the ten achievement-oriented Ss and the ten
failure-oriented Ss in the Assessment Condition

Game	Motivation	Estimated* Probability Index	Average† Deviation Index	Geographic‡ Index
Ring Toss	Achievement-oriented	.16	1.00	2.13
	Failure-oriented	.12	1.01	2.11
Penny Pitch	Achievement-oriented	.19	1.13	2.04
	Failure-oriented	.18	.88	1.73
Horse Race	Achievement-oriented	—	.88	1.77
	Failure-oriented	—	1.13	1.99
Puzzle	Achievement-oriented	.20	1.06	2.13
	Failure-oriented	.27	.94	2.03
Grand mean	Achievement-oriented	.19	1.02	2.02
	Failure-oriented	.19	.99	1.97

Note: Low scores represent preference for intermediate level of difficulty.
* Analysis of variance shows a significant effect for games ($F = 10.00$, $df = 2/36$, $p < .001$) and for motivation $\times$ games interaction ($F = 3.75$, $df = 2/36$, $p < .05$).
† Analysis of variance shows a weak motivation $\times$ games interaction effect ($F = 1.77$, $df = 3/54$, $p < .20$).
‡ Analysis of variance shows no significant effects.

negative linear function of the probability of success. Figure 1 contains the graphs of the mean values of success for the achievement-oriented and failure-oriented Ss. Also shown in Figure 1 is a theoretical or $1-P_s$ line based on the estimated probabilities obtained from all Ss in the Assessment Condition. The estimated values are reasonably linear; the possibility of nonlinearity was rejected on the basis of visual inspection. To test the hypothesis that the slopes of the three lines were equal, the slope of the regression line of the estimated values was computed for each S. The mean slope for the ten achievement-oriented Ss was 6.09. The mean slope for the ten failure-oriented Ss was 4.37. The slope of the $1-P_s$ regression line was computed for each S in the Assessment Condition. The mean slope for the twenty Ss in the Assessment Condition was 5.04. (This group provided estimates of P_s but not of the monetary value of success.) A simple analysis of variance of the differences between slopes showed that the null hypothesis of equal slopes must be rejected ($F = 3.54$, $df = 2/37$, $p < .05$). Comparisons between

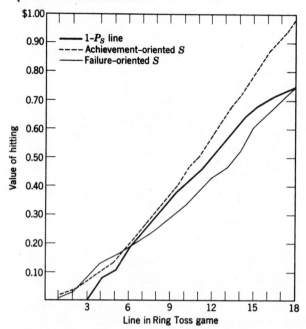

Figure 1   Monetary values of hitting assigned to various distances in the Ring Toss by achievement-oriented and failure-oriented *S*s in the Behavior Condition and a $1-P_s$ line based on the probability of success (P_s) estimates made by all *S*s in the Assessment Condition.

the slopes were made using the *t*-technique described by Cochran and Cox (1957). The slope of the achievement-oriented *S*s was found to be significantly larger than the slope of the failure-oriented *S*s ($t = 2.44$, $p < .05$) and the slope of the $1-P_s$ line ($t = 2.44$, $p < .05$). The failure-oriented *S*s were not found to have a slope significantly smaller than the slope of the $1-P_s$ line ($t = 1.02$, $p < .20$). The mean slope of the estimated values of success for all the Behavior Condition *S*s (5.23) is approximately equal to the $1-P_s$ line for all the Assessment Condition *S*s (5.04).

DISCUSSION

Expectancy of Success. The hypothesis that achievement-oriented *S*s see all tasks as easier (having higher expectancies of success) than failure-oriented *S*s is only partly confirmed; the relationship appears to depend on the type of game. In the ESP Game, where no cues about the actual probabilities were available, the achievement-oriented Ss did give "win" responses more often than failure-oriented Ss. However, in the Ring Toss Game and the Penny Pitch Game, no difference was observed in the estimates of difficulty given by each of the two motivation groups. Both these games had a fixed origin (a point at which success is certain) and a constant interval between tasks (in inches). In the Pencil Maze, the achievement-oriented Ss estimated higher probabilities than did the failure-oriented Ss for the harder puzzles, but not for the easier ones. The origin for the Pencil Maze is fairly well fixed (there is a point at which success is certain), but the interval between puzzles is not a fixed attribute of the game, and, in fact, many Ss commented on the disparity of certain intervals. It seems that some condition of real or apparent ambiguity is a prerequisite to strong motivational determination of expectancy.

Both the achievement-oriented and the failure-oriented Ss seriously overestimated the objective probabilities. Although the data are not adequate for a thorough comparison of estimated and actual probabilities, some data from the Ring Toss will serve as an illustration. A total of fifty or more shots were taken from lines 12, 15, and 18 in the Ring Toss. At line 12, fifteen of the ninety-five attempts, or 16%, were successful. The mean estimated probability of success at line 12 was .49. At line 15, twelve of the eighty-six attempts, or 14%, were successful. The mean estimated probability of success at line 15 was .32. At line 18, six of the fifty-five attempts, or 11%, were successful. The mean estimated probability of success at line 18 was .24.

Risk-Taking Behavior. The hypothesis that in the Behavior Condition the achievement-oriented Ss would select tasks of intermediate difficulty more often than the failure-oriented Ss was clearly confirmed. No matter which of the three indices was used, the achievement-oriented Ss generally had lower index scores. However, of the three indices, the Distribution Index yielded the most consistent results. For the Estimated Probability Index, the Ring Toss did not show the predicted difference. For the Geographic Index, the Horse Race Game did not show the predicted difference.

In the Distribution Index, the median of the distribution of task-choices is defined as the point of intermediate risk. The model predicts that achievement-oriented Ss will prefer tasks with expectancies near .50, while the failure-oriented Ss will avoid such tasks. There is no evidence that the median of the distribution of task choices is a task with a .50 expectancy of success. Rather, the median of the distribution is the most intermediate task in *another* sense; it is the median risk being taken by other Ss (remember the Ss do watch each other). This makes sense if we view these games as *competitive*. Thus a "calculated" or intermediate risk is the average aspiration of your competitors.

What is the apparent difficulty at this median task? The median tasks for Behavior Condition Ss were: 13.6 for Ring Toss, 5.9 for the Penny Pitch, and 6.1 for the Pencil Maze. The extrapolated subjective probabilities of these median tasks are (from Table 1), respectively, .41, .46, and .40. The median task for the Horse Race Game (either condition) is 3.5, the point at which the objective probability is .35. Thus, the most successful index, the Distribution Index, defines as the intermediate point tasks with subjective probabilities somewhat below the .50 mark.

The Assessment and Behavior Conditions were devised because it was expected that the probability estimation procedure would have some effect on the risk-taking behavior of the Assessment Condition Ss. Assessment procedures appear to have eliminated the predicted differences between motivation groups which were observed in the Behavior Condition. The process of estimating the probabilities of success may have seriously altered the meaning of the task. Instead of being concerned with doing well in the game in relation to some implicit standard of excellence, the Ss were concerned with checking the accuracy of their probability estimates—so that they would be expected to select tasks without regard for the *risk* involved.

The hypothesis that the estimated values of success are a negative linear function $(1-P_s)$ of the estimated probabilities of success was generally supported. The value estimates were linear, and the average slope of all the value estimates was approximately equal to the slope of the $1-P_s$ line. However, the slope of the achievement-oriented Ss' value estimates was somewhat larger than the slope of the $1-P_s$ line. Thus, the value estimates do not seem to represent incentives alone, but rather, incentive and motive, or what Lewin has called *valence*.

In Lewin's model (1951, p. 273), positive valence is the total attractiveness of a goal. It is a joint function of the goal properties and of tension in the person corresponding to that goal. In the present language, positive valence would be a product of motive and incentive value of success. The slope of the achievement-oriented Ss' value estimates (6.09) is a product of the slope of the $1-P_s$ line (5.04), and a constant (1.21), which could represent the average strength of the motive to achieve. The slope of the failure-oriented Ss' value estimates (4.37) is a product of the slope of the $1-P_s$ line (5.04), and a constant (.87), which could represent the lower average strength of the motive to achieve in this group.

This study provides positive evidence for the risk-taking model, using the thematic apperception measure of *n* Achievement originally developed by McClelland, et al. (1953). Atkinson, et al. (1960) and Atkinson and Litwin (Chapter 5) used a Test of Insight measure of *n* Achievement developed by French (1958) that is similar to the thematic apperception measure. The high degree of agreement between the results of the present study and those using the Test of Insight strongly suggests that the two instruments measure the same construct.

SUMMARY

Forty male undergraduates played games in which they had to select one from a set of tasks varying in difficulty. There were two experimental conditions: one in which the Ss estimated the probabilities of success before playing the games, the other in which no probability estimates were obtained.

In the Behavior Condition (no probability estimates), achievement-oriented Ss selected tasks of intermediate difficulty significantly more often than did failure-oriented Ss. Achievement-oriented Ss gave higher probability estimates than did failure-oriented Ss, but not in games where objective cues were present. Estimates of the amount of money that should be awarded as a prize for hitting the target in a Ring Toss Game were interpreted as estimates of valence, and shown to be a product of motive and incentive value.

The Relationship of Persistence at a Task
to Expectation of Success
and Achievement-Related Motives

The present study investigates the relationship of persistence at a task both to its apparent difficulty and to the relative strength within an individual of the motives to achieve success and to avoid failure (Feather, 1960). The situation to be considered is one in which a subject comes to an objectively insoluble puzzle either believing it to be easy or very difficult. He works at this achievement task under test conditions and suffers repeated and consistent failure in his attempts to get the solution. Persistence is measured in terms of the total time or total trials which the subject works at the task before he turns to an alternative achievement activity. The former measure is sometimes referred to in the literature as temporal persistence; the latter is analogous to resistance to extinction.

The hypotheses of the present investigation are developed from the theory of achievement motivation together with certain additional assumptions. This theory (Chapter 2) relates characteristics of motivated behavior to the interaction of relatively stable personality dispositions (motives) and more transient situational influences (expectations and incentive values). As such, this approach belongs to a class of "expectancy-value" theories which all involve somewhat similar concepts (Feather, Chapter 3). Within this context, the present research attempts to clarify the relationship of persistence at a task to expectations and motives by providing answers to the following two questions:

Reprinted and abridged by permission of the author and the American Psychological Association from the *Journal of Abnormal and Social Psychology*, 1961, 63, 552–561. This paper is based upon a doctoral dissertation submitted to the Department of Psychology at the University of Michigan in 1960 for which the author was awarded the first annual Donald G. Marquis Dissertation Prize.

1. How is persistence at a task affected by the initial subjective probability of success among subjects in whom the motive to achieve success is stronger than the motive to avoid failure $(M_S > M_{AF})$? Do such subjects tend to persist longer at the task when it initially appears easy to them than when it initially appears very difficult?

2. Conversely, how is persistence at a task affected by the initial subjective probability of success among subjects in whom the motive to avoid failure is stronger than the motive to achieve success $(M_{AF} > M_S)$?

The present investigation goes beyond the earlier studies of French and Thomas (1958) and Atkinson and Litwin (Chapter 5) in its attempt to vary both motive and expectation simultaneously. Furthermore, it provides assumptions about the dynamics of changing motivation as expectations of success and failure change, and an explicit analysis of why the subject stops performing the task.

THEORETICAL ASSUMPTIONS

Consider a subject who is performing the initial achievement task. It is assumed that he will continue to persist at this task as long as total motivation to perform it is stronger than total motivation to perform the alternative available to him.

Total motivation to perform the initial achievement task is attributable to the following component motivation[1]: *(a)* achievement-related motivation to perform the task, and *(b)* extrinsic motivation to perform the task. Similarly, since the alternative is also an achievement task, total motivation to perform it is attributable to analogous component motivations.

Achievement-related motivation to perform a task refers to the *resultant* of motivation to achieve success at the task and motivation to avoid failure at the task. According to the theory of achievement motivation, these two motivations summate algebraically to give *positive* achievement-related motivation (approach) for subjects in whom the motive to achieve success is stronger than the motive to avoid failure (i.e., when $M_S > M_{AF}$), and *negative* achievement-related motivation (avoidance) for subjects in whom $M_{AF} > M_S$. Further, achievement-related motivation whether positive or negative is at its maximum

[1] It should be noted that a distinction is made between motivation, which refers to a particular act or response, and motive. Differences in strength of motive (a latent disposition of personality) are assumed to be only one factor influencing the strength of motivation, the other influences being level of expectation and incentive value.

when subjective probability of success at the task is intermediate (i.e., when $P_s = .50$) and decreases monotonically as P_s becomes either smaller or larger than .50. If achievement-related motivation were the only motivation elicited in the situation, it is apparent that a subject with stronger motive to avoid failure should not even undertake performance of an achievement task. Instead he should avoid the task and choose activities which do not arouse anxiety about failure. In contrast, a subject with stronger motive to achieve success should show some positive interest in performing an achievement task.

The concept of extrinsic motivation to perform a task is introduced to account for the fact that the subject is in a social situation in which he has the role of a subject in an experiment and knows he is expected to make some attempt at the task. In any test situation there are certain extrinsic constraints that influence the subject to perform the task irrespective of the nature of his achievement-related motivation. Studies by French (1955), and by Atkinson and Raphelson (1956) have shown, for example, that other motives like n Affiliation are sometimes systematically related to task performance in a situation where no achievement orientation is given but cooperation is requested. The usual social constraints (i.e., desire for approval, fear of disapproval) provide an important source of motivation for subjects in whom $M_{AF} > M_S$. If these subjects are to perform the task at all, some positive motivation must exist to oppose their tendency to avoid an achievement task. For subjects in whom $M_S > M_{AF}$, the extrinsic motivation to perform an assigned task enhances their normally positive motivation to perform achievement-related tasks. In both cases, task performance may be considered overdetermined, that is, the result of two or more different kinds of motivation to perform or not to perform the task (cf. Atkinson and Reitman, 1956).

In the light of this analysis of the components of total motivation, the basic condition for performance of the initial task rather than the alternative task is as follows:

Initial Task		*Alternative Task*	
Achievement-related motivation	$+$ Extrinsic motivation	$>$ Achievement-related motivation	$+$ Extrinsic motivation

It is assumed that the subject will turn to the alternative achievement task when:

Initial Task		*Alternative Task*	
Achievement-related motivation	$+$ Extrinsic motivation	$<$ Achievement-related motivation	$+$ Extrinsic motivation

How then does total motivation to perform the initial achievement task become weaker than total motivation to perform the alternative, so that the subject gives up persisting at the initial task and turns to the alternative? To permit derivation of hypotheses the following three assumptions are made:

1. Both extrinsic motivation to perform the initial task and extrinsic motivation to perform the alternative task are assumed to be constant across experimental conditions.

2. Extrinsic motivation to perform the initial task is assumed to be stronger than extrinsic motivation to perform the alternative task. This is a strong assumption that at least acknowledges the fact that the subject is asked by the experimenter to begin the initial task first.

3. The subjective probability of success for the alternative achievement task is assumed to be constant across experimental conditions. Hence, achievement-related motivation to perform the alternative task is a positive constant for subjects in whom the motive to achieve success is stronger (i.e., when $M_S > M_{AF}$), and has a negative constant value for subjects in whom $M_{AF} > M_S$.

It follows that any decrease in total motivation to perform the initial task must be related to change in achievement-related motivation to perform the initial task. Since, in the theory of achievement motivation, the motives to achieve success (M_S) and to avoid failure (M_{AF}) are considered relatively *stable* dispositions of the personality, change in achievement-related motivation to perform the initial task must be mediated by variation in the subject's expectation of success at the task as he works at it unsuccessfully. Repeated unsuccessful attempts at the initial task are assumed to produce successive decreases in subjective probability of success at the task (P_s). Decrease in P_s is thus the basic dynamic principle assumed to mediate decrease in total motivation to perform the initial task.

The following two specific assumptions are made about this decrease in expectation of success:

1. When the task is presented as a test of skill, reduction in P_s to a particular value is assumed to require more unsuccessful attempts at the task when P_s is initially high than when P_s is initially low.[2]

2. The rate at which decrease in P_s occurs is assumed not to be systematically related to the strength of either the motive to achieve success (M_S) or the motive to avoid failure (M_{AF}).

[2] This assumption is consistent with the distinction between tasks involving skill and tasks involving a degree of external control (e.g., chance) presented by James and Rotter (1958).

Hypotheses. The following four hypotheses are tested in the present investigation:

HYPOTHESIS 1 states that when the motive to achieve success is stronger than the motive to avoid failure $(M_S > M_{AF})$, persistence at the initial achievement task should be greater when initial subjective probability of success is high (i.e., some $P_s > .50$) than when initial P_s is low (i.e., some $P_s < .50$).

HYPOTHESIS 2 states that when $M_{AF} > M_S$, persistence at the initial achievement task should be greater when initial P_s is low (i.e., some $P_s < .50$) than when initial P_s is high (i.e., some $P_s > .50$).

HYPOTHESIS 3 states that when initial P_s is high (i.e., some $P_s > .50$), subjects in whom $M_S > M_{AF}$ should persist longer at the initial achievement task than subjects in whom $M_{AF} > M_S$.

HYPOTHESIS 4 states that when initial P_s is low (i.e., some $P_s < .50$), subjects in whom $M_{AF} > M_S$ should persist longer at the initial achievement task than subjects in whom $M_S > M_{AF}$.

The detailed derivation is presented for Hypotheses 1 and 2 only. The derivation of Hypotheses 3 and 4 follows the same line of argument.

Derivation of Hypothesis 1. Consider a subject in whom the motive to achieve success is stronger than the motive to avoid failure (i.e., $M_S > M_{AF}$), and to whom the initial achievement task is presented as easy (i.e., some $P_s > .50$). For this subject, achievement-related motivation to perform the task is *positive* (approach) and becomes increasingly positive as his subjective probability of success (P_s) at the task falls to .50 with successive failures. Hence, total motivation to perform the initial task should increase as the task appears more difficult to the subject up to the point at which his $P_s = .50$. At this point positive achievement-related motivation and, hence, total motivation to perform the task would be maximum. Thereafter, as P_s gets lower and the task appears more and more difficult to the subject, positive achievement-related motivation decreases until at some low level of P_s total motivation to perform the initial task becomes weaker than total motivation to perform the alternative. The subject should then quit the initial task and turn to the alternative.

In contrast, if the initial task were presented to this subject as very difficult (i.e., some $P_s < .50$), there would be an immediate decrease in the positive achievement-related motivation to perform the task as his P_s drops with repeated failure. Hence, total motivation to perform the initial task would decrease immediately. In this condition it should take fewer unsuccessful attempts at the task to reduce P_s to the low level at which total motivation to perform the initial task becomes less than total motivation to perform the alternative. Hence, we would expect a subject in whom $M_S > M_{AF}$ to persist longer at the initial achievement task when his P_s is initially high than when his P_s is initially low.

Derivation of Hypothesis 2. Consider a subject in whom the motive to avoid failure is stronger than the motive to achieve success (i.e., $M_{AF} > M_S$), and to whom the initial achievement task is presented as easy (i.e., some $P_s > .50$). For this subject, achievement-related motivation to perform the task is *negative* (avoidance) and becomes increasingly negative as his P_s at the task drops to .50 with repeated failure. Hence, total motivation to perform the initial task should decrease as the task appears more difficult to the subject up to the point at which his $P_s = .50$, where negative achievement-related motivation would be maximum. At this point total motivation to perform the initial task should therefore be minimum. It follows that if the subject is to quit the task at all, he should do so as his P_s at the task falls to .50, since it is during this stage of task performance that total motivation to perform the task is decreasing.

In contrast, if the initial task were presented to this subject as very difficult (i.e., some $P_s < .50$), there would be an immediate decrease in negative achievement-related motivation as his P_s drops with repeated failure. Hence, total motivation to perform the initial task would increase immediately, and the subject should continue to perform the task indefinitely. We would therefore expect a subject in whom $M_{AF} > M_S$ to persist longer at the initial achievement task when his P_s is initially low than when his P_s is initially high.

In the preceding analysis, differences in persistence have been related to differences in the way in which total motivation to perform the initial achievement task changes with decrease in P_s as a subject experiences repeated failure at the task. The different types of change in total motivation are summarized in Table 1 in relation to differences in motive and differences in initial P_s.

Adequate tests of the hypotheses of the study clearly require development of procedures which communicate to the subjects that they are expected to perform the initial achievement task first, but that they may feel free to move on to the alternative achievement task whenever they choose to do so. If extrinsic motivation to perform the initial task were very strong in relation to extrinsic motivation to perform the

Table 1

Changes in total motivation to perform the initial achievement task
as P_s decreases in relation to differences in motive ($M_S > M_{AF}$ and
$M_{AF} > M_S$) and differences in initial subjective probability
of success ($P_s > .50$ and $P_s < .50$)

Initial P_s	Motive Relationship	Change in Total Motivation as P_s Decreases
$> .50$	$M_S > M_{AF}$	Increase followed by decrease
$< .50$	$M_S > M_{AF}$	Immediate decrease
$> .50$	$M_{AF} > M_S$	Decrease followed by increase
$< .50$	$M_{AF} > M_S$	Immediate increase

alternative task, none of the differences in persistence predicted here
would be expected to occur.

METHOD

Subjects. Thematic apperceptive stories under neutral conditions and Mandler-Sarason Test Anxiety Questionnaire provided measures of strength of n Achievement (M_S) and Test Anxiety (M_{AF}) for 89 male college students from an introductory psychology course at the University of Michigan in 1959.[3] The TAT was administered according to the standard procedure (McClelland, Atkinson, Clark, and Lowell, 1953). Six pictures were presented in the following order (using numbers assigned by Atkinson, 1958a): 2, 48, 1, 7, 100, 24. Interscorer reliability for scoring n Achievement was .93.[4]

In subjects classified High n Achievement-Low Test Anxiety (in terms of median splits) it was assumed $M_S > M_{AF}$; in subjects classified Low n Achievement-High Test Anxiety it was assumed $M_{AF} > M_S$.

Task. A task consisting of four items and labeled the Perceptual Reasoning test was presented to 34 of these preselected subjects in individual test sessions of one hour duration. Subjects were randomly assigned so that approximately half of each of the High n Achievement-Low Test Anxiety and Low n Achievement-High Test Anxiety groups came to the first item of the Perceptual Reasoning test with a high initial subjective probability of success (P_s); the other half came to the first item with a low initial P_s. The procedure

[3] The author wishes to thank Charles P. Smith for administering the TAT and Test Anxiety Questionnaire.
[4] The author wishes to thank William Larkin for his assistance in scoring the TAT protocols.

adopted in assigning subjects guaranteed that the experimenter would be unaware when testing a subject for persistence of his *n* Achievement and Test Anxiety scores. The initial P_s for each item of the test was experimentally induced by using fictitious group norms and the subject could leave each item as he wished and turn to the next one in the series.

Each item of the Perceptual Reasoning test involved a line diagram approximately 1.5 inches square printed on a white card 6 in. × 4 in. Copies of a particular item were stacked in a pile 2 inches high and the four piles of cards were placed in line on the desk immediately in front of the subject. The piles were designated 1–4 from left to right, and the subject could not see the content of any item until he began to work at it, i.e., the precise content of the alternatives to which he could turn if he wished to quit an item was unknown to him.

For each item the subject's task was to trace over all the lines of the diagram with a red pencil according to two rules: he was not permitted to lift his pencil from the figure; he was not permitted to trace over any line twice. It is a simple matter to construct figures for which the problem is *insoluble* but which are sufficiently complex so that the subject is unable to see this. The subject was allowed to take as many trials at an item as he wished. If he wanted another trial at the item, he simply took another copy of the same item from the top of its pile and worked at it. The following instructions to the subject summarize the restrictions placed on task performance:

> Naturally there are certain restrictions involved in this test. You can only work at an item for 40 seconds at a time, and I shall be timing you on that. But you can have as many of these 40-second trials as you want. If you fail on a trial, that is if you don't succeed in tracing over all the lines in the figure, you will then have the choice of continuing or going on to the next item. If you want to go on to the next item, you should let me know at once. Once you've stopped working at an item you can't go back to it again. If you want to continue with the item, you should turn the *failed* copy face downwards. You can then take another copy of the same item from the pile and you will again have 40 seconds to work at that.

Obviously, for an insoluble item, each trial the subject took resulted in failure. Using this procedure, one can obtain two measures of persistence for an insoluble item: total time spent in working at the item; and number of trials taken at the item before turning to the next one in the series. The former measure is akin to the typical temporal measure used in studies of persistence; the latter is analogous to resistance to extinction.

It will be noted that the alternative activity to which the subject could turn was another *achievement* task similar in content to the one at which he had been working.

Of the four items involved in the Perceptual Reasoning test the first and third were *insoluble,* the second and fourth items were soluble.

Experimental Induction of Subjective Probability of Success. The following instructions were given:

> Now the four items vary in difficulty. Some are harder than others, and you're not expected to be able to solve all of them, but do the best you can. Before I present each item I'm going to let you know the percentage of college students who are able to pass that item. . . . Well, let's look at the norms for the first item. These go by age. How old are you? The tables show that at your age level——per cent, that is approximately——per cent of college students are able to get the solution.

Table 2 presents the fictitious norms for each of the four items of the Perceptual Reasoning test that were reported to Groups A, B, C, and D. These norms were assumed to be sufficiently different to determine differences in initial P_s for each of the four items. It should be noted that initial P_s on items following the first may be influenced not only by the norms reported to the subject but also by the subject's actual experience with the preceding items.

Table 2

Fictitious percentages* of success reported to subjects in the experimental induction of initial difficulty for each of four test items

Group	*n* Achievement	Test Anxiety	1	2	3	4
A	High	Low	70	50	5	50
B	High	Low	5	50	70	50
C	Low	High	70	50	5	50
D	Low	High	5	50	70	50

(header spanning columns: Motivation over *n* Achievement/Test Anxiety; Reported percentages of success for each of four items over 1, 2, 3, 4)

* Actual percentages reported deviated slightly from tabulated values in that they were given to one decimal place to add to authenticity (e.g., 69.4%).

The following final instructions were given before Item 1 was presented to the subject:

> Try to get the solution if you can. It's quite OK for you to take as many 40-second trials as you want at the item. But remember that the four items do vary in difficulty; some are harder than others and you may not be able to solve all of them. So if you should feel that you're not getting anywhere with the item, you should let me know at once so that we can move on to the next one. Here is Item 1. You should find it fairly easy/difficult.

For each insoluble item the subject was timed from when he started the item until when he nominated to try the next item in the set. When he quit an insoluble item, the copies of the item he had attempted were stacked to one side out of sight and their number was later recorded.

Effectiveness of Reported Norm Procedure. After reporting the fictitious group norm, but before presenting the item, the experimenter gave the following instruction: ". . . I'm also going to ask you to let me know what you think your own chances are of solving the problem. You can do this very simply by marking a number along this scale. I'll get you to do this before I present each item and I'll also get you to check here how confident you are about that estimate." To obtain the probability estimates a 20-point rating scale was used, numbered from 0 to 100 in steps of five. The subject made his rating of confidence in his probability estimate on a five-category Likert-type scale ranging from "Not certain at all" to "No doubt about it at all."

Time Limits for Insoluble Items 1 and 3. Data concerning persistence at Item 1 were from the very outset considered more crucial for the test of the hypotheses, since results for other items would be complicated by differential sequence effects. For this reason each subject was allowed to persist at Item 1 for 20 minutes (if he so desired) so as to increase the possibility of obtaining a wide variance in persistence scores. If the subject was still persisting at Item 1 after 20 minutes, it was suggested that he move on to Item 2. This interruption procedure for Item 1 necessarily introduced a time differential for Item 3, some subjects having more time to work at this item than others, depending on how long they had worked at Item 1. Subjects still working at Item 3 were interrupted at approximately 15 minutes before the hour to allow sufficient time for administration of a postperformance questionnaire.

Postperformance Questionnaire. Finally, the experimenter administered a questionnaire to each subject specifically designed to provide information about the assumptions involved in the hypotheses. The majority of questions were presented in Likert-type form and were related to Item 1. When the subject had completed the questionnaire he was thanked for his participation in the experiment, commended on his performance at a fairly difficult task, and requested to keep details of the experiment in confidence. A report of the experiment was sent to each subject at a later date.

RESULTS

The basic data relevant to the hypotheses of the present investigation are the persistence scores of the four groups in terms of time and trials for the first insoluble item (Item 1). The results of analysis of persistence scores for the second insoluble item (Item 3) are presented in less detail, since the necessity for unanticipated interruption of a sizable number of extremely persistent subjects on the first and third items, and the possibility of uncontrolled sequence effects, make interpretation of results for the third item equivocal.

Analysis of Persistence at Item 1. Since time and trials scores are perfectly correlated for Item 1, only the analysis of persistence trials is presented. By persistence trials is meant the number of trials the subject took at Item 1 before he quit to move on to the second item or before he was interrupted. The median of these persistence trials at Item 1 for all subjects is 20 with a range from 2 to 41+.[5] Persistence trials for subjects of each of Groups A, B, C, and D are classified as high and low in terms of whether they are above or below this median, and the resulting frequencies are presented in Table 3. Below Table 3 are presented the results of a partitioned χ^2 analysis (Sutcliffe, 1957) applied to these data.

Table 3 shows that only the χ^2 representing the interactive effect of

Table 3

Number of subjects who were high and low in persistence on Item 1 in relation to stated difficulty of the task and nature of motivation

	Motivation			Persistence Trials	
Group	*n* Achieve-ment	Test Anxiety	Stated Difficulty of Task	High (above median)	Low (below median)
A	High	Low	70% (easy)	6	2
B	High	Low	5% (difficult)	2	7
C	Low	High	70% (easy)	3	6
D	Low	High	5% (difficult)	6	2

Partition of χ^2

Source	Value	df	p
Motivation × persistence	.12	1	>.05
Expectation × persistence	.12	1	>.05
Motivation × expectation × persistence	7.65	1	<.01
Total	7.89	3	<.05

[5] The + indicates that the subject had to be interrupted. Due to the interruption procedure some scores are open-ended. Hence, results are classified on the basis of median splits and relationships in the resulting frequency tables analyzed using χ^2 as the basic statistic.

motivation and expectation on persistence is significant $(p < .01)$. While the proportion of subjects classified high in persistence *increases* as the reported norm varies from 5% to 70% (i.e., from difficult to easy) for subjects high in n Achievement and low in Test Anxiety, this proportion *decreases* for subjects low in n Achievement and high in Test Anxiety with the same variation in the reported norm. This implies a basic difference in the way persistence is related to the initial difficulty of the item among subjects in whom $M_S > M_{AF}$ versus subjects in whom $M_{AF} > M_S$.

Relationships in Table 3 are clearly consistent with Hypotheses 1, 2, 3, and 4. Subjects in whom it is assumed that $M_S > M_{AF}$ (the High-Low subjects) show greater persistence at the task when the reported norm defines it as easy (70% norm) than when the norm defines it as difficult (5% norm). This result supports Hypothesis 1 in implying that subjects in whom $M_S > M_{AF}$ tend to persist longer at the item when initial expectation of success is high rather than low. In contrast, subjects in whom it is assumed that $M_{AF} > M_S$ (the Low-High subjects) show greater persistence at the task when the reported norm defines it as difficult (5% norm) than when the norm defines it as easy (70% norm). This result supports Hypothesis 2 in implying that subjects in whom $M_{AF} > M_S$ tend to persist longer at the item when initial expectation of success is low rather than high. Furthermore, among subjects for whom the reported norm defines the item as easy, the proportion of subjects showing high persistence is greater for those classified as high in n Achievement and low in Test Anxiety. This result is consistent with Hypothesis 3 in implying that, when the initial expectation of success is high, subjects in whom $M_S > M_{AF}$ tend to persist longer at the item than subjects in whom $M_{AF} > M_S$. Finally, among subjects for whom the reported norm defines the item as difficult, the proportion of subjects showing high persistence is greater for those classified as low in n Achievement and high in Test Anxiety. The result is consistent with Hypothesis 4 in implying that, when the initial expectation of success is low, subjects in whom $M_{AF} > M_S$ tend to persist longer at the item than subjects in whom $M_S > M_{AF}$.

Analysis of Persistence at Item 3. Persistence data for Item 3 compared across Groups A, B, C, and D show no significant trends. However, when comparisons of persistence scores for Items 1 and 3 are made within the same group, subjects of Group B (High-Low subjects) persist longer at Item 3 which for them is defined by the reported norm as easy than at Item 1, which is defined by the norm as difficult. This change is consistent with Hypothesis 1. Subjects of Group C (Low-

High subjects) persist longer at Item 3, which for them is defined by the reported norm as difficult than at Item 1, which is defined by the norm as easy. This change is consistent with Hypothesis 2. However, when ambiguous comparisons of persistence scores are excluded (due to the interruption procedure), there is a tendency for all subjects to persist longer at Item 3 than at Item 1. This suggests that an influence common to all subjects might have operated to increase persistence at Item 3.

When such an influence is assumed and ambiguous differences in persistence scores (due to the interruption procedure) are excluded, the data support the qualified prediction that Groups A and D should at least tend to increase relatively less in persistence from Item 1 to Item 3 than do Groups B and C. However, this result is equivocal since, as a result of limitations of time, subjects of Group A and D who persisted relatively longer at Item 1 may not have had the same opportunity to increase in persistence at Item 3 as did subjects of Groups B and C.

Analysis of Supplementary Data. Analysis of data concerned with effectiveness of experimental procedures supports the assumption that the different reported norms determined widely different initial subjective probabilities of success. The probability estimates given by subjects in all four groups tend to follow the reported norms very closely. Data obtained from the postperformance questionnaire are generally consistent with assumptions involved in hypotheses. For example, subjects in all four groups report decreases in estimates of probability of success as they work at Item 1 with repeated failure. This decrease is consistent with the basic dynamic assumption that expectation of success should diminish with repeated failure at the task. In addition, there is no evidence that the rate of decrease in probability estimates with failure at Item 1 differs between the two motivation conditions (High-Low subjects versus Low-High subjects). This implies that rate of decrease in P_s is independent of the relative strength of M_S and M_{AF} within the individual.

DISCUSSION

Where the present investigation permits unequivocal test of the four hypotheses (i.e., for Item 1), results are consistent with predictions. Furthermore, postperformance questionnaire data generally support the basic assumptions involved in these predictions.

The investigation stands in marked contrast to the typical trait studies of persistence and extinction studies with human subjects, since hypotheses are based on a consideration of personality and situational factors in interaction. Trait studies of persistence typically concentrate on the relatively stable aspects of persons by looking for consistencies in behavior and they tend to neglect the role of the situation. In contrast, extinction studies usually attempt to relate persistence of behavior to characteristics of the acquisition stage and they tend to ignore the influence on resistance to extinction of relatively stable personality characteristics. The contribution of the present study is to investigate persistence as a phenomenon determined by the interaction of both personality and situational influences.

The present investigation also differs from the usual extinction investigation by using a task that could be seen by the subject as involving personal skill (cf. James and Rotter, 1958) and that provided a relatively inexhaustible range of alternative responses following failure. In contrast, extinction studies with humans have often used tasks in which the subject may see success and failure as largely beyond his control (e.g., the Humphreys' apparatus) and where the response is restricted to a particular action (e.g., pulling down a lever). Furthermore, in the present investigation initial expectation of success was varied by using fictitious norms. In contrast, in extinction studies the expectation may be considered as based mainly on frequency and pattern of reinforcement and nonreinforcement in the acquisition series.

The theoretical analysis may be extended to a consideration of persistence under conditions that differ from those of the present investigation in important respects. The general paradigm of the persistence situation is that in which the subject has some expectation of attaining a goal, is unrestricted in the number of attempts he can have at attaining it, and has an alternative activity to turn to as he wishes. Within this general framework the following differences may be noted which in turn imply specific types of persistence situation worthy of investigation:

1. Performance of the alternative to which the subject may turn may involve motives that are the same or different from those involved in the performance of the activity at which he is presently engaged. The persistence situation studied in the present investigation is one in which initial task and alternative activity belong to the same class of activity. Total motivation to perform the initial task and total motivation to perform the alternative task are both attributable to the *same* motivational components. In contrast, we can consider a type of persistence situation in which the initial task and the alternative task do

not belong to the same class of activity, i.e., where the alternative is *motivationally different* in the sense that total motivation to perform the alternative is influenced by motives which are not involved in performance of the initial activity. Investigations of persistence by French and Thomas (1958) and by Atkinson and Litwin (Chapter 5) appear to fall in this latter class, since in both of these studies the alternative activity to which the subject can turn does not necessarily involve achievement-related motivation.

2. The situation does or does not involve types of motivational tendency in which incentive values and expectations are assumed to be dependent. In the achievement context dependencies are assumed between the positive incentive value of success and the subjective probability of success, and between the negative incentive value of failure and the subjective probability of failure (cf. Feather, 1959a, 1959b). But, in the more general case (e.g., efforts to get food when hungry), there would be no dependency between incentive value and expectation, and, hence, no increase to a maximum motivation followed by a decrease as expectation of goal attainment (P_g) changes from $P_g > .50$ to $P_g < .50$ (as occurs for achievement-related motivation). Instead we would expect motivation to perform the activity to decrease continuously with decrease in the strength of expectation of goal attainment, providing strength of motive and incentive remained constant.

3. Persistence situations may differ according to whether or not the incentive is objectively present. One can consider a persistence situation in which the incentive is actually in view, e.g., young children attempting to overcome an obstacle in order to get a candy. In the present investigation and in the human extinction type of study, the incentive is not objectively present. In the Perceptual Reasoning test, the subject has to solve the puzzle; he cannot see the solution. In the extinction situation the reinforcement does not appear in the extinction series. Hence, it is possible for the subject to develop the expectation that there is in fact no incentive, e.g., that the puzzle is insoluble or that the experimenter has "fixed" the apparatus so that no more reinforcements will occur. In other words, the subject may conceive of these situations as beyond his control, as not involving skill. Consequently, special care is required to ensure that the subject retains the belief that only his efforts will influence the outcome.

These three differentiating characteristics, in combination, yield the eight specific types of persistence situation summarized in Table 4. The persistence situation investigated in the present study corresponds to 5, i.e., performance of the alternative involves the same kind of

Table 4

Types of persistence situation according to whether or not the
alternative is motivationally the same or different from the
present activity, dependencies between incentives values
and expectations exist or do not exist, and the
incentive is objectively present or absent

Persistence Situation	Alternative (motivationally same or different)	Dependency Between Expectation and Incentive Value (present or absent)	Incentive (objectively present or absent)
1	Same	Present	Present
2	Different	Present	Present
3	Same	Absent	Present
4	Different	Absent	Present
5	Same	Present	Absent
6	Different	Present	Absent
7	Same	Absent	Absent
8	Different	Absent	Absent

motivation as the activity at which the subject is presently engaged,
dependencies are assumed between incentive values and expectations,
and the incentive is not objectively present. In contrast, the persistence
situation studied by French and Thomas (1958) and by Atkinson and
Litwin (Chapter 5) corresponds to 6, since performance of the alternative in these studies probably involves different motivation from that
involved in the activity at which the subject is engaged. It should be
possible to construct experimental situations corresponding to the other
six cases and to analyze persistence behavior in each of these in terms
of the interaction of motives, expectations, and incentives. Such an
approach would require (a) specification of the nature of the motives,
expectations, and incentives involved in the situation; (b) measures of
the strength of these motives, expectations, and incentives; (c) assumptions concerning how these basic variables combine to determine the
various component motivations; (d) specification of the manner in
which expectation changes with experience at the activity; and (e)
assumptions concerning the resolution of the set of component motivations into a resultant motivation.

The present study has shown that this strategy does work for the type
of persistence situation investigated here. Detailed specification of the

components of total motivation to perform a task in relation to total motivation to perform the available alternative, in conjunction with a dynamic principle of expectation change, has permitted differential predictions about persistence. This type of analysis, which takes account of both personality dispositions and situational influences in interaction according to an "expectancy-value" model, may also be required to explain persistence in the other types of situation.

SUMMARY

This investigation examines the relationship of persistence at a task both to its apparent difficulty and to the relative strength within an individual of the motives to achieve success and to avoid failure. A subject performs a task presented to him as part of an important test, undergoes repeated failure at it (because it is in fact insoluble), but may turn to an alternative achievement task whenever he desires. Strength of motive to achieve success is assessed by the TAT *n* Achievement procedure; strength of motive to avoid failure is assessed by Mandler-Sarason Test Anxiety Questionnaire. Apparent difficulty of the task (i.e., initial expectation of success) is varied by use of fictitious group norms. Persistence is measured by total trials or total time the subject works at the task before turning to the alternative.

Hypotheses are derived from the theory of achievement motivation with additional assumptions. . . . Results are generally consistent with hypotheses and with assumptions involved in the predictions.

As a guide to future research, a theoretical scheme is presented in which different classes of persistence situations are identified. The present investigation indicates the importance of specifying the components of total motivation to perform a task in relation to the components of total motivation to perform the alternative when attempting to predict degree of persistence. The theoretical analysis suggests the possibility of conceptualizing each component motivation in "expectancy value" terms, and the importance of change in expectation as a dynamic principle mediating change in motivation. The factual evidence clearly provides a demonstration that persistence can be conceptualized as an interaction of personality dispositions and situational influences.

9.

Persistence at a Difficult Task
with Alternative Task of Intermediate Difficulty

The present investigation of persistence is concerned with a situation
in which an individual works at an achievement task presented to him
as very difficult. He knows that he can turn, whenever he so chooses, to
another task of the same type which is described as intermediate in
difficulty (i.e., 50/50 probability of success). The initial achievement
task is, in fact, objectively insoluble and the person undergoes repeated
failure in his attempts to get the solution. Within this context, persistence is studied in relation to the relative strength within the individual
of the motives to achieve success and to avoid failure. Persistence is
measured by the total number of trials the person works at the initial
achievement task before turning to the alternative.

Results of an earlier study (Feather, Chapter 8) indicate that subjects
classified as high in n Achievement and low in Test Anxiety persist
longer at an achievement task when it is presented to them as easy than
as very difficult. In contrast, subjects classified as low in n Achievement
and high in Test Anxiety do just the reverse. No attempt was made in
this earlier study to specify the difficulty level of the alternative to
which the subject could turn when he so desired. The present study is
designed to fill this gap and specifies an alternative of intermediate
difficulty. The investigation also provides a further test of the theoretical approach adopted.

Two hypotheses are investigated.

HYPOTHESIS 1 states that, when the initial achievement task is presented as very difficult (subjective probability of success, $P_s < .50$) and
the alternative achievement task as intermediate in difficulty ($P_s = .50$),
subjects in whom the motive to avoid failure is stronger than the
motive to achieve success ($M_{AF} > M_S$) should persist longer at the

Reprinted by permission of the author and the American Psychological Association
from the *Journal of Abnormal and Social Psychology*, 1963, **66**, 604–609.

initial task than subjects in whom the motive to achieve success is stronger than the motive to avoid failure $(M_S > M_{AF})$. In accordance with the earlier theoretical derivation (Chapter 8, p. 122) total motivation to perform the initial, subjectively very difficult task should *increase* for subjects in whom $M_{AF} > M_S$ as they undergo repeated failure, but should *decrease* for subjects in whom $M_S > M_{AF}$. Furthermore, since the alternative task is described as intermediate in difficulty, achievement-related motivation to perform this task should have a maximum *negative* value for subjects in whom $M_{AF} > M_S$, and a maximum *positive* value for subjects in whom $M_S > M_{AF}$, when $P_s = .50$. Hence, for the former subjects in whom $M_{AF} > M_S$, total motivation to perform the alternative task should be relatively weak; the alternative task should provoke a high level of anxiety about failure which dominates any achievement interest. In marked contrast, for the latter subjects in whom $M_S > M_{AF}$, total motivation to perform the alternative task should be relatively strong; the alternative task should elicit a high degree of achievement interest which dominates any anxiety about failure. It follows from these considerations that subjects in whom $M_{AF} > M_S$ should persist at the initial achievement task longer than subjects in whom $M_S > M_{AF}$. Since the alternative task is presented as intermediate in difficulty, we would expect these differences in persistence between the two types of subjects to be quite pronounced.

HYPOTHESIS 2 states that, when the initial achievement task is presented as very difficult $(P_s < .50)$, persistence should be positively related to initial expectation of success among subjects in whom $M_S > M_{AF}$, but there should be no relationship between persistence and initial expectation of success among subjects in whom $M_{AF} > M_S$. Although the initial task is described to subjects as very difficult, we would expect their initial expectations of success to differ, some subjects having higher expectations than others. Persistence should relate positively to initial expectation of success among subjects in whom $M_S > M_{AF}$ since, for these subjects, total motivation to perform the initial task should decrease as expectations of success fall with repeated failure. The higher the initial expectation of success, the more unsuccessful attempts at the task it should take to reduce expectation to the low level at which total motivation to perform the initial task becomes less than total motivation to perform the alternative (Chapter 8, p. 120). However, there is no basis in the present theory for predicting a definite relationship between persistence and initial expectation of success among subjects in whom $M_{AF} > M_S$, when their initial expectations are very low ($P_s < .50$). In fact, under such conditions, these subjects should persist at an achievement task indefinitely[1] (p. 122).

Both Hypothesis 1 and Hypothesis 2 assume that initial expectations for success for the initial achievement task are very low ($P_s < .50$) among the subjects tested.

METHOD

The basic procedure is essentially the same as that used in the earlier investigation. Scores for n Achievement (M_S) and Mandler-Sarason Test Anxiety scores (M_{AF}) were obtained for 60 male students in introductory, undergraduate courses at the University of New England. The author administered the Thematic Apperception Test (TAT) under neutral conditions according to the standard procedure (McClelland, Atkinson, Clark, and Lowell, 1953). Six pictures were presented in the following order (using numbers assigned by Atkinson, 1958a): 2, 48, 1, 7, 100, 24. Interscorer reliability[2] for scoring n Achievement was .89. In subjects classified as high in n Achievement and low in Test Anxiety (using median splits) it was assumed $M_S > M_{AF}$; in subjects classified as low in n Achievement and high in Test Anxiety it was assumed $M_{AF} > M_S$. A score of 8 and above was designated High n Achievement; a score below 8 was designated Low n Achievement. A score of 83 and above was designated High Test Anxiety; a score below 83 was designated Low Test Anxiety.

A subject's Test Anxiety score was obtained by summing his scores on the individual items of the Test Anxiety Questionnaire. As in the previous investigation, these item scores were obtained by dividing the rating scale for each item into five equal parts and by scoring responses from one to five in the direction of increasing anxiety.

Some three months after this initial testing the test of persistence was administered to each of the 60 subjects in individual sessions. The procedure adopted ensured that the experimenter was unaware, when testing a subject for persistence, of his n Achievement and Test Anxiety scores. The first two items of the Perceptual Reasoning test were used in the present study. These two items

---

[1] Future elaboration of the theory of persistence in achievement contexts will need to explain why subjects in whom $M_{AF} > M_S$ ever stop working at a very difficult achievement task (Feather, 1960, pp. 183–186). Such an elaboration might consider as possible factors a decrease in extrinsic motivation to perform the initial task with performance and the development of other motivational tendencies associated with alternatives.

[2] The author wishes to thank Catherine Macleod for her assistance in scoring the TAT protocols and for her administration of the test of persistence. The present study was conducted as part of her Honors program (Macleod, 1961). The author also wishes to thank Graeme Halford for scoring the Test Anxiety Questionnaires.

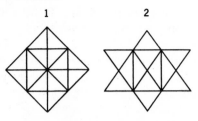

Figure 1   Item 1 (insoluble) and
Item 2 (soluble) from the Perceptual
Reasoning test.

consist of the unicursal puzzles presented in Figure 1. For each item the subject
is required to trace over all the lines of the diagram without lifting his pencil
from the paper and without tracing over any line twice. Detailed instructions
for administration of this test are presented in the earlier paper (Feather,
Chapter 8). Item 1 is, in fact, insoluble and the subject can work at it for as
many trials as he chooses, failing at each attempt, before he decides to turn to
Item 2. Each subject was allowed to persist at Item 1 for up to 20 minutes (if
he so desired) so as to increase the possibility of obtaining a wide variance in
persistence scores. It was necessary to suggest to 12 subjects who were still
persisting at Item 1 after 20 minutes that move on to Item 2. This second item
is soluble and quite easy. All subjects were able to solve it. A subject could not
see the content of Item 2 until he began to work at it, but he knew that the
item was similar in kind to Item 1.

Initial subjective probabilities of success for Items 1 and 2 were induced by
reporting fictitious group norms. The following instructions were given to the
subject before he began working at Item 1:

> The two items that I'm going to give you today vary in difficulty. The
> first item is very difficult. In fact, only about 5% of University students are
> able to pass it, so the chances of success are very low indeed. The second
> item is of average difficulty. About 50% of University students are able to
> pass it, so the chances of success are 50/50.

Thus, in contrast to the previous study, a subject knew the difficulty level of
the alternative task in advance.

As in the previous investigation, estimates of probability of success and ratings of confidence in these estimates were obtained from subjects prior to
performance at Item 1 as a check on the effectiveness of the fictitious group
norm procedure. Probability estimates and confidence ratings related to the
middle and terminal stages of performance at Item 1, along with other information relevant to assumptions involved in the hypotheses, were obtained
from a postperformance questionnaire administered at the end of the experimental session.

RESULTS

Analysis of Persistence Data. The distribution of persistence trials at Item 1 for the 60 subjects tested in the present investigation has a range from 1 to 48+[3] and a median of 9.5. Persistence trials for subjects classified as High n Achievement-Low Test Anxiety and for subjects classified as Low n Achievement-High Test Anxiety are designated as high and low in terms of whether they are above or below this median. The resulting frequencies are presented in Table 1.

Table 1

Number of subjects who were high and low in persistence on Item 1 in relation to stated difficulty of the task and nature of motivation ($N = 36$)

Motivation			Persistence Trials	
n Achievement	Test Anxiety	Stated Difficulty of Task	High*	Low†
High	Low	5% (difficult)	6	12
Low	High	5% (difficult)	10	8

Note: $\chi^2 = 1.80$, $df = 1$, ns ($p < .10$, one-tailed test).
* Above median.
† Below median.

Table 1 does not provide definite support for Hypothesis 1. The results indicate that the proportion of subjects who show high persistence at Item 1 is greater for those subjects classified as low in n Achievement and high in Test Anxiety than for those subjects classified as high in n Achievement and low in Test Anxiety. This difference in proportions is consistent with Hypothesis 1 in implying that when the initial task is presented as very difficult and the alternative task is described as intermediate in difficulty, subjects in whom $M_{AF} > M_S$ tend to persist longer at the initial task than subjects in whom

---

[3] The + indicates that the subject had to be interrupted. Due to the interruption procedure some scores are open-ended. Hence, results are classified on the basis of median splits and relationships in the resulting frequency tables analyzed using χ^2 as the basic statistic.

$M_S > M_{AF}$. However, the difference in proportions is not statistically significant ($\chi^2 = 1.80$, $df = 1$, $p < .10$, one-tailed test).

Table 2 presents data concerning the relationship of persistence to estimates of probability of success given prior to performance at Item 1 by subjects classified as high in n Achievement and low in Test Anxiety, and by subjects classified as low in n Achievement and high in Test Anxiety. These probability estimates are designated as high or low in terms of whether they are above or below the median of the distribution for all subjects. This median probability estimate is 16.5. Table 2 also

Table 2

Number of subjects who were high and low in persistence on Item 1 in relation to initial estimates of probability of success for Item 1 and nature of motivation
($N = 36$)

Motivation			Persistence Trials	
n Achievement	Test Anxiety	Initial Probability Estimate for Item 1	High*	Low†
High	Low	High	6	3
		Low	0	9
Low	High	High	5	4
		Low	5	4

Partition of χ^2		
Source	χ^2	df
Motivation $\times$ persistence	1.80	1
Probability estimate $\times$ persistence	4.05‡	1
Motivation $\times$ probability estimate $\times$ persistence	4.05‡	1
Total	9.90§	3

* Above median.
† Below median.
‡ $p < .05$.
§ $p < .02$.

presents the results of a partitioned χ^2 analysis (Sutcliffe, 1957) applied to these data.

Results in Table 2 support Hypothesis 2. The partition of χ^2 indicates that the two motivation groups (High-Lows versus Low-Highs) differ significantly ($\chi^2 = 4.05$, $df = 1$, $p < .05$) with respect to the relationship of persistence at Item 1 to initial estimates of probability of success. In Table 2 the positive relationship between persistence and probability estimates is highly significant ($p < .005$, Fisher exact test, one-tailed) among subjects classified as high in n Achievement and low in Test Anxiety. In contrast, Table 2 shows that there is no evidence for a relationship between persistence and probability estimates among subjects classified as low in n Achievement and high in Test Anxiety. These data are consistent with Hypothesis 2 in implying that, when the initial achievement task is presented as very difficult ($P_s < .50$), persistence should be positively related to initial expectation of success among subjects in whom $M_S > M_{AF}$, whereas there should be no relationship between persistence and initial expectation of success among subjects in whom $M_{AF} > M_S$.

Finally, Table 3 presents data concerning the relationship of persistence to initial estimates of probability of success for all 60 subjects tested in the present study.

Table 3

Number of subjects who were high and low in persistence on Item 1 in relation to initial estimates of probability of success for Item 1 ($N = 60$)

Initial Probability Estimate for Item 1	Persistence Trials	
	High*	Low†
High*	20	10
Low†	9	21

Note: $\chi^2 = 8.08$, $df = 1$, $p < .01$, two-tailed test.
* Above median.
† Below median.

Table 3 shows that there is a statistically significant tendency ($\chi^2 = 8.08$, $df = 1$, $p < .01$) for subjects with high initial probability estimates to persist longer at Item 1 than subjects with low initial probability estimates, and conversely. No such relationship was found in the earlier study (Feather, Chapter 8).

In summary, the results obtained from an analysis of persistence trials for Item 1 support Hypothesis 2 but do not provide definite support for Hypothesis 1.

Analysis of Supplementary Data. The following results obtained from analysis of responses to the postperformance questionnaire are of interest in their bearing upon assumptions involved in the theoretical derivation of the hypotheses and in providing suggestions for future research.

PROBABILITY ESTIMATES. Means of the probability estimates obtained from the 60 subjects both prior to performance at Item 1 and from the postperformance questionnaire for the middle and terminal stages of performance at Item 1 show an initial increase followed by a decrease. These mean probability estimates for the three different stages of performance at Item 1 are as follows: Prior to performance, $M = 20.37$, $SD = 16.63$; middle stage of performance, $M = 28.00$, $SD = 21.20$; terminal stage of performance, $M = 19.95$, $SD = 21.90$. These means differ significantly ($F = 7.29$, $df = 2/118$, $p < .005$) and the trend is independent of n Achievement and Test Anxiety. Apparently subjects become more "optimistic" about their chances of success once they have worked at Item 1 for a number of trials. After a certain number of failures, however, expectations of success begin to decline. This tendency for probability estimates to rise initially did not appear in the earlier study (Chapter 8), where estimates decreased from prior to performance through the middle to the terminal stage of performance. It is interesting to note that, as in the previous study, probability estimates tend to exceed the 5% reported norm. This general tendency to overestimate low probabilities has been found in previous research (cf. Cohen, 1960; Feather, 1963a; Preston and Baratta, 1948).

PREFERENCE FOR ITEM 1 VERSUS ITEM 2. Data from the postperformance questionnaire indicate that subjects who showed high persistence at Item 1 tend to select Item 1 when asked which of Item 1 (5% difficulty) or Item 2 (50% difficulty) they would have chosen to work at if they had been given the choice at the beginning of the test session. In contrast, subjects who showed low persistence at Item 1 tend to prefer Item 2. The positive relationship between persistence at Item 1 and choice of Item 1 in the postperformance questionnaire is evident in Table 4, and is statistically significant ($\chi^2 = 5.34$, $df = 1$, $p < .05$).

DISCUSSION

The above results, taken in conjunction with those of the earlier study, provide strong support for the type of theoretical analysis of the persistence situation employed in both investigations in the derivation

Table 4

Number of subjects choosing Item 1 or Item 2 in the postperformance
questionnaire in relation to degree of persistence at Item 1 ($N = 60$)

	Persistence Trials	
Choice in Questionnaire	High*	Low†
Item 1 (5% difficulty)	17	9
Item 2 (50% difficulty)	12	22

Note: $\chi^2 = 5.34$, $df = 1$, $p < .05$, two-tailed test.
* Above median.
† Below median.

of hypotheses. The interesting difference between the results of the two
investigations is that whereas in the earlier study no general relationship was found between persistence at Item 1 and probability estimates
given by subjects prior to performance at the item, the present investigation reveals a general tendency for subjects to persist longer at Item 1
when their estimated probabilities of success are high rather than low
(Table 3). The results show that this positive relationship between
persistence and probability estimates is very apparent for subjects
classified as high in *n* Achievement and low in Test Anxiety, but does
not occur for subjects classified as low in *n* Achievement and high in
Test Anxiety (Table 2).

One would expect a general trend of this nature if, among subjects
tested, a high proportion were those in whom the motive to achieve
success is stronger than the motive to avoid failure $(M_S > M_{AF})$. There
are, in fact, good reasons for expecting a predominance of subjects at
university level in whom $M_S > M_{AF}$, and a greater predominance of
such persons in Australian as opposed to American universities. The
proportion of high school students proceeding to university is lower in
Australia than in the United States. Selection for university undergraduate work tends to be more stringent, perhaps too stringent. It is
reasonable to suppose that many students who perform poorly at
examinations do so partly because they become highly anxious under
test conditions. These students are selected out and do not proceed to
university (cf. Atkinson and Litwin, Chapter 5, p. 89). Such considerations lead one to expect that Australian freshmen may have lower Test
Anxiety scores than American freshmen. A comparison of Test Anxiety
scores from the earlier study (American students) with scores from the

present study (Australian students) supports this prediction. The respective mean Test Anxiety scores are as follows: Earlier study, $M = 97.92$, $SD = 22.64$; present study, $M = 83.97$, $SD = 19.04$. The difference between these means is highly significant ($F = 15.23$, $df = 1/147$, $p < .001$). When this result is taken in conjunction with the relatively high ratings of achievement concern and the relatively low ratings of anxiety about failure at Item 1 given by subjects in the postperformance questionnaire, the supposition is strengthened that a large proportion of subjects in the present study are subjects in whom $M_S > M_{AF}$. This may account for the failure to obtain statistically significant support for Hypothesis 1 in the present study (Table 1), when differences in persistence between subjects from the contrasting motivation groups are examined. The group of subjects classified as low in n Achievement and high in Test Anxiety may include some in whom the motive to avoid failure is not stronger than the motive to achieve success but rather the reverse. Future research is needed in test development to improve the basis for selecting subjects in whom $M_S > M_{AF}$ as contrasted to those in whom $M_{AF} > M_S$. If the Test Anxiety scale is to be used again in relation to the study of persistence, it appears that research with Australian students will need to study more extreme groups on the Test Anxiety continuum.

The results of the present study indicate that estimates of chances of success at Item 1 tend to rise and then fall with repeated failure at the task. This trend did not occur in the earlier study where these estimates tended to decrease with successive failure experiences. The initial rise in probability estimates obtained in the present study may relate to the earlier finding (Feather, 1960) that subjects are less confident about their probability estimates prior to performance of a task when the task is presented as very difficult than as easy. Estimates of probability of success given by a subject after the fictitious norm has been reported but before he has seen the content of an item may change once the task is available to him, i.e., the structure of the task should influence his expectation of success (Feather, 1963a). In the present study this influence seems to have produced an initial "optimism" among subjects. As subjects become more familiar with the task we would expect them to become more confident about their estimates of probability. Results from the present study do indicate that subjects tend to be more confident about their probability estimates for the middle and terminal stages of performance than about the estimates they gave prior to performance at Item 1. The respective mean confidence ratings are as follows: Prior to performance, $M = 2.22$, $SD = .69$; middle stage of performance, $M = 2.78$, $SD = .79$; terminal stage of performance, $M = 2.85$, $SD = .96$. The difference between these means is highly significant ($F = 13.80$, $df = 2/118$, $p < .001$). Clearly, future research needs to consider the different factors which may influence change in expectation of success with repeated failure at a task. As indicated previously (Chapter 8), specification of the rate and manner of change in expectation of success with repeated failure is essential if predictions about persistence are to be made in the present theoretical context.

Finally, it is interesting to note that when subjects were asked in the postperformance questionnaire which of Item 1 (5%) or Item 2 (50%) they would have chosen if they had been given the choice at the beginning of the test session, subjects who showed high persistence at Item 1 tended to choose Item 1, while subjects who showed low persistence at Item 1 tended to choose Item 2 (Table 4). It is possible that subjects in stating a preference for Item 1 were attempting to justify their extreme persistence at Item 1 to the experimenter. Alternatively, one can argue that total motivation to perform Item 1 was not entirely reduced for highly persistent subjects and remained at a sufficient level to influence their later preference. Certainly, highly persistent subjects tend to give higher probability estimates for the terminal stage of performance than do less persistent subjects (correlation of persistence trials with probability estimates for the terminal stage of performance is $r = .53$, $df = 58$, $p < .001$). Such an explanation is similar to the Lewinian concept of persisting tension following an uncompleted task. In a sense, Item 1 has not been completed; the subject has not succeeded because the task is insoluble. Total motivation to perform Item 2 has, however, been dissipated since the problem has been solved and expectation of success is now certain. Thus, as in the studies by Ovsiankina and Lissner (Lewin, 1935), we would expect the nondissipated total motivation to perform Item 1 to persist and later to influence a preference for the item. Future research might well be directed towards an analysis of the Lewinian literature on uncompleted tasks with a view to discovering whether this area of investigation which has been based on a "tension" model can be conceptualized using the "motive-expectancy-value" framework adopted in the present study.[4]

SUMMARY

Sixty male Ss were tested individually for persistence at an insoluble task presented to them as very difficult. They experienced repeated failure at the task but could turn to a similar task described as inter-

---

[4] See Atkinson and Cartwright (1964) and Atkinson (1964, Chapter 10) for a theoretical development along the line suggested here. (The Editors.)

mediate in difficulty whenever they wished. Differences in persistence at the initial task were examined between Ss high in n Achievement and low in Test Anxiety (HL) and Ss low in n Achievement and high in Test Anxiety (LH). Results show that: *(a)* persistence is positively related to initial estimates of probability of success *(P$_s$)* at the task for HL Ss *(p* < .005), but there is no relationship between persistence and initial estimates of P_s for LH Ss; *(b)* estimates of P_s tend to rise initially and then to fall following repeated failure *(p* < .005); *(c)* Ss who persisted at the initial task show a later preference for that task *(p* < .05). Results are discussed in terms of the "motive-expectancy-value" model.

10. ROBERT W. MOULTON

Effects of Success and Failure
on Level of Aspiration as
Related to Achievement Motives

In studies of level of aspiration behavior, it has been observed that the most typical reaction to a success experience is a moderate rise in level of aspiration and that the usual reaction to failure is a moderate drop in level of aspira*ion. However, a minority of subjects, on occasion, react to success or failure in an apparently paradoxical manner. That is, they respond to failure by raising level of aspiration and to success by lowering it. A model of risk taking recently developed by Atkinson (Chapter 2), which is a modified form of the resultant valence conception (Lewin, Dembo, Festinger, and Sears, 1944), clearly implies that reactions to success and failure, whether they are typical or atypical, are predictable from a knowledge of individual differences in the relative strength of motives to achieve success (M_S) and to avoid failure (M_{AF}). The study being reported is an attempt to provide a test of these implications.

In Atkinson's model, the attractiveness of a particular task is a resultant of approach and avoidance "tendencies." The strength of the approach tendency is assumed to equal: Motive $\times$ Expectancy $\times$ Incentive. Motive refers to a general disposition to strive for success (M_S) when confronted with an achievement situation. Expectancy is defined as subjective probability of success (P_s) for the task in question, and the incentive value of the task is assumed to equal $1 - P_s$. The strength of the avoidance tendency is also expressed as: Motive $\times$ Expectancy $\times$ Incentive. In this case, motive refers to a disposition to avoid failure (M_{AF}). If expectancy is again expressed as P_s, incentive is defined as the minus value of P_s. With this series of assumptions it can be shown that

Reprinted by permission of the author and the American Psychological Association from *Journal of Personality and Social Psychology*, 1, May 1965, 399–406. This study was supported by a research grant from the Department of Education, University of California, Berkeley.

maximum motivation, either to approach or to avoid, is aroused by tasks which have a P_s of .50 (Atkinson, Chapter 2).[1] When individuals whose motive to approach success exceeds their motive to avoid failure (approach oriented) are presented with a set of achievement tasks which vary in subjective probability of success, they will tend to choose the task which has a subjective probability closest to .50. On the other hand, individuals for whom the avoidance motive is preponderant (avoidance oriented) will seek to avoid achievement tasks because all such tasks tend to arouse avoidance tendencies in these individuals. However, if forced to make a choice from among a set of achievement tasks, avoidance-oriented individuals will tend to select tasks for which P_s is as far from .50 as possible, thus selecting tasks from either the easy or the difficult range. This aspect of the model has been confirmed by previous studies (Atkinson, Bastian, Earl, and Litwin, 1960; Atkinson and Litwin, Chapter 5; McClelland, 1958b; Mahone, Chapter 12).

Success or failure on a task may change its attractiveness because subjective probability of success for the task is thereby altered. Thus, if the individual were to succeed on a task he initially perceived to be very difficult, P_s should increase and move toward .50. If he were to fail a task initially perceived to be easy, P_s for the task should decrease and move closer to .50. In both instances, the task should become relatively more attractive for approach-oriented individuals and should evoke a stronger avoidance tendency in avoidance-oriented individuals. On the other hand, success on a task initially perceived to be easy should widen the gap between P_s for the task and the .50 value. Failure on a task initially perceived to be difficult will have the same effect. In these latter instances, the task should become less attractive to the approach-oriented subject and should now evoke a relatively weaker avoidance tendency in the avoidance-oriented subject. It can be shown with this series of assumptions that the model predicts differential persistence on "easy" and "difficult" tasks in the face of failure or success for approach-oriented versus avoidance-oriented individuals. Feather (Chapter 8; Chapter 9) has been able to confirm several of these implications. The study being reported was designed to provide a test of the model as it applies to the effects of success and failure on *selection* of tasks of varying levels of difficulty.

In the study being reported, the subject was presented with three tasks presumably varying widely in level of difficulty: one was easy ($P_s = .75$), one was difficult ($P_s = .25$), and one was of intermediate

---

[1] The incentive value of failure can also be defined as $1 - P_f$ where P_f is the subjective probability of failure. $P_s + P_f$ is assumed to be equal to 1.00.

difficulty ($P_s = .50$). He was asked to perform the task of intermediate difficulty. If he succeeded, he would then be expected to perceive these tasks as less difficult for him than he had originally thought. That is, P_s for both remaining tasks should increase and, consequently, P_s of the difficult task should now be closer to .50 than P_s of the easy task. Analogously, if the subject were to fail the task of intermediate difficulty, the resultant P_s for the easy task should be closer to .50 than P_s for the difficult task. Following either success or failure on the task of intermediate difficulty, the subject was asked to choose which one of the two remaining tasks he would like to perform. This choice should be predictable from a knowledge of the relative strengths of M_S and M_{AF}. Consider first the case of the approach-oriented $(M_S > M_{AF})$ individual. Since he tends to prefer tasks with a P_s close to .50, he should select the difficult task after success and the easy task after failure. These choices would be equivalent to raising of level of aspiration after success and lowering of level of aspiration after failure (the typical shift). What kinds of choices are to be expected after success and failure for the avoidance-oriented $(M_{AF} > M_S)$ subject? If, as assumed, he attempts to avoid tasks with a P_s of .50, he may select the difficult task following failure and the easy task following success, thus raising level of aspiration following failure and lowering it after success (the atypical shift). The prediction was that avoidance-oriented subjects in the present study would show the atypical shift in level of aspiration more frequently than would the approach-oriented subjects.

A further hypothesis was tested involving the group of subjects who do *not* show a clear preponderance of M_S or M_{AF} (ambivalent group). If motives which presumably determine the nature of the choice after success or failure are of roughly equal strength, then these individuals might be expected to show evidence of conflict with respect to the choice. A check on this possibility was made by looking for evidence of indecision about the choice of task following success or failure among these subjects.

Within the design of the study being reported it was possible to gather data on level of aspiration *prior* to success or failure on the tasks in question. Thus, it was feasible to obtain data which might contribute to further examination of several other issues which have arisen in research aimed at validating the Atkinson model. Atkinson et al. (1960) report a tendency for the avoidance-oriented subjects to avoid intermediate risks by selecting the difficult alternatives with a higher frequency than the easy alternatives. Evidence is provided that the task used in that study was, inadvertently, so difficult that the easiest possible alternatives had a P_s not far removed from .50. Thus, in effect, the easy alternatives were not available, so avoidance-oriented subjects utilized the only remaining defensive alternatives—the difficult range.[2] It would be expected that if the range of possible aspirations is symmetrical, so that the subject could move equally as far from a P_s of .50 by choosing an easy task as he could by choosing a difficult one, a roughly equal proportion of avoidance-oriented subjects would choose the easy and the difficult tasks. An attempt was made to provide a test of this assumption in the study being reported.

The issue of initial task preferences is complicated by yet another factor. Atkinson (Chapter 2) has argued that subjective probability of success for the avoidance-oriented individual tends to be a systematic underestimate of "objective" probability of success. Feather (1963a; Chapter 17) offered supportive experimental evidence for this assumption. The implication is that, even given a range of tasks which are "objectively" symmetrical with respect to probability of success, one could predict a preference for the difficult range on the part of the avoidance-oriented subjects. This prediction follows because the tendency of the avoidance-oriented subjects to bias P_s downward would inevitably reduce the range of easy tasks and expand the range of difficult tasks. In the present study, an effort was made to minimize this factor by attempting to convince the subjects that P_s for each of three experimental tasks (symmetrically distributed with $P_s = .25$, $P_s = .50$, $P_s = .75$) could be clearly and accurately estimated in advance. To the extent that this technique is effective in reducing bias, the easy and difficult alternatives should be equally desirable to the avoidance-oriented subjects as ways of avoiding the intermediate task on the initial choice, and thus a roughly equal proportion of these choices (easy versus difficult) should be expected within the avoidance-oriented group.

The initial choices of members of the ambivalent group were also examined, though no predictions were possible from the risk-taking model under investigation. However, the behavior of this group should provide some preliminary ideas about the kinds of choices that are likely to occur when other than achievement-related motives, as defined in the present study, are presumably determining the choice.

At this point the overall design of the study being reported will be

---

[2] Another possible explanation suggested by Atkinson, Bastian, Earl, and Litwin (1960) for the relative preference for the difficult range shown by the avoidance-oriented subjects is that such preferences are more "socially desirable" than choices in the easy range. The issue of "social desirability" as it applies to this problem as well as the manner in which it may affect the "atypical shift" will be dealt with in the Discussion section of this paper.

reviewed briefly in order that the rationale for, and implications of, several aspects of the procedure can be presented. Of particular importance is the manner in which success and failure inductions were assigned. Subjects were presented with three tasks and informed that the tasks were easy, difficult, and of intermediate difficulty and were asked to indicate on which of the tasks they would prefer to work. Irrespective of his initial choice, each subject was then required to work on the task of intermediate difficulty.[3]

When the subjects had completed their work on the task of intermediate difficulty, those who had initially chosen the easy task were told that they had failed; those who chose the difficult task were told that they had succeeded. Half of those subjects who chose the intermediate task were told that they had succeeded and half that they had failed; with the first of these subjects told that he had succeeded, the second that he had failed, and so on. The particular assignments of success and failure inductions were adopted in order to be sure that the atypical change in level of aspiration always involved a shift from the task originally chosen. Thus, the atypical shift could not be explained simply as a perseveration on the initial choice. This procedure may have reduced the number of instances in which shifts in level of aspiration appeared atypical. This assumption is based on the reasoning that for subjects who initially chose the easy or difficult task and were subsequently required to work on the task of intermediate difficulty there may have been generated a task tension (that is, the Zeigarnik effect) which would not be discharged by working on the task of intermediate difficulty. It could thus be argued that any differences obtained between approach and avoidance groups with respect to the frequency of atypical shifts might be explained in terms of variations in strength of tendencies to persist in the direction of the initial choice. This problem can be dealt with by examining the pattern of typical and atypical shifts among subjects who initially chose the task of intermediate difficulty. In these instances there can be no argument that choice of task following success or failure is influenced by a tendency to repeat the initial choice. If clear differences in frequency of atypical shifts between approach and avoidance groups occur among those subjects who initially chose the task of intermediate difficulty, then it would seem quite plausible to interpret the differences in terms of the Atkinson model.

[3] The decision to ask each subject to work on the intermediate task first, regardless of his initial choice, was made on the basis of pretest data which suggested that P_s could be more easily manipulated in a manner clear to the subject if he worked on this task first. Subjects seemed to accept easily the explanation offered for this procedure.

METHOD

Subjects were 93 male students drawn from the junior and senior classes of a suburban high school. They were required to participate in the study. As in previous studies, the *n* Achievement measure developed by McClelland, Atkinson, Clark, and Lowell (1953) and the high school form (Mandler and Cowen, 1958) of the Mandler-Sarason (1952) Test Anxiety Questionnaire (TAQ) provided measures of motive to achieve success (M_S) and motive to avoid failure (M_{AF}). A picture form of the *n* Achievement measure was administered under standard neutral conditions (McClelland et al., 1953) with pictures presented in the following order (using numbers assigned by Atkinson, 1958a, p. 832): 2, 8, 1, 7. The *n* Achievement protocols were scored by a coder who had acquired the requisite level of skill through work with the practice materials presented in Atkinson (1958a). These scores correlated .88 with those of a second expert coder who also scored the protocols.

Subjects were ranked on both measures with the highest scores given a rank of 1, and so on. Differences between ranks were computed by subtracting, algebraically, the subject's rank score on *n* Achievement from his rank score on TAQ. For a given subject, if the result of this operation was a *negative* number, he stood relatively higher in the TAQ distribution than in the *n* Achievement distribution. If the result was *positive,* he ranked relatively higher in *n* Achievement. The distribution of rank-difference scores was divided into thirds. The 31 subjects with the highest positive rank-difference scores constituted the approach-oriented group ($M_S > M_{AF}$). The 31 subjects with the highest negative rank-difference scores constituted the avoidance-oriented group ($M_{AF} > M_S$). For the remaining 31 subjects, it was assumed that M_S and M_{AF} were roughly equivalent in strength; these subjects constituted the ambivalent group. Results of these measures were not known by the experimenter during the remainder of the study.

Following the group administration of the motivation measures, subjects were seen individually and given the following general instructions:

> I am studying certain aspects of ability in high school students. Here in this file [the experimenter pointed to a box containing a large number of file folders] I have a number of tasks. As you know, if you have less ability, a particular task will be harder for you, and if you have more ability, it will be easier. We already have some information about your abilities from the school files, but we need a little more in order to tell how hard these tasks will be for you. I want to ask you a few questions and then give you a short test which will help me to assess your ability.

The experimenter then asked the subject about his general grade-point average and about his average in math and in science. The experimenter then administered a short test comparable to the Similarities subtest of the WISC and, after "scoring" this test, stated:

Now with the other information and your score on this test you just took I can judge your ability to do these tasks very accurately. All of these tasks are of the same type; the only difference is that they differ in how difficult they are. Let's see now [the experimenter selected three file folders and placed them in front of the subject], for students of *your* ability, there are three chances in four that you will do well on this easy task. You therefore have a 75% chance on this one. This second task is of medium difficulty; you have one chance in two of succeeding, that is, you have a 50% chance of succeeding. This task is difficult; there is one chance in four for students of your ability to succeed, that is, you have a 25% chance of success. Remember [pointing] this is the easy one, this is the one of medium difficulty, and here is the hard one. Which one of these three would you like to work on; the one with three chances of four of succeeding, the one with one chance out of two, or this one with one chance out of four of succeeding? Which one would you prefer to do?

After the subject made his choice, the experimenter said:

You chose the [easy, medium, difficult] task. Well, we have found that we can learn most about students' abilities if we start everyone on the task of medium difficulty, the one on which you have a 50–50 chance of success. All right? Here is the idea. The letters of these words have been mixed up. Your task is to rearrange the letters to form the name of a fruit, vegetable, color, or type of cloth. Rearrange as many words as you can as fast as you can. Do not spend too long on any one word. Do you understand? You may start now.

The experimenter made a show of timing the work and, after telling the subject to stop, he "scored" the tests and announced the results. All subjects who had chosen the easy task and alternate subjects who had chosen the intermediate task were told at this point (failure instructions):

Well, you didn't do as well as we predicted you would do. I guess that you did not use the best strategy. You're not as good at these tasks as we expected from the previous information.

All subjects who had chosen the difficult task and alternate subjects who had chosen the intermediate task were told at this point (success instructions):

You did very nicely. You must have used the best strategy. You're better at these tasks than we expected from the previous information.

Following success or failure instructions, the subjects who had originally chosen the easy or difficult task were told:

Originally you chose the difficult [easy] task; you have worked on the medium difficulty task, and you did [did not do] well. Now I am going to ask you to work on *one* more of the remaining two tasks, either the easy or difficult task. Although you originally chose the difficult [easy] task, feel free to change your mind if you wish. This time you will *definitely* work on the one you choose. So, on which one of the two would you like to work?

Subjects who had originally chosen the task of intermediate difficulty were told at this point:

Originally you chose the medium difficulty task and you worked on that one and did [did not do] well. Now I'm going to ask you to work on *one* more of the remaining two tasks, either the easy or difficult task. Feel free to choose either one. On which one of the two would you like to work?

After the choice was made, each subject was asked to indicate what he thought were the new probabilities of success for the remaining tasks. He was given a simple diagram numbered from 0.00 to 1.00 and asked to indicate the points on the diagram which represented the new P_s level.[4] He was then asked the following:

When you chose the easy [difficult] task to do next, did you have any trouble making the decision? Were you at all tempted to choose the difficult [easy] task?

The subject then performed another scrambled word task; it was "scored"; he was told he had done reasonably well on the last task and asked if he had any questions about the study. He was also given specific instructions not to discuss the study with other students, and our inquiries indicated that this injunction was obeyed.

RESULTS

The major hypothesis of the study involved the prediction that atypical shifts in level of aspiration following success or failure occur more frequently among subjects whose motivation to avoid failure exceeds motivation to approach success than among subjects who show the opposite motive pattern. From results presented in Table 1, it can be seen that 15 subjects made the atypical shift and that this shift occurred more frequently among subjects whose resultant motivation was avoidance oriented. The difference between the approach and avoidance group was clearly significant ($p < .01$). It is also evident that the atypical shift is relatively rare among subjects for whom there is not a clear preponderance of approach or avoidance motivation. In fact, the ambivalent group differed significantly from the avoidance group in this respect ($p < .05$).

[4] As expected, success always resulted in an increase in reported P_s for both remaining tasks, and failure resulted in a decrease in P_s for both remaining tasks.

Table 1

Type of shift in level of aspiration as related to resultant motivation

Resultant Motivation	Type of Shift		
	Atypical	Typical	N
Avoidance-oriented	11	20	31
Ambivalent	3	28	31
Approach-oriented	1	30	31
Total	15	78	93

Avoidance-oriented versus approach oriented, $\chi^2 = 8.37$†
Avoidance-oriented versus ambivalent, $\chi^2 = 4.52$*

* $p < .05$.
† $p < .01$.

Table 2

Initial task preferences and subsequent typical versus atypical shifts
as related to resultant motivation

Resultant Motivation	Difficulty Level of Tasks Initially Chosen			
	Intermediate	Extremes		N
		Easy	Difficult	
Approach-oriented	23 (0)	1 (1)	7 (0)	31
Avoidance-oriented	14 (6)	9 (3)	8 (2)	31
Ambivalent	17 (2)	0 (0)	14 (1)	31
Total	54	10	29	93

Approach-oriented versus avoidance-oriented; choice of intermediate difficulty
task versus choice of either the easy or difficult task, $\chi^2 = 5.43$*

Note: Numbers in parentheses refer to the frequency of atypical shifts following
a particular initial choice.
* $p < .02$.

Table 2 presents data relevant to the occurrence of the atypical shift as related to the task initially chosen. It can be seen that 6 of 14 subjects in the avoidance-oriented group who initially chose the intermediate task made the atypical shift following success or failure while none of the corresponding 23 subjects in the approach-oriented group made the atypical shift. The difference is clearly significant ($\chi^2 = 8.82$, $p < .01$). Note also (Table 2) that among subjects in the avoidance-oriented group the frequency of atypical shifts following an initial choice of the intermediate difficulty task was 43% and among those who chose the easy or difficult task the frequency of atypical shifts was 29%.

Each of the motive measures considered independently was signifi-cantly related in the expected direction to the occurrence of the atypi-cal shift (see Table 3). Thus, 13 of 15 subjects who made the atypical

Table 3

Type of shift in level of aspiration as related to test anxiety and n Achievement

		Type of Shift		
		Atypical	Typical	N
Test anxiety				
High		13	34	47
Low		2	44	46
	Total	15	78	93
		$\chi^2 = 7.70\dagger$		
n Achievement				
High		3	44	47
Low		12	34	46
	Total	15	78	93
		$\chi^2 = 5.29*$		

* $p < .05$.
$\dagger$ $p < .01$.

shift were above the median on TAQ ($p < .01$), and 12 of 15 below the median on n Achievement ($p < .05$).

It was predicted that subjects in the ambivalent group would show evidence of conflict with respect to the postsuccess or postfailure choices. These results are presented in Table 4. Of the 24 subjects who reported conflicted choices, a majority and a statistically significant proportion fell in the ambivalent group ($p < .05$).

Data on the initial choices made before the success or failure experi-

Table 4

Conflicted shifts in level of aspiration as related to resultant motivation

Resultant Motivation		Conflicted	Not Conflicted	N
		Shifts in Level of Aspiration		
Avoidance-oriented		7	24	31
Ambivalent		13	18	31
Approach-oriented		4	27	31
	Total	24	69	93

Ambivalent group versus approach and avoidance groups combined, $\chi^2 = 5.12$*

* $p < .05$.

ences are also presented in Table 2. Members of the avoidance-oriented group showed a relative preference for the easy and difficult task in contrast to the approach-oriented subjects, who tended to select the task of intermediate difficulty. This difference was generated primarily by the fact that the avoidance-oriented subjects selected the easy task with greater frequency than did the approach-oriented group. Subjects in the ambivalent group also avoided the easy task, but they exceeded both of the other groups with respect to the frequency with which they chose the difficult task in preference to the other two (see Table 2).

DISCUSSION

As predicted by Atkinson's model, the atypical shift in level of aspiration occurred more frequently among the avoidance-oriented than among the approach-oriented subjects. The fact that this relationship retains significance among just those subjects who initially chose the task of intermediate difficulty would seem to make it clear that the results cannot be interpreted in terms of differences between the two motive groups in strength of tendency to persist with respect to their initially chosen task, an issue clearly raised by the nature of the experimental design. The atypical shift was also relatively infrequent among members of the ambivalent group although, as predicted, these subjects did show evidence of greater frequency of conflict or indecision with respect to the direction of change in level of aspiration. This group of findings represents the first clear confirmation of the effects of success and failure on shifts in level of aspiration implicit in the model.

The relatively low frequency of atypical shifts (36%) among subjects in the avoidance-oriented group, for whom this behavior was specifically predicted, requires consideration. As indicated earlier the nature of the design was such that subjects who initially chose the easy or difficult task were required to change from the task initially chosen if they were to make the atypical shift following success or failure. It is possible that this requirement may have tended to lower the proportion of atypical shifts among these subjects. This assumption is tentatively supported by the fact that within the avoidance-oriented group there was a somewhat greater (though not statistically significant) proportion of atypical shifts following an initial choice of the intermediate task than following an initial choice of either easy or difficult. However, even for those subjects in the avoidance-oriented group who initially chose the intermediate task a minority (43%) show the atypical shift. One possible explanation of why even these subjects failed to show a high proportion of atypical shifts was suggested by the spontaneous remarks made by some subjects who, when asked about the choice they had made, expressed the idea that it would not have been "sensible" or would have been "weird" to pick an easy task after success or a difficult task after failure, even though they had been inclined to do so. Thus, the atypical shift may have low "social desirability" and, even among the avoidance-oriented subjects who initially chose the task of intermediate difficulty, those with strong needs to act in a "socially desirable" manner will not show this behavior.

It is of interest to note in this connection that subjects in the ambivalent group, for whom M_S and M_{AF} are presumed to be of roughly equal strength, were shown to make the atypical shift less frequently than did avoidance-oriented subjects. In the ambivalent group, it could be argued that motives other than M_S or M_{AF} must have determined the nature of responses to success and failure, and it seems plausible to assume that when achievement-related motives were not the determining factors, the choices were influenced by the greater social desirability of the typical shift. An implication of this argument is that if the apparent "social desirability" of the atypical shift could be increased, the ambivalent group might show a significantly greater proportion of atypical shifts than the approach-oriented subjects whose behavior in these situations is presumably clearly controlled by "intrinsic" achievement-related motivations. In further studies, attempts to control the social-desirability factor by independent measurement of individual differences in need to behave in a socially desirable manner, or through experimental attempts to counteract the low social desirability of the atypical shift, should be useful in deciding these questions.

The exploratory data gathered on presuccess or prefailure choices provide encouraging results. Subjects in the avoidance-oriented group chose the easy or difficult task with greater frequency than the approach-oriented group, as expected. Of greater interest was the fact that in contrast to previous work, subjects in the avoidance-oriented group chose the easy task as often as they chose the difficult one. Recall that several aspects of the procedure were aimed at producing just this effect. P_s for the easy and difficult tasks was set equidistant from .50 and an attempt was made to minimize the tendency of avoidance-oriented subjects to bias P_s downward. These results are, of course, only tentative support for the assumptions tested because there is no assurance at this point that these findings are clearly attributable to the fact that bias was reduced by the operations involved. A more definitive test would involve a study in which the instructions intended to reduce the degree of bias would be retained for one experimental group and omitted for another experimental group. In such a study, it would be predicted that, among the avoidance-oriented subjects, a greater proportion would choose the difficult task when instructions intended to counteract bias were omitted than when these instructions were included.

Finally, the initial choices of members of the ambivalent group in the present study tentatively suggest that when M_S and M_{AF} are of roughly equal strength, preferences for tasks of relatively low P_s are predominant. The suggestion that the social desirability of such choices may strongly affect the behavior of this group would seem to warrant further investigation.

SUMMARY

Atkinson's risk-taking model predicts that individuals high in fear of failure and low in need for achievement may react in an atypical manner to success or failure experiences; i.e., they may raise their level of aspiration following failure and lower it after success. An experimental situation was designed to test these predictions and confirmation of this aspect of the model was obtained. Effects of instructions intended to reduce the degree to which these Ss subjectively underestimate probability of success were also examined. Results tentatively suggest that such instructions increase the proportion of low as contrasted to high levels of aspiration in this group.

PART III

Applications and Social Implications

11. JOHN W. ATKINSON

Notes Concerning the Generality
of the Theory of Achievement Motivation

This paper, except for minor editorial changes, was distributed in-
formally as a dittoed memo April 15, 1959. It contains some guiding
hypotheses that have since been explored with profit in the chapters
cited and other hypotheses concerning child training that appear
worthy of study.

1. The so-called "risk-taking model" is presented as a general theory
of achievement motivation (Chapter 2).

2. It is expected that hypotheses from the theory will apply whenever
achievement-related behavior is under consideration in relation to a
series of tasks ordered in terms of difficulty (that is, P_s).

3. This means that the social psychological problems of vocational
aspiration, social mobility, etc. can be considered by recognizing that
the hierarchy of occupations (which according to Inkeles and Rossi
(1956) is stable across all modern industrialized societies) is a continuum of "tasks" which differ in "difficulty" (i.e., probability of success) and also in "incentive value" (i.e., status accorded persons holding
those occupations). It is known that greater prestige is accorded persons
in higher occupations. That is, I_s (the value of success in an occupation)
is inversely related to the P_s. It is assumed that the relationship of I_s
and P_s is $I_s = 1 - P_s$.

4. Litwin (Chapter 7) has explored one important implication of
the $M_S \times P_s \times I_s$ formulation. He obtained estimates of P_s in a Ring
Toss Game by having Ss state how many times out of ten they thought
they could hit the target from each line. He then calculated the I_s value
for each task according to the assumption $I_s = 1 - P_s$. He then asked
Ss who were high and low in n Achievement to report how large a monetary prize should be offered for success at each line. His results (ideal-
ized) are shown in Figure 1.

The "subjective value" or "valence" of success (Va_s) is a joint func-

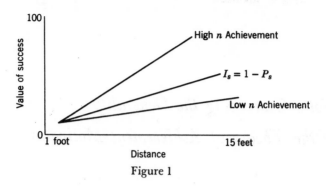

Figure 1

tion of incentive value and strength of motive (that is, $Va_s = M_S \times I_s$). This is the major implication of the multiplicative relationship between Motive and Incentive Value in the theoretical formulation. $M_G \times I_g$ is a general theory of "valence" or "utility." The major prediction from this conception is that the slope of Va_s in relation to increasing difficulty of task will be steeper, the stronger M_S is. In other words, when achievement motive is strong, the individual is progressively more pleased with success as difficulty of task increases. When achievement motive is weak, the increase in satisfaction with increasing difficulty is much less apparent, i.e., the slope is flatter.

5. Jewish and Italian high school boys were asked to indicate whether they would be pleased or disappointed should they eventually end up in certain occupations (Strodtbeck, McDonald, and Rosen, 1957). The occupations were chosen to represent six levels of status on the usual hierarchy of occupations: (1) doctor, advertising executive; (2) druggist, jewelry store owner; (3) bank teller, bookkeeper; (4) carpenter, auto mechanic; (5) mail carrier, bus driver; (6) night watchman, furniture mover.

Results showed that the slope of satisfaction was steeper for Jewish boys than Italian boys and steeper for middle-class boys than for working-class boys. The slope for upper-class boys was slightly less steep than that for middle-class boys. A typical result showing what the data looked like is the comparison of the percent "pleased" responses for middle-class boys in the two ethnic groups (Table 1).

These (and other results of this study) are particularly exciting, because independent studies have shown n Achievement to be stronger among Jews than Italians and stronger in the middle class than in the working class (or upper class).

6. In a study by Rosen (1959), the Winterbottom (1958) training

Table 1

Occupation Level	Italians	Jews
1	57	71
2	47	55
3	37	17
4	40	19
5	5	2
6	3	1

After Strodtbeck, McDonald, and Rosen (1957), with permission of the author and the American Sociological Association.

items dealing with independence and mastery were used in interviews with mothers. (Parental expectations for independence and mastery at an early age have been shown by Winterbottom to be related to n Achievement in 8 to 10-year-old children in the Ann Arbor area.) In addition, this study assessed n Achievement in high school boys by thematic apperception. The results are as expected:

(a) Average age at which independence and mastery is expected according to reports of mothers about child-training practices: Jews, 6.83 years; Italians, 8.03 years. This is the largest difference in a table containing other ethnic groups ($p < .01$).

(b) Mastery and independence training also expected earlier in middle class than in working class: middle class, 6.31 years*; working class, 7.64–7.59 years; ($p < .001$).

(c) n Achievement has been shown higher in the middle class than in the working class in three earlier studies (Douvan, 1956; Rosen, 1956; Milstein, 1956); and in this study (Table 2).

Table 2

	Social Class (Hollingshead Index)				
	Highest			Lowest	
	I–II	III	IV	V	
n Achievement	10.55	11.26	9.01	8.32	($p < .005$)

(After Rosen (1959) with permission of author and American Sociological Association.)

* Contains also a small number from "upper" class.

(d) *n* Achievement stronger among Jews than Italians: Jews, 10.53; Italians, 9.65. (The study contains results for other ethnic groups as well and shows ethnicity related to *n* Achievement ($p < .05$), but social class much more strongly related to *n* Achievement).

7. Implications: The theoretical model for achievement motivation can be extended to cover the problems of vocational aspiration (Chapter 12) and of social mobility (Chapter 13). To date, there is a rather striking agreement among these and other studies that have examined the age at which independent mastery is expected in children, the TAT *n* Achievement score, and estimates of satisfaction in attaining certain occupational goals.

The slope of the satisfaction curve in relation to increasing difficulty of task can be taken as an index of the strength of achievement motive. In other words, individual differences (or group differences) in *n* Achievement can be inferred from the estimates persons make of how pleased they would be to succeed at certain levels of difficulty. This appears to be the most promising alternative method for assessing strength of *n* Achievement in light of the failure of more direct objective test methods to yield scores having the same predictive significance as TAT *n* Achievement scores (Chapter 14). For example, a student who reports much greater pleasure in getting an A in a course than a C has a stronger achievement motive than one for whom the differential in pleasure is less.

8. What are the implications of the theoretical model for estimates of how much pain (or punishment) should be experienced for failing to succeed at different levels of difficulty? According to the model ($Va_f = M_{AF} \times I_f$), the stronger the motive to avoid failure (i.e., the stronger the disposition to anxiety in achievement-stress situations), the steeper the slope of Va_f in relation to difficulty.

A person strong in M_{AF} should think failure at an easy task extremely painful (shameful, embarrassing, punishable). The slope should be steep. A person who is weak in this motive should not think failure at easy tasks much more blameworthy than failure at more difficult tasks.

9. Can behavior of mothers toward their own children be explained in terms of the relative strength of M_S and M_{AF} *in the mothers?* According to the model, when M_S is the stronger motive in the mothers the following should occur:

(a) Praise and other rewards for success should be generally much stronger than shame, blame, and punishments applied for failure.

(b) The mother should show a very clear differentiation in amount of reward for accomplishment depending upon the difficulty of the task the child has attempted; but she should not show as clear a differentiation in amount of punishment (probably shame) for failure at different levels of difficulty. This will be relatively mild in any case.

(c) The mother should encourage the child to be realistic and approach tasks that the child has about a 50–50 chance of mastering. Success at this level should be followed by expecting the child to try something a little harder next time, etc., ... (This is the derivation for changes in level of aspiration following success and failure.)

(d) The mother's vicarious motivation for the child should be generally positive toward competitive activities and activities requiring skill. Hence, she should encourage moving toward these kinds of situations generally (Feld, 1959).

However, when M_{AF} is the stronger motive within the mother,

(a) Punishment for failures should generally be more intense across all activities than are rewards for accomplishment.

(b) Differential punishment for failure at easy versus difficult tasks should be very marked, while differential rewards for varying degrees of success should be less marked (the slope hypothesis).

(c) The mother should encourage the child to "play it safe" or to "shoot for the moon" (daydream) rather than attempt tasks of intermediate risk. She should not encourage a "realistic" orientation towards achievement.

(d) The vicarious motivation of the mother is essentially anxious and avoidant. She should not encourage competitive activities nor attempting tasks which require skill. She should (if anything) impose restrictions on the child's spontaneous attempts at mastery or perhaps be very inconsistent in sometimes expecting exceptional accomplishments, while at other times expecting virtually nothing.

10. In this regard, Winterbottom's (1958) results appear to be generally consistent:

(a) Mothers of boys who are high in n Achievement tend to expect earlier development of mastery and independence and appear to be actively involved in getting the child to learn how to do things.

(b) Mothers of boys who are low in n Achievement are more restrictive.

(c) Mothers of boys who are high in n Achievement report offering stronger rewards for accomplishment. (However there is no evidence of less punishment than other mothers.)

(d) Teachers report that boys who are high in n Achievement appear to take *greater pride* in their accomplishments. (This would be the *capacity* for pleasure in success that is called Motive in the theoretical formulation.)

11. What is needed? Research relating parental attitudes and training practices to development of "sense of pride in accomplishment" versus "sense of shame for failure" in the child. The former is the "achievement motive," the latter is "test anxiety" (Feld, 1959).

12. CHARLES H. MAHONE

Fear of Failure and
Unrealistic Vocational Aspiration

This study is concerned with the application of a theory regarding fear of failure to the problem of vocational choice. Atkinson's usage (Chapter 2) is followed in regard to fear of failure, which is defined as a motivational disposition to be anxiously concerned about avoiding failure. This disposition has been measured by two kinds of instruments: (a) the self-report measure of achievement-related anxiety, such as the Mandler-Sarason Test Anxiety Scale (Mandler and Sarason, 1952) or the Achievement Anxiety Scale (Alpert and Haber, 1960); and (b) the scoring of thematic apperception stories for achievement imagery (McClelland, Atkinson, Clark, and Lowell, 1953). In the latter case, fear of failure is inferred from low n Achievement scores, for achievement anxiety is likely to be higher than positive achievement motivation for this group.

Two of the major factors that determine a person's suitability for a particular vocation are ability and interest. Therefore, if one is to be considered realistic in his choice of occupation, he should have ability commensurate with that required for substantial success in the occupation, and his interest pattern should be congruent with that of most people in his chosen field. The thesis of this paper is that persons who are fearful of failure tend to be unrealistic in their vocational choice with respect to both ability and interest.

With respect to the factor of interest, at least two studies (Atkinson, 1953; McClelland and Liberman, 1949) have shown that persons with relatively high fear of failure (as inferred from low n Achievement) tend to avoid consideration of achievement-related information. Fear-

Reprinted with some abridgement by permission of the author and the American Psychological Association from the *Journal of Abnormal and Social Psychology*, 1960, **60**, 253–261. The author is appreciative of the grant made for this study by the H. H. Rackham School of Graduate Studies at the University of Michigan.

ful persons should therefore show a relative lack of relevant information concerning the kinds of interest satisfaction to be found in the various occupational areas. They should thus be likely to choose occupations only remotely related to the kinds of gratifications that they desire and expect to find in their vocations.

As for the ability factor, two considerations underlie the prediction. As in the case of interest, the fearful person may be expected to lack information concerning his own ability and that required for his choice of occupation. The second reason is based on theory regarding the level of aspiration of the fearful person. Atkinson (Chapter 2) has offered a theoretical model for predicting level of aspiration from the relative strengths of fear of failure and need for achievement. . . .

Applying this theory to level of aspiration, the fearful person (more strongly motivated to avoid failure than to achieve success) should tend either to overaspire or to underaspire (i.e., to avoid the intermediate range of the risk continuum). This prediction has been confirmed in several studies of risk-taking behavior in the experimental laboratory on simple competitive games (Atkinson and Litwin, Chapter 5; Clark, Teevan, and Ricciuti, 1956; Litwin, Chapter 7; McClelland, 1958b). As yet, however, there is no theoretical basis for differentially predicting under- versus overaspiration.

Let us regard the level of ability required by a person's vocational choice as an index of his level of aspiration. The fearful person may then be expected to aspire either to an occupation which he feels very confident about attaining (underaspiration) or to an occupation which he considers very difficult to attain (overaspiration). That is, he should avoid the choice of an occupation that represents an intermediate risk of failure for him—the most "realistic" choice in the sense that it falls within the "most probable" range of achievement (Lewin, Dembo, Festinger, and Sears, 1944). It is in this sense that the person fearful of failure is likely to be "unrealistic" with respect to ability in his vocational choice.

Hypotheses. The following hypotheses are therefore offered:

HYPOTHESIS 1. A person who is fearful of failure tends to choose a vocation that is unrealistic in terms of the discrepancy between his own ability and the ability judged suitable for the occupation to which he aspires.

This is the most general hypothesis regarding ability, and the confirmation of this hypothesis should constitute evidence consistent with the parts of the theory concerning risk-taking and/or lack of information.

HYPOTHESIS 2. A person who is fearful of failure tends to choose a vocation that is unrealistic in terms of the discrepancy between his own *perceived* ability and the level of ability that he *perceives* as being suitable for the occupation to which he aspires.

This hypothesis rules out consideration of amount and accuracy of information, and the confirmation of this hypothesis should constitute evidence consistent with the risk-taking model.

HYPOTHESIS 3. A person who is fearful of failure tends to be inaccurate in his estimation of his own ability.

This hypothesis rules out consideration of risk, and the confirmation of this hypothesis should constitute evidence supporting the assumptions concerning lack of information as a determinant of unrealistic vocational choice.

HYPOTHESIS 4. A person who is fearful of failure tends to choose a vocation that reflects a pattern of interests discrepant from his own.

Since interest does not involve risk-taking behavior, the confirmation of this hypothesis should constitute evidence supporting the assumptions concerning lack of information as a determinant of unrealistic vocational choice.

METHOD

Subjects. The Ss were 135 male college students drawn from introductory courses in psychology, French, and mathematics at the University of Michigan. They were volunteers from a larger group of approximately 330 male Ss who had participated in another research project which involved the administration of the thematic apperceptive measure of *n* Achievement and the Achievement Anxiety Scale. In addition, the present Ss were asked to answer the Strong Vocational Information Blank and a vocational information questionnaire.

Vocational Information Questionnaire. This questionnaire consisted of a series of questions designed to tap various factors associated with the Ss' vocational choice. The most relevant items of information for the present study were obtained from questions that asked S to state: (*a*) his vocational objective; (*b*) an estimate of the ability required for each of a number of listed occupations; (*c*) an estimate of his own general ability relative to that of his fellow students; (*d*) what his vocational choice would be if ability were not a limiting consideration; and (*e*) which occupation in the above-mentioned list of occupations resembled most closely his own vocational choice. On the basis of pretest information on the vocational choices of a sample of 200 college students, the list of occupations was formulated so as to include, if not the actual stated vocational choice, at least a closely related occupation to that chosen by each *S*. It was the *S*s' estimate of the level of ability required for this listed occupation which constituted the measure of estimated ability required for own vocational choice.

n **Achievement Scale.** Fear of failure has been defined conceptually as a relatively stronger disposition to avoid failure than to approach success. In order to assess this variable, it was necessary to use measures of both positive and negative achievement motivation. The *n* Achievement test, the measure of positive achievement motivation, consisted of a set of six pictures recently included in a national survey by the Survey Research Center at the University of Michigan (Veroff, Atkinson, Feld, and Gurin, 1960). The pictures were selected so that the stories could be scored for the achievement, affiliation, and power motives (Atkinson, 1958a). The test was administered under neutral classroom conditions (McClelland, et al., 1953). The stories were scored for *n* Achievement by three trained scorers, each of whom scored stories to two pictures. A check on the reliability of scoring was made by having another experienced scorer score all six stories for a group of 30 *S*s. The rank order correlation between the latter scorer's total scores and the combined scores of the three original scorers was $+.80$. The mean *n* Achievement score for the present sample was 5.0, and the best median cutting point for both the larger group as a whole and the present sample was between 4 and 5, which placed 67 *S*s above the median (High *n* Achievement) and 68 *S*s below the median.

Debilitating Anxiety Scale. The measure of achievement anxiety (motivation to avoid failure) used was the Debilitating Anxiety Scale (Alpert and Haber, 1960). This scale is a part of the more general Achievement Anxiety Scale, which was designed in an attempt to refine the Mandler-Sarason Test Anxiety Scale by differentiating debilitating and facilitating anxiety. An early validation study on this instrument showed the Debilitating Anxiety Scale to correlate $+.79$ ($N = 40$) with the Test Anxiety Scale ($N = 40$), and, like the latter, to correlate negatively with college grades and performance on achievement and aptitude tests (Alpert, 1957).

The Debilitating Anxiety Scale measures *S*'s awareness of the extent to which anxiety interferes with the efficiency of his performance in achievement test situations. An illustrative item is: "In a course where I have been doing poorly, my fear of a bad grade cuts down my efficiency." The scale consists of ten such items, and *S* is asked to respond by indicating, on a five-point scale, how often he experiences the described situation. A score of 50 represents the highest degree of debilitating anxiety. For the present sample scores ranged from 12 to 39 with a mean of 25.9, and the best median cutting point was between 25 and 26. The best median cutting point for the larger group, however, was between 26 and 27. Since the larger group was more heterogeneous and representative of the college population as a whole, the latter cutting point was used, yielding 59 *S*s in the present sample who scored above the median (High Anxiety) and 76 *S*s who scored below the median.

The product-moment correlation between *n* Achievement and Debilitating

Anxiety was $+.09$ ($N = 135$). When Ss were grouped according to their position above or below the median score on both n Achievement and Debilitating Anxiety, 31 Ss were classified as High n Achievement-High Anxiety, 36 as High n Achievement-Low Anxiety, 28 as Low n Achievement-High Anxiety, and 40 as Low n Achievement-Low Anxiety.

RESULTS

Judgments of Unrealistic Vocational Choice (with Respect to Ability). The first hypothesis requires some evaluation of the discrepancy between S's general ability and the ability required in order to achieve his vocational objective. Because no adequate information was found in the literature concerning the level of ability required in various occupations, clinical judgments were employed as the major criteria in determining realism of vocational choice with respect to ability. Two clinical psychologists, both having considerable experience in vocational counseling, made independent judgments of the realism of the vocational choice of each of the Ss on the basis of the following information:

ACE[1] score (total of the verbal and quantitative scores expressed as a percentile), grade point average for the preceding semester, class, major field, vocational choice, and "ideal" choice (i.e., the vocational choice that would be made if ability were not a consideration). The information on "ideal" choice was included to permit judgments of "underaspiration" in cases where the student was judged to have sufficient ability for a particular vocation, even though he rejected it because of perceived lack of ability.

The judges were asked to assign each S to one of five categories: Probably Overaspiring, Perhaps Overaspiring, Probably Realistic, Perhaps Underaspiring, Probably Underaspiring. They were also asked to indicate whether they were Very Confident, Moderately Confident, Moderately Doubtful, or Very Doubtful about their assignments in each case. The investigator, who has had three years experience as a trainee in vocational counseling, made independent judgments for each S to provide a basis for resolving disagreements between the two expert judges.

The three judges were in agreement with one another in 71–81% of the cases in judging the S to be either "realistic," "overaspiring," or "underaspiring." With the investigator making the deciding judgment in case of disagreement between the two expert judges, the final ratings

[1] American Council on Education test of verbal and quantitative aptitude.

consisted of 80 Ss judged to be realistic, 45 judged to be overaspiring, and 10 judged to be underaspiring. Each of the three judges agreed with these final ratings in at least 81% of the cases. In the analysis, ratings of overaspiration and underaspiration were combined in a single "unrealistic" category.

According to the first hypothesis, Ss who are high in achievement motivation and low in anxiety about failure should be judged more realistic in aspiring to vocations that are commensurate with their ability than Ss who are low in achievement motivation and high in anxiety. The relative frequency of realistic and unrealistic persons in the various motivational groups are all in the predicted direction (Table 1). A highly significant difference is found between the High n Achievement-Low Debilitating Anxiety group and the Low n Achievement-High Debilitating Anxiety group $(\chi^2 = 7.96, df = 1, p < .003)$.

Table 1

n Achievement and debilitating anxiety related to all clinical judgments of realistic and unrealistic vocational choice ($N = 135$)

n Achieve-ment	Anx-iety	N	Real-istic	Unreal-istic	Anxiety	N	Real-istic	Unreal-istic
			Clinical Judgments				Clinical Judgments	
High	High	31	48%	52%	High	59	44%	56%
High	Low	36	75*	25*	Low	76	71	29
Low	High	28	39*	61*			$\chi^2 = 10.1$	
Low	Low	40	68	32			$p < .001$	
					n Achieve-ment			
					High	67	63	37
					Low	68	56	44
		* $\chi^2 = 7.96$					$\chi^2 = 1.09$	
		$p < .003$					$p < .15$	

* Significance levels reported in this table are based on one-tailed tests since the direction of the differences was predicted.

Debilitating Anxiety alone also discriminates between Realistic and Unrealistic groups $(\chi^2 = 10.1, df = 1, p < .001)$, but n Achievement alone does not.

Also, since the clinical judgments are obviously a rather gross and imperfect measure, a more refined analysis was made using only ratings on which both expert judges were not only in agreement but rated themselves as being either "Very Confident" or "Moderately Confident." There were 58 judgments, including 38 "realistic," 19 "overaspiring," and one "underaspiring."

In this more rigorous analysis (Table 2), n Achievement by itself is

Table 2

n Achievement and debilitating anxiety related to confident, agreed-upon clinical judgments of realistic-unrealistic vocational choice ($N = 58$)

n Achievement	Debilitating Anxiety	N	Clinical Judgments		Debilitating Anxiety	N	Clinical Judgments	
			Realistic	Unrealistic			Realistic	Unrealistic
High	High	9	56%	44%	High	21	33%	67%
High	Low	18	94*	06*	Low	37	80	20
Low	High	12	17*	83*	$\chi^2 = 15.0$			
Low	Low	19	74	26	$p < .0005$			

n Achievement

	N	Realistic	Unrealistic
High	27	81	19
Low	31	52	48

$\chi^2 = 5.68$
$p < .01$

* $\chi^2 = 15.5\dagger$
$(p < .0005)$

* Significance levels reported in this table are based on one-tailed tests since the direction of the differences was predicted.
† Yates correction was used in obtaining this chi square value because of the small N.

significantly associated with judged reality of vocational choice ($\chi^2 = 5.68$, $df = 1$, $p < .01$). The degree of association between unrealistic aspiration and Debilitating Anxiety is also very much enhanced ($\chi^2 = 15.0$, $df = 1$, $p < .0005$), and the difference between the High n Achievement-Low Anxiety and the Low n Achievement-High Anxiety groups is striking ($\chi^2 = 15.5$, $df = 1$, $p < .0005$).

It may be noted in Table 2 that when Ss are classified according to both n Achievement and Anxiety, the distinctive group is the one low in *n* Achievement and high in Anxiety, which is clearly more unrealistic than the other three groups combined ($\chi^2 = 12.0^2$, $df = 1$, $p < .0005$).

Subjective Goal Discrepancy. The second prediction was that Ss who are fearful of failure should avoid choosing occupations that they perceive as requiring the same level of ability as they perceive in themselves. Instead, they should favor occupations that they perceive as requiring either more or less than their own perceived ability. In order to test this hypothesis, it was necessary to obtain a measure of each S's estimate of his own ability and his estimate of the level of general ability necessary in order to attain his occupational goal. On the initial questionnaire all Ss were asked: "What percentage of the undergraduates at the University of Michigan do you feel have sufficient *general ability* (i.e., verbal and quantitative ability) to attain the following occupational goals, provided they were motivated to do so?" As a measure of their perception of their own ability, they were also asked: "Irrespective of your own grade point average, where do you think you stand in relation to your fellow students in *general ability?*" Both of these estimates were made relative to "fellow students" so that they would be comparable.

The subjective goal discrepancy, then, is the difference between the S's estimate of his own ability and his estimate of the ability required for his vocational objective. The formula for the discrepancy score is the perceived percentage of students with higher ability than S minus the perceived percentage of students with sufficient ability to attain S's vocational goal. The range of discrepancy scores was from -48 (own ability seen as superior to that required by job) to $+85$ (own ability seen as inferior to that required by job). The median discrepancy score was $+7$, if the direction of discrepancy is taken into account. If only the absolute size of the discrepancy is considered, the median discrepancy is ± 12.

This index is somewhat problematic, however, in that it raises the question of whether the best test of the hypothesis is made using the median cutting point, which takes into consideration the direction of the discrepancy, or the median cutting point which disregards direction. If one assumes that the Ss are responding to the question of estimating ability required by various occupations by estimating the *average* ability required, then the theoretical model for risk-taking behavior would certainly call for the cutting point which disregards the direction of discrepancy, since this estimate would be analogous to an estimate of intermediate risk, and thus large negative discrepancies would represent underaspiration. If, however, the Ss are making estimates in

---

[2] Computed with Yates correction because of the small N.

terms of the *minimum* ability required, then this kind of estimate provides no basis for determining underaspiration, for occupations probably differ markedly in the range of ability levels which they can productively use. In this case negative discrepancies would have to be regarded as realistic, regardless of size. Since the basis on which Ss arrived at their estimates is not known, analysis of the data was made both considering and disregarding the direction of the discrepancy.

When the direction of the discrepancy was considered, the median cutting point was +8, in terms of which 71 Ss were classified as "realistic," and 63 were classified as "unrealistic," which, in this case, means only overaspiring (i.e., positive discrepancies[3]). When the direction of the discrepancy was disregarded, the median cutting point was ±13, in terms of which 68 Ss were classified as "realistic," and 66 were classified as "unrealistic," which, in this case, includes both overaspiring (positive discrepancies) and underaspiring (negative discrepancies) Ss.

In the positive discrepancy analysis (Table 3), the hypothesis is con-

Table 3

n Achievement and debilitating anxiety related to positive
subjective goal discrepancy (overaspiration)

n Achievement	Anxiety	N	Positive Goal Discrepancy		Anxiety	N	Positive Goal Discrepancy	
			High	Low			High	Low
High	High	30	53%	47%	High	58	57%	43%
High	Low	36	31*	69*	Low	76	39	61
Low	High	28	61*	39*				
Low	Low	40	48	52	$\chi^2 = 3.97$			
					$p < .03$			
					n Achievement			
					High	66	41	59
					Low	68	53	47
		* $\chi^2 = 5.69$			$\chi^2 = 1.92$			
		$p < .01$			$p < .10$			

* Significance levels reported in this table are based on one-tailed tests since the direction of the differences was predicted.

[3] The total *N* here is only 134 because one S failed to provide an estimate of his own ability.

firmed for the combination of n Achievement and Debilitating Anxiety ($\chi^2 = 5.69$, $df = 1$, $p < .01$). Debilitating Anxiety alone is also significantly related to this index of overaspiration ($\chi^2 = 3.97$, $df = 1$, $p < .03$), but n Achievement alone is not. In the absolute discrepancy analysis (both over- and underaspirants considered unrealistic), none of these associations reached the .05 level of significance when the distribution of absolute discrepancies is divided at the median ± 13. However, if we accept a more stringent definition of the "realistic" category which includes *only the least discrepant third of the distribution* of absolute goal discrepancies (± 8), as suggested in a study by Atkinson and Litwin (Chapter 5), then Debilitating Anxiety alone ($\chi^2 = 5.36$, $df = 1$, $p < .02$) and the High n Achievement-Low Anxiety versus Low n Achievement-High Anxiety comparison ($\chi^2 = 7.0$, $df = 1$, $p < .005$)

Table 4

n Achievement and debilitating anxiety related to absolute subjective goal
discrepancy (intermediate third versus combined positive
and negative extremes)

n Achievement	Anxiety	N	Absolute Goal Discrepancy		Anxiety	N	Absolute Goal Discrepancy	
			Mid-third	Ex-tremes			Mid-third	Ex-tremes
High	High	30	30%	70%	High	58	24%	76%
High	Low	36	50*	50*	Low	76	43	57
Low	High	28	18*	82*		$\chi^2 = 5.36$			
Low	Low	40	38	62		$p < .02$			
					n Achievement			
					High	66	41	59
					Low	68	29	71
	* $\chi^2 = 7.0$					$\chi^2 = 2.07$		
	$p < .005$					$p < .10$		

* Significance levels reported in this table are based on one-tailed tests since the direction of the differences was predicted.

show highly significant relationships with subjective goal discrepancy (Table 4). n Achievement alone does not reliably discriminate between the mid-third realistic group and the over- and underaspirant groups combined. However, the trends are all in the predicted direction, and it is very clear that the only group heavily represented in the "realistic" category is the High n Achievement–Low Anxiety group.

Inaccuracy in Estimation of Own Ability. In the initial questionnaire, Ss were asked to estimate their standing in general ability in comparison with fellow students, in terms of percentile rank, which would then be directly comparable to Ss' actual percentile scores for combined verbal and quantitative ability on the ACE. One measure of unrealism (or inaccuracy) is the discrepancy between the percentile ranks of the S's estimate of his ability and his actual ability; the latter percentile rank was subtracted from the former. The ranks for measured ability ranged from the 4th to the 99th percentile, with a median at the 61st percentile. The percentile discrepancies ranged from —47 (underestimation) to +75, with a median· absolute discrepancy of ±16. There were 35 negative discrepancies and 99 positive discrepancies.[4] The median cutting point was between ±15 and ±16, yielding 68 Ss classified as "inaccurate" and 66 Ss classified as "accurate" in estimating their own ability.

The third hypothesis states that Ss with high achievement motivation and low anxiety are more accurate in estimating their own general level of ability than are Ss with low achievement motivation and high anxiety. This prediction was confirmed ($\chi^2 = 3.52$, $df = 1$, $p < .04$). Debilitating Anxiety and n Achievement taken singly were not significantly related to accuracy of estimate (Table 5). The major difference in Table 5 is between the Low n Achievement–High Anxiety group and the other three groups combined ($\chi^2 = 4.6$, $df = 1$, $p < .02$).

Unrealistic Vocational Choice (with Respect to Interest). At the same time that the judges made their rating of the realism of vocational choice with respect to ability, they also indicated the primary and secondary vocational areas on the Strong interest test which they felt would reflect the interest pattern most congruent with the S's vocational choice. On the basis of the S's scores in these designated areas, as evaluated in terms of the pattern analysis suggested and used by Darley (1941), plus his score on the specific occupational key related to his vocational choice, the investigator divided the Ss into two approximately equal groups. One group ($N = 66$) was considered to be nondiscrepant in their interest patterns (i.e., inventoried interests were

---

[4] The total N here is only 134 because one S failed to provide an estimate of his own ability.

Table 5

n Achievement and debilitating anxiety related to inaccuracy
in estimate of own ability

n Achievement	Anxiety	N	Inaccuracy High	Inaccuracy Low	Anxiety	N	Inaccuracy High	Inaccuracy Low
High	High	30	46%	54%	High	58	57%	43%
High	Low	36	44*	56*	Low	76	46	54
Low	High	28	67*	33*				
Low	Low	40	47	53			$\chi^2 = 1.41$	
							$p < .15$	
					n Achievement			
					High	66	45	55
					Low	68	56	44
		* $\chi^2 = 3.52$					$\chi^2 = 1.46$	
		$p < .04$					$p < .15$	

* Significance levels reported in this table are based on one-tailed tests since the direction of the differences was predicted.

congruent with vocational choices) and the other group ($N = 69$) was considered to be discrepant (i.e., inventoried interests were not congruent with vocational choices).

n Achievement alone was found to be significantly related to congruence (or reality) of interest pattern in the expected direction ($\chi^2 = 4.55$, $df = 1$, $p < .02$), and a significant difference was also found between the High *n* Achievement–Low Anxiety group and the Low *n* Achievement–High Anxiety group ($\chi^2 = 3.50$, $df = 1$, $p < .04$). Anxiety alone, however, was not significantly related to realism of interest pattern (Table 6).

Relationships Among Indices of Unrealism. The relationships among the indices of unrealism about ability are all in the expected direction, and three of the five comparisons are statistically significant beyond the .05 level. The dimensions that do not appear to be significantly related are the Clinical Judgments and both the Positive and the Absolute Subjective Goal Discrepancy. The relationships between the unreal-

Table 6

n Achievement and debilitating anxiety related to realistic-unrealistic vocational choice (with respect to interest)

n Achievement	Anxiety	N	Interest Realistic	Interest Unrealistic	Anxiety	N	Interest Realistic	Interest Unrealistic
High	High	31	61%	39%	High	59	47%	53%
High	Low	36	56*	44*	Low	76	50	50
Low	High	28	32*	68*			$\chi^2 = .12$	
Low	Low	40	45	55			$p < .40$	
					n Achievement			
					High	67	58	42
					Low	68	40	60
		* $\chi^2 = 3.50$					$\chi^2 = 4.55$	
		$p < .04$					$p < .02$	

* Significance levels reported in this table are based on one-tailed tests since the direction of the differences was predicted.

istic interest index and the ability indices are also all in the expected direction, but only one of the relationships with Interest, that of Absolute Goal Discrepancy, is statistically significant ($\chi^2 = 3.00$, $df = 1$, $p < .05$).

Ability, Fear of Failure, and Indices of Unrealism. The results show that measured ability (ACE percentile score) is significantly related (negatively) to Debilitating Anxiety ($\chi^2 = 11.8$, $df = 1$, $p < .001$), but is not related to n Achievement. Ability is also significantly associated with all of the indices of unrealism related to ability ($p < .005$ in all cases). In every case the group low in ability is typically more unrealistic than the group high in ability. However, ACE percentile score is not significantly related to Interest Reality.

DISCUSSION

Because of the association between high measured ability and low Debilitating Anxiety, it is very difficult to distinguish between the relationships of ability and those of motivation to the three ability-related dimensions of unrealistic vocational aspiration. This kind of distinction is desirable, however, in view of the possibility that the relationships of ACE score to Clinical Judgments and to Inaccuracy in Estimating Own Ability are artifacts resulting from the fact that measured ability was directly involved in arriving at these two indices.

In view of this possibility, it is important to determine whether or not fear of failure is related to Clinical Judgments and Inaccuracy in Estimating Own Ability independent of level of ability. For this reason, an analysis of covariance was accomplished to determine whether the average level of anxiety in "Realistic" and "Unrealistic" groups was different (as predicted) when the groups were equated by this statistical procedure on ACE score. The results clearly show that fear of failure is related to Clinical Judgments ($N = 135$) when ability is held constant ($F = 5.40$; $df = 1/132$; $p < .02^5$). This means that it would *not* be possible to account for the relationship between fear of failure and judgments of unrealistic vocational aspiration solely in terms of a possibly artifactual relationship between judgments of unrealistic aspiration and ability. An analysis of covariance was not made using the Inaccuracy index to categorize realistic and unrealistic groups because an inspection of the chi square tables indicated that no relationship between this index and the motivation measures remained when Ss high and low on the ACE were considered separately. Most of the relationship between this index and the fear of failure measure reported in Table 6 should be attributed to the relationship of both kinds of variables to the general ability measure.

Let us now consider the relationship between low intelligence and high anxiety about failure, since the interaction of these two variables is probably of substantial importance in the prediction of unrealistic vocational aspiration. One reason why we might expect these variables to be related is that relatively low intelligence may cause a person to have more early failure experiences and thus to become more fearful of failure. A second and perhaps even more important factor is that anxiety about achievement has on numerous occasions been shown to interfere with performance on aptitude tests (Alpert and Haber, 1960; Sarason and Mandler, 1952; Zweidelson, 1956). Since our measure of ability, the ACE test, is just such a performance test taken under competitive conditions, we should expect that high anxiety would lead to performance decrements, i.e., lower ACE test scores. For this reason, when we control for measured ability in the analysis of covariance we

---

⁵ One-tailed test.

are probably overcontrolling. Not only are we ruling out the effect of innate ability on fear of failure, but we are in all likelihood also ruling out the effect of fear of failure on the performance measure of innate ability. Thus, we have good reason to believe that the relationship of fear of failure to unrealistic vocational aspiration, independent of the effect of innate ability, is even stronger than the results of the analysis of covariance show it to be.

The results of the present study confirm the applicability of the principles found in the laboratory study of level of aspiration to aspiration in real life.

SUMMARY

Vocational aspiration is considered in the context of theory having to do with motivational determinants of level of aspiration. Persons who are fearful of failure are presumed to be generally avoidant in their behavior in competitive achievement situations. On the one hand, such a person should avoid consideration of achievement-related information, and, on the other hand, he should prefer speculative ventures, where his probability of success is quite low (overaspiration), or safe ventures, where his probability of success is quite high (underaspiration). In contrast, persons who are relatively strong in motivation to achieve success should tend to prefer ventures where the probability of success is intermediate.

Measures of both achievement motive and achievement-related anxiety were used in the present study. The Ss were 135 male college students. They were classified as "realistic" or "unrealistic" in vocational aspiration in terms of each of four criteria: *(a)* judgments by clinical psychologists based on the discrepancy between the S's own measured ability and the ability judged to be required by the S's vocational choice; *(b)* the discrepancy between the S's estimate of his own ability and his estimate of the ability required to attain his vocational goal; *(c)* the S's inaccuracy in estimating his own ability; and *(d)* the discrepancy between the S's interest pattern and his vocational aspiration. On each criterion of realistic versus unrealistic vocational aspiration, significantly more Ss who were low in achievement motivation and high in achievement-related anxiety were classified as unrealistic, than Ss who were high in achievement motivation and low in achievement-related anxiety. Thus, the major hypothesis was clearly supported.

13. HARRY J. CROCKETT, JR.

The Achievement Motive
and Differential Occupational
Mobility in the United States

Among persons for whom roughly equal opportunity for mobility may
be said to exist (e.g., persons from similar regional, occupational, and
educational backgrounds), particular persons actually do rise in the
occupational hierarchy while others do not, or fall. Empirical research
directly concerned with this phenomenon of differential mobility is
not extensive (Lipset and Bendix, 1959). Evidence from a variety of
sources does, however, support the notion that motivation may play a
key role in the occupational mobility of persons sharing broadly similar opportunity. Many community studies and sample survey studies
have documented the existence of divergent belief-value systems as between social class groups.[1] For present purposes, it is important to note
that beliefs and values conducive to achievement striving in the occupational sphere are found to be more typical of the middle class than
of the working class. Yet these studies also show that important proportions of both social class groups subscribe to beliefs and values at
variance with the typical belief-value system of their own group. Hyman (1953, pp. 426–442) has presented an analysis linking the belief-

Reprinted with some abridgement by permission of the author and the American
Sociological Association from the *American Sociological Review*, 1962, 27, 191–204.
This chapter is an expanded version of a paper read at the annual meetings of the
Southern Sociological Society in Miami, Florida, April 5–8, 1961. The data for this
study were made available by the Survey Research Center of the University of Michigan; I wish to thank Angus Campbell and Gerald Gurin for extending this courtesy
to me. Grateful acknowledgement is also made to Richard L. Simpson for his critical
reading of an earlier version of this paper.
[1] See Centers (1941); Davis, Gardner, and Gardner (1949); Drake and Cayton (1945);
Hollingshead (1949); Hyman (1953); Kornhauser (1939); Warner and Lunt (1942);
West (1945).

value systems of different classes to different motivations characteristic
of the separate classes. Beliefs and values, according to his analysis, are
internalized and operate as determinants of achievement striving. To
explain individual deviation from social class norms, Hyman uses the
reference group concept: psychological identification with another class
is said to account for the internalization of the beliefs and values of
that class as part of the deviant individual's motivations. Thus, within
both the middle class and the working class, persons may acquire motivations either more or less conducive to achievement striving in the
occupational sphere.

A number of other researches provide evidence that motivation may
be an important determinant of differential occupational mobility.
Warner and Abegglen (1955), in their study of the American business
elite, while explicitly disavowing any attempt to estimate the relative
contribution of motivation to the careers of mobile respondents, nevertheless make clear their conviction that the contribution is not negligible. Seeman (1958) has examined the relationship of motivation to
mobility among a group of school administrators. Several other studies
present data on parent-child relationships and family structure as they
relate to the development of different motivations for mobility.[2]
Finally, Rosen (1956) has presented one rationale for expecting achievement motivation to be especially relevant to the mobility process.

While all of the studies noted above carry the implication that motivation may be an important requisite of differential occupational mobility, empirical measurement of the contribution of specific motives
to the mobility process is lacking. As a first step toward providing such
empirical knowledge, the present study focuses upon the role of the
achievement motive in the mobility process in our society, using the
thematic apperceptive (TAT) measure of the achievement motive developed by McClelland and his co-workers.[3]

The TAT measure of achievement motive and a theory of achievement motivation (Atkinson, Chapter 2) have been evolved in experimental laboratory studies, typically with college students as subjects.
Since the present study represents the first assessment of the achieve-

[2] See Douvan and Adelson (1958); Dynes, Clarke, and Dinitz (1956); Ellis (1952);
Strodtbeck (1958). Although these studies reach inconsistent conclusions regarding
the type of parent-child interaction leading to strong motivation for mobility, the
implication is clear that motivation is an important variable in differential mobility.
[3] McClelland, Atkinson, Clark, and Lowell (1953). The achievement motive is conceived as an enduring personality disposition to strive for success in situations where
performance is to be evaluated in terms of some standard of excellence. The disposition, it is assumed, is learned, so that its strength may vary as between individuals.

ment motive as a variable affecting the occupational mobility of individuals in the larger social setting, the applicability of this variable to the larger social setting merits discussion.[4] . . .

An empirical foundation for applying the theory of achievement motivation (Chapter 2) to the study of occupational mobility may now be offered. The data linking the model to the study of occupational mobility are obtained from studies of the prestige ratings of occupations in samples representative of our national population, and of various subgroups within it, over a time span of more than twenty-five years. Numerous studies demonstrate the existence of an occupational prestige hierarchy which is remarkably stable over time, and which is perceived in highly similar fashion by persons from all strata in our society.[5]

Let us grant that the occupational system is generally perceived by Americans as hierarchically structured in terms of the prestige attached to various occupations. In order to justify the relevance of the theory of achievement motivation for prediction of occupational mobility, it must now be shown that the higher prestige occupations are actually perceived both as having greater incentive value and as being more difficult to attain (lower expectancy of success) than the lower prestige occupations.

Is the perception of the personal satisfaction to be gained from jobs higher in the prestige hierarchy generally greater than that from jobs lower in the hierarchy? Strodtbeck, McDonald, and Rosen's (1957) study of youths in the New Haven area provides evidence for a strongly affirmative answer to this question. The boys were presented a list of twelve occupations representative of the entire range of the occupational prestige hierarchy. They were asked to state whether they would be pleased or displeased to have each of these jobs as adults, and whether their parents would be pleased or displeased if they had such jobs as adults. The percentage of pleased responses for each occupation, for both self-reports and guesses about parents, increased markedly from low prestige occupations to high prestige occupations. Rosen (1959) reports similar findings for a sample of mothers in four northeastern states. These findings suggest that the incentive value attached to successful attainment of different occupations increases with incre-

---

[4] The present discussion will demonstrate the empirical relevance of the theory of achievement motivation to differential mobility. For a thorough discussion of the methodological problems arising in the use of the thematic apperceptive method in a national sample survey, see: Veroff, Atkinson, Feld, and Gurin (1960).

[5] See Brown (1955), Centers (1953), Counts (1925), Deeg and Paterson (1947), Bendix and Lipset (1953, pp. 411–426), Smith (1943).

ments in the prestige of occupations. In fact, prestige ratings are probably the best estimate available of the generally accepted incentive values of success in different occupations.

National data are available regarding the perceived difficulty associated with occupations at various prestige levels. In the National Opinion Research Center (NORC) study (Bendix and Lipset, 1953), respondents were asked:

When you say that certain jobs have excellent standing, what do you think is the one main thing about such jobs that gives this standing?

Two responses stressing the degree of difficulty connected with such jobs, ranked third and sixth, respectively, among eleven categories of responses emerged: (1) Preparation requires much hard work, education, and money; (2) it requires intelligence and ability. Several other studies provide similar evidence that jobs rated high in prestige are perceived to be more difficult to attain than jobs rated low in prestige (Brown, 1955; Mahone, Chapter 12; Simpson and Simpson, 1960).[6]

It seems clear, then, that the occupational prestige hierarchy is invested with the properties essential for the application of the model of achievement motivation. The occupational prestige hierarchy may be identified as a series of "tasks" involving both increasing incentive value (increasing prestige) and increasing difficulty (decreasing probability of success). Thus, the implications of the theory of achievement motivation derived from experimental analysis of behavior can be appropriately applied to the behavior of individuals in relation to occupational striving.

The general hypothesis derived from the model regarding differential occupational mobility is clear: strong achievement motive should lead to more "realistic" striving, to greater effort, and to greater persistence than weak achievement motive, and, as a consequence, to greater accomplishment in the occupational sphere. "Common sense"

---

[6] Respondents in Brown's study described high ranking occupations as "better" than others, and two of eleven response categories seen to characterize these jobs stressed the "difficulty" variable. In the Simpson and Simpson study, evaluations of occupations ranked in the NORC study by a panel of raters resulted in a strong positive association between perceived degree of difficulty of a job and its prestige ranking. A secondary analysis by the writer of data kindly supplied by Mahone (Chapter 12) showed a rank order correlation between college students' estimates of probability of success in selected occupations and the prestige rankings of the occupations to be —.85. Among college men in whom *n* Achievement was high and anxiety low, the correlation was —.90. (See Crockett, 1960).

might suggest such a notion; yet common sense might equally well predict that strong achievement motive would lead to unrealistically high aspirations, and hence to less accomplishment.[7] The theory of achievement motivation goes beyond common sense by specifying the variables involved in the hypothesized relationship, and the functional relationships between them.

METHOD

This study is a secondary analysis of national sample survey data (Gurin, Veroff, and Feld, 1960; Veroff, et al., 1960). The original sample included 2,460 respondents selected according to strict probability methods to yield a representative sample of persons 21 years of age or older residing in private households in the United States. Measures of motive strength, however, were obtained from a randomly selected subsample, of which a total of 715 were males. Responses to the thematic apperception test, from which scores on the achievement, affiliation, and power motives were derived, were judged inadequate by the original investigators for 118 of these respondents, yielding a total of 597 men as potential cases for use in the present study. The procedures for selecting the respondents included in the present study will be discussed subsequently.

The methodological problems encountered in adapting a method of measurement which was standardized in experimental settings for use in a survey study have been thoroughly examined in a paper by the original investigators; they conclude that a level of measurement adequate for research purposes is attained (Veroff et al., 1960).[8] It should be emphasized that a disproportionate number of respondents from the lower social strata and the older age groups gave inadequate responses to the motive questions, responses which could not legitimately be assigned a motive score. This disproportionate loss of respondents from particular demographic groups imposes a restriction on generalization of the findings of the present study, but it does not affect the testing of hypotheses concerning relationships between motive strength and occupational mobility within the present sample. Moreover, data to be presented subsequently indicate that generalization of present results may well be admissible.

Occupational mobility is assessed in this study through comparison of the prestige of the respondent's occupation at time of interview with the prestige of the occupation of the father during the period when the respondent was

---

[7] I am indebted to Richard L. Simpson for this latter suggestion.

[8] They reason also that relationships between strength of achievement motive and other variables in the present sample should be lower than those typically obtained in the laboratory situation.

growing up.[9] About a third of the potential respondents gave their father's occupation as "farmer," thus inextricably lumping together farm owner-operators of varying degrees of affluence, tenant farmers, farm laborers, and share croppers. The 193 cases falling in this group were deleted from the sample. In addition to farm-reared respondents, it was necessary to exclude 36 other potential cases: 23 because their fathers' occupations were not ascertained, two because their own occupations were not ascertained, and 11 who gave "student" as their occupation.[10]

A sound empirical basis for assigning prestige scores to occupations is presented in the NORC study (Bendix and Lipset, 1953).[11] On the basis of the NORC prestige scores, four categories of prestige were constituted; only four categories were used in order to obtain subgroups of sufficient size for the type of analysis contemplated.[12] The distributions of respondents high and low in

[9] It is recognized that this measure may introduce error. Typically, the occupation given for the father is the most prestigeful of all the occupations he may have had. The respondent, however, may sometime hold occupations either more or less prestigeful than his occupation at the time of interview. Consequently, both over- or underestimations of intergenerational mobility can result from this measure. There appear to be no compelling *a priori* reasons to indicate that the two types of error should accrue disproportionately to persons scoring high or low in achievement motive. Hence, it is assumed that error from this source is randomly distributed within the groups to be studied. For a discussion of this question see Lipset and Zetterberg (1954).

[10] To preserve Ns, the writer also coded a number of cases which had not been coded in the original study (respondents who were unemployed or retired), and recoded a number of cases originally coded "not ascertained." These changes in the coding of occupations made by the writer do not appear to have introduced substantial error, since checks of the occupational distributions in the present sample and other recent national samples show generally comparable results.

[11] Successful use of the NORC prestige indices has been made by Lenski and by Empey. See Empey (1956); Lenski (1954).

[12] The use of these four categories of prestige reduces the sensitivity of discrimination between the prestige of occupations considerably. At several points in the present scheme, assignments of occupations to particular prestige categories are made which might be changed, either upward or downward, had more detailed occupational data been available. For example, no discrimination was attempted within the skilled occupations because sufficient detail to warrant such judgments was generally lacking. All skilled workers are assigned to the Lower Middle prestige category. Similarly, all businessmen are assigned to either the High or the Upper Middle prestige categories, even though some should probably fall below these levels. Despite these sources of error in classification, the discrimination obtained using prestige indices is superior to that afforded, for example, by either the standard census category or the manual-nonmanual schemes. For example, occupations classifiable in the Professional or Business census categories may fall in either the High or Upper Middle prestige categories. Occupations classifiable in the White Collar census category may be assigned to the Upper Middle, Lower Middle, or Low prestige categories. Occupations classifiable in the Service census category may be assigned to either the Lower Middle or Low prestige categories.

strength of achievement motive,[13] in relation to occupational prestige category of father, are given in Table 1.

Table 1

Distribution of respondents high and low in strength of achievement motive, in relation to occupational prestige category of father

Occupational Prestige Category of Father	Prestige Scores	Strength of Achievement Motive	N (368)
High	78–93	High	20
		Low	11
Upper Middle	69–77	High	50
		Low	43
Lower Middle	61–68	High	67
		Low	52
Low	33–60	High	60
		Low	65

The reliability of the writer's prestige coding procedure was assessed by two separate internal reliability checks in which the writer's coding was compared with sample codings made by two other sociologists,[14] as well as by an external check. The internal checks showed the prestige scoring procedure to have a coding reliability of around 80 per cent with regard to prestige category placement, and of about +.85 with regard to correlation of prestige scores.[15]

As an external check on the reliability of the prestige scoring, an analysis of results based only on those respondents whose own occupations or whose fathers' occupations actually appear in the NORC (Bendix and Lipset, 1953) ratings was conducted. Results of this analysis, to be presented subsequently, were fully comparable to the results based on the total sample.

Since the original sample from which the respondents are selected was drawn by a cluster sampling technique, statistics based on random sampling assumptions are not applicable (Kish, 1957). Tests of the significance of differ-

[13] In keeping with conventional usage in analysis of achievement motive data, "high" and "low" achievement motive groups are formed by cutting the distribution of motive scores at the median. The median for all respondents giving adequate motive protocols in the original study is used here; hence, the Ns in the high and low motive groups in the present sample are unequal.

[14] The writer is indebted to Elton F. Jackson and Ernest Harberg for this work.

[15] The overall reliability of slightly better than 80 per cent correct placement in prestige category may be compared with a coding reliability reported by Lenski of better than 90 per cent prestige category placement. See Lenski (1954).

ence between proportions, used throughout the analysis, are therefore based on cluster sampling variances rather than random sampling variances.[16]

Reference has already been made to the view of the original investigators that observed relationships between achievement motive and other variables in this sample should be underestimates of the actual relationships in the population. Attention should also be called to the fact that the national sample under study here, while selected by a cluster sampling technique, is probably less homogeneous in important respects than are most samples used in experimental research as well as most field studies which conventionally employ statistics based on the assumption of random sampling. Thus, the test of association used in the present study, based on estimates of standard error for clustered rather than random samples, is interpreted as conservative relative to tests employed in other research reports. In light of these several considerations, differences which attain the .10 level of significance in the predicted direction[17] will be spoken of as indicating meaningful trends, and those which attain the .05 level of significance will be taken as evidence of substantial relationships. In addition, the over-all consistency of results relative to predictions, irrespective of significance level, will be considered in evaluation of the findings.

RESULTS

The research hypothesis is that respondents with strong achievement motive will show greater upward mobility and less downward mobility than respondents weak in achievement motive. The relationships between strength of achievement motive and occupational mobility among sons of fathers in each of the prestige levels are shown in Table 2. Expectations concerning differential upward mobility are clearly supported among sons of fathers in both the Low prestige category ($p < .04$) and the Lower Middle prestige category ($p < .06$), but not among sons of fathers in the two higher prestige categories. Only in the Lower Middle prestige category is there evidence of a trend supporting the expectation that downward mobility would be more

[16] Cluster sampling variances for the present sample were computed by the Sampling Section of the Survey Research Center. For formulas and rationale, see Kish and Hess (1959).

[17] Since the hypotheses tested here are derived from a theory concerning the influence on behavior of strength of achievement motive, which is already supported by considerable experimental evidence, the expected directions of relationships are clearly specified in advance. Therefore, a one-tailed test of significance is considered appropriate.

Table 2

Strength of achievement motive and occupational mobility*

Occupational Prestige Category of Father	Strength of Achievement Motive	N (368)	Below	Difference	Same	Difference	Above	Difference
High (78–93)	High	(20)	55%		45%		—	
						−0		
	Low	(11)	55		45		—	
Upper Middle (69–77)	High	(50)	42		32		26%	
				−0				+3
	Low	(43)	42		35		23	NS
Lower Middle (61–68)	High	(67)	16		41		43	
				+12				+18
	Low	(52)	28	$p < .16$	47		25	$p < .06$
Low (33–60)	High	(60)	—		33		67	
								+21
	Low	(65)	—		54		46	$p < .04$

* A plus sign indicates a percentage point difference in the direction predicted. A minus sign indicates a percentage point difference in the direction opposite to that predicted. Probabilities for percentages based on *N*s less than 25 are not presented. Since directional predictions are derived from theory, a one-tailed test is used. The remaining tables in this paper present one-tailed tests identical to the test used in the present table.

evident in the low achievement group, and there it is not statistically significant ($p < .16$).

Strong indication that the above results are not produced by the prestige scoring procedures employed is afforded by analysis of data for only those respondents whose own occupations or whose fathers' occupations were rated in the NORC (Bendix and Lipset, 1953) study (Table 3). The table shows, among respondents for whom prestige coding was most precise, results highly comparable to those obtained previously for the full sample.

Can it be argued that differences in mobility attributed to strength of achievement motive reflect the effect of general level of motive strength on mobility? Are persons with strong motivation, whether deriving from achievement motive or from other motives, likely to show greater upward mobility and less downward mobility than persons with weak general motivation? A check on this possibility is made

Table 3

Strength of achievement motive and occupational mobility among respondents whose own occupation or whose fathers' occupations were rated in the National Opinion Research Center Study*

Occupational Prestige Category of Father	Strength of Achievement Motive	N (146)	Occupational Prestige Category of Respondent in Relation to that of Father					
			Below	Difference	Same	Difference	Above	Difference
High (78–93)	High	(12)	50%		50%	+5	—	
	Low	(11)	55		45		—	
Upper Middle (69–77)	High	(8)	50	+7	12		38%	+12
	Low	(23)	57		17		26	
Lower Middle (61–68)	High	(17)	24	+12	29		47	+15
	Low	(25)	36		32		32	
Low (33–60)	High	(26)	—		31		69	+40
	Low	(24)	—		71		29	p < .02

* Analysis for each specific group (i.e., respondents whose own occupations and whose fathers' occupations were rated in the earlier study, respondents whose own occupations only were rated, and respondents whose fathers' occupations only were rated) is precluded because of the small number of cases. Even with the three groups combined, the Ns for sons of fathers in the Lower Middle, Upper Middle and High prestige categories are too small to afford tests of significance.

possible by data concerning the affiliation and power motives,[18] which were also obtained in the original study.

Comparison of the relationships between strength of affiliation motive and mobility (Table 4) with those between strength of achievement motive and mobility (Table 2) show achievement motive much more strongly related to upward mobility than affiliation motive among those reared in the two lower prestige categories. Only among sons of fathers in the Upper Middle prestige category is the relationship between affiliation motive and upward mobility stronger than that

[18] The affiliation motive is characterized as a disposition to establish, restore or maintain positive relationships with others. The power motive is characterized as a disposition to seek control over the means of influencing others. Detailed discussions of each of these motives are to be found in Atkinson (1958a).

between achievement motive and upward mobility. With regard to downward mobility, both affiliation motive and achievement motive show relatively slight negative relationships.

Table 4

Strength of affiliation motive and occupational mobility

Occupational Prestige Category of Father	Strength of Affiliation Motive	N (368)	Occupational Prestige Category of Respondent in Relation to that of Father					
			Below	Differ-ence	Same	Differ-ence	Above	Differ-ence
High (78–93)	High	(18)	61%		39%		—	
	Low	(13)	46		54	−15	—	
Upper Middle (69–77)	High	(48)	46		23		31%	
	Low	(45)	51	+5 NS	38		11	+20 $p < .06$
Lower Middle (61–68)	High	(66)	15		50		35	
	Low	(53)	30	+15 $p < .13$	34		36	−1
Low (33–60)	High	(50)	—		38		62	
	Low	(75)	—		48		52	+10 $p < .20$

Analysis of the relation of power motive to mobility discloses even less support for the notion that motive strength in general, rather than strength of achievement motive specifically, influences mobility (Table 5). The table shows essentially no difference in mobility between groups high and low in power motive.

Thus, it appears quite clear that the relationships shown to exist between strength of achievement motive and occupational mobility cannot be interpreted as deriving from the factor of strong general motivation.

There remains now the possibility that other variables which current knowledge indicates are positively and causally related to mobility may also be positively and causally related to strength of achievement motive: for instance, age level, amount of education,[19] region of birth,

---

[19] Studies of national samples show age level and education level, along with occupation level of origin (which is controlled throughout all analyses in this study), are important variables related to occupational mobility. See Centers (1953); Glick (1954); Lenski (1958).

Table 5

Strength of power motive and occupational mobility

Occupational Prestige Category of Father	Strength of Power Motive	N (368)	Occupational Prestige Category of Respondent in Relation to that of Father					
			Below	Difference	Same	Difference	Above	Difference
High (78–93)	High	(12)	50%		50%		—	
	Low	(19)	58		42	+8	—	
Upper Middle (69–77)	High	(44)	50		32		18%	
	Low	(49)	47	−3	28		25	−7
Lower Middle (61–68)	High	(55)	24		45		31	
	Low	(64)	20	−4	41		39	−8
Low (33–60)	High	(63)	—		44		56	
	Low	(62)	—		43		57	−1

rural-urban residence background, race, religion, nativity, marital status, and the presence of children in the home.[20]

The relationship between strength of achievement motive and each of the other above-noted variables has been examined, in each case with occupational prestige level of origin controlled (Crockett, 1960). In general, these relationships do not indicate the serious likelihood of inflated positive results regarding strength of achievement motive and occupational mobility. Some consistent trends which might lead to inflated results were noted, however, in the relationships between strength of achievement motive and age, education, and marital status. It is also possible that inflated results might be produced by the combined effects of several of these variables.

Consequently, two sets of variables are used to select precision-matched groups from respondents classified high and low in strength of achievement motive.[21] The relatively small size of the sample, coupled with the rapid attrition of cases in precision-matching as the

[20] Other factors might also be involved in such a spurious relationship, but the ones cited are the only variables for which measures are available.

[21] This procedure, rather than cross-tabulation within each variable of interest, is used in order to avoid excessively small *N*s.

number of variables involved increases, means that cases can be matched on only three variables at a time. In light of the observed relationships cited above, the following two sets of variables are used to form precision-matched groups: (1) occupational category of origin, age level, and amount of education; (2) age level, marital status, and the presence of children in the home. Both of the precision-matched groups are formed by means of a random selection technique.

Table 6

Strength of achievement motive and occupational mobility; respondents matched on occupational prestige category of father, age, and level of education*

Occupational Prestige Category of Father	Strength of Achievement Motive	N (302)	Occupational Prestige Category of Respondent in Relation to that of Father					
			Below	Differ-ence	Same	Differ-ence	Above	Differ-ence
High (78–93)	High	(10)	50%		50%	−0	—	
	Low	(10)	50		50		—	
Upper Middle (69–77)	High	(36)	44	−6	28		28%	+3 NS
	Low	(40)	38		37		25	
Lower Middle (61–68)	High	(54)	17	+11 $p < .20$	42		41	+17 $p < .10$
	Low	(50)	28		48		24	
Low (33–60)	High	(51)	—		35		65	+16 $p < .11$
	Low	(51)	—		51		49	

* In the case of sons of fathers in the two middle prestige categories, the Ns in the High and Low achievement motive groups are unequal because the two categories were pooled for matching purposes here. This enabled a larger number of respondents to be included in the analysis.

Table 6 shows that results parallel to the initial findings, even with somewhat reduced samples, are obtained when the effects of age, occupational prestige level of origin, and education level are simultaneously controlled through precision-matching. Consistent trends in the direction predicted are found with regard to upward mobility among sons of fathers in the Low prestige category ($p < .11$) and the Lower Middle prestige category ($p < .10$), but not among sons of fathers in the two higher prestige categories. Respondents high in achievement motive are again less likely (although the trend is not significant) to be downwardly mobile among sons of fathers in the Lower Middle prestige category, but this relationship does not appear among persons reared in the Upper Middle or High prestige categories.

The same pattern of results is obtained when life cycle variables (i.e., age, marital status, and the presence of children in the home) are controlled by precision matching, again with a reduction in sample size (Table 7). The table shows strength of achievement motive posi-

Table 7

Strength of achievement motive and occupational mobility; respondents matched on age, marital status, and the presence of children in the home

Occupational Prestige Category of Father	Strength of Achievement Motive	N (300)	Occupational Prestige Category of Respondent in Relation to that of Father					
			Below	Difference	Same	Difference	Above	Difference
High (78–93)	High	(18)	56%		44%		—	
	Low	(10)	60		40	+4	—	
Upper Middle (69–77)	High	(34)	35		35		29%	
	Low	(38)	40	+5 NS	37		24	+5 NS
Lower Middle (61–68)	High	(53)	15		47		38	
	Low	(43)	26	+11 $p < .20$	49		26	+12 $p < .18$
Low (33–60)	High	(45)	—		31		69	
	Low	(59)	—		56		44	+25 $p < .03$

tively and significantly associated with upward mobility among sons of fathers in the Low prestige category ($p < .03$). Among respondents whose fathers held occupations in the Lower Middle prestige category, there is a positive but not significant relationship between achievement motive strength and upward mobility, and an insignificant negative relationship between achievement motive strength and downward mobility. Among sons of fathers in the two higher prestige categories, the relationships between strength of achievement motive and occupational mobility are again very slight.

It will be recalled now that respondents who did not give adequate responses to the thematic apperceptive test of motive strength have been excluded from all previous analyses. Moreover, it was reported earlier that these omitted respondents were disproportionately representative of the lower socio-economic strata and of the older age groups. The original investigators (Veroff, et al., 1960) suggest that failure to produce a meaningful TAT protocol is probably indicative of weak motivation. If respondents omitted from analysis because of inadequate motive responses are presumed to be for the most part low in strength of achievement motive, then in pattern of mobility these omitted respondents should be more similar to respondents low in achievement motive than to those high in achievement motive. The distributions given in Table 8 show the expected trends. The deleted respondents have rates of upward mobility that are actually lower than the rates of the respondents classified low in achievement motive in two

Table 8

Comparison of occupational mobility among achievement motive groups and respondents omitted from analysis because of inadequate motive protocols*

Occupational Prestige Category of Father	Strength of Achievement Motive	N (383)	Occupational Prestige Category of Respondent in Relation to that of Father		
			Below	Same	Above
Upper Middle (69–77)	High	(50)	42%	32%	26%
	Low	(43)	42	35	23
	Omitted	(8)	50	38	13
Lower Middle (61–68)	High	(67)	16	41	43
	Low	(52)	28	47	25
	Omitted	(15)	20	47	33
Low (33–60)	High	(60)	—	33	67
	Low	(65)	—	54	46
	Omitted	(23)	—	61	39

* Excludes omitted respondents who were sons of farmers, or for whom information regarding own occupation or father's occupation was not codable. There were no omitted respondents whose fathers held occupations in the High prestige category.

of the three comparisons, and a downward mobility rate that is greater than that of respondents classified low in achievement motive in one of two comparisons. Only in the case of downward mobility from the Lower Middle prestige category is the mobility rate of the omitted respondents more similar to that of respondents with strong achievement motive than with weak achievement motive. Given these relationships, it is suggested that the results of this study may be generalized to the adult male population of the United States who were not reared on farms.

DISCUSSION

The several analyses presented above show strength of achievement motive clearly related to upward mobility among sons of fathers in the two lower prestige categories but not among sons of fathers in the two higher prestige categories.[22] Because detailed exploration of the possible explanations for this finding requires the introduction of many new data, such exploration is reserved for a subsequent paper. Suffice it to say here that the explanation, in my judgment, is to be found in the differential effect of education level upon mobility in the higher versus lower prestige groups. Among sons of fathers in the two lower prestige categories, while higher education will certainly have a tremendous positive effect upon upward mobility, higher education is in fact not essential to upward mobility.[23] This means that strength of achievement motive, quite apart from education level attained, may play an important part in upward mobility. Among sons of fathers in the two higher prestige categories, on the other hand, higher education is virtually essential to upward mobility (or stability).[24] Therefore, among these respondents, factors which affect the attainment of higher education must have a greater effect upon subsequent mobility than is the case among respondents in the two lower prestige groups. Consequently, the effect of strength of achievement motive is obscured among persons reared in the two higher prestige categories, while it comes through clearly among persons reared in the two lower prestige groups. As noted above, a subsequent paper will deal with this matter more fully.[25]

In contrast to results for strength of achievement motive, strength of affiliation motive among sons of fathers in the Upper Middle prestige category was positively associated with upward mobility ($p < .06$). This finding is consistent with recent arguments (Miller and Swanson, 1958; Riesman, 1950; Whyte, 1956), which stress the implications of broad changes in the social structure for the personality structure of

---

[22] The reader is reminded of the earlier discussion of levels of significance appropriate to this research. If tests of significance are disregarded, the clear relationship alluded to can be seen by comparison of percentage points differences between the high and low achievement motive groups.

[23] Of the upwardly mobile persons from the two lower prestige levels, 65 per cent had only a high school education or less.

[24] Of the stable persons from the High prestige level, only 7 per cent had a high school education or less; of the upwardly mobile persons from the Upper Middle prestige level, only 13 per cent had a high school education or less.

[25] See Crockett (1964) (The Editors.)

occupationally successful persons. The large-scale, bureaucratic work setting, which rewards cooperative and harmonious relationships, is replacing the small-scale, entrepreneurial work setting in which individual, competitive effort is more rewarded. As a consequence, the person with relatively strong affiliation motive is now expected to be more occupationally successful than the person with strong motive to achieve. The results of the present study suggest, however, that the shift in the dynamics of the mobility process anticipated by these writers has not yet occurred in marked degree. For among two thirds of the respondents (sons of fathers in the two lower prestige groups) occupational advancement is associated with strength of achievement motive but not with affiliation or power motives.

Notice must now be taken of the fact that the expectation concerning strength of achievement motive and downward mobility was not supported (although, in general, trends in the predicted direction were found). The argument offered previously regarding the absence of predicted relationships among persons reared in the two higher prestige categories is clearly relevant here. If other factors are relatively important to mobility among these persons, then the effect of strength of achievement motive must be reduced. However, no "explanation" is available to account for the absence of the predicted relationship among persons reared in the Lower Middle prestige category, where, presumably, "other" factors are less important relative to strength of achievement motive.

Throughout this paper it has been assumed that strong achievement motive is one of the antecedents of occupational mobility among persons sharing equal opportunity. It can be argued, however, that the experience of upward mobility may produce an increase in strength of achievement motive. Empirical substantiation of one or the other interpretation is not possible in the present study because time-sequential data are lacking. Nevertheless, the issue merits consideration.

Practically all students of human behavior appeal to some concept of motivation in their explanations of human action. Agreement on this point arises from the widely acknowledged utility of breaking up the flux of human behavior into identifiable sequences of action which differ in direction, vigor, and persistence through time, and terminate when some end-state or goal is reached. If it is maintained that strength of achievement motive is a consequence of differential occupational mobility rather than one of its determinants, then motivation for other goals must be invoked to explain those action sequences which eventuate in differential mobility. The question then becomes: What other motives are we led to posit, from intuition or theoretical conception, as more likely determinants of the effort and persistence it takes to get ahead in the occupational sphere than the achievement motive, which we already know from experimental evidence to be an effective determinant of action when performance is evaluated as good (success) or poor (failure)?

To raise this question is to reveal the meager extent of our knowledge of the relationships between any motivational factors and social mobility. Mention has already been made of current theoretical stress upon affiliation motivation as a source of occupational mobility. Present evidence, however, does not lend substantial support to this position. Seeman (1958) has proposed that "goals which are not status goals in themselves, and which are assumed to be intrinsically valuable to the respondent in contrast to the value of status betterment . . ." (p.365). may provide motivation for mobility. He cites as examples of such goals, family interest and community and friendship ties. Although research linking these motives, or indeed any others that may be advanced, to occupational mobility is lacking, the position taken here does not deny that in different persons many different motives may influence mobility. Rather, it argues that there should be a systematic relationship between strength of achievement motive and occupational mobility in our society.

In short, the theoretical model of achievement motivation developed by Atkinson (Chapter 2) is the only carefully worked out motivational scheme currently available which has direct relevance for the analysis of the mobility process. Lipset and Bendix (1959), while noting in anticipation of a study such as this one that the thematic apperceptive measure of achievement motive employed here has "exciting implications for social analysis," stress the fact that "there is no evidence that motivation (of the sort measured by the technique mentioned above) results in higher occupational achievement among those with equal opportunity" (p.247). The present study is the first to provide empirical evidence on a national scale that strength of achievement motive, assessed by thematic apperception, is an important personality factor contributing to occupational mobility. Perhaps, then, the most important practical implication of this study is that the thematic apperceptive method for assessment of motivation, which has been undergoing development and refinement since 1948, now appears a useful technique for incorporating personality variables in survey studies of sociological interest. Finally, the present study illustrates the potential fruitfulness of simultaneous consideration of individual personality factors and social structural factors in the analysis of occupational mobility.

SUMMARY

This study examines the influence of strength of achievement motive on intergenerational occupational mobility in the United States. The theory of achievement motivation, shown to be relevant to the study of occupational mobility, predicts that strength of achievement motive— among persons sharing equal opportunity—will be positively associated with upward occupational mobility and negatively associated with downward occupational mobility. In the national sample studied, the expected results are clearly attained with regard to upward mobility among persons reared in the lower social strata, but predicted relationships are not found among persons reared in the middle and upper social strata. The hypothesis concerning strength of achievement motive and downward mobility is not supported. The results indicate the fruitfulness of considering personality variables in conjunction with social structural variables in the study of occupational mobility.

14. JAMES N. MORGAN

The Achievement Motive
and Economic Behavior

Recent developments in the psychology of personality and motivation promise to be of some real use in improving our ability to explain economic behavior. These have focused on relatively few variables, variables which have been at least roughly measured and which are intended to explain the dynamics of behavior of reasonably normal individuals. At some point, presumably, it is advantageous to give up a little of the parsimony and elegance of economic theories about the behavior of consumers, workers, and businessmen, for improvement in ability to explain and predict that behavior.

This article provides some empirical evidence that one such variable, the motive to achieve, may have real value in improving our explanation of several crucial forms of economic behavior in a representative cross-section of the population. If so, implications as to policies to increase economic growth in both the short and long run may result. This is not the first example of quantitative use of psychology in economics.

OPTIMISM AND SPENDING

One main stream of development has been under way for some time, connected particularly with the name of George Katona (1960). It can be inadequately summarized as follows: events and new information impinge on individuals. The individuals have varied backgrounds and insights, and each interprets what he sees and hears, occasionally reshaping his attitudes, expectations, and sometimes his explicit plans for the future. If the attitude changes are important, there may then be

Reprinted from *Economic Development and Cultural Change*, 1964, **12**, 243–267, by permission of author and of The University of Chicago Press. Copyright 1964 by The University of Chicago.

important changes in behavior. Among the attitudes which are likely to change similarly for large groups at the same time, and to affect behavior, the most important are those which can be classed as optimism, confidence in the future, willingness to commit funds to durable goods and future payments, versus uncertainty, worry, desire to remain liquid and keep commitments short. The former should lead to greater spending by consumers, the latter to restraint. Rarely, uncertainty can shift into fear with pressure to act, as in the case of runaway inflation, but normally it is confidence rather than fear which leads to consumer action.

Much has been done to measure the relevant attitudes and the relevant behavior using a series of surveys, reinterviews, and panels. As the data accumulate, the evidence becomes increasingly convincing that this is a fruitful way to improve our understanding of short-run dynamics of consumer behavior.

ACHIEVEMENT MOTIVATION AND ECONOMIC BEHAVIOR

In explaining longer run changes in behavior, attitudes are more difficult to use because it is necessary to untangle the causal model. Attitudes can result from behavior and experiences as well as cause them. However, according to psychological theory, there are stable personality dispositions or motives which do not change rapidly, if at all, over time, and which should affect behavior. Within a generation, they can help explain differences in behavior and in the way in which people respond to environmental changes, including government policies. Between generations, they can help explain global changes.[1]

Two developments in psychology have improved the possibility of fruitful progress in explaining economic behavior. First, the long descriptive lists of human motives have given way to disciplined empirical research of a few. Leaving aside the mundane desires for physical comforts, empirical study has focused attention on three basic "needs": achievement, affiliation, and power. Second, valid methods have been developed for measuring these personality characteristics, and they have been shown to be related to human behavior in systematic empirical studies in and out of the laboratory (Atkinson, 1958a; Veroff, Atkinson, Feld, and Gurin, 1960).

[1] For a pioneering attempt in the field of economic development, see McClelland, *The Achieving Society* (1961).

Clearly, the most directly relevant of these "needs" for explaining economic behavior is the need for achievement or achievement motive. This motive is defined as a tendency to strive for success in situations involving an evaluation of one's performance in relation to some standards of excellence. A person with a strong motive to achieve tends to derive satisfaction from overcoming obstacles by his own efforts. He takes calculated risks, rather than playing long shots or being overly cautious. Compared with the need for affiliation—to give and receive affection—or for power—to control the means of influencing the behavior of others and not be under their control—the need for achievement seems most likely to be associated with upward mobility, long hours of work, desires to accumulate capital and educate one's children, and entrepreneurial activity.

Perhaps the most interesting implication of the concept of need for achievement refers to situations involving risks. There is a satisfaction in doing difficult things well, and the satisfaction increases with the difficulty. At the same time, the mathematical expected value of any risky venture becomes smaller, the smaller the probability of success. It is this combination of motives, the desire for ordinary economic gain, and the desire for the satisfaction of achieving something difficult which leads to the derivation that those with strong need for achievement should take calculated risks, with somewhat less expected value than some safer alternatives (Atkinson, Chapter 2).

Atkinson's model argues that it is the product of the strength of achievement motive, times the incentive value of success (which is proportionate to the difficulty of the task) that determines the subjective value or attractiveness of success at a particular activity. The payoff in any theory is its ability to predict behavior. The fact that successful businessmen score high on measures of the achievement motive is not convincing by itself. Current studies under way at the Survey Research Center are attempting to explain *differences* in the output of individuals in an entrepreneurial type of occupation on the basis of the Atkinson model.

We report here some results from a national cross-section where a crude but theoretically sound measure of achievement motive was used, along with a number of other explanatory factors, to explain various aspects of individual behavior. The achievement motive was selected for study both because it appeared more directly relevant to economic behavior, and because a promising method of measuring it in an interview was available.

MEASUREMENT OF THE NEED FOR ACHIEVEMENT

In the experimental study of motivation, motives are usually measured by the use of a projective technique calling for a controlled elicitation of imaginative material, usually by asking a standard series of questions about each of a set of pictures, getting the individual to create a story around each. Scoring methods were developed for these Thematic Apperception Test (TAT) protocols by comparing stories produced when the achievement motive, for instance, was purposely aroused with those when it was not (McClelland, Atkinson, Clark, and Lowell, 1953; Atkinson, 1958a).[2]

While these TAT protocols have been used in field interviews, both with injured workers in Michigan and with a national sample, they are difficult for uneducated and not very verbal people, require elaborate adjustment for the lengths of the stories, and take a good deal of interviewing time (Gurin, Veroff, and Feld, 1960; Morgan, Snider, and Sobol, 1959; Veroff, et al., 1960). On the other hand, direct attempts to measure the motive through attitudinal questions have not been particularly successful (Decharms, Morrison, Reitman, and McClelland, 1955; Rosen, 1958; McClelland, 1958a; See also Chapter 5).

There was reason to believe, however, that an indirect measure of the motive to achieve could be derived from a relatively simple procedure suggested by Atkinson (Chapter 11). In a discussion of the implications of his assumption that the subjective value or attractiveness of success at an activity is a multiplicative function of strength of achievement motive and incentive value of success (difficulty), he pointed out that both laboratory experiments and comparisons of ethnic groups indicated a tendency for groups known to be high in achievement motive to assign substantially higher reward value to difficult than to easy tasks. The differential reward value assigned to difficult versus easy tasks was much less marked in groups known to be low in achievement motive. This general result is clearly implied by the assumption that strength of motive multiplies incentive value of success to determine the attractiveness or subjective value of success for a particular individual. Atkinson then summarized the results of several investigations. Unpublished laboratory work by Litwin (see Chapter 7) showed that college students did, in fact, assign higher monetary prize values to

---

[2] It should be noted that while the basic motive is enduring, the momentary strength of motivation can be heightened and lessened by situational factors.

ring toss games, which all agreed were more difficult, and that subjects higher in TAT measures of achievement motive showed the greatest discrimination in assigning prize values to difficult versus easy tasks. From this Atkinson concluded: "The slope of the satisfaction curve in relation to increasing difficulty of task can be taken as an index of the strength of achievement motive."

Additional evidence has made this statement more persuasive. At least among college students, it was shown that popular estimates of the proportion who could succeed at different occupations were negatively correlated (—.85) with the prestige rankings or general standing of those occupations (Crockett, Chapter 13). Here again is the inverse relationship between probability of success and an index of incentive value of success.[3] Furthermore, an examination by the same writer of various occupational prestige rankings found them all positively correlated with one another at levels between .88 and .98, providing "strong evidence that the occupational prestige system for at least some thirty years past has been perceived in a highly similar manner by Americans from every strata of society." (Crockett, Chapter 13; see also Inkeles, 1960.)

An index of strength of the achievement motive should then be provided by the extent to which an individual places high values on succeeding in the difficult high-prestige occupations and low values on succeeding in the easy occupations. This, Atkinson has pointed out, had already been reported by Strodtbeck, McDonald, and Rosen (1957). These investigators had shown that Jewish high school boys differentiated more strongly between different occupations than Italian boys when asked how they would feel if they should end up in one or another occupation; and middle-class boys were more discriminating than working-class boys. Other studies employing the TAT measure of achievement motive had also already shown Jews to be stronger than Italians and middle-class boys to be stronger than working-class boys (Rosen, 1959; Douvan, 1956; Milstein, 1956; Veroff, et al., 1960).

This technique for assessment of strength of achievement motive was adapted for the present research. We asked the following question about "most people": "We are interested in how people compare occupations. How do you think most people would feel if a boy of

[3] Atkinson and O'Connor (1963) have found a correlation of —.90 between prestige index of occupations and the average probability of success estimated by high school students. The students were asked, in reference to each of twenty-five different occupations, "What percentage of students at this school have sufficient general ability (i.e., verbal and quantitative ability) to attain the following goals, provided they were motivated to do so?" (The Editors.)

theirs chose each of these types of work?" Table 1 gives the occupations used, together with the National Opinion Research Center's rankings (Barber, 1957), the scale rankings we used, and the average rankings which actually came from our sample. We gave our respondents a

Table 1

Occupation prestige rankings from NORC study used in building
the achievement index and derived from this study

Occupation*	NORC Score	Scale Score Used for Index	Average Score in This Study†
Night watchman	47	1	1.25
Auto mechanic	59	2	2.31
Carpenter	65	3	2.30
Mail carrier	66	4	2.15
Bus driver	68	5	1.75
Bookkeeper	68	6	2.54
Drugstore owner	69	7	3.33
High school teacher	80	8	3.19
Doctor	93	9	3.96

* Social worker was also included, not to use in deriving the index, but to see how people evaluated the occupation. The average evaluation for social workers fell in the middle at 2.41.

† Using an index ranging from 1 for "not happy" to 5 for "delighted."

choice among: not happy, wouldn't mind, happy, very happy, and delighted, hoping to spread the replies and distinguish the strong differences.

It is clear that changes have occurred since 1950 in the rankings of auto mechanics and carpenters, who moved up, and bus drivers and high school teachers, who moved down. It is possible that some of these shifts resulted from differences in questions, but they are meaningful in light of what happened to relative earnings in these occupations.

Table 2 provides information on the spread of the evaluation scores and the relation of the scores for each occupation to the education of the spending unit head. It is clear that the differences between mean scores are significant, and that while those with more education make stronger distinctions between occupations, the occupational differences persist through all education groups.

Our index of achievement motivation was based on the scale score in the central column of Table 1, derived from the NORC rankings. A

Table 2

Occupation evaluation (mean scores within education of head and distribution by occupation)

A. Mean Score for Each Occupation Within Education of the Head

Education of Head		Night Watchman	Auto Mechanic	Carpenter	Mail Carrier	Bus Driver	Bookkeeper	Drug-store Owner	High School Teacher	Doctor
None	0	1.86	2.90	2.97	2.48	2.25	2.82	3.10	3.29	3.71
1–8 grades	1	1.02	2.52	2.55	2.42	1.92	2.70	3.28	3.20	3.82
9–11 grades	2	1.36	2.30	2.31	2.10	1.72	2.56	3.38	3.14	3.94
12 grades	3	1.42	2.29	2.31	2.13	1.76	2.53	3.41	3.20	3.99
12 grades and nonacademic training	4	1.28	2.17	2.20	2.26	1.61	2.47	3.39	3.20	4.06
College, no degree	5	1.31	2.16	2.06	2.00	1.61	2.37	3.28	3.29	4.08
College, bachelor's degree	6	1.25	2.02	1.92	1.83	1.54	2.30	3.25	3.14	4.14
College, advanced degree	7	1.15	1.88	1.72	1.75	1.52	2.15	3.18	3.16	4.27
	All	1.25	2.31	2.30	2.15	1.75	2.54	3.33	3.19	3.96

B. Distribution of Evaluation Scores Within Each Occupation

Evaluation Scores		Night Watchman	Auto Mechanic	Carpenter	Mail Carrier	Bus Driver	Bookkeeper	Drug-store Owner	High School Teacher	Doctor
Not happy	1	66	19	17	22	43	9	5	4	2
Wouldn't mind	2	22	38	43	43	35	38	18	18	8
Happy	3	7	30	29	25	14	40	33	39	20
Very happy	4	1	6	4	4	2	7	22	22	26
Delighted	5	0	2	3	1	1	2	18	11	40
Do not know; not ascertained	9	4	5	4	5	5	4	4	6	4
	Total	100	100	100	100	100	100	100	100	100

better index could presumably be developed by using the rankings from our own study.

The extent to which an individual differentiated between occupations on the basis of their prestige was measured by the slope of the regression of the evaluation index (1 for not happy to 5 for delighted) on the prestige scale score (1 to 9). The regression coefficient indicates the increase in the evaluation index as one increases the prestige of the occupation.

One might ask how we know that we are measuring anything more than a mere evaluation of occupations. It must be kept in mind that the slope index is a measure of a particular kind of differentiation among occupations, one that rates the difficult high-status occupations much more highly than the easier ones. It is not merely valuing certain occupations but valuing them differentially. It is not variability in valuations but a particular relation to particular occupations. The index is the steepness of the gradient, the extent of differentiation between occupations when arranged in a particular order.

In spite of all this, of course, it is possible that the index does not represent achievement motivation. The reader who prefers to regard it as a summary measure of a particular kind of occupational evaluation is free to do so. However, it will prove more difficult to interpret the findings coherently. Also, in order to avoid defensiveness by the respondent or focus on his own occupation, we asked about "most people" and "a boy of theirs," thus allowing a projection of the respondent's feelings to others. An assumption behind the present index, then, is that it is a projective measure, leaving the respondent free to express his own feelings without appearing to do so. There may remain some tendency for those in low-status occupations to be defensive about their own occupations and think people would be satisfied for their sons to go into it, particularly if they have less exposure to people in other occupations. This would produce some downward bias in the index for those with low education or in unskilled occupations, or on the farm.

The limited number of occupations used, the use of previous rankings rather than those implied within this study, were the result of the pioneering nature of the study and competing objectives. If an inexpensive, rough measure produced some significant relations, then it was felt further investigation would be justified.

While the ultimate test of a variable is in its predictive ability, it is always useful to attempt an assessment of validity. In national samples interviewed in the field, test-retest measures are not feasible. Relationships with other measures of the same concept are inconclusive, particularly if the validity of the other measure is uncertain.

In a sample of 73 pretest interviews, the index of need for achievement was related to a score indicating the number of evidences (mostly in attitudes and plans) of upward mobility, and a low but positive significant correlation was found. A better measure of actual striving would presumably have been more highly correlated with the need for achievement.

In a class of 64 psychology students at the University of Michigan, the need-achievement index proved to be uncorrelated with a TAT measure of achievement motive. There were some problems with the administration of the protocols, and it is possible that the range of occupations relevant for a cross-section of the population was largely below the interest range of college students. The actual index measures for the students were much higher than for our cross-section, twice as many in the group over .35, and no students in the group under .15. Other attempts to correlate the two measures have been more successful. More impressive, however, is the general agreement between the TAT measures and the slope measure in their correlations with other demographic and background factors such as religion.

THE DATA

The necessary data for developing an index of the achievement motive and relating it to behavior were collected in interviews with nearly 3,000 heads of spending units in early 1960. They represent a national probability sample, although higher sampling fractions were used for certain low-income units where the head was of working age, and weights were applied to offset differences in sampling and response rates, thus to provide unbiased estimates.[4] Since a large number of behavior variables were measured, as well as numerous explanatory factors, the data provide an opportunity to see what background characteristics seem to be associated with high need for achievement, and what forms of behavior are associated with (caused by) high motive to achieve.

RELATION OF PARENTAL BACKGROUND TO ACHIEVEMENT MOTIVATION

Unravelling causal processes in human affairs requires coming to grips not only with the problem of the direction of causation, but of

---

[4] The full analysis of the determinants of income and of intergenerational changes, which was the main purpose of the study, can be found in Morgan, David, Cohen, and Brazer (1962).

the possibility of chains of causation, where A causes B, and B in turn causes C. Both the theory of achievement motivation and some rudimentary evidence argue that early independence training leads to the development of high levels of need for achievement. Early independence training does not mean neglect or freedom, but insistence on self-reliance and praise for the child when he does things that are difficult at his age (Winterbottom, 1958).

Theory and some evidence argue that, once established, the basic level of an individual's achievement motivation is relatively stable (Moss and Kagan, 1961). In a cross-section survey, relying on the

Table 3

n Achievement index within education of fathers
(percentage distribution of spending unit heads)

| Education of Fathers | n Achievement Index | | | | | Per Cent of Spending Units |
	.35 and Higher	.34-.15	.14 and Lower	Not Ascertained	Total	
None	19	41	35	5	100	4
1–8 grades	30	46	21	3	100	59
9–11 grades	33	42	23	2	100	6
12 grades	40	43	15	2	100	10
Some college	38	48	10	4	100	4
College degree	41	42	12	5	100	3
All spending unit heads*	29	45	22	4	100	100

* Includes 14 per cent of spending unit heads whose fathers' education was not ascertained.

respondent's memory about his own past, it is not possible to assess his early childhood training, but we can look at the demographic facts. Tables 3 through 5 show that the index of need for achievement is higher for those whose fathers were more educated, in white-collar jobs, and lived in large cities and in the Northeast. The implication is that successful parents may have provided the kind of early childhood training which led to high achievement orientation of their children.

The relation of the achievement motive to religion might be considered a parental background factor, since people seldom change their major denominational affiliation. The Jews tend to score highest, then the nonfundamentalist Protestants, the Catholics, and the fundamentalist Protestants, in that order. The differences are small and barely significant, however.

Within a single country, the variety of racial, religious, and cultural

Table 4

n Achievement index within occupation of fathers
(percentage distribution of spending unit heads)

Occupation of Fathers	.35 and Higher	.34-.15	.14 and Lower	Not Ascertained	Total	Per Cent of Spending Unit Heads
Professionals	40	47	9	4	100	5
Managers	41	37	22	0	100	2
Self-employed businessmen	35	46	15	4	100	12
Clerical and sales workers	41	48	10	1	100	6
Artisans, foremen, and craftsmen	33	44	19	4	100	14
Operatives	29	48	23	0	100	12
Unskilled laborers, service workers	22	43	30	5	100	14
Farmers	24	45	27	4	100	28
Government protective workers	30	53	17	0	100	1
Not ascertained	27	43	15	15	100	6
All spending units	29	45	22	4	100	100

Table 5

n Achievement index within regions and size of places where heads
grew up (percentage distribution of spending unit heads)

Regions Where the Head Grew Up	.35 and Higher	.34-.15	.14 and Lower	Not Ascertained	Total	Per Cent of Spending Unit Heads
Northeast	37	42	18	3	100	21
North central	27	50	21	2	100	28
South	28	45	23	4	100	34
West	29	38	27	6	100	9
Outside the United States	28	46	19	7	100	6
All spending unit heads	29	45	22	4	100	100
Size of Places Where the Head Grew Up						
Farms	21	47	28	4	100	32
Small towns	32	44	21	3	100	34
Large cities	35	45	17	3	100	32
Several places; other	23	46	29	2	100	2
All spending unit heads	29	45	22	4	100	100

backgrounds is limited, and the survey from which the data come did not attempt to measure ethnic background. Religious and major racial factors, however, were available. Early findings by Rosen and others had indicated higher levels of achievement motivation for Jews than Protestants and for Protestants than Catholics (Rosen, 1959). However, these studies had been done on restricted populations, usually middle and upper income groups in the Northeast. National sample TAT data from a Survey Research Center study indicated that in other areas and among lower income groups, Catholics had higher measures of achievement motivation than Protestants (Veroff, Feld, and Gurin, 1962). The authors suggest that as a minority group, Catholics may have their achievement motives aroused more constantly than Protestants. The fact that it was the low-income Catholics who had the highest motive scores supported this inference. At any rate, the dangers of relying on small special subgroups of the population for broad generalizations is well illustrated by the difference in conclusions between Rosen and Veroff and others.

Since some later analysis uses the attitude about the connection between hard work and success, it is interesting to note that Negroes and Jews are more likely to be fatalistic and suggest luck or help from friends may matter, although the vast majority of every group believes in the efficacy of hard work. Those who have moved up in occupational status or remained in their father's high status are also more likely to believe that hard work pays off.

INTERCORRELATIONS OF THE ACHIEVEMENT MOTIVE WITH OTHER EXPLANATORY FACTORS

The achievement motive is, by assumption, a relatively stable, enduring characteristic of the individual. Hence, one does not expect later events to change the achievement motive and, by that path, behavior. However, it is still useful to look at intercorrelations which could make the assessment of the separate importance of the achievement motive difficult.

In order to reduce the complexity and provide a maximum chance for relations to show, we compare the 29 per cent with high index of achievement motive (slopes of .35 or more) with the 22 per cent with a low index (slopes of less than .15) and refer to them as Highs and Lows, ignoring the 49 per cent in the middle.

The Highs are twice as likely to have entered college as the Lows (30 versus 15 per cent) and two-and-a-half times as likely to have

graduated (15 versus 6 per cent). Their parents were also more educated, too, of course.

The Highs are more likely than Lows to supervise other people (28
versus 19 per cent), but less likely to be self-employed (16 versus 20
per cent), because farmers, who are generally not high on our index,
make up much of the self-employed group. Perhaps the index is less
appropriate for farmers, whose contacts with other occupations are
more limited.

The Highs are slightly more likely to be married (71 versus 67 per
cent). Unmarried males are twice as likely to be Lows (15 versus 8 per
cent). Highs are somewhat more likely to have more education than
their wives (37 versus 23 per cent). Aside from some small differences
which could be attributed to educational levels, the Highs do not seem
to be older or younger or concentrated in any particular region. The
Highs are more likely to be white (93 versus 86 per cent) (see Merbaum,
1960, 1961).

RELATION OF THE ACHIEVEMENT MOTIVE TO ECONOMIC BEHAVIOR

With this background, and keeping in mind the treacherous problem
of causal chains and direction of causation and the nature of our index
measure, we turn now to some relations between the index of achievement motive and various types of economic behavior.

We have already noted that Highs are less likely to be farmers, more
likely to supervise other people. They are also a little *more* likely to
work in companies with ten or more employees (83 versus 75 per cent).

The Highs are three times as likely as the Lows to have *started* in a
high-status occupation and to have stayed there (15 versus 5 per cent).
Almost as many Lows as Highs moved up from their first occupation to
a better one (29 versus 31 per cent). The Highs are much less likely to
have started in a low-status occupation and remained there (9 versus 28
per cent). These relations are stronger among younger people. The
combined results of these tendencies is to produce *no* overall relation
between the achievement motive and occupational mobility during the
individual's career.

Perhaps the mobility results have to do, then, with the change from
the *father's* occupation. Using the usual crude grouping of occupations
into three groups, however, we find that the Highs are somewhat less
likely to be in the same occupational level as their fathers, but they are
about as likely to have moved to a lower as to a higher occupation. In
many cases, their fathers were already in high-status occupations.

If we exclude the farmers and government protective workers, there is a slight (nonsignificant) tendency for the Highs to have higher level occupations than their fathers (44 versus 38 per cent). However, if we focus separately on two groups under the greatest economic pressure to move, farmers and unskilled workers, there does appear a tendency for sons with high achievement motive scores to move to higher status occupations (see Table 6).

Table 6

Occupation of head within selected groups by occupation of
father and index of need for achievement

Occupation of Head	Father Was a Farmer; n Achievement Index of Head		Father Was an Unskilled Worker (laborer, operative);* n Achievement Index of Head	
	Less Than .15	.35 or More	Less Than .15	.35 or More
Professional, technical	6	9	4	10
Other white collar	15	20	15	26
Craftsmen, foremen	13	17	12	23
Operatives, laborers, service workers	38	32	38	36
Farmers	23	15	5	1
Other (government protective workers, housewives, widows, not ascertained)	5	7	6	4
Total	100	100	100	100
Per cent of spending unit heads	8	7	7	6
Per cent of farmers' sons	36	23		
Per cent of sons of unskilled workers			31	22

* For the Highs, the father was more likely to have been an operative than an unskilled laborer (i.e., somewhat better off within the group).

The attitudes of the two groups are in keeping with their income, educational, and occupational levels. One interesting finding is that Highs are more likely to have opinions, for instance, about tax support for colleges (80 versus 70 per cent). Among those with an opinion, the Highs are more likely than the Lows to favor support for students with ability (34 versus 19 per cent), and less likely to urge support based on need alone (15 versus 21 per cent).

The Highs are not particularly more mobile geographically. Indeed, slightly fewer Highs than Lows have lived in two or more different states since their first full-time regular jobs (33 versus 37 per cent), while only a few more are farm people who moved to a large city (18 versus 12 per cent).

No particular association appears between the achievement motive and change of religion from that of the father's. Seven out of ten have the same religions as their fathers, and those who change do so in both directions, regardless of their index of achievement motive. Remember, however, that the Highs attend church more frequently (58 versus 47 per cent attend twice a month or more).

The major difference in intergenerational change is in education, where the Highs are more likely than the Lows to have had more education than their fathers (48 versus 24 per cent), in spite of the fact that their fathers had more education to start with.

Finally, and consistent with the higher education of those with high achievement motivation, there is a strong tendency for those with more education to be planning ahead. An index was created based on the number of evidences of planning and foresight in the interview, based on questions about hospitalization insurance, savings, feeling of ability to plan ahead, planning purchases, planned retirement age, and planned sources of additional retirement income. The Highs average 3.7, as against 2.7 for the Lows.[5]

MEASURE OF ANCILLARY VARIABLES

The theory relating achievement motivation to behavior involves two other intervening variables. These two variables are the incentive value of the expected outcome and the expectancy (subjective probability) that a particular course of action will lead to that outcome. Behavior is thought to be a joint result of the levels of all three (Chapter 2).

Variations in the incentive value of economic success are uncontrolled, difficult to measure, and perhaps not so different from one person to another within one culture. The major factor affecting a person's desire for more income might be the number of other persons dependent upon him, which we have used as a separate predictor in many of our analyses.

The subjective probability that working hard, or getting more education, or accumulating capital would pay off can vary from individual to individual, and the theoretical model says that it may interact with the motive value to determine actual behavior. Hence, we attempted to measure the expectancy and used a joint classification of our individ-

[5] The index of planning has a standard deviation of 1 63, and the *N*s are 464 for Highs and 382 for Lows. Hence, regardless of qualifications about the sample design, the difference is highly significant. See also Green and Knapp (1959).

uals on both motive and expectancy in much of the analysis. Our measure of expectancy was based on a single, simple question, "Some people say that people get ahead by their own hard work; others say that lucky breaks or help from other people are more important. What do you think about this?"

The theory was that those who had a high need for achievement, *and* believed that hard work would result in success, would work the hardest. The problem remains that the expectancy is an attitude which can change as a result of experience. The joint motive-expectancy mix should affect current behavior. However, past behavior or current situations which result from the past behavior have resulted from the combination of the stable motive and whatever expectancies existed when the behavior took place. Thus, if we find that income from capital, resulting from saving and accumulation, is related both to our index of need for achievement and to the belief that hard work pays off, the causal direction is relatively clear for the motive, but could go in either direction for the belief that hard work pays off. The belief in hard work reinforced by successful application remains, but a man who believed in hard work and failed may have lost his confidence that work is rewarded.

It is useful to remember that minority groups, particularly the visible minorities like Negroes, are more likely to feel that luck or help from friends make a difference, and for them perhaps this reflects reality. In general, however, the belief that hard work will be rewarded is predominant in this country.

It is quite possible that in other countries reliance on luck may be more widespread, the incentive value of economic success as compared with success as a priest or a general or a scholar may be lower, and the proportion with high achievement motivation may be different. Only carefully designed comparative studies will tell (McClelland, 1961).

MULTIVARIATE ANALYSIS OF WORK AND EARNINGS

In view of the correlation of our index of need for achievement with education and income, and the correlation of education and income with age, it is more convincing to look at analysis which simultaneously takes account of these other variables. To some extent, this is unfair, because if high achievement motivation is what has led to educational achievement and high income, we allow these things to take credit for something ultimately attributable to motivational forces.

On the other hand, it must also be kept in mind that in spite of the theory, it is possible that experience does change people's level of achievement motive, or that our measure is measuring attitudes toward occupations rather than toward achievement. At any rate, it is useful to look at the relations between the need for achievement index and the various behavior measures, taking account of other factors correlated with both of them.

Capital income, including imputed income on net equity in an owned home, results largely from saving and accumulation. Some is inherited, but within age-education groups rather randomly. Both income from which capital can be accumulated and achievement motivation are related to education, the latter either because the road to success requires education, or because the educational system inculcated achievement values. Hence, we must control on education. Capital accumulation also depends on fhe period of years over which it can be accumulated (or inherited), so we control on that. Farmers and businessmen have special coercion to accumulate capital, and our measure of their capital income is weak. The resulting Table 7 shows a per-

Table 7

Mean capital income within age, occupation, education,
and *n* Achievement index (for spending units)

Occupation, Age, Education of Heads	*n* Achievement Index			Per cent of Spending Units
	.35 and Higher	.34–.15	.14 and Lower	
Retired	$1,587	$1,217	$ 950	11
Not farmers, self-employed businessmen, or retired				
18–34				
0–11 grades	110	90	79	10
12 grades	117	118	100	9
Some college	249	182	147	8
35 or older				
0–11 grades	553	461	402	29
12 grades	691	664	514	12
Some college	1,415	1,094	761	10
Farmers	1,835	1,928	1,784	6
Self-employed businessmen	2,280	1,729	1,590	5

sistent relation between an index of need for achievement (based on the extent of differentiation between difficult and easy occupations) and capital income.

It should be said that more complex multivariate analyses for two separate age groups, 30 to 39 and 50 to 64, found no significant relation between income from self-accumulated capital (net of inheritances) and a combination of need for achievement and attitudes toward hard work. However, a pattern remained, the groups were small, and the other variables probably took credit which ultimately belonged to the motivational variable.

A challenge relevant to some people is the overcoming of a disability. Table 8 shows that among those who report some disability, there is a tendency for those high on the index of achievement motive to report less limitation on their work. An alternative interpretation of the findings is that those high on achievement motivation are more annoyed by minor disabilities and more likely to report them; but it remains a plausible hypothesis that they also do more to overcome their disabilities.

Table 9 summarizes three more multivariate analyses, giving only the coefficients for the combinations of achievement motive and beliefs about the efficacy of hard work. Combining the first of each pair of columns with the mean provides unadjusted subgroup averages, and combining the second of each pair with the mean provides standardized estimates of what the effects of the classifying grouping would be if each subgroup were the same as the others on all the other characteristics, e.g., age, education, race, physical condition, family composition, and so forth. Whether the head of a spending unit works is so dominated by other pressures that no significant effect of the motive to achieve appears, although the small differences are all in the expected direction.

The hourly earnings (annual earnings divided by estimated hours worked during the year) shows a highly significant relation to the motive-expectancy grouping, even after adjustments for:

Education and age	Extent of unemployment in state
Sex	Supervisory responsibility
Occupation	Race
Population of city	Interviewer's rating of ability to
Urban-rural migration	communicate
Movement out of Deep South	Past geographic mobility
Physical condition	Reported rank and progress in school

Table 8

Extent of limitation of disabled unit heads: effects of spending unit
heads' attitude toward hard work and *n* Achievement index

Attitude Toward Hard Work, *n* Achievement Index	N	Extent of Limitation Mean = .56*	
		Unadjusted Deviations	Adjusted Deviations†
Hard work is equal to or more important than luck; n Achievement index is in:			
High range (.35 or higher)	107	−.18	−.08
Middle range (.34–.15)	193	.00	−.01
Low range (.14 or lower)	90	.10	.04
Hard work is less important than luck; n Achievement index is in:			
High range (.35 or higher)	27	−.16	−.06
Middle range (.34–.15)	67	−.14	−.14
Low range (.14 or lower)	55	.06	.12
Scores not ascertained	40	.56	.33
F-ratio			2.07

* The questions were: "Have you had an illness, physical condition, or nervous condition which limits the type or amount of work you can do? How does it limit your work?" Limitation was scored on a three-point scale: 0 = moderate limitation; 1 = severe limitation; 2 = complete limitation.

† Adjusted = determined simultaneously in a multivariate analysis with age, education, etc. These can be thought of as the coefficients in a multiple regression of variables which take the value one if the individual belongs to that subgroup, otherwise, zero. They have been adjusted so that the weighted mean of the coefficients for any one classification is zero, making the constant term in the regression equation the grand mean of the dependent variable.

When the analysis was restricted to white, male, nonfarmer spending unit heads who worked in 1959, the pattern remained, but the differences were not significant.

The results for hours worked, something presumably more subject to involuntary outside forces, such as the standard working week and involuntary unemployment, are significant only at the 5 per cent level, using a crude F-test, but in the expected direction. The eleven other factors taken into account in this analysis were not quite the same. For

Table 9

1959 work experience of spending unit heads: effects of spending unit heads' attitudes toward hard work and n Achievement index

Attitudes Toward Hard Work n Achievement Index	Probability of Working Mean = 0.86		N	Hourly Earnings Mean = $2.29		Hours Mean = 2092	
	Unadjusted Deviations	Adjusted Deviations*		Unadjusted Deviations	Adjusted Deviations*	Unadjusted Deviations	Adjusted Deviations*
Hard work is equal to or more important than luck; n Achievement index is in:							
High range (.35 or higher)	.03	.01	630	$ .32	$ .12	28	28
Middle range (.34–.15)	.00	.00	921	.06	.01	39	25
Low range (.14 or lower)	.00	.00	440	-.32	-.17	10	-29
Hard work is less important than luck; n Achievement index is in:							
High range (.35 or higher)	.05	.01	120	-.04	-.05	0	18
Middle range (.34–.15)	-.01	-.01	228	-.26	-.01	-151	-72
Low range (.14 or lower)	-.07	-.03	139	-.52	-.05	-231	-181
Index not ascertained	-.13	-.02	90	.01	-.16	22	73
F ratio		.78			2.91†		2.54‡

* Adjusted = determined simultaneously in a multivariate analysis with age, education, race, etc.
† Significant at a probability level of .01.
‡ Significant at a probability level of .05.

instance, they included the hourly earnings, but left out sex and the past mobility factors. In all the multivariate analysis presented here, there were other more directly relevant explanatory factors with higher significance levels than achievement motivation, of course.

An analysis of money saved by home production of food and home repairs showed no relationship to our motive-expectancy classification. Perhaps achievement orientation leads to focusing on the main job, rather than on relatively unproductive work around the house.

MULTIVARIATE ANALYSIS OF EDUCATION

Turning now to something more under the control of the individual, perhaps, than hours of work, Table 10 provides the results of four multivariate analyses of education, in each of which the "achievement motive-attitude toward hard work" factor proved highly significant, even after adjusting for some things, which could be argued to be themselves the results of high achievement motivation.

In the case of the education of the respondent himself, the possibility remains that his education has affected his verbal responses even to a projective question, so that the causation is reverse to that we hypothesized. It is interesting that adjustments for the education and occupation of the head's father, the head's age, and the number of brothers and sisters he had all have a substantial effect in reducing the apparent importance of the achievement motive, indicating that they are correlated both with the head's education and with his index of achievement motive. However, if they *led* to the early independence training that created the high achievement motivation, we have understated the importance of achievement motivation as a link in the causal chain. After all, how else does one explain the persistence and effort needed to secure the education?

The completed education of the respondent's children, even after adjustments for the respondent's education and eleven other factors (a total of 71 other subclasses), remains significantly related to our motive-expectancy classification of the father. Here there can be no question about the causal direction, though the exact way in which the parental influence operates cannot be discovered with these data.[6]

[6] Both the theory and evidence summarized by Atkinson (Chapter 11) would indicate that parental influence operated through early independence training of children and focus on the child's mastery of tasks. See Winterbottom (1958); see also Rosen (1959) where ethnic groups and social classes known from other evidence to be high on motive to achieve also reported expectations of mastery of tasks by their children at earlier ages.

Table 10

Education of spending unit heads and their children: effects of spending
unit heads' attitudes toward hard work and n Achievement index

Attitude Toward Hard Work, n Achievement Index	Education of Heads Mean = 2.82*			Education Completed by Children Who Are Finished with School; Mean = 11.82†		
	N	Unadjusted Deviations	Adjusted Deviations‡	N	Unadjusted Deviations	Adjusted Deviations‡
Hard work is equal to or more important than luck; n Achievement index is in:						
High range (.35 or higher)	714	.52	.28	190	.96	.32
Middle range (.34–.15)	1,070	.09	.05	334	.08	.03
Low range (.14 or lower)	511	–.36	–.23	169	–.51	–.25
Hard work is less important than luck; n Achievement index is in:						
High range (.35 or higher)	132	.08	.08	34	1.29	.75
Middle range (.34–.15)	270	–.70	–.49	100	–.96	–.32
Low range (.14 or lower)	177	–.96	–.48	72	–1.20	–.26
Index not ascertained	122	.04	.34	40	–.28	–.26
F-ratio			16.06§			2.89§

Table 10 (Cont.)

Attitude Toward Hard Work, n Achievement Index	Education Planned for Boys 20 and Under Mean = 5.15*			Education Planned for Girls 20 and Under Mean = 4.77*		
	N	Unadjusted Deviations	Adjusted Deviations‡	N	Unadjusted Deviations	Adjusted Deviations‡
Hard work is equal to or more important than luck; n Achievement index is in:						
High range (.35 or higher)	282	.45	.22	261	.42	.20
Middle range (.34–.15)	401	.09	.00	389	.06	.03
Low range (.14 or lower)	198	–.32	–.13	183	–.29	–.15
Hard work is less important than luck; n Achievement index is in:						
High range (.35 or higher)	53	–.04	–.06	44	.20	.17
Middle range (.34–.15)	93	–.56	–.37	97	–.43	–.27
Low range (.14 or lower)	70	–.76	–.01	63	–.88	–.35
Index not ascertained	331	–.42	–.17	32	–.20	.00
F-ratio			3.77§			3.33§

* Education scores on an eight-point scale: 0 = no education; 1 = 0–8 grades; 2 = 9–11 grades; 3 = 12 grades; 4 = 12 grades and nonacademic training; 5 = some college; 6 = bachelor's degree; 7 = college, advanced degree.
† Education scored in years: 12 = high school diploma; 16 = college degree, etc.
‡ Adjusted = determined simultaneously in a multivariate analysis with age, race, etc.
§ Significant at a probability level of .01.

Finally, there are significant relations with the amount of education parents plan for their boys and girls, even after adjustments for thirteen other classifications, containing 85 subgroups.

SUMMARY

The index, then, has effects on many forms of behavior, even after taking account of many other factors, through some of which it may also be operating indirectly. The belief that hard work pays off also seems to have an effect, though it is strongest where it may be a result rather than a cause, i.e., in its relation to the education the respondent completed some time ago.

Could the index still be a result rather than a cause, or an occupational evaluation rather than a measure of personality disposition to strive for achievement? Had the index been related to the education of the respondent, but not to that of his children, we might have thought so—the index reflecting only attitudes influenced by the formal education received. But the fact that the index also helps predict the completed education of children, plans for education of younger children, income from savings, hourly earnings, and the extent of planning ahead, increase the credibility that we have tapped something else, particularly since the respondent's education was taken into account in the analyses.

The cumulative impression of these relationships is that the measure of achievement motive, combined with that of the subjective expectation that hard work pays off, are related to a variety of relevant economic behaviors in a meaningful way. Adjustment, and even overadjustment for intercorrelations with other influences, reduces the apparent size of the effects and occasionally reduces them below the levels necessary for crude significance tests, but in general the results suggest that the achievement motive and beliefs about the probabilities of hard work being rewarded are related to the economic behavior of individuals within a culture.

The possibility is thus opened for international comparisons which combine within-country and between-country analyses. The power of such analyses is, of course, far greater than those to which McClelland (1961) has largely had to resort, comparing whole countries with one

---

(1959) where ethnic groups and social classes known from other evidence to be high on motive to achieve also reported expectations of mastery of tasks by their children at earlier ages.

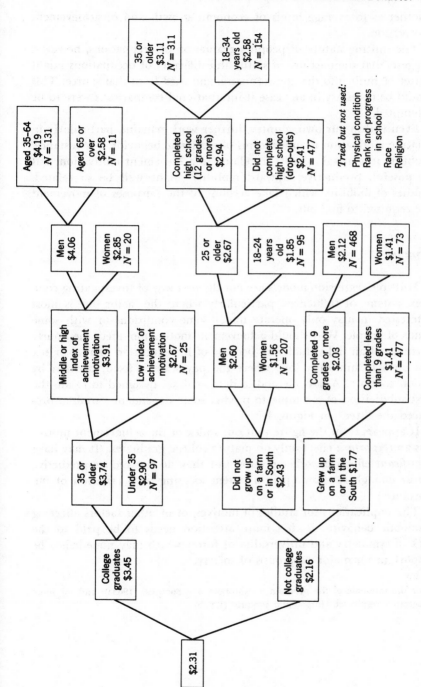

Figure 1   Average hourly earnings for heads of spending units who had income in 1949. *Source:* Survey Research Center Study 678.

another as to average levels of economic growth and of achievement motivation.

The shifting nature of people's evaluation of occupations, however, suggests that the measure of status and difficulty of occupations might better be built into the questionnaire, and used from that source. This would be necessary in any case if international comparisons were to be attempted.

Even within our own country, further work remains, particularly in relating motivation to other forms of economic behavior. For instance, mobility in general appears unrelated to achievement motivation, but purposeful, productive, upward mobility might well be so related. Studies of mobility which take account of the purposes of movement are required to find out.

ADDENDUM

Multiple regression models are not the best way of investigating complex systems of influences, particularly where the factor one is most interested in may only operate under some conditions or with some kinds of people. Why should achievement motivation affect the hourly earnings of an individual who because of his education or race or sex has open to him only jobs where the pay scale is fixed, perhaps by union contract? A new method of data analysis, designed to locate the best subdivision of a sample to predict some dependent variable, produced the "tree" in Figure 1.[7]

It appears from the figure that our index of the achievement motive has an *important* effect only on mature college graduates. (It may have *significant* effects on other groups, but they do not reduce predictive errors enough to show up in a system focusing on a criterion of importance.)

The implications for studies of motives, or of other factors affecting economic behavior, is that more attention needs to be paid to the lack of symmetry and universality of forces which may nonetheless be important for major subgroups of society.

---

[7] For the rationale of the program, see Morgan and Sonquist (1963a); and for some illustrative results see Morgan and Sonquist (1963b).

15.
PATRICIA O'CONNOR, JOHN W. ATKINSON, AND MATINA HORNER

Motivational Implications
of Ability Grouping in Schools

The desirability of employing some form of ability grouping to enhance learning in the schools is a question of current interest and
controversy. Advocates of ability grouping often argue from general
observations that the wide variability in abilities represented in the
traditional unselected class produces a situation which very often stifles
the enthusiasm of the student of high ability because he is insufficiently challenged, and one which engenders discouragement and
apathy in the student of low ability because he repeatedly fails to meet
the standards set by his more able peers. It is generally assumed by
proponents of ability grouping that narrowing the range of capabilities
in a class would be a spur to learning and interest in schoolwork. Those
who take a negative view of ability grouping frequently tend to minimize the issue of achievement and emphasize instead potentially unde-
sirable social consequences, (e.g., the establishment of an intellectual
elite, the threat to the self-esteem of students assigned to the lower
ability groups, etc.) The question obviously has many sides. Equally
obvious is the need for more and better empirical information related
to the various arguments and suppositions which now influence decision making on this problem.

The impetus for the present investigation was provided in part by
the desire of teachers and administrators in a Midwestern city to learn
something about the consequences of their experimental program in
ability grouping, and in part by the implications of recent research on
achievement-oriented behavior, particularly the theory of achievement
motivation (Chapter 2) which has evolved in experimental and societal

This study was supported by the Cooperative Research Program of the Office of
Education, United States Department of Health, Education, and Welfare. Other
phases of the research are reported by Atkinson and O'Connor (1963). We wish to
acknowledge the assistance of Irene Brock and the cooperation of Mr. Russell West
and the Ann Arbor school system for making this study possible.

studies (see McClelland, Atkinson, Clark, and Lowell, 1953; Atkinson, 1958a, McClelland, 1961).

This study was undertaken to explore some of the motivational implications of ability grouping as manifested in scholastic achievement and reported interest in schoolwork among students who differ substantially in the nature of their motivation to achieve. As suggested in earlier chapters, there is much in the contemporary literature on the effects of individual differences in achievement motive (*n* Achievement) and Test Anxiety (Sarason, Davidson, Lighthall, Waite, and Ruebush; 1960) to suggest that ability grouping should enhance motivation for schoolwork in some, but not all, students.

Application of Theory of Achievement Motivation to Problem of Ability Grouping. We make two assumptions in our analysis of motivational implications of ability grouping, guided by the theory of achievement motivation. First, following the lead of ideas developed by Festinger (1954) in an analysis of the social comparison process, we assume that feelings of success and failure in day-to-day schoolwork are largely a consequence of evaluating one's own performance relative to the performance of others in the same class. This means that in the traditional class, which is heterogeneous in ability, the very intelligent child will almost always consider himself a standout performer and the least endowed child will almost never have this experience of success. Second, we assume that individual differences in intelligence probably represent the best estimate of individual differences in expectancy of success (e.g., of being a standout performer) which students bring to their schoolwork.

According to the theory of achievement motivation, neither the positive tendency to achieve success nor anxiety and the tendency to avoid failure should be very strongly aroused in a student when the probability of success relative to peers is either very high or very low. This means, then, that achievement-related motivation is not likely to be strongly aroused for a considerable number of students in the class where all levels of ability are represented. It also implies that both positive interest in achievement and anxiety about failure should be more strongly aroused in a homogeneous, ability-grouped class. For when the student of high intelligence is surrounded by classmates of equally high endowment, his own expectancy of success (i.e., of being a standout performer) must be lower than when he is substantially higher in ability than most of his peers. Similarly, the less endowed student surrounded by peers of comparable ability now should find himself with an increased expectancy of success relative to his peers.

For many students, then, *homogeneous ability grouping should provide a competitive achievement situation more nearly approximating one of intermediate probability of success, or intermediate difficulty, than the traditional heterogeneous class.* Both effort and anxiety should be more apparent when ability grouping is employed, and both should be generally weaker when students of diverse abilities are members of the same class.

Whether or not ability grouping will enhance school performance or produce a decrement in performance should depend upon the relative strength of the motive to achieve success (*n* Achievement) and motive to avoid failure (Test Anxiety) within the individual student. According to theory, an increase in positive interest leading to enhancement of performance should occur for students who are highly motivated to achieve but weak in the disposition to be anxious when they are subjected to ability grouping. However, students who are more strongly disposed to be anxious about failure than motivated to achieve success *may* be less adequately motivated under a program of ability grouping than in the heterogeneous class. For in them, the arousal of anxiety may be substantially stronger than the arousal of positive motivation to achieve. Thus performance and interest may decline under ability grouping. (See Figure 3, Chapter 20, for graphic representation of these ideas.)

Hypotheses. The specific hypotheses tested are the following:

HYPOTHESIS 1. Students in whom the motive to achieve success (*n* Achievement) is relatively strong in relation to the motive to avoid failure (Test Anxiety) *(a)* will show more growth on measures of scholastic achievement when they are placed in a homogeneous ability group than when they remain in a group in which student ability is more heterogeneous; and *(b)* when placed in a homogeneous group will show more growth on measures of scholastic achievement than will students in whom the motive to avoid failure is strong in relation to motive to achieve success.

HYPOTHESIS 2. Students in whom the motive to avoid failure is relatively strong in relation to the motive to achieve success will show *less* growth on measures of scholastic achievement when they are placed in a homogeneous ability group than when they remain in a group in which the abilities are more heterogeneous.

HYPOTHESIS 3. Students in whom the motive to achieve success is relatively strong in relation to the motive to avoid failure will report greater interest in class activities, and a greater interest compared with the previous year, when they are placed in a homogeneous ability group than when they remain in a group in which abilities are more heterogeneous; and these students, when placed in a homogeneous group, will show greater interest and greater increase in interest than students in whom the motive to avoid failure is strong in relation to motive to achieve success.

HYPOTHESIS 4. Students in whom the motive to avoid failure is relatively strong in relation to the motive to achieve success will report less interest, and less interest relative to the previous year, when they are placed in a homogeneous ability group than when they remain in a group more varied in ability.

METHOD

Subjects. This study was carried out during three academic years in the sixth-grade classes of three schools. Prior to sixth grade all students had been in classes in which students were not intentionally grouped according to ability or past achievement. During the first two years of the study, ability grouping was introduced on an experimental basis in the sixth-grade classes of two schools. The basic plan of the study is to compare measures of achievement and interest in sixth grade of students experiencing homogeneous ability grouping for the first time, with comparable measures obtained from students in control classes, who continued (as in fifth grade) in classes that were heterogeneous in ability.

Decisions concerning criteria for grouping and assignment of students to special and regular sections in the ability-grouped schools had been made by school personnel. In each of the schools in which homogeneous ability grouping was employed, one of three sixth-grade classes was a special advanced section; the other two classes were considered *regular* sections. In School A, intelligence test score was the primary criterion for placement in the advanced section. In School B, performance on achievement tests was given top priority. But judgment of teachers concerning individual students was an important factor in deciding who should be in special advanced and *regular* sections in both schools. The composition of the experimental group (homogeneous in ability) and control group (heterogeneous in ability) is shown in Table 1.

All students in each of the sixth-grade classes were tested. Students for whom an intelligence test score (California Mental Maturity Test) and scores on both n Achievement and Test Anxiety were obtained numbered 206 in the homogeneous classes and 233 in the heterogeneous classes. These Ns are depleted in the analysis of results for reasons later specified.

Measurement of Motivation. Four verbal cues were presented by a female E under neutral conditions to elicit imaginative stories. These were later scored for n Achievement by PO, whose scoring reliability is above .90. Each cue was

Table 1

Composition of experimental group (classes homogeneous in ability)
and control group (classes heterogeneous in ability)

| School | Experimental Group (Homogeneous in Ability) | | |
	1959	1960	1961
A	1 advanced section 2 regular sections	1 advanced section 2 regular sections	— —
B	1 advanced section 2 regular sections	— —	— —
	Control Group (Heterogeneous in Ability)		
	1959	1960	1961
A	—	—	4 classes
C	—	3 classes	3 classes

Note: In 1961 school A returned to heterogeneity of ability in sixth grade, but school B instituted a team-teaching method in 1960 and 1961, which made classes unsuitable for this research either in the experimental or control groups. For this reason, a third school, C, as comparable to A and B as seemed possible in the school system was chosen to enlarge the size of the control group.

placed at the top of a page in the test booklet which provided suggestions for the writing of stories. The verbal cues were identical for all Ss with the single exception that the characters presented in the lead were of the same sex as the subject. The instructions and verbal cues employed to elicit stories are shown in Table 2.

Table 2

Instructions and verbal cues employed to elicit thematic apperceptive stories
from sixth-grade children*

Making Up Stories

We will all spend the next few minutes making up stories and writing them on the pages which follow.

Each page has a suggestion to start off the story. Then there is space for you to make up the rest of the story.

To help you, there are other suggestions printed on the page for each story with space for you to fill in.

The first suggestion is "Tell what is happening."

The second suggestion is "Tell what happened before."

The third suggestion is "Tell what is being thought about and what is wanted by the people in your story."

The last suggestion is "Tell what will happen."

(continued)

When we begin, we will all read the suggestion for a story together. Then if you will make up a story by filling in the spaces, we will all finish together. We will spend about two minutes answering each of the questions. That will mean a total of eight minutes for each story.

Let's turn to the first page and read the suggestion together.

Verbal cues: (words in parentheses substituted for girl subjects.)

1. This story is about a brother and sister playing a game. One of them is a little ahead of the other.

2. This story is about a boy (girl) sitting at his (her) desk in a school room.

3. This is a story about a father and his son (mother and her daughter) talking about something important.

4. This is a story about a boy (girl) working on something in his (her) room. A friend is watching.

---

* Earlier use of this technique with young children is described by Lowell in McClelland, et al. (1953) and by Winterbottom (1958).

Following the administration of the *n* Achievement measure, a preliminary form of the Test Anxiety Questionnaire (TAQ) for children developed by Sarason (Sarason, et al., 1960, p. 306) was read aloud. The Test Anxiety score consists of the number of items in which S endorsed as self-descriptive some statement reflecting a symptom of anxiety in the classroom.

To provide a single index of the strength of motive to achieve (*n* Achievement) relative to strength of motive to avoid failure (Test Anxiety), raw scores on both measures were converted to standard scores. The standard scores were based on the distribution of scores obtained from the sixth-grade students in a given school in a given year. Separate distributions were made for boys and girls. An index of *resultant motivation to achieve* was computed by subtracting the standard score for Test Anxiety from the standard score for *n* Achievement. A high score (*n* Achievement-Test Anxiety) implies that the motive to achieve success is substantially stronger than the motive to avoid failure. A low score implies either very weak resultant motivation to achieve or that the motive to avoid failure is in fact stronger than the motive to achieve and the resultant tendency is avoidant.

Derivation of an index of motivation for each student relative to scores obtained by members of his class level in a particular school and year assumes that there are not marked differences in motive strength between the populations of the three schools or between the population of the sixth grades in the same school during different years. In the light of the known sensitivity of these tests to conditions prevailing at the time of administration, it is assumed that any obtained differences in motive scores between groups are more likely to be the result of the conditions than of stable group differences in personality.

Reported Interest in Schoolwork. During the last month of the school year a questionnaire concerning interest in schoolwork was administered by another female *E*. It consisted of two parts. The first part is comprised of 20 items describing twenty activities which were undertaken in the sixth-grade by students in our sample. Students were asked to place an ✕ on a line scale at any point for each item. At either end of each line and at the center, the phrases "like very much," "neither like nor dislike," and "dislike very much" were introduced as reference points. The items were:

1. Writing stories and letters
2. Studying how climate influences the way people live in other parts of the world
3. Studying the universe and our solar system
4. Punctuating sentences
5. Making relief maps
6. Studying the way people live in the arid regions or dry lands
7. Multiplying and dividing with fractions
8. Working on panel discussions and debates
9. Painting with water colors
10. Studying weather forecasting
11. Answering questions in the *Weekly Reader* or *Junior Scholastic*
12. Studying the causes of tornadoes and hurricanes
13. Writing poems
14. Doing problems on the blackboard
15. Studying about the soil
16. Doing book reports
17. Reciting in class
18. Doing story problems in arithmetic
19. Reading stories
20. Working in the spelling workbook

A similar format was employed for 11 other items included to elicit evidence of a change in interest in schoolwork between the fifth and sixth grades. The descriptive phrases for this second set of items were "much more interesting this year," "about the same in interest as last year," and "much less interesting this year." Broad categories of activities common to the fifth and sixth grades were each rated in a single item. Each item was preceded by the words, "In comparison with our work in fifth grade, our work this year in _____ is." The items were:

21. Arithmetic
22. Science
23. Language
24. Reading
25. Spelling
26. Social studies

The remaining items were rated on a line scale anchored in the phrases "much more than last year," "about the same as last year," and "much less than last year." They were:

27. In general I like school this year. . . .
28. In comparison with last year I feel I am learning. . . .
29. In comparison with last year, I like to talk with my parents about what I am studying in school. . . .
30. In comparison with last year, I like the other students in my class. . . .
31. In comparison with last year, I am trying to do my best in school. . . .

For scoring, the lines were divided into five equal segments and scores of from 1 to 5 were assigned for each answer. Scores were summed over items yielding two final scores—one representing reported interest for the sixth grade (items 1 to 20) and the other, interest in the sixth grade as compared with the fifth grade (items 21 to 31). High scores indicate high reported interest and greater interest in sixth than fifth grade.

Standardized Tests of Ability and Achievement. The California Mental Maturity test, regularly given in January to the third and sixth grades as part of normal school procedure, was the measure of intelligence employed in the present study. When both scores were available for a given S, the higher of the two scores was used to define the level of ability. When only one score was available that score was used. As measures of achievement, the scores on the California Achievement Tests for Upper Elementary grades given in January to the fifth and sixth grade were utilized.

Evidence That Experimental Classes Were in Fact More Homogeneous in Ability than Control Classes. It was necessary to examine the assumption that classes defined as homogeneous in ability were, in fact, more homogeneous in ability than the control classes. If homogenization of ability had been accomplished, a student's IQ would be more similar to the median IQ within his class than to the median IQ score of all sixth-grade students in his school. The percentage of students in each of the nine "homogeneous" and ten "heterogeneous" classes whose IQ score was more similar to the median IQ for his class was determined. The resulting percentages were ranked and a Mann-Whitney U test of differences between ranks was computed for the experimental and control classes. The results show that the classes intended to be "homogeneous in ability" were significantly more homogeneous in ability than those intended to be "heterogeneous in ability" ($U = 13.5; p < .02$).

Despite efforts of school personnel to produce classes that were homogeneous in ability, some students with relatively high intelligence were assigned to regular sections, and some students with relatively low intelligence were assigned to the advanced sections. Our examination of IQ distributions showed that if homogenization in terms of IQ alone had been consistently employed, students with an IQ of 125 or above would have been placed in special advanced sections and students with lower IQ scores in regular sections. To sharpen the analysis of differences between experimental and control groups, we have excluded from subsequent analysis those students of the experimental group who were misplaced according to this arbitrary criterion—21 per cent of the experimental group.

The experimental group, as purified by this analysis, consists of students with IQ scores of 125 and above, who had been assigned to special advanced sections and students with IQ scores of 124 and below, who had been assigned to regular sections. In the control group, students having IQ substantially above 125 or below 124 are all members of the same class.

RESULTS

Performance on Achievement Tests. In Table 3, the percentage of students scoring above the median for this sample on the California Achievement Test of Reading and Arithmetic is reported for the fifth and sixth grades. Students in the experimental (homogeneous) and control (heterogeneous) groups are classified according to strength of resultant motivation to achieve.

Table 3

Percentage of students who scored above the median of the sample on California Achievement Tests administered in sixth and fifth grades

n Achievement-Test Anxiety	Homogeneous Classes			Heterogeneous Classes		
		Per Cent Above Median			Per Cent Above Median	
	N	6th	5th	*N*	6th	5th
Reading						
High	(45)	69	58	(64)	69	80
Moderate	(51)	41	45	(71)	45	61
Low	(59)	46	22	(67)	30	42
Arithmetic						
High	(45)	73	44	(64)	67	75
Moderate	(51)	45	37	(71)	42	61
Low	(59)	32	25	(67)	44	45

Note: Median breaks made separately for boys and girls.

Looking at the results for all levels of intelligence combined, we fail to find any marked difference between the homogeneous and heterogeneous groups on sixth-grade achievement tests. The percentage of *S*s at comparable levels of motivation who score above the median on sixth-grade tests is so similar for the two treatments that inspection alone permits the inference of no difference. The only substantial trend on sixth-grade achievement tests is the consistent tendency for *S*s high in resultant motivation to achieve to perform better than those low in resultant motivation to achieve.

Can we conclude from this that the grouping procedure had no effect on scholastic performance? The answer to this question is provided by examination of achievement test scores attained in the fifth grade. At each level of motivation, students who were later assigned to the homogeneous ability groups in sixth grade scored *lower* on the fifth-grade achievement tests of reading and arithmetic than students who continued in heterogeneous classes in sixth grade. In other words, the control group in the present study scored higher on these achievement tests than the experimental group, *before* the grouping procedure had been introduced.

This unanticipated result may be explained in part by the fact that a larger percentage of the control group scored 125 or above on intelligence. Fifty per cent of the heterogeneous group as compared with 37 per cent of the homogeneous group scored that high in intelligence. But this is not a sufficient explanation, for when the scholastic achievements in fifth grade of the three levels of intelligence were considered separately, it was apparent that students in the heterogeneous group generally had an initial advantage.

Considering the proportion of Ss who scored above the median in both years, the *growth* in the homogeneous ability group appears to be greater than in the heterogeneous group. There is a general tendency for a larger proportion of the homogeneous group to score above the median in the sixth than in the fifth grade. Just the opposite is true for Ss in the heterogeneous group.

The marked discrepancy between the initial positions of the experimental and control groups introduced a difficulty in assessing the effects of method of grouping on growth. The most obvious solution to the problem was to determine, for each subject, the number of months gained in grade level between the two testings. Thus a growth of 6.6 to 7.6 would be considered equivalent to a growth of 7.6 to 8.6. This method could be justified only if raw changes in growth were *not* associated with fifth-grade score. To make a rough check on this requirement, the proportion of students whose fifth-grade scores were above and below the median for their sex and who showed above median growth for their sex was determined. This comparison showed that 69 per cent of students with low fifth-grade reading scores showed above median growth, while only 22 per cent of students with high fifth-grade scores showed above median growth. The relationship between fifth-grade arithmetic score and amount of growth was much less pronounced.

It is apparent that the California Achievement Test imposes limitations on measurable growth for the students in this study. In the fifth grade, the median total reading score falls at about the 90th percentile and median total arithmetic score, at about the 80th percentile on national norms. A large percentage of students are performing at a level so high in the fifth grade that little further growth could be demonstrated.

To provide a measure of growth between fifth and sixth grade that would control for initial position, the following steps were taken. An estimate of the mean increase in grade level was determined for students having different initial grade levels in fifth grade. Since students classified moderate in resultant motivation to achieve were not explicitly included in any of the hypotheses to be tested, they were employed to provide an estimate of average growth as related to initial fifth-grade position. The mean growth attained by moderately motivated students classified homogeneous and heterogeneous was weighted equally.

The results of this analysis showed that high score on the fifth-grade achievement tests was associated with low growth between the fifth and sixth grades as measured in school-year units (10 months). The estimates of mean growth associated with initial standing in fifth grade obtained from students moderate in resultant achievement motivation provide a basis for a simple classification of the relative growth shown by all other students. *The amount of growth shown by a student in reading or arithmetic was classified high (meaning above average) if his gain between fifth and sixth grade exceeded the mean gain for persons at a fifth grade level comparable to his own.*

In the subsequent analysis of performance, students classified as moderate in resultant achievement motivation are not considered, since they were employed to provide the criterion of high growth for students with different initial or fifth-grade standing. Furthermore, the analysis is restricted to Ss for whom scores on both achievement tests were available in both fifth and sixth grade and Ss whose fifth grade scores fell within the range of scores for which there were a sufficient number of Ss moderate in achievement motivation to define high or low growth.

The growth shown by each student between the fifth and sixth grades on reading and arithmetic was classified as high (above average for his fifth-grade level) or low (below average for his fifth-grade level). To provide a single overall estimate of growth, each S was classified as showing high growth on both, one or neither of the two achievement tests, California Reading and Arithmetic.

Table 4 presents the final results of this analysis. Subjects are classified with regard to intelligence, motivation, and treatment. Since the more intelligent students showed greater growth in general, the criterion employed in comparisons between intelligent students who differ in

Table 4

Percentage of students showing above median growth in reading and arithmetic on California Achievement Test

n Achievement– Test Anxiety	*N*	Homogeneous Classes Per Cent High	*N*	Heterogeneous Classes Per Cent High
		IQ 125 and Above		
		Both Areas		*Both Areas*
High	(24)	71	(37)	46
Low	(10)	50	(27)	37
		IQ 113–124		*Both or*
		Both or One Area		*One Area*
High	(11)	90	(17)	41
Low	(17)	65	(19)	58
		IQ 112 and Below		
High	(8)	88	(8)	38
Low	(23)	52	(14)	36

High Motivation: Homogeneous versus Heterogeneous

High IQ	3.65
Moderate IQ	6.93
Low IQ	4.00

$$\chi^2 = \overline{14.58} \quad p < .01$$

Low Motivation: Homogeneous versus Heterogeneous

High IQ	.51
Moderate IQ	.18
Low IQ	.95

$$\chi^2 = \overline{1.64} \quad \text{n.s.}$$

Homogeneous Group: High Motivation versus Low Motivation

High IQ	1.34
Moderate IQ	2.45
Low IQ	3.12

$$\chi^2 = \overline{6.91} \quad p < .10$$

(continued)

Heterogeneous Group: High Motivation versus Low Motivation

High IQ	.51
Moderate IQ	1.00*
Low IQ	.00
	n.s.

* Lows exceed Highs.

motivation is more stringent than for the two lower levels of intelligence. Since the results for boys and girls considered separately were similar, the results for boys and girls are combined in a single analysis.

The combined effect of comparisons made separately and evaluated by the chi square test at each level of intelligence confirms the following hypotheses:

1. Students who are high in resultant motivation to achieve (n Achievement-Test Anxiety) show greater growth when assigned to a class that is homogeneous in ability than when assigned to a class that is heterogeneous in ability ($\chi^2 = 14.58$, $df = 3$, $p < .01$).

2. Students who are high in resultant motivation to achieve show greater growth in a homogeneous ability group than students who are low in resultant motivation to achieve ($\chi^2 = 6.91$, $df = 3$, $p < .10$).

There is, however, no support for the hypothesis that homogeneous grouping would be disadvantageous for students low in resultant motivation to achieve. If anything, there is also a tendency for the performance of students low in resultant motivation to achieve to be better under homogeneous than heterogeneous conditions at all levels of intelligence. But the combined effect of these differences is not statistically significant ($\chi^2 = 1.64$, $df = 3$, n.s.)

Finally, there is no evidence that the difference in resultant motivation to achieve had any effect on growth between fifth and sixth grade in the heterogeneous classes. The observed differences are small, inconsistent, and not statistically significant. No formal hypothesis was stated concerning effect of motivation on growth in the heterogeneous group, because the method of grouping did not differ for them. Hence, there was no reason to suppose that motivation would have a *differential* effect on performance in the fifth and sixth grades. This does not mean that achievement-related motivation had no effect on their scholastic achievement. Table 3 has already shown the generally expected effect of the difference in motivation on level of performance in both the fifth and sixth grades. Table 4, in contrast, shows evidence of differential *growth* only within the classes that are homogeneous in ability.

Reported Interest in Schoolwork. Since girls tended to score higher than boys òn the interest questionnaire, scores were divided at the median for each sex separately before combining the results. Considering the results for all students in the homogeneous and heterogeneous groups without regard to differences in motivation, there is no evidence that either treatment produces greater overall interest in present activities or greater change of interest between fifth and sixth grades. Forty-nine per cent of Ss in the heterogeneous group and 44 per cent in the homogeneous group score high (above the median) in present interest ($\chi^2 = .66$), and 50 per cent of each group score high (above the median) on interest in sixth-grade compared with interest in fifth grade. When interest of Ss who differ in achievement motivation is considered, however, it is evident that homogeneous grouping *does* produce substantial differences in degree of interest that are related to the motivational dispositions of students.

Table 5

Percentage of students high, moderate, and low in resultant achievement motivation reporting above median interest in sixth-grade activities

n Achievement-Test Anxiety	Homogeneous Classes		Heterogeneous Classes	
	N^*	Per Cent Above Median	N	Per Cent Above Median
High	(18)	61	(78)	53
Moderate	(22)	55	(82)	44
Low	(22)	18	(73)	51
			χ^2	p (one-tail)
Homogeneous: high versus low motivation			7.78	$<.005$
Heterogeneous: high versus low motivation			.15	—
High motivation: homogeneous versus heterogeneous			.31	—
Low motivation: heterogeneous versus homogeneous			7.28	$<.005$

* The interest questionnaire was introduced in the second year of the study, and was therefore obtained from only one of the homogeneous ability-grouped classes.

Table 5 shows the predicted higher interest of Ss high in resultant achievement motivation as compared with those low in resultant achievement motivation within the homogeneous group ($\chi^2 = 7.78$, $p < .005$). Individual differences in achievement-related motivation do not, however, influence interest in the heterogeneous groups. There is a slight tendency for Ss high in motivation to report higher interest in the homogeneous group, but this difference is not significant ($\chi^2 = .31$, n.s.). On the other hand, the hypothesis that Ss low in resultant achievement motivation would respond to the more competitive situation as less attractive is confirmed in the comparison between comparable groups in the homogeneous and heterogeneous classes ($\chi^2 = 7.28$, $p < .005$).

Table 6

Percentage of students high, moderate, and low in resultant
achievement motivation reporting above median
interest in sixth as compared with fifth grade

	Homogeneous Classes		Heterogeneous Classes	
n Achievement-Test Anxiety	N	Per Cent Above Median	N	Per Cent Above Median
High	(18)	78	(78)	56
Moderate	(22)	41	(82)	43
Low	(22)	36	(73)	52
			χ^2	p (one-tail)
Homogeneous: high versus low motivation			6.86	$<.005$
Heterogeneous: high versus low motivation			.29	—
High motivation: homogeneous versus heterogeneous			2.79	$<.05$
Low motivation: heterogeneous versus homogeneous			1.67	$<.10$

In Table 6 parallel comparisons are made for reported interest in general activities of sixth grade, relative to interest in similar activities in fifth grade. Again we find that interest is positively related to resultant motivation to achieve in the homogeneous classes ($\chi^2 = 6.86$, $p < .005$) but not in the heterogeneous classes. The trends shown by the high and low motivation groups between the two treatments are consistent with our hypotheses. Students who are strong in resultant motivation to achieve report significantly greater interest in sixth as compared to fifth grades when they are in homogeneous ability-grouped classes ($\chi^2 = 2.79$, $p < .05$ (one-tail test)). Students low in resultant motivation to achieve report near significantly less interest in sixth as compared to fifth grade when they are in homogeneous ability-grouped classes ($\chi^2 = 1.67$, $p < .10$ (one-tail test)).

Although the number of cases is small in the homogeneous group, it is important to determine whether or not the level of ability of students influences the findings. The theory of achievement motivation implies that motivation will be associated with reported interest in the same manner for students in the advanced and the regular sections, since in all sections the level of ability is more homogeneous than in the control group. However, it might be argued that the advanced and regular sections differ in status. Since high motivation tends to be associated with high intelligence, the obtained results concerning interest could be generated by bright children, who tend to be highly motivated, finding greater satisfaction in the high-status class and other children, tending to be lower in motivation, finding less satisfaction in a class with low status. To examine this possibility, the results for high IQ students in advanced sections and lower IQ students in regular sections were examined separately in relation to their respective control groups in the traditional heterogeneous classes. Table 7 shows that the effect of homogeneous ability grouping on the interest of students who are high and low in resultant motivation to achieve is present among both highly intelligent students placed in special advanced sections and less intelligent students in regular sections.

Table 7

Percentage of students high, moderate, and low in resultant achievement motivation reporting above median interest in sixth as compared with fifth grade. Students of high, moderate, and low intelligence reported separately

n Achievement–Test Anxiety	*N*	Homogeneous Classes Per Cent Above Median	*N*	Heterogeneous Classes Per Cent Above Median
		High IQ		
High	(6)	67	(45)	60
Moderate	(11)	27	(39)	44
Low	(5)	40	(31)	61
		Moderate and Low IQ		
High	(12)	83	(33)	51
Moderate	(11)	55	(43)	42
Low	(17)	35	(42)	45

DISCUSSION

The results of this investigation indicate that placement in homogeneous ability groups does not lead to general enhancement or decline in interest or learning. Rather, motivational dispositions of the individual interact with treatment so that the effect for some students is advantageous and for others disadvantageous. Students high in resultant achievement motivation (i.e., High n Achievement and Low Test Anxiety) show greater growth in scholastic achievement and greater interest in school work given the challenge of an ability-grouped class. Those low in resultant achievement motivation (the more anxious students) show a decline in interest when placed in the homogeneous ability groups, but no marked difference in scholastic achievement. It would appear that they perform as well as before but at greater personal cost.

Differences associated with motivation are obtained both for students of high ability placed in special advanced sections and for students of lower ability placed in homogenized regular sections. If these results are confirmed in subsequent studies, it would appear that achievement motivation should become one of the more important factors to be considered in determining which students should be assigned to homogeneous ability groups to maximize interest and learning.

Under natural circumstances, the motivational impact of ability grouping is experienced by students in the upper quarter of a high school class, when they later constitute the freshman class at college, and then again when members of the upper quarter of the senior class of the college find themselves classmates in graduate school. This sometimes would account for the phenomenon of the "late blooming" student who finds himself finally challenged at college and also the often inexplicable academic difficulties confronted by students of high ability when surrounded by equally talented peers for the first time.

SUMMARY

Hypotheses derived from the theory of achievement motivation were tested in sixth-grade classes in which ability grouping had been introduced. An ability-grouped class was conceived as one in which the probabilities of success and failure were more nearly equal for most students than one in which ability grouping had not been imposed. It was predicted that ability grouping would have differential effects on growth as measured by standardized tests of achievement and on interest in schoolwork depending upon the relative strength of motive to achieve and disposition to be anxious about failure. Results supported the prediction that students who were relatively high in *n* Achievement would show greater interest and enhancement in learning when they were grouped by ability than when they were not. Ability grouping did *not* produce the expected decrement in performance among students who were relatively high in Test Anxiety, but there was evidence of a significant decline in interest in schoolwork among anxious students placed in ability-grouped classes.

PART IV

Critical Problems

n Achievement, Test Anxiety, and Subjective Probability of Success in Risk-Taking Behavior

This study is one of a series of studies designed to validate a theoretical model (Chapter 2) relating individual differences in motivation and risk-taking behavior. . . .

The present experiment is designed to extend earlier research in two ways. First, subjective probability of success will be measured directly by asking the subject to state his confidence in a decision he must make. Second, by use of a sequential decision task in which the probability of success goes from low to high as the subject is presented with more relevant information, it is possible to derive a new hypothesis from the Atkinson model relevant to changes in subjective probability of success. This experiment seeks to obtain data relevant to the following questions:

1. Will subjects tend to make decisions at levels of subjective probability of success that will maximize their resultant motivation?
2. What are the effects of n Achievement and Test Anxiety on overall levels of subjective probability of success?
3. What is the relationship between resultant motivation and changes in the subjective probability of success as it goes from low to high?

As subjects for whom it is assumed the motive to achieve success is greater than the motive to avoid failure go from levels of subjective probability of success below .5 to .5, they should tend to increase their resultant motivation. However, any increase in subjective probability

Reprinted with some abridgement by permission of the author and the American Psychological Association from the *Journal of Abnormal and Social Psychology*, 1963, **66**, 413–418.

of success beyond .5 should result in a decrease in resultant motivation for these subjects. If it is assumed that subjects tend to state a subjective probability of success that will maximize their resultant motivation, we should expect that subjects for whom it is assumed the motive to achieve success is greater than the motive to avoid failure should increase subjective probability of success rapidly up to a level of subjective probability of success of .5, and should then tend to decrease their rate of increase in subjective probability of success after a level of subjective probability of success of .5 is reached. Subjects for whom it is assumed the motive to avoid failure is greater than the motive to achieve success should show the opposite pattern of changes in subjective probability of success.

METHOD

Subjects. One hundred and fifteen male subjects were obtained from the introductory psychology course at the University of Michigan during the fall semester of the 1959–1960 academic year. Subjects were run in groups that varied in size from 5 to 10.

Procedure. The experimenter and a female assistant were present during the test session. The subjects were told they were to be given a series of tests. The *n* Achievement Test was then administered with standard neutral instructions (McClelland, Atkinson, Clark, and Lowell, 1953, p. 98). Pictures 2, 5, 9, and 24 were presented in that order (Atkinson, 1958a). The Test Anxiety Questionnaire (TAQ) was then given.

After the subjects had completed the TAQ they were presented with a lithographed booklet entitled *Michigan Decision-Making Abilities Test.* The subjects were then presented with a standard probability learning experiment after the method of Jarvik (1951).[1]

Sequential Decision Experiment. The following printed instruction appeared in the test booklet:

This is another test of decision-making ability. Please write your name and code number in the space provided.

The test administrator has a deck which contains 50 cards. The deck definitely contains circles and may have in addition a certain number of squares. These are the only kinds of cards which the deck can have. The deck is well shuffled and the cards are not placed in any kind of order. You will have to decide how many circles there are in the entire deck. There can be either 5, 10, 15, 20, 25, 30, 35, 40, 45, or 50 circles in the deck. One of

---

[1] The results of the probability learning experiment will not be discussed in this paper. They are not relevant to the theory and data analysis being discussed here.

these ten possibilities is the correct answer. The cards will be shown to you one at a time. *You will be allowed only a single decision.* It is up to you to decide when the best time to make your decision has been reached. You can make your decision at any point in the presentation of cards. Your performance will be evaluated by a scoring system. You will receive more points for a correct decision if you make it earlier in the series. In other words, the sooner you make your decision, the more points you will receive if it is correct. However, you will receive zero points if the decision you make is incorrect. Obviously, the more cards you look at, the better chance you will have to make the correct decision. On the other hand, the longer you delay your decision, the fewer the number of points you will receive for the correct decision.

There is a second part to this experiment. Before each card is presented to you, you should check the appropriate position on the 100-point confidence scale. This should represent your confidence in the correctness of your decision if you had to make it before the next card is shown to you. Be sure you check all fifty of these scales at the appropriate time. *Remember you are allowed only a single decision.* When you feel that the best time to make your decision has arrived, write your decision next to the confidence scale for the coming trial. For example, if you wish to make your decision after the fortieth card is shown to you, place your answer next to the 41st scale. Feel free to ask any question you may have about these instructions.

The subjects recorded their responses on a set of 50 11-point scales with the 0, 50, and 100% positions marked. Each confidence response was assigned 1 of 21 values from 0 to 100 in units of 5.

Treatment of Data. Of the 115 subjects who were selected from the subject pool, 93 arrived for the experimental sessions. Two subjects were discarded from the analysis, as they came late and completed only part of the *n* Achievement Test. The TAQ was scored by a procedure outlined by Atkinson and Litwin (Chapter 5). The *n* Achievement Test was scored by the writer. The *n* Achievement Test was scored again by the writer after a three-month period. The rank-order test-retest correlation was .93 ($N = 91$). The product-moment correlation between *n* Achievement and TAQ was .05 ($N = 91$), a result previously reported by Atkinson and Litwin, and Feather (1960), indicating no relationship between these measures under neutral conditions.

Subjects were assigned to motive groups on the basis of their scores on the two motive measures. The groups were composed, respectively, of subjects who scored above the median in *n* Achievement and in the highest quartile of the TAQ ($N = 11$); above the median in *n* Achievement and in the lowest quartile of the TAQ ($N = 13$); below the median in *n* Achievement and in the highest quartile of the TAQ ($N = 11$); and below the median in *n* Achievement and in the lowest quartile of the TAQ ($N = 9$).

RESULTS

Confidence statements between 30 and 70 were selected *a priori* to represent intermediate levels of subjective probability of success. The number of subjects in each motive group who made their decision when their confidence levels were between 30 and 70 or less than 30 and above 70 was obtained. There was no tendency for subjects for whom it is assumed the motive to achieve success is greater than the motive to avoid failure to decide at confidence levels between 30 and 70 more often than subjects for whom it is assumed the motive to avoid failure is greater than the motive to achieve success. (Four of the 13 subjects in the High *n* Achievement-Low Test Anxiety group decided at levels of confidence between 30 and 70, and 4 of the 11 subjects in the Low *n* Achievement-High Test Anxiety group decided at levels of confidence between 30 and 70.) A further examination of confidence at the trial of decision was made by obtaining the distribution of confidence statements for all subjects at the trial of decision. Table 1 presents the number of subjects in each motive group who made their decision in the first, second and third, and fourth quartiles of the distribution of reported confidence at the trial of decision.

Table 1

Number of subjects in first, second, third, and fourth quartiles of the distribution of reported confidence at the trial of decision

n Achievement	Test Anxiety	Q_1 (100)	Q_4 (<65)	$Q_{2 \text{ and } 3}$ (65–95)
High	High	7	1	3
High	Low	2	0	11
Low	High	3	4	4
Low	Low	0	4	5

The Low *n* Achievement-High Test Anxiety subjects tend to decide in the first and fourth quartiles of the distribution while the High *n* Achievement-Low Test Anxiety subjects tend to decide in the intermediate quartiles of the distribution. This difference is statistically significant by a one-tailed Fisher exact test ($p < .05$). It is of some interest to see whether the significant difference between these two groups is attributable to either or both of the motivational variables, *n*

Achievement and Test Anxiety. A comparison between the High *n* Achievement and Low *n* Achievement subjects in tendency to make their decisions in the intermediate quartiles yields a nonsignificant χ^2 ($\chi^2 = .80$, $df = 1$, $p > .05$). A comparison between the High Test Anxiety subjects and Low Test Anxiety subjects in tendency to decide in the intermediate quartiles of the distribution yields a significant χ^2 ($\chi^2 = 7.38$, $df = 1$, $p < .01$). The Test Anxiety variable is therefore the major contributor to the significant difference between the High *n* Achievement-Low Test Anxiety and Low *n* Achievement-High Test Anxiety groups.

The intermediate quartiles of the distribution of reported confidence at the trial of decision fall within a confidence range between 65 and 95. Consequently, although the High *n* Achievement-Low Test Anxiety subjects tend to decide in the intermediate quartiles of the distribution, their decisions tend to occur at levels that are higher than would be expected on the basis of Atkinson's model. One possible explanation for these unexpected results involves Festinger's (1957) theory of cognitive dissonance. The subject is instructed to write his decision next to the confidence scale for the following trial. Consequently, the confidence statements at the trial of decision actually are postdecisional measures of confidence and may be increased by the subject's attempt to reduce postdecisional cognitive dissonance. In order to test for this possibility, the confidence statements at the trial preceding the trial of decision were examined. The confidence statements at this trial are presumably uninfluenced by postdecisional attempts to reduce cognitive dissonance. The mean confidence at the trial preceding the trial of decision for the High *n* Achievement-Low Test Anxiety subjects is 78.1. Therefore, these subjects are still substantially above the theoretically expected level of subjective probability of success of .5. Furthermore, the mean trial at which 50% confidence is reached is 18.1 for the High *n* Achievement-Low Test Anxiety subjects, and the mean trial of decision for these subjects is 27.3. Consequently, the High *n* Achievement-Low Test Anxiety subjects are deciding on the average about nine trials after they have reached the 50% confidence level. These analyses of confidence at the trial preceding the trial of decision indicate that the unexpectedly high values of confidence at the trial of decision for the High *n* Achievement-Low Test Anxiety subjects cannot be attributable solely to the effects of postdecisional cognitive dissonance.

A plot of the mean confidence over trials by trial blocks of 12, 13, 13, and 12 is presented for each of the motive groups in Figure 1. Examination of Figure 1 shows that the two High *n* Achievement groups tend to have higher confidence ratings than the two Low *n* Achieve-

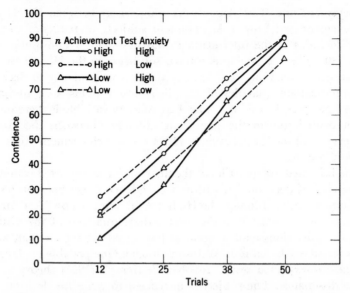

Figure 1   Mean confidence in four motive groups by trial blocks of 12, 13, 13, and 12.

ment groups. Differences in Test Anxiety do not appear to be consistently related to the overall level of confidence ratings.

The inferences drawn from the qualitative analysis of data in Figure 1 are statistically supported by an analysis of variance performed on the mean confidence over all trials for each subject. Table 2 presents a summary of this analysis.

The analysis presented in Table 2 leads to two conclusions: High n Achievement tends to increase the overall level of subjective probability of success. Test Anxiety is unrelated to the overall level of subjective probability of success. An analysis of variance performed on the confidence statements at the trial of decision reveals the same pattern of results. That is, High n Achievement subjects tend to have higher confidence at the trial of decision than Low n Achievement subjects (F for n Achievement $= 7.87$, $df = 1/36$, $p < .01$). In the analysis of variance of confidence at the trial of decision, only the n Achievement variable is significant.

The final analysis is concerned with differential rates of increase in confidence up to the 50% confidence level and after the 50% level of confidence has been attained. Data for the statistical analysis of rates of change in subjective probability of success were obtained in the following manner: First, the rate of increase in confidence up to the stated

Table 2

Analysis of variance of mean confidence ratings

Source		df	MS	F
Anxiety (A)		1	58.1	<1
Achievement (Ach)		1	1047.7	5.74*
Ach $\times$ A		1	43.9	<1
Error		28	182.6	
	Total	31		

Note: Three subjects were discarded from the High *n* Achievement-High Test Anxiety group and one subject was discarded from the Low *n* Achievement-Low Test Anxiety group. These four subjects checked their confidence ratings in terms of an incorrect decision they had made, rather than the decision they would make. They all ended the task with 0 confidence. In order to achieve orthogonality, this analysis is performed on a random sample of eight subjects drawn from each motive group.

* $p < .05$.

level of confidence of 50% was obtained by dividing the trial number at which a confidence value equal to or greater than 50 was first attained, by 50. Second, the rate of increase in confidence after the 50% level was obtained by dividing the difference between the trial number at which the highest confidence was first attained and the trial number at which a confidence level of at least 50 was first attained, by the highest level of confidence attained minus 50. Finally, the second measure was subtracted from the first. When the resulting value is negative, the growth rate of confidence has been more rapid up to 50% confidence than after 50% of confidence has been reached. Table 3 presents the mean values of this measure for the four motive groups.

A one-tailed *t* test comparing the High *n* Achievement-Low Test Anxiety subjects with the Low *n* Achievement-High Test Anxiety subjects on the rate measures reported in Table 3 reveals that they are significantly different ($t = 1.72$, $df = 22$, $p < .05$). This finding indicates that subjects for whom it is assumed the motive to achieve success is greater than the motive to avoid failure tend to approach .50 subjective probability of success rapidly, and then decrease their rate of increase in subjective probability of success, relative to subjects for whom it is assumed the motive to achieve success is less than the motive to avoid failure. As in the case of the analysis of the data presented in Table 1, it is of interest to discover the contribution of the two

Table 3

Means for analysis of differential growth rate of confidence before and after
a subjective probability of success of .50 is reached

| n Achievement | Test Anxiety | | |
	High	Low	
High	.01	—.08	—.04
Low	.21	.07	+.15
	.11	—.02	

motivational variables, n Achievement and Test Anxiety, to the significant difference that has been obtained. The one-tailed t test comparing the High n Achievement subjects with the Low n Achievement subjects for the rate measure presented in Table 3 reveals a significant difference ($t = 1.76$, $df = 42$, $p < .05$). The t test comparing the Low Test Anxiety subjects with the High Test Anxiety subjects is nonsignificant ($t = 1.31$, $df = 42$, $p > .05$).

DISCUSSION

The results of this experiment are equivocal in support of the suggested theoretical relationship between subjective probability of success and resultant motivation in different motive groups. The data on changes in confidence tend to support the theoretical relationship suggested by Atkinson's model. However, the data on confidence at the trial of decision are only equivocal in support of the theoretical relationship. These results are in agreement with those of Atkinson and Litwin (Chapter 5) in that High n Achievement-Low Anxiety subjects tend to take intermediate risks when intermediate is defined in terms of the median of the frequency distribution of goal setting behaviors. However, intermediate goal setting, as measured by confidence statements, does not coincide with the theoretically expected value of .5. If these results are replicated in other risk-taking situations, they would suggest that subjects for whom it is assumed the motive to achieve success is greater than the motive to avoid failure prefer intermediate risks, but do not necessarily prefer situations where the subjective probability of success is .5.

The finding that n Achievement positively relates to subjective probability of success supports the previous research of Pottharst (1955) and Atkinson, Bastian, Earl, and Litwin (1960). There has been no previous research on the effect of Test Anxiety on subjective probability of success. Therefore, the results neither contradict nor support past research, but they fail to support Atkinson's (Chapter 2) conjecture that high Test Anxiety would decrease the overall level of subjective probability of success.

SUMMARY

This study was concerned with the effects of *n* Achievement and Test Anxiety on risk-taking behavior and subjective probability of success in a sequential decision task. The principle findings were as follows: *S*s who scored high on *n* Achievement and low on Test Anxiety tended to make their decisions in the intermediate quartiles of the distribution of reported confidence at the trial of decision more often than *S*s who scored high in Test Anxiety and low in *n* Achievement. High *n* Achievement tends to bias the overall level of subjective probability of success upward. *S*s who scored high in *n* Achievement and low in Test Anxiety tended to increase confidence rapidly up to the level of 50% confidence, and then decrease their rate of increase in confidence after the 50% level of confidence had been attained, in comparison to *S*s who scored low in *n* Achievement and high in Test Anxiety.

17. N. T. FEATHER

The Relationship of Expectation of Success to n Achievement and Test Anxiety

In a recent investigation (Feather, 1963a), subjects were required to estimate their chances of successfully completing an anagrams task prior to actual performance. They were provided with fictitious information about the average probability of success of a peer group who had performed the task in the past. The results indicated that subjects' initial estimates of probability of success at the task were *positively* related to facilitating anxiety and *negatively* related to debilitating anxiety as assessed by the Achievement Anxiety Test (Alpert and Haber, 1960). The correlations were very low, but in the predicted direction. Initial estimates of probability of success were not, however, positively related to n Achievement assessed by the TAT procedure. It is possible that this predicted positive relationship would appear in a test situation where instructions imply that success at the task is by no means certain and where there are fewer reality constraints than in the situation investigated in the previous study. The experiment reported in the present paper was designed to explore this possibility.

The present experiment is a modification of a study by Sarason (1961) in which he examined the effect of the interaction of instructions and anxiety on the solution of a difficult task (namely, solving complex anagrams). Sarason used two different sets of instructions. Subjects given the first set were told that solving anagrams is directly related to intelligence level. But they were also informed that high school students of above average intelligence, and most college students, should be able to complete the task successfully in the time allowed. Subjects

Reprinted by permission of the author and the American Psychological Association from the *Journal of Personality and Social Psychology*, 1965, 1, 118–126. Parts of this paper were written while the author was Visiting Scientist and Research Associate at the University of Michigan under the sponsorship of the Institute of Science and Technology and the National Science Foundation (Project GS-9 on "Determinants of Human Choice," under the direction of J. W. Atkinson and J. David Birch.)

given the second set of instructions were told that the anagrams were harder than most and that they may not be able to finish all of them. We assume that these instructions influence subjects' initial expectations of success so that those given the first set of instructions begin the task with a high expectation of success, believing it to be easy and well within their competence, while those given the second set of instructions begin the task with a lower expectation of success, believing it to be moderately difficult. If we assume that expectations of success in this second condition are relatively closer to a 50–50 subjective probability of success (P_s), then it follows from Atkinson's model (Chapter 2) that both achievement motivation and motivation to avoid failure would be elicited at greater strength when the second set of instructions is employed.

It is predicted that subjects' initial estimates of probability of success at the task will be *positively* related to *n* Achievement where the task is presented as moderately difficult (i.e., where achievement motivation is assumed to be elicited at a relatively high level). The positive relationship may be less evident, however, where the task is presented as easy (i.e., where strength of achievement motivation is assumed to be relatively weak). The basis of the above prediction is that presented in the previous paper (Feather, 1963a). Specifically, it is assumed that subjects high in *n* Achievement have in the past performed relatively better than subjects low in *n* Achievement, in situations where achievement motivation has been aroused (Atkinson, 1958a; McClelland, 1961), particularly where it has been aroused at a high level. This superiority in past performance would act as a frame of reference to determine relatively higher initial expectations of success among subjects high in *n* Achievement when they come to a task which can be seen as providing the opportunity for exercising personal skill and the possibility of a praiseworthy accomplishment.

In line with the results of the previous study (Feather, 1963a), we also predict that subjects' initial estimates of probability of success at the task will be negatively related to Test Anxiety assessed by the Test Anxiety Questionnaire (Mandler and Sarason, 1952), since Test Anxiety scores and debilitating anxiety scores are positively correlated (Alpert and Haber, 1960). This negative relationship may be rather more apparent where the task is presented as moderately difficult (i.e., where motivation to avoid failure is assumed to be elicited at a relatively high level). This prediction is based on the assumption that, when the task is complex, subjects high in Test Anxiety have generally performed less well in stressful situations than subjects low in Test Anxiety (Mandler and Sarason, 1952; Sarason, 1961; Sarason, 1963), particularly when a high level of motivation to avoid failure has been aroused.

This inferior past performance would tend to determine relatively lower initial expectations of success among subjects high in Test Anxiety when they are presented with a complex task under test conditions.

Finally, we assume that once subjects are involved in performance of a task, the frequency and patterning of their actual successes and failures will become the dominant influence in shaping their expectations. Hence the predicted relationships between estimates of probability of success and either *n* Achievement or Test Anxiety should become less apparent once expectations of success have been modified by task performance (cf., Feather, 1963c).

METHOD

Subjects were 168 male, external students attending a vacation school in psychology at the University of New England in 1962.[1] These subjects first completed the Test Anxiety Questionnaire (Mandler and Sarason, 1952). A subject's Test Anxiety score was obtained by summing his scores on the individual items of the Test Anxiety Questionnaire. As in previous investigations (e.g., Feather, 1963b) these item scores were obtained by dividing the rating scale for each item into five equal parts and by scoring responses from one to five in the direction of increasing anxiety.

One week after administration of the Test Anxiety Questionnaire subjects were tested for *n* Achievement under neutral conditions according to the standard procedure (McClelland, et al., 1953). The following four pictures were presented: 2, 48, 1, and 7 (using numbers assigned by Atkinson (1958a)). Interscorer reliability[2] for scoring the TAT *n* Achievement was $r = .89$.

Following the measurement of *n* Achievement, subjects were presented with an anagrams test. Two different sets of instructions, corresponding to those used by Sarason (1961), were randomly distributed among subjects to vary initial expectation of success. In the Moderately Difficult experimental condition the instructions were as follows:

> On the next page you will see a set of disarranged words (anagrams). Your job will be to rearrange each group of letters so that they make a meaningful word. Start when you are so instructed. Stop at the stop signal.
>
> Most of you probably have worked anagrams. The task on the next page works the same way. These anagrams, however, are harder than most you have seen in books and magazines. Consequently, you may not finish all of

---

[1] The total group was split into two separate groups of approximately equal size for purposes of testing.

[2] The writer wishes to thank Graeme Halford for his assistance in the reliability check.

them, and you may find some of the anagrams very difficult. If this happens, don't worry about it. No one will find the anagrams easy.

In the Easy experimental condition the instructions were the same as above, except for the second paragraph, which was as follows:

Ability to organize material such as the letters on the next page has been found to be directly related to intelligence level. High school students of above average intelligence (IQ greater than 100) and most college students should be able successfully to complete the task. You will have 18 minutes in which to complete it.

Before commencing the task all subjects were required to estimate their chances of solving all the anagrams by checking a 5-inch scale numbered from 0 to 100 in equal steps of twenty, with the statement, "No chance at all" at one extreme of the scale; the statement, "An even chance" at the middle of the scale; and the statement, "Completely certain" at the other extreme of the scale. This procedure provided a measure of a subject's expectation of success prior to task performance. In a postperformance questionnaire subjects were also required to estimate what they considered their chances of success to be when they had worked at the test for 9–10 minutes (about half the total time allowed), and just before they were asked to stop working at the test. This procedure provided measures of a subject's "middle" and "terminal" expectations of success (i.e., expectations modified by task performance).

All subjects worked for 18 minutes at the same set of 13 difficult anagrams, which are listed in Sarason's report (1961). Eighty-two subjects worked under the instructions for the Moderately Difficult condition; 86 subjects worked under the instructions for the Easy condition.

The mean n Achievement and Test Anxiety scores for subjects in the Moderately Difficult and Easy conditions were as follows: for the Moderately Difficult condition, mean n Achievement = 4.49, SD = 4.04, mean Test Anxiety = 95.82, SD = 25.59; for the Easy condition, mean n Achievement = 2.92, SD = 4.37, mean Test Anxiety = 96.21, SD = 28.78.[3]

RESULTS

Table 1 presents the correlations of initial, middle, and terminal probability estimates with n Achievement and Test Anxiety scores for

---

[3] The mean n Achievement score of subjects in the Moderately Difficult condition is significantly greater than the mean n Achievement score of subjects in the Easy condition. Since subjects were randomly assigned to each condition, this difference may be considered accidental rather than as reflecting a systematic influence. When the n Achievement distributions are matched by deleting subjects, the analysis of results indicates the same trends as described below, but the relationships involving n Achievement scores are somewhat attenuated because of the restriction in the range of n Achievement scores.

Table 1

Correlations of probability estimates with n achievement and test anxiety for moderately difficult ($N = 82$) and easy ($N = 86$) experimental conditions

Probability Estimate	Moderately Difficult Condition		Easy Condition	
	n Achievement	Test Anxiety	n Achievement	Test Anxiety
Initial	.20*	−.27†	−.20	−.39‡
Middle	.12	−.04	−.14	−.19
Terminal	−.05	−.06	−.11	−.03

* $p < .05$, one-tailed test
† $p < .01$, one-tailed test
‡ $p < .0005$, one-tailed test

both experimental conditions. Initial probability estimates were those obtained prior to task performance. Middle and terminal probability estimates were those obtained in the postperformance questionnaire, and related to the middle and terminal stages of performance. Table 2

Table 2

Mean initial probability estimates in relation to n Achievement

n Achievement	Moderately Difficult Condition			Easy Condition		
	M	SD	N	M	SD	N
High	.45	.23	19	.56	.30	13
Upper Middle	.45	.19	22	.56	.11	21
Lower Middle	.40	.23	27	.55	.18	19
Low	.30	.19	14	.63	.23	33

presents mean initial probability estimates for approximate quarters of the *total* distribution of n Achievement scores. n Achievement scores of 8 and above were classified as High, from 4 to 7 as Upper Middle, from 1 to 3 as Lower Middle, and below 1 as Low. Table 3 presents mean initial probability estimates for approximate quarters of the *total* distribution of Test Anxiety scores. Test Anxiety scores of 117 and above were classified as High, 96 to 116 as Upper Middle, 75 to 95 as Lower Middle, and below 75 as Low.

Table 3

Mean initial probability estimates in relation to Test Anxiety

Test Anxiety	Moderately Difficult Condition			Easy Condition		
	M	SD	N	M	SD	N
High	.29	.17	18	.45	.23	20
Upper Middle	.40	.17	22	.60	.16	22
Lower Middle	.47	.25	22	.60	.24	22
Low	.45	.24	20	.69	.16	22

In general, the results shown in Tables 1, 2, and 3 support the predictions. In the first place, Table 1 indicates that initial probability estimates and n Achievement scores are positively correlated in the Moderately Difficult condition ($r = .20$, $df = 80$, $p < .05$). This positive relationship is also apparent in Table 2, where the mean initial probability estimate for the Moderately Difficult condition is greater when n Achievement is high than when it is low. These results imply that, in a situation which is assumed to elicit a relatively high level of achievement motivation, subjects high in n Achievement tend to have relatively higher expectations of success prior to task performance. Initial probability estimates and n Achievement scores are not positively related in the Easy condition. In fact, the relationship is negative ($r = -.20$), and would be statistically significant if a one-tailed test were applied. This negative relationship is also evident in Table 2, where the mean initial probability estimate for the Easy condition is less when n Achievement is high than when it is low. The correlation of initial probability estimates with n Achievement scores differs significantly between the two experimental conditions ($z = 2.58$, $p < .01$). These results imply that in a situation which is assumed to elicit a relatively low level of achievement motivation, subjects low in n Achievement may tend to have relatively higher expectations of success prior to task performance.

An important assumption involved in the foregoing prediction is that subjects should tend to perceive the task in the Moderately Difficult condition as fairly difficult, as one which permits the opportunity for personal accomplishment which can be evaluated against standards of excellence. In contrast, we assume that subjects should tend to perceive the task in the Easy condition as relatively easy, as one for which successful performance should be possible for most people. In terms of the theory (Chapter 2), these assumptions imply that a higher level of achievement motivation would be elicited in the Moderately Difficult condition. The results do indicate that the mean initial probability estimate is significantly lower in the Moderately Difficult condition ($M = .41$ for Moderately Difficult condition, $M = .59$ for Easy condition, $F = 27.77$, $df = 1/166$, $p < .001$). Hence the different instructions appear to have determined the expected difference in subjects' initial expectations of success, although the mean initial probability estimate in the Easy condition is not as high as we had anticipated. According to Atkinson's model, P_s values of .41 and .59 would be associated with *equal* levels of achievement motivation for an individual in a test situation. The results do indicate, however, that there is a significant positive correlation in the Moderately Difficult condition ($r = .25$, $df = 80$, $p < .025$, one-tailed test) between performance scores (number of anagrams correctly solved) and n Achievement scores, but no significant relationship between these scores in the Easy condition ($r = -.11$, $df = 84$, n.s.). This result suggests that in an achievement situation where a deliberate attempt is made to reduce anxiety about failure by reassurance (as in the Moderately Difficult condition), a positive relationship between n Achievement scores and performance may be more apparent.

Table 1 also shows that initial probability estimates and Test Anxiety scores are negatively correlated in the Moderately Difficult condition ($r = -.27$, $df = 80$, $p < .01$) and in the Easy condition ($r = -.39$, $df = 84$, $p < .0005$). This negative relationship is also evident in Table 3 where the mean initial probability estimates for both Moderately Difficult and Easy conditions are less when Test Anxiety is high than when it is low. These results are consistent with predictions and with the evidence of the previous study (Feather, 1963a). They imply that subjects high in Test Anxiety tend to have relatively lower expectations of success prior to performance of a complex task in a test situation. Contrary to prediction, there is no evidence that the negative correlation between initial probability estimates and Test Anxiety is higher in the Moderately Difficult condition. In fact, the reverse occurs although the difference in correlations is not statistically significant. The lower negative correlation in the Moderately Difficult condition may reflect the influence of the greater reassurance provided by the instructions for this condition. Subjects were told not to worry if they encountered some very difficult anagrams. This instruction would tend to reduce anxiety about failure. Such a reassuring instruction may have the effect of reducing the magnitude of the negative incentive value of failure (I_f) across the entire range of subjective probabilities (P_f), and hence would determine lower levels of motivation to avoid failure. This would be an example of a situational effect on value (Feather, 1959a, Chapter 3).

Table 4

Mean initial probability estimates in relation to n Achievement and Test Anxiety

n Achievement	Test Anxiety	Moderately Difficult Condition			Easy Condition		
		M	SD	N	M	SD	N
High	High	.43	.14	20	.56	.19	19
High	Low	.47	.25	21	.56	.22	15
Low	High	.28	.18	20	.51	.21	23
Low	Low	.45	.23	21	.68	.19	29

In Table 4 mean initial probability estimates are presented for the simultaneous classification of n Achievement and Test Anxiety. Subjects are classified as high or low in n Achievement or Test Anxiety according to whether they are above or below the median of the respective total distribution of scores. n Achievement scores of 4 and above are classified as high, below 4 as low. Test Anxiety scores of 96 and above are classified as high, below 96 as low.

Table 4 represents the joint influence of n Achievement and Test Anxiety. The mean initial probability estimates differ significantly for both the Moderately Difficult condition ($F = 3.37$, $df = 3/78$, $p < .05$) and the Easy condition ($F = 3.28$, $df = 3/82$, $p < .05$). For both experimental conditions, subjects classified as high in n Achievement and low in Test Anxiety tend to have higher initial probability estimates than subjects classified as low in n Achievement and high in Test Anxiety; although this difference is negligible in the Easy condition where it is overshadowed by the relatively high mean initial probability estimate for subjects classified as low in both n Achievement and Test Anxiety. This relatively high mean reflects the negative correlation of initial probability estimates with both n Achievement and Test Anxiety in the Easy condition. In a sense, subjects low in both n Achievement and Test Anxiety are behaving realistically since they rate their chances quite highly when told that the task should, in fact, be easy.

Finally, the results in Table 1 show that neither middle nor terminal probability estimates are significantly correlated with n Achievement or Test Anxiety scores. This lack of significant relationships is consistent with the assumption that once a person is involved in performance of a task, his present performance becomes the dominant influence in shaping his expectations of success. Whereas prior to performance his expectations may tend to be shaped by his past history of success and failure in similar situations, once he begins the task the frequency and patterning of present success and failure will assume the major role in determining expectations. The effect of present performance on expectations is, in fact, evident in the correlation of performance scores with middle and terminal probability estimates obtained in the postperformance questionnaire. We would expect these estimates to be influenced by success and failure at the task, those subjects with relatively high performance scores being those with relatively high middle and terminal probability estimates. Table 5 presents the correlations of initial,

Table 5

Correlations of probability estimates with task performance

Probability Estimate	Moderately Difficult Condition	Easy Condition
	Task Performance	Task Performance
Initial	.31*	.14
Middle	.60†	.55†
Terminal	.60†	.61†

* $p < .005$, one-tailed test
† $p < .0005$, one-tailed test

middle, and terminal probability estimates with performance scores for both experimental conditions.[4] The highly significant positive correlations of performance scores with middle and terminal probability estimates are taken as indicating the modifying effect of success and failure at the task on expectations of success.

DISCUSSION

These results generally support predictions and are consistent with the underlying assumptions. They suggest that in order to predict the relationship between expectation of success prior to task performance

[4] The positive correlation of performance scores with initial probability estimates in the Moderately Difficult condition parallels the positive relationship of persistence scores to initial probability estimates in a previous investigation (Feather, 1963b, Chapter 9) where an insoluble task was presented to subjects as very difficult.

and achievement-related motives, one requires two main types of information. First, it is necessary to determine whether the situation is one which would arouse achievement motivation or anxiety about failure. Second, one would need to know what the effect of this aroused motivation is likely to have been when subjects performed similar tasks in the past under conditions similar to those now present. In particular, has this aroused motivation determined relatively more success than failure in the past, or vice versa? We believe that subjects tend to categorize performance situations in terms of their past experience. For example, a subject high in n Achievement might tend to categorize a situation, where he has the opportunity to excel, as one in which he usually does rather well in comparison to others. In contrast, a subject high in Test Anxiety might tend to categorize the same test situation as one in which he usually performs badly, particularly if the task is complex.

In general, there are probably several cues in a test situation to which a subject responds when estimating his chances of success prior to task performance. The important cues are those which have been consistently associated with his success and failure in the past. Some cues may have similar implications about present performance; other cues may have conflicting implications. For example, a subject high in Test Anxiety may feel pessimistic about his chances of success at a complex task since he has done poorly when working at complex tasks in test situations in the past. But the task may be verbal in character and he may have found that in the past he has often excelled at verbal activities. Thus the verbal nature of the task may determine some optimism about chances of success. In this example the different characteristics of a complex, verbal task have different implications for present performance. For other cases task characteristics may have similar rather than conflicting implications for present performance. Somehow the subject has to resolve these implications when he estimates his chances of success at the task. Future research might investigate which features of a test situation have greatest weight in determining a subject's initial expectation of success. It is likely that they would be those characteristics of the situation which have been closely and reliably related to the quality of task performance in the past.

Since ability measures are customarily taken as important predictors of performance, the above line of argument suggests that subjects with high verbal ability may tend to report relatively high initial probability estimates in both the Moderately Difficult and Easy experimental conditions. The anagrams test is verbal in nature. Subjects with high verbal ability may therefore react to it in terms of their generally superior performance on previous verbal tasks, and estimate their chances of success as fairly high. Table 6 presents data relevant to this prediction. Scores on the Test AL were available for the majority of subjects. This test was developed by the Australian Council for Educational Research as an advanced level test of verbal ability. Table 6 shows that initial probability estimates are positively related to scores on Test AL in the Easy condition but not in the Moderately Difficult condition. Performance scores on the anagrams test and scores on Test

Table 6

Correlations of probability estimates and task performance with verbal ability for Moderately Difficult ($N = 73$) and Easy ($N = 73$) experimental conditions

Variable	Moderately Difficult Condition Verbal Ability (Test AL)	Easy Condition Verbal Ability (Test AL)
Initial probability estimate	.01	.30†
Middle probability estimate	.09	.21*
Terminal probability estimate	.09	.10
Task performance	.24†	.23†

* $p < .05$, one-tailed test
† $p < .01$, one-tailed test

AL are positively correlated for both experimental conditions.[5] Thus the results for the Easy condition support our prediction, while those for the Moderately Difficult condition do not. It is possible, however, that the instructions for the Moderately Difficult condition, in implying that the anagrams were harder than most usually encountered, may have suggested to subjects that their past experience specifically at anagrams (and more generally at verbal tasks) would not be a reliable guide to present performance. They could, however, still perceive the task as a challenge and respond to it in terms of how they met similar challenges in the past. In this respect, motives to achieve success and to avoid failure would be important influences on performance, and we would therefore expect present expectations of success to relate to these motives as predicted.

---

[5] Verbal ability scores are negatively correlated with Test Anxiety scores for both experimental conditions (for Moderately Difficult condition, $r = -.30$, $p < .01$; for Easy condition, $r = -.26$, $p < .01$). These negative relationships are consistent with previous results reported by Sarason (1963).

One rather unexpected finding in the present study is the negative correlation between initial probability estimates and n Achievement scores in the Easy condition. In terms of the preceding argument, this result suggests that subjects low in n Achievement may tend to perform better than subjects high in n Achievement in situations where a task is presented as easy and is, in fact, easy. As indicated previously, we would not expect a situation of this type to elicit much achievement motivation, so superior performance may reflect the operation of other types of motivation (e.g., desire for social approval). It is possible also that subjects high in n Achievement may be relatively uninterested in this type of situation, and may not feel it worthwhile to try very hard to do well. In studies reported by Atkinson (1958a, pp. 288–305) and by McClelland (1961, pp. 217–221), subjects low in n Achievement tended to perform better at a task than subjects high in n Achievement, when the chances of winning were high (3/4). Differences were not, however, statistically significant. Atkinson (1955, p. 502) also found in an earlier study that subjects low in n Achievement tended to have relatively higher performance scores under relaxed conditions than subjects high in n Achievement but differences were not statistically significant. Further research is needed in this area.

An alternative interpretation of the positive correlation of initial probability estimates and n Achievement scores in the Moderately Difficult condition and the negative correlation of these scores in the Easy condition is in terms of Brody's (Chapter 16) assumption that subjects will tend to state a subjective probability of success that will maximize their resultant motivation. According to the theory of achievement motivation, this would be at a subjective probability of .50 for subjects in whom the motive to achieve success (M_S) is stronger than the motive to avoid failure (M_{AF}). The results do show that the mean probability estimates of subjects high in n Achievement and low in Test Anxiety are close to .50 in both the Moderately Difficult and the Easy conditions (Table 4). If we assume that these subjects tend to be those in whom $M_S > M_{AF}$, then these results would be consistent with the above interpretation. However, this line of argument would also imply that subjects in whom $M_{AF} > M_S$ should tend to state either very low or very high probabilities.[6] If we assume that subjects low in n

[6] We assume that these subjects would not maximize their resultant negative motivation but, in fact, would tend to minimize this motivation. Brody's statement is rather ambiguous in this respect. We interpret his principle as a maximizing of resultant positive motivation by subjects in whom $M_S > M_{AF}$, and a minimizing of resultant negative motivation by subjects in whom $M_{AF} > M_S$. This interpretation is consistent with his prediction about changes in confidence ratings (Brody, Chapter 16, p. 252).

Achievement and high in Test Anxiety tend to be those in whom $M_{AF} > M_S$, then these subjects should tend to avoid stating probabilities of .50. But while the results in Table 4 for the Moderately Difficult condition are consistent with this prediction, those for the Easy condition are not. In any case, the assumption that subjects in whom $M_S > M_{AF}$ should state probabilities so as to maximize resultant positive motivation, and subjects in whom $M_{AF} > M_S$ should state probabilities so as to minimize resultant negative motivation, needs some further clarification. Atkinson applies the theory to risk-taking behavior where a subject is required to perform an achievement task which varies in difficulty. In making a choice, the subject commits himself to task performance at a particular level of difficulty (e.g., to throwing the ring at a chosen distance from the peg in a ring toss situation). This type of situation appears to be different from one in which a subject is required to state probabilities and where there may be no necessary commitment to action. Furthermore, in Atkinson's theory, subjective probabilities are assumed to influence strength of motivation which then determines choice, whereas Brody appears to reverse the causal sequence in assuming that a preference for a maximum (or minimum) level of motivation determines the stated probability. Just why subjects would prefer a maximum (or minimum) level of motivation needs further clarification.

We do not, however, wish to deny the possibility of "motivational" types of effect. Brody's (Chapter 16) experiment is of value in suggesting this kind of interpretation. It may be argued, for example, that the results of the present study demonstrate the influence of *subjective attractiveness* of success and *subjective repulsiveness* of failure on a person's probability statements.[7] Within each experimental condition subjects high in the motive to achieve success (M_S) may tend to perceive success as more attractive then do subjects low in the motive to achieve success. This relatively higher perceived attractiveness may tend to dominate the judgments of probability of success made by subjects who are high in M_S such that these judgments are more "wishful" than reality-oriented. Such effects should be especially likely in situations

---

[7] Subjective attractiveness of success (or positive valence or utility of success) may be conceptualized in Atkinson's model as the multiplicative product of motive to achieve success (M_S) and positive incentive value of success (I_s). Similarly, subjective repulsiveness of failure (or negative valence or utility of failure) may be conceptualized as the multiplicative product of motive to avoid failure (M_{AF}) and negative incentive value of failure (I_f) (Atkinson, 1964). In Atkinson's model $I_s = 1 - P_s$ and $I_f = -P_s$. We believe, however, that incentive values may depend on the nature of the situation (e.g., test versus nontest) as well as upon the difficulty of the task (Feather, 1959a, Chapter 3).

where reality constraints are few and where the positive incentive value of success (I_s) tends to be high (e.g., in the Moderately Difficult situation). Subjects high in M_S may, as it were, react autistically by stating high probability estimates, expressing the hope that they may succeed at a task for which success is seen as very attractive. This argument would imply a positive correlation between initial probability estimates and n Achievement scores, assuming these latter scores reflect strength of M_S. This positive correlation should be especially apparent in the Moderately Difficult condition where perceived attractiveness of success should tend to be relatively high because of the higher I_s.

Similarly, within each experimental condition subjects high in the motive to avoid failure (M_{AF}) may tend to perceive failure as more repulsive than do subjects low in the motive to avoid failure. This relatively higher perceived repulsiveness may determine lower judgments of probability of success among subjects who are high in M_{AF}. These effects should be especially likely in situations where reality constraints are minimal and where the negative incentive value of failure (I_f) tends to be high (e.g., in the Easy situation). Subjects high in M_{AF} may, as it were, react defensively by stating low probability estimates, since failure would not be so repulsive if the task were accepted as fairly difficult.[8] This argument would imply a negative correlation between initial probability estimates and Test Anxiety scores, assuming these latter scores reflect strength of M_{AF}. This negative correlation should be especially evident in the Easy condition where perceived repulsiveness of failure should tend to be relatively high because of the higher I_f.

The above type of interpretation therefore assumes an *autistic biassing* of judgments of probability of success among subjects high in M_S, especially under conditions where I_s is high (i.e., where the task is presented as difficult), and a *defensive biassing* of these judgments among subjects who are high in M_{AF}, especially under conditions where I_f is high (i.e., where the task is presented as easy). In general, the results of the present experiment are consistent with this interpretation, although it also has difficulty in accounting for the obtained negative relationship between initial probability estimates and n Achievement scores in the Easy condition.

This alternative interpretation could be tested further by presenting an achievement task to subjects at a number of different levels of

---

[8] Probability statements are public in that the subject knows that the experimenter will see them. The subject's response may therefore also be influenced by his concern about how the experimenter will react to the probability estimate which the subject reports.

difficulty and investigating relationships between motive assessments and initial probability estimates. The predicted *positive* relationship between initial probability estimates and *n* Achievement should be stronger when the task is presented as very difficult, than as moderately difficult, than as easy. The predicted *negative* relationship between initial probability estimates and Test Anxiety should be stronger when the task is presented as easy, than as moderately difficult, than as very difficult.[9] These predictions are clearly different from those which would follow from the type of theoretical analysis developed in the present paper which sees the relationships as reflecting the influence of past experience in related situations and which considers differences in past performance in terms of Atkinson's theory of achievement motivation. Our present theoretical approach would predict that the strongest positive relationship between initial probability estimates and *n* Achievement scores, and the strongest negative relationship between initial probability estimates and Test Anxiety scores, should both occur when the task is presented as moderately difficult. Here then is an instance where the alternative theoretical approaches imply different predictions. These predictions now await experimental test.

The experiment investigated the prediction that Ss' expectations of success prior to task performance would be positively related to *n* Achievement in a situation providing the opportunity for personal accomplishment. It was also predicted that these initial expectations would be negatively related to test anxiety but that, following task performance, relationships would be less apparent. In a test of these predictions, 168 male Ss rated their chances of success before commencing an anagrams task. The task was presented as "moderately difficult" to 82 Ss and as "easy" to 86 Ss. In a postperformance questionnaire, Ss rated their chances of success for the middle and terminal stages of performance. Results supported predictions and were interpreted in terms of the influence of past experience in related situations, and as also possibly reflecting the effect of subjective attractiveness of success and subjective repulsiveness of failure on intitial expectations.

[9] Table 1 does in fact indicate a higher negative relationship between initial probability estimates and Test Anxiety scores in the Easy condition.

The Influence of Testing Conditions
on Need for Achievement Scores
and Their Relationship to Performance Scores

This study presents evidence concerning two important assumptions underlying past research on the need for achievement (*n* Achievement). First, it was assumed explicitly in the development of the *n* Achievement scoring system that "achievement imagery" in thematic appercep- tion reflects *only* achievement motivation (McClelland, Atkinson, Clark and Lowell, 1953, p. 3; McClelland, 1958a, p. 14; 1961, p. 39). Second, it has been assumed tacitly in some studies relating *n* Achievement to performance that *S*s having high *n* Achievement are similar on the average to *S*s having low *n* Achievement. That is, the two motivation groups have been compared on the assumption that all *other* factors were equal (Atkinson, 1958b; French, 1955). Atkinson and Reitman (1956, p. 361) call attention to this assumption but do not pursue its implications in the interpretation of their results.

The assumption that "achievement imagery" reflects *only* achieve- ment motivation should be investigated for several related reasons. First, as Ritchie (1954) has pointed out, the demonstration by McClel- land, et al. (1953) that achievement imagery is produced by achieve- ment motivation does not prove that achievement imagery is produced *only* by achievement motivation. Second, it has been argued cogently that an intervening variable should be defined not solely in terms of responses (as with *n* Achievement) but in terms of antecedent conditions as well (Brown and Farber, 1951). Third, a manifest content analysis ignores the possibility that "achievement imagery" could represent the disguised expression of an unacceptable wish, such as aggression toward

This chapter is adapted from an unpublished Ph.D. dissertation (Smith, 1961), carried out at the University of Michigan, in which procedures and results are reported in considerably greater detail. Some new material is included in the present version.

siblings, instead of achievement motivation. In short, the assumption that there is a set of responses in fantasy that uniquely reflect a particular motivational state runs counter to the prevalent view that a wide variety of possible responses can be attached through learning to antecedent conditions and/or inner states (cf. Farber, 1954).

There is also experimental evidence which calls this assumption into question. For example, French (1955) found that n Achievement scores obtained under different conditions had different properties. In one condition, she offered an "extrinsic" incentive of free time to heavily scheduled Ss in an Officers' Candidate School for high performance on a digit-letter substitution test. A significant positive relationship was found between performance for the "extrinsic" incentive and n Achievement scores obtained following instructions designed to arouse extrinsic motivation. French also found that n Achievement scores obtained under these extrinsic conditions *(a)* did not relate to n Achievement scores for the same Ss obtained under natural achievement-oriented testing conditions, and *(b)* were significantly higher than the n Achievement scores of similar Ss obtained under relaxed conditions. If French's incentive was really extrinsic to achievement, then her results (the high level of achievement imagery and the correlation of n Achievement scores with *extrinsically* motivated performance) suggest that under some conditions n Achievement scores may reflect extrinsic motivation instead of, or in addition to, achievement motivation. Other studies (Birney, 1958; Douvan, 1956; Field, 1951) suggest the possibility that extrinsic motives, such as a desire for the approval of the experimenter, for a monetary prize, or for social acceptance may under certain conditions augment the amount of achievement imagery in projective stories.

If "achievement imagery" sometimes reflects extrinsic motivation, then it is important to identify the conditions under which n Achievement scores can be considered valid measures of achievement motivation. The present study reexamines the effect on n Achievement scores of instructions designed to arouse extrinsic motivation. An attempt is made to assess the *perceived* effects of the motivation-arousing procedures in order to determine whether the "extrinsic" instructions do, in fact, introduce incentives other than achievement incentives.

It is also important to investigate the assumption that high and low n Achievement groups are similar in other respects than their achievement motivation. When the performance of these groups is contrasted under various conditions, it is important to know that obtained differences are due only to differences in achievement motivation. Ss with high and low n Achievement have, in fact, been shown to be similar with respect to quantitative ability (Atkinson and Reitman, 1956) and with respect to test anxiety (Atkinson, 1960; Atkinson and Litwin, Chapter 5). However, the two groups are not alike in other possibly important respects such as authoritarian tendencies (cf. McClelland, et al., 1953), which might interact with achievement motivation under certain conditions to influence performance differences between the two groups.

Theoretical Background of the Present Study. The theoretical foundation of the present study from which the hypotheses to be tested were derived will now be summarized. The *McClelland-Atkinson position* is represented by the following statements:

1. A *motive* is characterized as "a disposition to strive for a certain kind of satisfaction, as a capacity for satisfaction in the attainment of a certain class of incentives" (Atkinson, Chapter 2, p. 13). The achievement motive is conceived as a latent disposition which is manifested in overt striving only when the individual perceives performance as instrumental to a sense of personal accomplishment (Atkinson, 1953; 1958c; Atkinson and Raphelson, 1956; Atkinson and Reitman, 1956).

2. *Motivation* is defined as "the activated state of the person which occurs when the cues of a situation arouse the expectancy that performance of an act will lead to an incentive for which he has a motive" (Atkinson, 1958b, p. 304). Achievement motivation $= f$ (achievement motive $\times$ expectancy of an achievement incentive $\times$ value of the achievement incentive); (Atkinson, Chapter 2; 1958b).

3. An *achievement incentive* is present when a person anticipates that his skill and competence in the performance of a task will be evaluated, and that good performance will produce a feeling of pride in accomplishment (Atkinson, 1953; Chapter 2).

4. Frequently a single act may lead to incentives for several different motives. In the case of such "overdetermined" performance, the *total* strength of motivation to perform the act is the combined strengths of the different kinds of motivation aroused (Atkinson and Reitman, 1956).

5. A positive relationship between strength of achievement *motive* and performance level is maximized when Ss are led to expect that performance will lead to an achievement incentive but not to other kinds of incentives. The relationship is minimized *(a)* when little or no achievement motivation is aroused for performance, or *(b)* under "multi-incentive" conditions when achievement motivation is aroused for performance, and *in addition,* other motives uncorrelated with *n* Achievement (i.e., extrinsic motives) are also aroused (Atkinson, 1958c;

Atkinson and Raphelson, 1956; Atkinson and Reitman, 1956). In the latter case, the relationship between n Achievement and performance will be reduced, assuming an asymptote for performance, when the total motivation of both the high and low n Achievement groups produces performance at the upper limit, even though the total motivation of the high n Achievement group is greater than that of the low n Achievement group.

The alternative or *multiple-determinant* view to be investigated here assumes in contrast to the McClelland-Atkinson position that specific responses, such as types of imagery, are *not* uniquely related to particular motives. According to this view, "achievement imagery" does not uniquely reflect striving for achievement incentives. Rather, it indicates strength of motivation for *any goal* which is to be attained by working hard or doing well at some task, whether the goal is money, being on time for an evening meal, or pleasing the experimenter.

Hypotheses. The following hypotheses derive from the two contrasting theoretical positions.

HYPOTHESES CONCERNING THE EFFECT OF EXPERIMENTAL PROCEDURES ON THE AMOUNT OF ACHIEVEMENT IMAGERY IN THEMATIC APPERCEPTION. According to McClelland and Atkinson, mean n Achievement scores should be higher when achievement incentives are emphasized (achievement-oriented conditions or multi-incentive conditions) than when no attempt is made to emphasize them (neutral conditions). According to the multiple-determinant assumption, mean n Achievement scores should be higher when achievement incentives are emphasized and *also* when extrinsic incentives are emphasized (extrinsic conditions) than when conditions are neutral. (Extrinsic conditions refer to conditions in which the attainment of *any kind* of incentive, other than achievement incentives, is dependent on working hard or performing well at some task, e.g., working rapidly in order to be on time for a meal.)

HYPOTHESES CONCERNING THE RELATIONSHIP BETWEEN n ACHIEVEMENT SCORES AND PERFORMANCE LEVEL. According to Atkinson, when *only* achievement motivation is aroused for performance (achievement-oriented conditions), the performance level of Ss with high n Achievement should be substantially higher than that of Ss with low n Achievement. As performance is directed toward other kinds of incentives *in addition to* achievement incentives (multi-incentive conditions), the superiority in performance of Ss with high n Achievement should diminish. When performance is directed entirely toward extrinsic incentives (extrinsic conditions), or when achievement incentives are minimized (relaxed conditions), there should be no difference between performance levels of Ss who differ in *n* Achievement.

According to the multiple-determinant position, the performance level of Ss with high *n* Achievement scores should be higher than that of Ss with low *n* Achievement scores whenever *n* Achievement scores are obtained immediately following performance for *any kind* of incentive which is attained by working hard or performing well at some task (i.e., under achievement-oriented, multi-incentive, or *extrinsic* conditions).

METHOD

Subjects. The Ss were 225 male students in introductory psychology at the University of Michigan who were participating in the experiment to fulfill a course requirement. Ss were assigned to experimental conditions on the basis of the compatibility of their time schedules. All data were not usable; the number of Ss varies for different measures: 218 for *n* Achievement scores, 217 for arithmetic scores, 215 for Test Anxiety scores.

Methods of Measurement. Scores for *n* Achievement were obtained from a thematic apperceptive measure administered according to standard procedures (Atkinson, 1958a, pp. 836–837). Six pictures, in the following order of presentation, were used for all conditions: (1) picture 7, "Boy with vague operation scene in background"; (2) picture 2, "Two men ('inventors') in a shop working at a machine"; (3) picture 9, "Good work, Bill! Man working on papers at office desk"; (4) picture 1, "Father-son"; (5) picture 46, "Man skiing down steep hill"; (6) picture 8, "Boy in checked shirt at a desk." Numbers and descriptions are taken from Atkinson (1958a, Appendix III). Three pictures (2, 9, and 46), which elicit a relatively high amount of achievement imagery, and three pictures (7, 1, and 8), which elicit a relatively low amount, were chosen on the basis of normative information (Atkinson, 1958a). Stories were scored without knowledge of the S or of the condition in which the story was written, using the scoring system given by Atkinson (1958a). All stories for 30 Ss were scored by another judge.[1] The product-moment correlation between the two sets of scores was .83. The percentage of agreement between the two scorers with regard to the presence of AI—the basic scoring category denoting achievement imagery—was .90.

Test anxiety scores were obtained from the Mandler-Sarason (1952) questionnaire. Each item was scored as a five-point scale (Mandler and Cowen, 1958).

Performance level was measured by 14 minutes of performance on a two-step arithmetic task, which required S to write down only his final answer, keeping intermediate calculations in his mind.

---

[1] John W. Atkinson.

Incentives for performance present in each experimental condition were assessed at the end of each session by means of a postperformance questionnaire which asked what satisfactions *S* sought from performance on the arithmetic test. Eighteen representative need satisfactions adapted from Murray (1938) and White (1951) were presented as possible "reasons" for working hard on the arithmetic task. Four items represented achievement satisfactions: "I wanted the satisfaction that accompanies a job well done." "I wanted to see myself as a person of high ability." "I wanted to compete with and do better than others." "I wanted to turn in an exceptional performance." Each of the other items represented a different kind of satisfaction (e.g., "I wanted to earn as much money as possible." "I wanted to establish and maintain warm friendly relationships with other people."). The kinds and relative strengths of the incentives sought by each *S* are indicated by the items he checked and by his ranking of the items in their order of importance for him.

Certain other tasks were also administered for the purpose of supplementary analyses which are not included in this report due to space limitations (see Smith, 1961; 1963).

Experimental Conditions. There were seven different experimental conditions, with approximately 30 *S*s in each. Of these, four were "neutral *n* Achievement prior to performance" or "A" conditions, which provided a baseline for comparison. In each of the "A" conditions, *n* Achievement scores were obtained under "neutral" conditions (i.e., no attempt was made either to relax or to arouse the *S*s' motivation) *preceding* arithmetic performance under "achievement-oriented," "multi-incentive," "extrinsic," and "relaxed" conditions. In three matching "aroused performance prior to aroused *n* Achievement" or "B" conditions, *n* Achievement scores were obtained *following* arithmetic performance under "achievement-oriented," "multi-incentive," and "extrinsic" conditions. Scores for *n* Achievement in the latter three conditions are considered to reflect aroused motivation even though no special instructions were given for the thematic apperceptive measure, on the assumption that motivation aroused for arithmetic performance is carried over to, and reflected in, the projective measure.

The experimental design enables the comparison of *n* Achievement scores obtained under neutral, achievement-oriented, multi-incentive, and extrinsic conditions. It also enables a comparison of the relationships between neutral *n* Achievement scores and performance under four different incentive conditions and between aroused *n* Achievement scores and performance under three different incentive conditions.

Achievement Conditions. In the Achievement conditions an attempt was made to introduce only achievement incentives for arithmetic performance. The thematic apperceptive measure either preceded (Condition IA) or followed (Condition IB) arithmetic performance under achievement-oriented conditions. The following achievement-oriented instructions were given for the arithmetic task:

Each of you will be assigned to an individual work room for this next test since it requires considerable concentration. . . . The tests you are taking today are similar to various tests which psychologists have developed to measure critical abilities such as intellectual alertness. . . . (cf. Atkinson and Reitman, 1956; McClelland et al., 1953, p. 102). *E* then read the instructions for the arithmetic task, assigned *Ss* to individual testing rooms, and told them to solve as many problems as possible in the time allowed. After 14 minutes each *S* was stopped and asked to return to the classroom. *Ss* were placed in individual testing rooms in order to minimize the arousal of expectancies of incentives other than achievement incentives (Atkinson and Reitman, 1956).

Multi-Incentive Conditions. In the Multi-Incentive conditions monetary incentives and proctoring of performance were added to achievement incentives. The thematic apperceptive measure either preceded (Condition IIA) or followed (Condition IIB) arithmetic performance under multi-incentive conditions. The multi-incentive orientation given for the arithmetic task was similar to the achievement orientation but made no mention of working alone, since the *Ss* were to work on the problems in a group. The *added elements of the multi-incentive orientation* were as follows: "Since I am interested in seeing your very best performance when you are actually putting out, I am going to award a prize of $5.00 to the person having the highest score on this test. . . . While the *Ss* were working, *E* paced around the room, attempting to look concerned about the *Ss'* performance, holding his stopwatch in full view. The procedures were intended to reproduce as nearly as possible the Multi-Incentive condition used by Atkinson and Reitman (1956).

Extrinsic Conditions. In the Extrinsic conditions an attempt was made to exclude achievement incentives and to introduce only the extrinsic incentive to finish quickly in order to get out in time for dinner. The thematic apperceptive measure either preceded (Condition IIIA) or followed (Condition IIIB) arithmetic performance under extrinsic conditions. *Ss* were deliberately scheduled late in the afternoon (i.e., 4:00 to 6:00 p.m.) so they would feel under pressure to hurry through the tasks in order to return to their dormitories or fraternities for the regularly scheduled evening meal. In Extrinsic Condition IIIA a "tartan preference task" (Knapp, 1958) was introduced following the neutral projective measure to fill time and to create additional time pressure for performance on the arithmetic task. In Extrinsic Condition IIIB, an additional "fill-in" task was introduced prior to arithmetic performance, requiring the *Ss* to state their preference for different kinds of foods. It was hoped that this task would heighten the salience of the extrinsic goal of getting out to dinner.

After the "fill-in" tasks, *E* looked at his watch, began to move rapidly, and gave the following extrinsic orientation for the arithmetic task: "Well, we'll have to move right along in order to finish by six. There are several more of these tasks which I'd like to have you work on. They'll take quite a while, but you can go as soon as you are finished. I think it will be possible to finish and get away early if you work hard. I think I'll have you do these arithmetic problems next. They are quite simple once you get the hang of them. Once again, I just need groups of scores on this task. You will not receive an individual score, so just work through the problems as quickly as possible so we can get on to the next tasks." The instruction sheet for this condition, in contrast to the others, had no spaces for the subject's name, age, or code number. Ss were assigned to individual testing rooms as for the Achievement conditions. They were unaware their performance was being timed. Fourteen minutes after starting each S, the E entered the room of that S and said: "Listen, this is taking too long. I think we'd better stop this and go on to the next task, so take your materials back to the other room." Ss were asked to put their names on their materials only after they had completed all the tasks in the session in order to maintain a feeling of anonymity as they worked on the tests.

Relaxed Condition. In Relaxed condition IVA, for which there is no matching "B" condition, an attempt was made to minimize the presence of all incentives. E greeted the Ss in an informal manner as they entered. After neutral administration of the projective measure, E tossed the protocols into a box, took off his jacket and loosened his tie, and told the Ss they were free to smoke. The tartan preference task was then introduced as a task which E wanted to use for his dissertation. (This was the only condition in which E implied that he was a graduate student. In the other conditions he stated that he was a member of the staff.) The following relaxed orientation was then given for the arithmetic task: "Next I'd like to get some information about some arithmetic problems. I'm afraid this will be kind of dull, but I hope you'll bear with me. I'd like to get a line on how long it takes to do these. They're pretty simple once you get the hang of them. Don't be alarmed at the size of the booklet. You won't have to work them all. . . . As I said before, what I'm interested in is groups of scores on these tasks. You won't receive an individual score. O.K. Go ahead and work on this awhile and then we'll go on to a couple of other things." The E then left the room and returned 14 minutes later to stop the Ss, who worked as a group rather than in individual testing rooms.

EFFECTIVENESS OF THE EXPERIMENTAL MANIPULATIONS

Since the testing of the hypotheses requires the creation of certain theoretically specified conditions, the first step in the analysis involved a check on the effectiveness of the experimental manipulations. An index of the *salience of achievement incentives for performance* in each condition was obtained from the postperformance questionnaire by giving each S a score based on the number of achievement items he had checked as his reasons for working hard on the arithmetic test, and the ranks—indicating order of importance—he assigned to the checked items. An achievement incentive that ranked first received 6 points, second, 5 points, and so on down to 1 point for an achievement incentive ranked sixth. The middle column of Table 1 shows the mean salience scores for each condition. The percentage of Ss in each condition whose scores

Table 1

Estimated proportion of overall motivation attributable
to achievement incentives

Condition	Overall Motivation			Salience of Achievement			Estimated Proportion*	
	Rank	Mean	Z_1†	Rank	Mean	Z_2	Z_1-Z_2	Rank
Achievement								
IA	3	4.00	+ .33	1	11.77	+1.45	−1.12	1
IB	5	3.70	− .66	5	8.27	− .49	− .17	3
Multi-Incentive								
IIA	1	4.39	+1.61	3	10.44	+ .72	+ .89	7
IIB	2	4.16	+ .85	2	10.59	+ .80	+ .05	4
Extrinsic								
IIIA	4	3.97	+ .23	4	9.40	+ .14	+ .09	5
IIIB	6	3.68	− .72	7	6.67	−1.36	+ .64	6
Relaxed								
IVA	7	3.41	−1.61	6	6.86	−1.26	− .35	2

* The rank of 1 indicates the highest proportion attributable to achievement
incentives.

† Z scores were obtained for each distribution using means as units of analysis:
$Z = (M_1 - \overline{M})/\text{SD}$.

on the salience index fall above the common median for all conditions was
also obtained for the purpose of chi square comparisons.

The self-report data from the post-performance questionnaire give the following information about the kinds of incentives for arithmetic performance
present in the different conditions:

1. Achievement incentives were reported to be significantly more salient in
the combined Achievement and Multi-Incentive conditions, in which achievement orientation was given, than in the combined Extrinsic and Relaxed conditions in which achievement-related cues were deemphasized ($x^2 = 17.54$,
$df = 1, p < .01$).

Fortunately, achievement salience was lowest in Extrinsic Condition IIIB,
an important precondition for studying whether there will be a positive relationship between extrinsically motivated performance and n Achievement
scores obtained following such performance.

2. A monetary incentive item ("I wanted to earn as much money as possible.") was checked significantly more often in the combined Multi-Incentive
conditions, in which a monetary incentive was offered, than in all other conditions combined ($p < .01$, Fisher-Yates exact test).

3. The extrinsic incentive item "to finish quickly in order to have time for
other things" was checked significantly more often in the combined Extrinsic
Conditions than in all other conditions combined ($x^2 = 113.21$, $df = 1$,
$p < .01$).

4. No strong incentives were reported in the Relaxed Condition.

These comparisons show that the procedures had the intended effects in general. However, effects for individual conditions were not always as clear-cut as was intended. In particular, achievement incentives were insufficiently salient in Achievement Condition IB and overly salient in Extrinsic Condition IIIA (Table 1).

An estimate of *overall strength of motivation for performance* was obtained from a question which asked the S to check on a scale how hard he had worked on the arithmetic test. Mean scores for different conditions are given in the first column of Table 1. A partial ordering of conditions based on this estimate is expected on the basis of the number of different incentives presented in different conditions, and places the Multi-Incentive Conditions first (achievement, affiliation, and monetary incentives), the Achievement and Extrinsic conditions (each with only a single incentive) intermediate, and the Relaxed condition, in which all incentives were minimized, last. Table 1 shows that within the "A" conditions the order is as expected. Means of the four "A" conditions are significantly different ($F = 5.00$, $df = 3$ and 122, $p < .005$). Within the "B" conditions the order is also as expected.

With information about the *salience* of achievement incentives and about *overall motivation,* an estimate of the *proportion of overall motivation for performance attributable to achievement incentives* was obtained in the following manner:

1. Conditions were ranked according to mean scores on the index of salience of achievement incentives, as in Table 1.

2. Conditions were also ranked according to mean scores on the index of strength of overall motivation, as in Table 1.

3. The salience index rank for a particular condition was compared with the overall motivation rank for that condition and the difference in comparative standing gave information about the proportion of overall motivation attributable to achievement incentives.

For example, Table 1 shows that Achievement Condition IA ranks first in achievement salience, but third in estimated overall motivation. Thus the two conditions ranked above Achievement Condition IA in overall motivation; namely, Multi-Incentive Conditions IIA and IIB must have had a smaller proportion of overall motivation contributed by achievement incentives.

The actual estimate was obtained by using differences between standard scores rather than between ranks, since standard scores reflect relative standing more sensitively. Table 1 shows the ranks of conditions in terms of the estimated proportion of overall motivation for performance attributable to achievement incentives. The order is meaningful in that in the four conditions in which extrinsic incentives were intentionally introduced—the Multi-Incentive and Extrinsic conditions—there is a lower proportion of overall motivation attributable to achievement incentives than in the other three conditions. This estimate orders conditions in terms of the *perceived* effects of the experimental manipulations rather than in terms of the objectively defined manipulations. This estimate will be related to performance level in analyses which follow.

Further information concerning the effectiveness of the experimental manipulations is provided by the actual arithmetic performance levels in different conditions. Conditions were ordered as follows in terms of the mean number of problems solved. Among the "neutral *n* Achievement prior to performance" or "A" conditions, the Achievement condition was highest (67.9), the Multi-Incentive Condition second (67.7), the Extrinsic condition third (56.2) and the Relaxed condition lowest (51.8). This order differs slightly from the expected order in that the Multi-Incentive condition produced the highest self-estimates of effort. The difference between the means is significant ($F = 4.37$, $df = 3$ and 118, $p < .01$). These differences between means of "A" conditions indicate that the experimental procedures had the intended effect in reducing the level of performance in the Relaxed condition. The "aroused performance prior to aroused *n* Achievement," or "B" conditions, were similarly ordered with Achievement highest (58.1), Multi-Incentive second (55.3) and Extrinsic lowest (52.1). Means were not significantly different ($F = .83$, $df = 2$ and 85, n.s.), and were not intended to be since it was hoped that all three groups would work hard but for different kinds of incentives.

Analysis of variance of arithmetic scores as a function of incentive orientations (I, II, III) and task order ("A" versus "B") reveals that significantly more problems were worked in the "A" conditions than in the "B" conditions ($F = 5.20$, $df = 1$ and 152, $p < .025$). This unexpected result suggests that when the thematic apperceptive measure *preceded* performance it accentuated the arousal of motivation for performance, a possibility worthy of further study.

RESULTS

Level of Achievement Imagery Expressed under Different Experimental Conditions.

The purpose of the following analyses is to determine whether *n* Achievement scores are higher than under neutral conditions only when achievement incentives are introduced or an extrinsic incentive is introduced. Table 2 shows that a mean *n* Achievement score of 9.23 was obtained under neutral conditions, 9.77 under achievement-oriented conditions, 10.13 under multi-incentive conditions, and 11.81 under extrinsic conditions. An analysis of variance reveals no significant difference among the four means ($F = 1.32$, $df = 3$ and 214, n.s.). Dunnett (1955) provides a one-sided test of probability for situations in which different treatment conditions are all expected to produce higher means than the control conditions, as in the present experiment. Of the three conditions in which aroused *n* Achievement scores were obtained, there is a tendency for *n* Achievement scores to be higher than in the neutral condition only under extrinsic conditions ($p < .10$, one-tailed test).

These results do not provide clear-cut support for either the McClel-

Table 2

Comparison of means of *n* Achievement scores obtained
under four different experimental conditions

	Conditions			
	Neutral (N = 127)	Achievement-Oriented (N = 30)	Multi-Incentive (N = 30)	Extrinsic (N = 31)
Total n Achievement score				
Mean	9.23	9.77	10.13	11.81
SD	6.39	6.70	6.20	7.34
n Achievement score from three low-cue pictures				
Mean	1.66	2.23	2.20	3.81
SD	3.92	3.96	3.97	4.19

Analysis of Variance

	Source	*df*	*MS*	*F*	*p*
Total n Achievement scores	Between	3	56.55	1.32	n.s.
	Within	214	42.90		
n Achievement score from low-cue pictures	Between	3	38.48	2.44	$p < .10$
	Within	214	15.75		

land assumption or the multiple-determinant assumption. However,
the tendency for *n* Achievement scores obtained under extrinsic conditions to be higher than scores obtained under neutral conditions is
consistent with the multiple-determinant position and contrary to the
McClelland assumption. It is important to note that the amount of
achievement imagery produced under extrinsic conditions is greater
than that produced under any other condition.

Scores obtained from pictures with strong and weak achievement
cues were next examined separately, since it is possible that strongly
cued pictures elicited a maximal amount of imagery under neutral
conditions and consequently were not sensitive to experimentally
heightened achievement motivation. On the other hand, pictures with
weak achievement cues should have elicited only a moderate amount of
imagery under neutral conditions. These pictures would be more
sensitive to any increase in achievement motivation (cf. Haber and
Alpert, 1958).

ACHIEVEMENT IMAGERY FROM PICTURES HAVING STRONG AND WEAK ACHIEVEMENT CUES. For strongly cued pictures, means of n Achievement scores obtained under the four different conditions are virtually identical (ranging from 7.57 to 7.97) and are not significantly different ($F = .11$, $df = 3$ and 214, n.s.).

Table 2 shows that for pictures with weak achievement cues there is a tendency for means of n Achievement scores to differ across the four experimental conditions ($F = 2.44$, $df = 3$ and 214, $p < .10$). Dunnett's test shows that when the three arousal conditions are compared with the neutral condition, only the mean of n Achievement scores obtained under extrinsic conditions is significantly higher than the mean of the neutral n Achievement scores ($p < .01$, one-tailed test). This result provides clear support for the multiple-determinant assumption.

n ACHIEVEMENT SCORES OF SUBJECTS WITH HIGH AND LOW TEST ANXIETY. A possible explanation for the failure of n Achievement scores obtained under achievement-oriented and multi-incentive conditions to be higher than those obtained under neutral conditions is that the former conditions may have aroused anxiety about failure in subjects with high Test Anxiety, and consequently may have inhibited their expression of achievement imagery (Atkinson and Litwin, Chapter 5). This possibility implies a stronger negative (or weaker positive) correlation between Test Anxiety scores and n Achievement scores obtained under achievement-oriented or multi-incentive conditions than between Test Anxiety scores and neutral n Achievement scores. The results do not support this hypothesis. The correlation of Test Anxiety scores with n Achievement scores obtained under neutral conditions is .11 ($N = 125$), under achievement-oriented conditions is .18 ($N = 30$), under multi-incentive conditions is .30 ($N = 30$), and under extrinsic conditions is $-.15$ ($N = 30$). There is, if anything, a stronger *positive* correlation between Test Anxiety and n Achievement scores obtained under achievement-oriented and multi-incentive conditions than between Test Anxiety and neutral n Achievement scores. Hence, there is no evidence that the arousal of anxiety about failure inhibited the expression of achievement imagery in thematic apperceptive stories.

n ACHIEVEMENT SCORES AND ARITHMETIC PERFORMANCE.[2] Mean arithmetic scores for Ss high and low in n Achievement are presented for the different experimental conditions in Table 3. Analyses of variance comparing motivation groups across conditions were carried out for

[2] Supplementary analyses, reported in Smith (1961), show essentially the same relationships between n Achievement and performance as those reported above when the effect of ACE quantitative ability scores on performance is controlled.

Table 3

Arithmetic performance of subjects with high
and low *n* Achievement scores

Neutral *n* Achievement		"A" Conditions			
		Achievement IA	Multi-Incentive IIA	Extrinsic IIIA	Relaxed IVA
High	N	16	18	15	15
	Mean*	70.69	58.39	56.47	52.07
	SD	24.75	23.41	18.27	22.30
Low	N	15	18	15	14
	Mean	64.93	76.94	55.93	51.43
	SD	18.82	22.40	26.48	20.45
Aroused *n* Achievement		"B" Conditions			
		Achievement IB	Multi-Incentive IIB		Extrinsic IIIB
High	N	15	16		16
	Mean	59.80	54.81		51.38
	SD	12.55	23.78		12.22
Low	N	15	14		15
	Mean	56.33	55.86		52.93
	SD	22.89	18.19		17.21

* Mean number of arithmetic problems solved correctly in 14 minutes.

the "A" and "B" conditions separately. For the four "A" conditions there is a significant difference between mean arithmetic scores due to experimental conditions ($F = 3.90$, $df = 3$ and 116, $p < .025$), but the effect of high versus low motivation was not significant ($F = .79$, $df = 1$ and 116, n.s.). For the three "B" conditions there were no significant effects due to the experimental conditions ($F = 1.10$, $df = 2$ and 82, n.s.) or to motivation groups ($F = .01$, $df = 1$ and 82, n.s.).

The results do not support the hypothesis derived from the multiple-determinant position that *n* Achievement scores obtained following extrinsically motivated performance will be related positively to such performance. There are no significant differences between performance levels of high and low *n* Achievement groups in either Multi-Incentive Condition IIB or Extrinsic Condition IIIB. In fact, in both conditions,

Ss with low *n* Achievement work slightly more problems on the average than Ss with high *n* Achievement (Table 3).

Similarly, the results appear on first examination to give only weak support to Atkinson's theory of motivation and performance. The mean performance level of Ss with high *n* Achievement is not significantly greater than that of Ss with low *n* Achievement in either Achievement Condition IA or Achievement Condition IB. Moreover, in neither the "neutral *n* Achievement prior to performance" conditions nor the "aroused performance prior to aroused *n* Achievement" conditions is there the expected interaction between achievement motivation and experimental conditions showing a larger positive difference between performance scores of high and low *n* Achievement groups in the achievement conditions than in the other conditions. However, the largest positive differences do occur in the achievement conditions as expected. The interaction values of F are 1.95 ($df = 3$ and 116, $p < .20$) for the "A" conditions, and .26 ($df = 2$ and 82, n.s.) for the "B" conditions. The only significant difference between means of arithmetic scores of Ss with high and low *n* Achievement scores in any condition is the unexpected negative difference in Multi-Incentive Condition IIA ($t = 2.48$, $df = 116$, $p < .02$, two-tailed test).

It does appear, however, that across conditions the *pattern of differences* between performance means of Ss with high and low *n* Achievement supports the following reformulation of Atkinson's position: as the proportion of overall motivation for performance which is attributable to arousal by achievement incentives increases, the strength of the positive relationship between *n* Achievement and performance will increase. To test this hypothesis conditions were ordered according to the size of the differences between mean arithmetic scores of high and low *n* Achievement groups (see Table 4). In support of the hypothesis, the analysis shows a high positive correlation (Rho $= .93$, $N = 7$, $p < .02$, two-tailed test) between this ordering of the conditions and the order of conditions based on the estimated proportion of overall motivation for performance attributable to achievement incentives. In other words, *as the estimated proportion of overall motivation for performance attributable to achievement incentives increases, the strength of the positive relationship between n Achievement scores and performance increases.* In fact, there is a tendency for *n* Achievement scores to be negatively related to performance in conditions in which an extrinsic incentive was present, which suggests that motives negatively correlated with *n* Achievement were aroused in those conditions. This analysis of the pattern of differences across conditions defines high and low *n* Achievement groups in terms of a median split within each

Table 4

Experimental conditions ranked according to the proportion of
overall motivation for arithmetic performance attributable
to achievement incentives and according to the size of
the difference between mean arithmetic scores of
subjects with high and low *n* Achievement

Condition	Proportion of Overall Motivation Attributable to Achievement Incentives* Rank	Differences between Means of Arithmetic Scores			
		High Achievement Low Achievement† Difference	Rank	High Achievement Low Achievement‡ Difference	Rank
Achievement IA	1	5.76	1	10.58	1
Relaxed IVA	2	.64	3	4.49	2
Achievement IB	3	3.47	2	3.47	3
Multi-Incentive IIB	4	− 1.05	5	− 1.05	5
Extrinsic IIIA	5	.54	4	.55	4
Extrinsic IIIB	6	− 1.55	6	− 1.55	6
Multi-Incentive IIA	7	−18.55	7	−14.36	7

* The rank of 1 indicates the highest proportion attributable to achievement incentives.

† Differences between High and Low groups are based on a division of the *n* Achievement scores at the median within each condition.

‡ Differences between High and Low groups are based on a division of the *n* Achievement scores at the median within each condition for the "B" conditions. For the four "A" conditions all neutral *n* Achievement scores were combined, and a common median was used to determine High and Low groups within particular "A" conditions.

condition. Another way of defining the high and low groups is possible for the "A" conditions. Since *n* Achievement scores in all the "A" conditions were obtained under neutral conditions, it is also possible to define high and low groups within each "A" condition in terms of a median split for all neutral *n* Achievement scores combined. When this is done, the differences between arithmetic means of Ss with high and low *n* Achievement are accentuated in the expected direction (Table 4). The correlation between conditions ordered according to these differences and according to the proportion of overall motivation for performance attributable to arousal by achievement incentives is even stronger (Rho = .96, *N* = 7, *p* < .02, two-tailed test).

DISCUSSION

Situational Determinants of Level of Achievement Imagery. The expectation based on the McClelland-Atkinson position that *n* Achievement scores would be higher under achievement-oriented conditions than under neutral conditions was not supported, although the difference was in the expected direction. Achievement salience scores from Condition IB suggest that the achievement-orientation may not have been fully effective, and therefore may not have provided a clear-cut arousal effect on level of achievement imagery. It is also possible that the use of a "relaxed" condition rather than a "neutral" condition as a baseline would have enabled the demonstration of the expected difference as in some prior studies (cf. French, 1955; McClelland, et al., 1953).

In the present study, as in that of French (1955), more achievement imagery was produced under extrinsic conditions than under any other condition. The fact that low cue pictures elicited higher *n* Achievement scores under extrinsic conditions than under neutral conditions was expected on the basis of the multiple-determinant position but not the McClelland-Atkinson position. This result is particularly striking in view of the fact that *(a)* the salience of achievement incentives was reported to be *lower* in the extrinsic condition (IIIB) than in the achievement-oriented (IB) and multi-incentive (IIB) conditions, *(b)* an extrinsic incentive to finish quickly so as to have time for other things was strongly present in the extrinsic condition and virtually absent in the other two conditions, and *(c)* the level of arithmetic performance was slightly lower in the extrinsic condition than in the other two conditions.

These results call into question the assumption that *n* Achievement scores reflect *only* achievement motivation. The possibility must now be considered seriously that "achievement imagery" can be produced by aroused states of motivation other than achievement motivation, especially in situations which call for instrumental acts typically associated with achievement motivation—such as working hard, fast, or carefully —which are directed toward some incentive or source of satisfaction which is extrinsic to pride in achievement per se. It would appear, for example, that *n* Achievement scores obtained from surveys (Veroff, Atkinson, Feld, and Gurin, 1960) and from folk tales and other literary products (cf. McClelland, 1958d) cannot automatically be assumed to reflect only achievement motivation, since the eliciting conditions for such materials are not controlled. Until these issues are clarified by further research, it would appear that n Achievement scores obtained under conventional testing conditions, in which extrinsic incentives are minimized, are likely to be the most valid measures of achievement motivation.

It must be noted, however, that the evidence for the multiple-determinant position is equivocal. In the first place, such a view also predicts that high n Achievement scores will be produced under achievement-oriented and multi-incentive conditions, a prediction which was not supported. Second, although achievement salience scores were lowest in Extrinsic Condition IIIB, achievement incentives were by no means eliminated completely by the experimental manipulations. Of the Ss in that condition, 58 per cent checked, "I wanted to see myself as a person of high ability," as a reason for working hard on the arithmetic test. Possibly the salience index, which is based on the *ranks,* as well as the number of achievement reasons checked, underestimated the salience of achievement incentives in Condition IIIB. Certainly it appears that the task itself may have generated some intrinsic achievement motivation despite attempts to reduce external cues suggestive of achievement. E may, in addition, have been unintentionally responsible for accentuating the level of achievement imagery produced under extrinsic conditions due to a flaw in the experimental design. Only in the extrinsic conditions were the Ss given the impression that they were expected to *complete* the arithmetic task and then interrupted after 14 minutes of performance. The procedure was intended to arouse motivation to finish quickly so as to leave as soon as possible. In fact, it may have inadvertently left the Ss with an unresolved tension to complete the task which was then expressed in the immediately following thematic apperceptive measure as heightened achievement imagery. (Research in progress by the author designed to check this possibility does indicate that Ss produce a somewhat, but not significantly, higher level of achievement imagery under achievement-orientation following interruption of performance than under regular achievement-orientation. Comparisons of these two groups with a neutral control group are not yet available.) For these reasons the high level of achievement imagery produced under extrinsic conditions must be regarded as equivocal support for the multiple-determinant position.

n Achievement and Arithmetic Performance Under Different Conditions. An analysis of differences between performance levels of high and low n Achievement groups within particular conditions does not provide direct support for either the McClelland-Atkinson position or the multiple-determinant position. The differences are generally in the direction expected by the McClelland-Atkinson position, however, and in the *opposite* direction from that expected by the multiple-determinant position. The slight negative relationship between extrinsically motivated performance and *n* Achievement scores obtained following extrinsic arousal is perhaps the strongest argument against the interpretation that the high level of achievement imagery in Extrinsic Condition IIIB reflects extrinsic motivation.

When self-report evidence concerning the relative effectiveness of the experimental procedures is taken into consideration, it is possible to test a reformulated statement of Atkinson's position. When performance levels *across conditions* are compared, it appears that the strongest positive relationships between *n* Achievement scores and arithmetic scores occur in conditions in which only achievement incentives for performance were introduced. More specifically, there is clear evidence that as the estimated proportion of overall motivation attributable to achievement incentives increases in different experimental conditions, the superiority in arithmetic performance of *S*s high in *n* Achievement over *S*s low in *n* Achievement increases.

The pattern of results for the achievement-oriented and multi-incentive conditions is similar to that obtained in similar conditions by Atkinson and Reitman (1956). In both studies, *n* Achievement scores are positively related to arithmetic scores under achievement-oriented conditions and negatively related under multi-incentive conditions. According to Atkinson and Reitman, *S*s with high *n* Achievement are expected to solve *more* problems than *S*s with low *n* Achievement under multi-incentive conditions, on the assumption that adding the incentives of a monetary prize and the *E*'s approval to the achievement incentives would be like adding a constant to both high and low motivation groups. Atkinson and Reitman, in discussing the unexpected negative relationship obtained in their multi-incentive condition, suggest that their high *n* Achievement group might have suffered a decrement in performance due to very intense motivation. The strong negative relationship obtained in the present study suggests the alternative possibility that motives such as a desire for money and approval, or resentment of *E*'s authority may have been aroused in the multi-incentive conditions and may be negatively correlated with *n* Achievement. In other words, the negative relationships between *n* Achievement and arithmetic performance obtained in the conditions in which extrinsic incentives were introduced imply that some motives aroused in these conditions were systematically stronger in *S*s having low *n* Achievement than in *S*s having high *n* Achievement. The finding calls into question the assumption in previous studies of performance level (e.g., Atkinson, 1958b) that extrinsic motives will be uncorrelated with *n* Achievement. It suggests that rather than assuming that high and low *n* Achievement groups will be like each other in all respects except achievement motivation, it might be better to conduct research in which *S*s with high *n* Achievement in one condition are compared with *S*s having high *n* Achievement in a different condition. For example, in tests of Atkinson's model for risk-taking (1957), it might be advisable to contrast the performance level of *S*s having high *n* Achievement and low Test Anxiety on a task where the probability of success is .50 with the performance level of similar *S*s on a task where the probability of success is .20.

Finally, the use of a postperformance questionnaire as an independent check on the effectiveness of the experimental procedures is a long-needed innovation in research on *n* Achievement. When, for example, performance scores of two different groups which have been given identical instructions turn out to be widely discrepant (O'Connor, 1959; Reitman, 1957), it is easier to interpret such results if there is *independent* evidence showing whether or not the intended conditions for performance were established.

SUMMARY

Evidence is presented concerning two assumptions underlying past research on *n* Achievement: first, that "achievement imagery" in thematic apperception reflects *only* achievement motivation; second, performance scores of *S*s high and low in *n* Achievement can be compared on the assumption that the two groups are similar, on the average, in all important respects other than achievement motivation. . . .

There were approximately 30 *S*s in each of seven different experimental conditions in which *n* Achievement scores and arithmetic performance scores were obtained under a variety of motivation-arousing orientations. The experimental manipulations were shown to be generally effective by means of a self-report questionnaire given at the end of each session.

The results showed that the highest *n* Achievement scores were produced under extrinsic conditions. For weak-cue pictures, significantly higher *n* Achievement scores were produced under extrinsic conditions than under neutral conditions. . . . Scores for *n* Achievement obtained under achievement-oriented and multi-incentive conditions were not significantly higher than those obtained under neutral conditions. . . .

The pattern of results across conditions clearly indicated that as the proportion of overall motivation for performance attributable to achievement incentives increases, the strength of the positive relationship between *n* Achievement and performance increases.

The results suggest that under some conditions *n* Achievement scores may reflect *extrinsic* motivation instead of, or in addition to, achievement motivation. The need for standardized conditions for obtaining optimally valid *n* Achievement scores is emphasized. The evidence is equivocal, however, since higher *n* Achievement scores were not also obtained under achievement-oriented and multi-incentive conditions than under neutral conditions.

Also called into question is the assumption made in some studies of motivation and performance that extrinsic motives will be uncorrelated with *n* Achievement. The present results strongly suggest the need in future research to control for motives negatively correlated with *n* Achievement which may be aroused under certain kinds of testing situations.

Neglected Factors in Studies
of Achievement-Oriented Performance:
Social Approval as Incentive
and Performance Decrement

Since the publication of *The Achievement Motive* by McClelland, Atkinson, Clark, and Lowell (1953), there have been a number of uniformly unsuccessful attempts to devise a new and better assessment device for this motive than the TAT. The present study must be added to the list. It represents an effort to exploit the behavioral implications of the theory of achievement motivation in the search for a simple, objective test of achievement motive. The general approach differs in one critically important respect from earlier attempts which are reviewed elsewhere (McClelland, 1958a; Atkinson, 1960). The construction of potentially useful test devices was explicitly guided by hypotheses derived from a theory which had been tested and supported in one or more earlier studies. Before the development of a theory specifying how achievement motive interacts with other factors to influence behavior, efforts to make a better test were guided by some misleading intuitive hypotheses grounded in conventional wisdom concerning the suggested meaning of the words "need for achievement," (e.g., a highly motivated person should set a very high level of aspiration, should consistently show a high level of performance and persistence at very difficult tasks, etc.).

Although the present theory-guided effort does not produce the new and better test—perhaps even *because* it does not—it serves to illustrate

This study and the preliminary work on which it is based were made possible by a grant-in-aid from Behavioral Research Service of the General Electric Company (1959–1960) and a graduate research and study grant from the General Elecric Foundation in 1961. We wish to express our gratitude to L. L. Ferguson and Herbert Meyer for their assistance in obtaining support for studies of achievement motivation.

how inseparable are problems arising in the construction of a test of personality and in the experimental analysis of behavioral processes. Instead of the new and better test, this study yields several unanticipated results and hypotheses about them. If substantiated in later work, this outcome will have served to enlarge considerably understanding of achievement-oriented behavior and bring us that much closer to the new and better tests we seek.

The plan of the study is simple. The strength of *n* Achievement and Test Anxiety were assessed using conventional methods. An achievement-oriented, individual test situation was employed to gain measures of each *S*'s speed of performance, risk-taking preference, and persistence in various activities. It was expected that previously observed relationships between *n* Achievement, Test Anxiety, and these dependent variables would be reproduced and that they would be interrelated in predictable ways. Then, it was presumed, one or another or some combination of these easily obtained behavioral measures might be pursued further as potentially a more useful and economical test of the achievement-related motives than the combination of TAT *n* Achievement and Test Anxiety Questionnaire presently employed. We supposed that the pattern of results would suggest which test had greatest sensitivity and the most fruitful next steps towards an objective test of achievement motive.

The results of earlier experiments have sensitized us to many often-ignored problems which arise when *S*s are tested individually (chiefly some loss of exact comparability of subtle situational factors among the various *S*s) and when a series of different tasks are presented to *S*s on one test occasion (chiefly loss of control over the conditions that are appropriate for each task because of uncontrolled or unknown sequence effects). We thus began this study anticipating that an attempt to replicate results obtained in earlier studies which had focused attention upon only one dependent performance variable might be marred by some loss of control of relevant conditions. The practical need for a standard test that can be administered individually overweighed these considerations.

AN ACHIEVEMENT RISK PREFERENCE SCALE (ARPS)

The main impetus for this study was provided by some encouraging preliminary results concerning a paired-comparison test of strength of achievement motive relative to strength of motive to avoid failure (O'Connor and Atkinson, 1962). Derivations from the theory provided the basis for selection of items. The scale, called ARPS, consists of a series of paired comparisons in which, according to theory, a person in whom $M_S > M_{AF}$ should favor one option and a person in whom $M_{AF} > M_S$ should favor the other. Two general derivations which give the rationale for a number of items are: *(a)* If $M_S > M_{AF}$, all activities in which performance is evaluated against some standard of excellence will be relatively attractive. If $M_{AF} > M_S$, those same activities will be relatively unattractive. *(b)* If $M_S > M_{AF}$, activities involving evaluation of performance will be more attractive when probabilities of success and failure are near equal than when they are discrepant. If $M_{AF} > M_S$, activities involving evaluation of performance will be more repulsive when probabilities of success and failure are near equal than when they are discrepant.

Some illustrative items based on these derivations are given in Table 1. In each case, the option marked with an asterisk is the one

Table 1

Sample items from an Achievement Risk Preference Scale (*$M_S > M_{AF}$)

---

1. *A. When I am reading a magazine and come across puzzles or quizzes, I often stop to try them.
   B. When I am reading a magazine and come across puzzles or quizzes, I rarely stop to try them.

2. A. If I were a pinch hitter, I'd like to come to bat when my team was losing 5 to 2.
   *B. If I were a pinch hitter, I'd like to come to bat when the score was tied.

3. *A. I become bored with tasks once I am sure I can do them.
   B. I enjoy tasks most when I am sure I can do them.

4. *A. I like playing a game when my opponent and I are equally skilled.
   B. I like playing a game when my opponent is much more skilled than I am.

5. A. When I am playing a game or participating in a sport, I am more concerned with having fun than with winning.
   *B. When I am playing a game or participating in a sport, I am very intent on winning.

---

which should be selected when $M_S > M_{AF}$. We do not include the whole scale in this report, because we do not wish to encourage the mere application of a device that requires substantially more systematic developmental work before it can be employed as a substitute for TAT *n* Achievement and the Test Anxiety Questionnaire combined. The sample items should be sufficient to spell out the line of attack for those who wish to undertake a similar approach to the problem of improving the assessment of motives.

Preliminary results with three forms of ARPS—one for college students, one for adults, one for children—are shown in Table 2. Each

Table 2

Percentage of Ss simultaneously classified high or low in n Achievement and Test Anxiety who scored high (above median) on ARPS*

n Achievement– Test Anxiety	College Men on College Form N	College Men on Adult Form N	Sixth-Grade Boys on Child Form N
High–Low	(24) 71%	(13) 85%	(41) 66%
High–High	(21) 52	(15) 47	(37) 22
Low–Low	(20) 50	(16) 56	(46) 46
Low–High	(22) 18	(12) 25	(45) 33
	$\chi^2 = 12.82$	$\chi^2 = 9.00$	$\chi^2 = 10.33$
	$p < .01$	$p < .01$	$p < .01$

* We are grateful to Harry Crockett, Robert Isaacson, and George Litwin for supplying data for these comparisons.

scale, containing 21 to 23 critical paired comparisons, yields a score representing the number of times S has selected options implying $M_S > M_{AF}$. In each preliminary study, Ss were classified in terms of standing relative to the median on n Achievement and Test Anxiety. Comparisons between the subgroups High n Achievement-Low Test Anxiety versus Low n Achievement-High Test Anxiety encouraged the view that ARPS should be employed in a study allowing comparison with the conventional tests in predicting certain characteristics of instrumental achievement-oriented action (speed, risk preference, persistence, etc.). Kasl (1962) employed the adult form with a group of 33 employees in a large industrial firm and found ARPS correlated .51 with the slope of reported satisfaction with occupations at different status levels, the index of strength of achievement motive developed earlier by Morgan (Chapter 14) in a study of economic behavior. Other less encouraging results with the children's form of ARPS are reported by Atkinson and O'Connor (1963).

Hypotheses. The theoretical conception from which specific predictions are derived is elaborated fully elsewhere (Chapters 2, 4, 8). Here we state the hypotheses and cite earlier studies which have confirmed them and which contain fuller discussion of their theoretical foundation.

HYPOTHESIS 1. Persons in whom the motive to achieve success (M_S) is relatively strong in relation to the motive to avoid failure (M_{AF}) will show a more marked preference for intermediate achievement risks (i.e., for tasks of intermediate difficulty) than persons in whom M_{AF} is relatively strong in relation to M_S (Atkinson, Bastian, Earl, and Litwin (1960); Atkinson and Litwin (Chapter 5); Litwin (Chapter 7); and McClelland (1958b) in reference to choice of level of difficulty in competitive games; Clark, Teevan, and Riccuiti (1956) in reference to aspiration for grades in a college course; Mahone (Chapter 12), in reference to vocational aspiration. In the present experiment, two devices are employed to assess risk preference in tasks requiring skill. One, first developed by Litwin (Chapter 7) is called a Decision-Making Test. It requires the S to examine quickly a set of tasks of the same general character, but which obviously differ in difficulty, and to make a rapid decision as to which one he will undertake to complete in a short time period. The second was the Achievement Risk Preference Scale, which also includes items indicating preference for achievement-related versus nonachievement-related activities.

HYPOTHESIS 2. Persons in whom the motive to achieve success (M_S) is strong relative to motive to avoid failure (M_{AF}) will perform an achievement-related task more rapidly and efficiently when it is presented as an important test of ability than persons in whom M_{AF} is strong in relation to M_S. We infer from previous research (namely, Atkinson and Reitman, 1956; Wendt, 1955; Atkinson and Raphelson, 1956; French, 1955; Smith, Chapter 18) that a positive relation between strength of assessed achievement motive and level of performance is most apparent when other incentives for rapid and efficient performance are minimized and the achievement-test character of a task is effectively stressed. This is also a condition in which persons strong in Test Anxiety have been shown to suffer performance decrements (Sarason, Mandler, and Craighill, 1952; Alpert and Haber, 1960; Atkinson and Litwin, Chapter 5.) In the present experiment it would have been ideal to reproduce the individual test condition prescribed by Atkinson and Reitman (1956) and employed by Smith (Chapter 18), but other requirements of the study made it necessary for the E (PO) to remain in the room with the S during performance of the achievement tasks.

HYPOTHESIS 3. Persons in whom the motive to achieve success (M_S) is strong in relation to the motive to avoid failure (M_{AF}) should be *less* persistent than persons in whom M_{AF} is strong in relation to M_S in their effort to solve a problem (actually an insoluble problem) that is initially presented to them as extremely difficult, *when there are other achievement activities to be undertaken as alternatives.* Studies by French and Thomas (1958) and Atkinson and Litwin (Chapter 5) have shown that achievement motive is positively related to persistence at an achievement task, and/or Test Anxiety is negatively related to persistence when the outcome is still in doubt and *when the alternative is a nonachievement-related activity.* But Feather (Chapters 8 and 9) has confirmed the above-stated implication of the theory of achievement motivation. In the present experiment, Ss are presented with a puzzle and given false norms which state that only 5 out of 100 college students have been able to solve it. They are also instructed that they may turn to a different puzzle whenever they so desire. We include this particular test of persistence because it is not obvious that a person who is highly motivated to achieve should ever show *less* persistence at a task than a person in whom anxiety (i.e., avoidant motivation) is stronger. Yet this is one of the predicted manifestations of preference for intermediate risk among Ss who are highly motivated to achieve.

Since the thematic apperceptive measure of *n* Achievement and the Test Anxiety Questionnaire have been the standard assessment devices in studies that have yielded the fund of evidence from which the theory of achievement motivation evolved, they are viewed as the validity criteria in the present study. . . . To provide a single indicator of the strength of M_S relative to M_{AF} (i.e., *n* Achievement minus Test Anxiety), the raw scores on each test were converted to standard scores and the standard score for Test Anxiety was subtracted from the standard score for *n* Achievement. We refer to this combination of scores as the criterion measure of *resultant achievement motivation.*

Use of a single indicator of the strength of motive to approach success in relation to the strength of motive to avoid failure is clearly justified by the logic of the theory of achievement motivation. When simplified algebraically, as pointed out by Edwards (1962), it states that the situational determinant of achievement-related motivation is represented by $P_s(1 - P_s)$, and the personality determinant is represented by $M_S - M_{AF}$. Resultant achievement motivation equals the product of personality ($M_S - M_{AF}$) and situational influences ($P_s (1 - P_s)$), where P_s (probability of success) is the measure of strength of expectancy of success in an activity and $1 - P_s$ is equivalent to I_s, the incentive value of success at that particular level of difficulty.

METHOD

Subjects. Subjects were recruited by announcement in the college newspaper and were paid at the rate of $2.00 per hour. Forty male subjects appeared for the first test period, but 5 of these Ss did not complete all other phases of the study. The effective N was thus reduced to 35.[1]

FIRST TEST PERIOD

Ss were tested individually in the first test period. It was devoted to the various objective test devices and measures of performance on achievement-related tasks.

Risk-Preference Task. When S arrived at the small test room, he was met by the E (PO) and asked to sit at a desk facing the wall. The E then administered Litwin's Decision-Making Test with the comment, "This is what I would like you to do first." The S then read the instructions for this task:

> In this test you are required to make decisions in situations involving risk of gain or loss. Your objective will be to make a decision in each situation presented which will be most likely to maximize your gain and minimize your loss.
>
> Although you will be asked to solve some problems or simple puzzles, this is *not* a test of your intelligence or of your problem-solving ability. In fact, it has more of the features of a game than a test.
>
> Each section of this test presents a series of problems or puzzles of a particular type. For example, one section presents arithmetic problems, another presents jig-saw puzzles, another has scrambled-letter puzzles and so on. The problem or puzzles within each section are presented in sets which vary in difficulty. Short, easy sets are presented first in each series and longer, more difficult sets are presented last.
>
> In each section you are to *select the one set you will work on* in the time allowed. (The time limit for each task will be one minute.) Your selection should be based on the following facts:
>
> (1) The *number of points* awarded for completing a set will be *proportional to the difficulty of the problems,* that is, the more difficult the problems, the higher the point payoff.
>
> (2) *No credit* will be given for partially completed or partially correct problems.

---

[1] Three Ss simply did not appear for the second test period. In addition, one S was eliminated because he reported having participated in a similar study previously, and another who had written obviously disturbed thematic apperceptive stories was eliminated before results were analyzed.

As a general rule, your experience with one series of problems will not be a good guide to the choice you should make on the next series, since the type of ability required in one series will differ quite a bit from the type of ability required in the next.

Following the general instructions, *S* opened the task booklet and confronted further instructions as to how the first task was to be accomplished and an example of it. Then he was specifically instructed:

> You are to select *one* _____ that you would like to try. You will then have *one minute* to work on the _____ you select. You must complete all the _____ correctly in order to receive credit.
>   When the signal is given to turn the page, look over the _____ quickly and choose the one you wish to try. You will have only 10–15 seconds to make your choice. As soon as you have made your choice, *circle the letter of the statement you are trying* (at the left).

When *S* indicated that he understood what was expected of him, *E* told him to go ahead and turn the page and look at the first set of tasks. Fifteen seconds were allowed for the decision as to which one of the set would be attempted, and then one minute was allowed for performance of the task. The *E* kept time. When one minute had elapsed, the *S* was told to turn to the next page, which described another task in a similar manner, and so on. There were four different kinds of tasks. Hence, the *S* made four relatively quick decisions as to what degree of difficulty he would attempt on each task.

When the Decision-Making Test had been completed, *E* said, "I'll put these aside for the man who is working on these games. He is interested in the kinds of risks people like to take in games." The *E* then led the *S* to another desk on which were several sharpened pencils, a manila folder containing several tests, and a folder of instructions which *E* then consulted.

Speed Task. The second task (letter-number substitution) was designed to yield a measure of *speed of performance*. When *S* was seated at the second desk, *E* gave the following achievement-oriented instruction:

> We will spend the rest of the time on a different study. We are working this year on developing tests similar to tests of ability you may have taken in the past. You probably know that psychologists are very much interested in the measurement of intelligence. Tests of intelligence are used widely to select students for college and for graduate and professional training. They are also used in the armed services and in business organizations to select men who will be likely to succeed in high-level positions. The usefulness of these tests has been repeatedly demonstrated. Men scoring high on tests of intelligence perform better on a variety of academic and professional activities than men scoring low.
>   Although the tests we have now are valuable, we are still attempting to construct better ones. As the number of applicants for college increases, it becomes even more important to have tests that will differentiate between

persons who are qualified for college training and those who are not. It is equally important to select men who will be most likely to succeed in the professional and business world. Today I am going to give you some tests which may be similar to some you have taken before.

The first test is the Letter-Number Substitution Test. Read the instructions on the first page.

The S then consulted instructions for the Letter-Number Substitution Test. The S's task was to substitute letters for a series of numbers following a coding system given on each page of the task booklet. For example, the coding system might have been:

MAZQFLODEP
1 2 3 4 5 6 7 8 9 0

and the task to substitute letters for series of numbers like 4 6 7 9 5.

The S was given three practice trials followed by a series of test trials. He was instructed to work as rapidly and as accurately as possible, turning to a new page only on the E's signal. The E timed the performance on each trial. Before the S began, E said,

> You see the task is to substitute letters for numbers according to the code as rapidly and accurately as possible. Your score will be the number coded correctly. There will be several trials and *the code will change on each trial*. This test seems to measure the ability to think rapidly and accurately. It is especially sensitive to the capacity for changing one's point of view and adopting a new approach. As I said, there will be three practice trials. Then there will be a series of test trials. Your score will be based on how well you do on the test trials. Any questions?

The E followed a prearranged schedule which defined how many letter-number substitutions should be accomplished by all Ss on a particular trial. Performance on each trial was timed by a stopwatch, and when S had completed the predetermined number of substitutions E called time and instructed S to turn to a new page. The measure of speed of performance is the total number of seconds required to complete the predetermined number of substitutions on six test trials. The number of substitutions was held constant for all Ss in order to prevent substantial variations in subjective feelings of success and failure since other tasks were to follow.

Persistence Task. The next task, a perceptual reasoning task, from which the measure of persistence is obtained, is described by Feather (Chapters 8 and 9). The instructions were adapted from Feather. The most critical instructions were:

> The four items in this test vary in difficulty. Some are harder than others, and you're not expected to solve all of them, but do the best you can. Before I give you an item, I shall let you know the percentage of college students who are able to pass it at your age level. This will give you an indication of its difficulty.

Here is item 1. (*E* refers to Table of Norms.) The tables show that for your age level, about 5% (4.8%, to be exact) of college students were able to get the solution. Try to get the solution if you can. But remember that these four items vary in difficulty, some are harder than others, and you might not be able to solve all of them. So if you feel you're not getting anywhere with an item, you should let me know at once, and we will move on to the next one. You can have as many trials as you like on any item. You should find this one fairly difficult.

Most important for creation of the proper experimental condition were the final instructions: (*a*) that there were four different items which differed in difficulty; (*b*) that the initial item was very difficult and likely to be solved by only 5% of college students; (*c*) that *S* was free to move on to another puzzle at any time. It is assumed that when *S*s are told that there are four items which differ in difficulty and then are given an extremely difficult one to begin with, all *S*s will anticipate that the other items are of more moderate difficulty.

If *S* had not elected to turn to another puzzle at the end of twenty minutes, *E* said, "We will have to go on to the second problem so that we will have time to finish everything we have to do." The second item was presented as one which 50% of college students could solve. It was easily solved by all *S*s within a few trials, providing an experience of success after a rather thwarting experience on the experimental task which had preceded. When *S* had solved the second puzzle, *E* then said that she had cut the length of the puzzle test to two items for everyone because she had one more task to present in the limited time. She assured *S* that her reason for stating initially that there would be four items was to allow direct comparison with earlier results on the first two puzzles when *S*s had been told there were four items. The *S*s accepted this as a reasonable explanation and showed no signs of feeling duped by the instructions.

Paired-Comparisons Scale of Risk Preference. At the close of the first test period, which had been cut short, *E* presented the Achievement Risk Preference Scale (ARPS) to the *S* and then *left the room while S read the instructions and completed the inventory.*

After ten minutes had elapsed, *E* returned to the test room, paid the *S* for his work in this test period, and asked him if he would like to participate in other studies at the same rate of pay. All *S*s expressed a willingness to be called again, but only 37 of the original 40 *S*s did, in fact, appear for the second test period several weeks later.

SECOND TEST PERIOD

The *S*s who had been tested individually in the first test period were scheduled in groups of 4 to 8 persons for the second test period. Scheduling difficulties prevented calling them all together, as would have been most desirable, for administration of the thematic apperceptive test of *n* Achievement and the Test Anxiety Questionnaire.

The original four *n* Achievement pictures designated in Atkinson (1958a, p. 832) as 2, 1, 8, and 7 (see also McClelland et al., 1953) were administered to obtain imaginative stories which yielded the measure of *n* Achievement. Nothing was done either to relax *S*s or to heighten their motivation prior to administration of the TAT measure. Standard procedure was followed for the test condition described as "Neutral" (McClelland et al., 1953; Atkinson, 1958a, pp. 836–837). Following this, the Test Anxiety Questionnaire developed by Mandler and Sarason (1952) was administered. This inventory calls for self-reports concerning symptoms of anxiety in test situations.

SCORES OBTAINED FROM VARIOUS TESTS

TAT *n* Achievement. Protocols were scored following the manual prepared by McClelland, et al. (1953), and Atkinson (1958a) by the *E* (PO), whose coding reliability exceeds .90. The range of obtained *n* Achievement scores was −1 to 14 with a median of 5. Raw scores were converted to standard scores to allow combination with standard Test Anxiety scores. Stories were also scored for *n* Affiliation yielding a range of 0 to 13 with a median of 2. Because *n* Affiliation figured centrally in the analysis of results in a way that had not been anticipated, another trained coder[2] also scored the stories. The rank-order coding reliability was .73 (*N* = 35), but examination of coding differences revealed only one major disagreement in coding. Without this case, which was referred to a third judge for resolution of the disagreement, the coding reliability was .86 (*N* = 34).

Test Anxiety. The Test Anxiety Questionnaire was scored by dividing each line scale into four equal intervals and assigning scores of 1 to 4 to each response with high score denoting strong anxiety response. Scores were summed to yield the total Test Anxiety score. Raw scores were converted to standard scores.

The rank-order correlation between *n* Achievement and Test Anxiety was −.12 (*N* = 35), between *n* Affiliation and Test Anxiety −.07 (*N* = 35), and between *n* Affiliation and *n* Achievement −.06 (*N* = 35). None of the correlations is significant.

Decision-Making Test. The score derived from this test represents degree of deviation from choice of tasks of intermediate difficulty. A low deviation score implies strong resultant achievement motivation. The theory of achievement motivation defines intermediate difficulty as the point at which subjective probability of success equals .50. In the Decision-Making Test, subjective probability of success is neither defined by instructions nor ascertained by self report from *S*s. It is defined indirectly by Litwin's (Chapter 7) distribution

[2] We acknowledge with thanks the assistance of Stuart Karabenick.

index. For each task, the median choice of Ss is ascertained, and the absolute discrepancy between the rank of the level of difficulty chosen by S and the rank of the median choice is determined. This deviation is then divided by the average deviation for that task to yield a score. Scores obtained in this way on each of the four tasks are then summed to provide a single index of degree of deviation of choices from intermediate difficulty.

Given the theory of achievement motivation, there is more justification for use of the obtained median choice of Ss who are high in resultant achievement motivation to define the point where probability of success equals .50 than the median choice of all Ss. Subjects in whom resultant achievement motivation is strong should approach the point of intermediate difficulty; but Ss who are strong in failure-avoidant motivation should avoid that point. If the range of difficulty of tasks presented to Ss is not symmetric, e.g., should the range of difficulty be restricted to very difficult to moderately difficult rather than from very difficult to very easy, the obtained median choice of a heterogeneous group of Ss would not, according to theory, fall at the point where P_s is .50. (An instance is reported in Atkinson, Bastian, Earl, and Litwin (1960).) And even when the range of difficulty is symmetric about $P_s = .50$, the theory of achievement motivation does not assume that Ss who are concerned about avoidance of failure will necessarily be equally distributed among preference for very easy and very difficult tasks. Hence, in the absence of an independent measure of probability of success, the most theoretically sound method of defining the point of intermediate difficulty is to employ the median choice of Ss who should approach the point where P_s equals .50, namely, those known to be strong in resultant achievement motivation. This procedure was followed in the present study as the basis for obtaining deviation scores for all Ss.

It might be argued that this procedure guarantees a positive relationship between preference for intermediate risk and the criterion measure of resultant achievement motivation. In fact, it does not; for Ss who are low in resultant achievement motivation (or avoidant in motivation according to TAT n Achievement and Test Anxiety) may distribute their choices about the median choice of those strong in resultant achievement motivation so that their median is, in fact, the same but the spread of scores is even more restricted. This result, clearly contrary to theory, can occur and would constitute a strong refutation of the hypothesis that preference for intermediate risk is a function of strength of resultant achievement motivation.

The deviation index employed must assume that there are no substantial differences among Ss in subjective probability of success at the various tasks employed. *It is an acknowledged weakness of this type of test that it does not provide an adequate measure of probability of success for individual Ss.*

Achievement Risk Preference Scale. The total score obtained for each S indicates the number of times (out of 23) that the alternative representing preference for intermediate versus extreme risk or some achievement risk versus no achievement risk is chosen. The range of the scores obtained was 6 to 20 with a median of 14.

Letter Substitution Test. The measure of *speed of performance* is the total time taken to perform a predetermined number of substitutions on six trials. The range of obtained time scores was 291 to 448 seconds, with a median of 368 seconds. A low time score implies strong resultant achievement motivation.

Perceptual Reasoning Test. The measure of *persistence* on an insoluble problem, presented to Ss as very difficult with other achievement tasks to be undertaken as alternatives, is the number of trials taken on the experimental task before turning to an alternative (or before being interrupted when the time limit was reached). Feather (Chapter 8) found that number of trials and time were so highly correlated in this task that either measure could be employed. The range of trials was 3 to 35 with a median of 10.5. A low number of trials (i.e., low persistence at an extremely difficult problem when other more moderately difficult problems are available as alternatives) implies strong resultant achievement motivation.

RESULTS

Table 3 shows the relationship between the criterion measure, *n* Achievement-Test Anxiety, and each of the other potential tests of achievement-oriented motivation. Only the relation of ARPS to the

Table 3

Effect of individual differences in resultant achievement motivation (TAT *n* Achievement-Test Anxiety) on risk preference, speed, and persistence on various achievement tests

n Achieve-ment-Test Anxiety	*N*	High on Achieve-ment Risk Preference Scale	Prefer Intermediate Risk (Decision-Making Test)	Fast Substitution Performance	Low Persistence When $P_s = .05$
High (Upper Quartile)	9	89%	44%	67%	67%
Moderate	17	35	53	59	47
Low (Lower Quartile	9	44	56	22	44
		$\chi^2 = 7.00$	n.s.	n.s.	n.s.
		$df = 2$			
		$p < .05$			

Note: In all comparisons, the distribution of dependent variable scores is divided at the median and the percentage reported refers to those behaving as specified by theory when $M_S > M_{AF}$.

criterion is as predicted and statistically significant. The measures of speed of performance and persistence[3] show insignificant trends in the predicted direction. The direction of the relation of the measure of preference for intermediate risk on the Decision-Making Test to the criterion, *n* Achievement-Test Anxiety, is opposite to that expected and insignificant. This dismal pattern of results defined the beginning point of an intensive analysis which is described in the following pages.

The Decision-Making Test, the test of speed of performance, and the puzzle task which yielded the measure of persistence were all administered under comparable conditions. The *E* was present to read instructions, observe performance, and keep time when that was called for by the nature of the task. From the theory of achievement motivation, we derive hypotheses that preference for intermediate risk (or difficulty), fast performance, and lack of persistence at the puzzle are expected behavioral symptoms of strong resultant achievement motivation. The *S* who expresses strong resultant achievement motivation in one of these tasks should also express it in the other two tasks. Table 4 shows that measures derived from the three performance tasks do, in fact, tend to be related to one another in the direction predicted. Those *Ss* who are least persistent at the insoluble puzzle (the nonobvious prediction from the theory of achievement motivation) do tend to work faster and more frequently prefer intermediate risk. The positive relationships among the three behavioral symptoms of resultant achievement motivation, while certainly modest, at least encourage the view that a standard behavioral test situation might be developed in which several different theoretically derived behavioral consequences of strong resultant achievement motivation are combined to yield a single measure of the relative strength within *S* of the two personality dispositions (motive to achieve and motive to avoid failure). This possibility is explored in Table 5.

When the inference of relatively strong resultant achievement motivation is based on positive evidence from two different performance measures, prediction of a third behavioral symptom of strong

---

[3] Feather (Chapter 9) repeated the experiment and obtained from *Ss* a measure of subjective probability of success immediately before performance. He reports substantial variation in subjective probabilities when the instruction that only 5 out of 100 college students can solve the problem was given. He shows that the predicted relationship is much more marked when the analysis of results is restricted to *Ss* who uniformly viewed probability of success at this task as very low (Table 2, Chapter 9). The present results are undoubtedly affected by some variations in subjective probabilities of success.

Table 4

Relationships among three performance measures of
resultant achievement motivation

Preference for Intermediate Risk	N	Speed of Performance	Persistence When P_s Is .05
		Fast	Low
High	18	67%	67%
Low	17	35	35

Speed of Performance	N		Persistence When P_s Is .05
			Low
Fast	18		61%
Slow	17		41

Note: According to theory, fast performance, preference for intermediate risk, and lack of persistence at an extremely difficult task when others are available are symptoms of strong resultant achievement motivation.

resultant achievement motivation is substantially improved. For example, among those who showed high speed of performance on the digit symbol substitution task, combined with low persistence at the very difficult puzzle ($N = 11$), 82% preferred intermediate risk on the Decision-Making Test compared to only 30% of those ($N = 10$), who would be classified weak in achievement motivation on the first two tasks. Yet preference for intermediate risk on the Decision-Making Test did not relate as predicted to the conventional measures, *n* Achievement–Test Anxiety. Three behavioral measures of achievement motivation are positively interrelated as predicted, but only two of them are positively related to the standard measures, *n* Achievement-Test Anxiety, and even then the relationship is weak. Why?

ARPS and Behavioral Symptoms of Achievement Motivation. A suspicion that relationships among the three performance measures might be attributable to some common influence other than resultant achievement motivation was heightened when it was found that scores from the ARPS (which did relate significantly to TAT *n* Achievement-Test Anxiety) were not related to any of the performance measures as predicted (see Table 6).

Table 5

Prediction of behavioral symptoms of resultant achievement motivation when *Ss* are simultaneously classified as strong or weak in achievement motivation on two other behavioral symptoms

Criterion measure of resultant achievement motivation: Speed of Performance and Risk Preference	N	Persistence When P_s is .05 Low
Strong on both	12	75%
Strong on one	12	42
Weak on both	11	36

$\chi^2 = 4.08$, $df = 2$, $p = .10 - .05$ (one tail)

Persistence and Risk Preference	N	Speed of Performance Fast
Strong on both	12	75%
Strong on one	12	42
Weak on both	11	36

$\chi^2 = 4.08$, $df = 2$, $p = .10 - .05$ (one tail)

Persistence and Speed of Performance	N	Preference for Intermediate Risk High
Strong on both	11	82%
Strong on one	14	43
Weak on both	10	30

$\chi^2 = 6.28$, $df = 2$, $p = .02$ (one tail)

Consideration of the possible effect of the immediate interpersonal relationship between *S* and *E* during performance of the three achievement activities, which we had obviously minimized in planning the experiment, directed attention to the possible confounding influence of *n* Affiliation in this experiment. Earlier studies have shown that performance is affected by *n* Affiliation when *E* appeals for cooperation and otherwise indicates that his immediate approval or disapproval of

Table 6

Relationship of scores on Achievement Risk Preference Scale and
three performance indicators of strong resultant achievement motivation

Score on ARPS	N	Fast Performance	Low Persistence When P_s is .05	Preference for Intermediate Risk
High	13	31%	46%	31%
Mid	8	63	75	63
Low	14	64	43	64

Note: On each performance measure, distribution of obtained scores divided at the median.

S may be contingent upon *S*'s willingness to comply with instructions to perform the tasks given him (e.g., French, 1955; Atkinson and Raphelson, 1956). Furthermore, Atkinson and Reitman (1956) and Smith (Chapter 18) have presented evidence to support the argument that when there are different kinds of incentive to perform a task (e.g., achievement, social approval, money, etc.), the relationship between level of performance (taken as a measure of strength of motivation) and independent measures of the strength of any particular motive (e.g., *n* Achievement) should be reduced, since the total strength of motivation expressed in performance of a task is then overdetermined. Strength of motivation to perform the task is then systematically influenced by several different kinds of motive and incentive at the same time.

The Effect of Strength of Affiliation Motive. Table 7 shows the relationship between TAT *n* Affiliation, ARPS, and each of the three behavioral symptoms of resultant achievement motivation. Immediately apparent is the fact that *n* Affiliation is positively related to each of the three measures derived from public performance of the *S* on tasks which required immediate interaction with the *E* who could observe what and how well he was doing. But *n* Affiliation is not positively related to the score obtained on the Achievement Risk Preference Scale, which *E* took privately.

Comparison of Table 7 with Table 3, which describes how the criterion measure of resultant achievement motivation (*n* Achievement-Test Anxiety) related to these same four variables, shows that: (*a*) the criterion measure of resultant achievement motivation (*n* Achievement-

Table 7

TAT *n* Affiliation scores in relation to four measures, which, according to
theory of achievement motivation, should be sensitive to differences
in strength of resultant achievement motivation

Strength of *n* Affiliation	*N*	High Score on ARPS	Intermediate Risk on Decision-Making Test	Fast Performance	Low Persistence When P_s Is .05
High	11	45%	82%	73%	73%
Moderate	12	50	50	42	58
Low	12	58	25	42	25
		n.s.	$\chi^2 = 7.40$ $df = 2$ $p < .05$	n.s.	$\chi^2 = 5.56$ $df = 2$ $p = .10 - .05$

Note: As in all previous comparisons, the distribution of scores on the four
dependent variables is divided at the median.

Test Anxiety) shows a substantial positive relationship to ARPS (the
task undertaken privately), but *n* Affiliation does not; *(b)* *n* Affiliation
shows more consistent positive relationships than the criterion measure
(*n* Achievement-Test Anxiety) with the three performance measures
obtained under conditions of immediate interaction between *S* and *E*.

Particularly striking, and disconcerting, are the fairly substantial
positive relationships between *n* Affiliation and lack of persistence at a
very difficult task and preference for intermediate difficulty on the
Decision-Making Test. We are led to the hypotheses that these two
behaviors should be sensitive measures of resultant *achievement* motivation only by the special assumptions of the theory of achievement
motivation namely, that the incentive value of success at a task (I_s) is
proportionate to the apparent difficulty of a task $(I_s = 1 - P_s)$, and
that (negative) incentive value of failure is proportionate to the apparent easiness of a task $(I_f = -P_s)$. Heretofore we have proceeded as if
these particular assumptions should refer uniquely to the amount of
pride one anticipates as a consequence of successful performance and
the amount of shame or embarrassment one anticipates as a consequence of incompetence. We have not seriously considered the possibility that the anticipated amount of any extrinsic reward that is
contingent upon accomplishment might also be related to the apparent
difficulty of a task in the same manner. The present result forces us to
consider the possibility that the amount of immediate social approval
from another person that is generally anticipated as a possible consequence of skillful achievement performance is also systematically related to the apparent difficulty of a task i.e., $I_{app} = 1 - P_s$.

While having appreciated the influence of other kinds of motives and incentives on performance of "achievement" tasks e.g., that strength of n Affiliation should influence performance when E urges cooperation or makes himself a visible source of approval and disapproval, we have always implicitly assumed that extrinsic sources of motivation would be constant, in a particular S, for all of the different kinds of tasks and performances required of him during an experimental period (see, for example, Chapter 8). We have assumed that a person strong in n Affiliation might be concerned about cooperating with E's demands, but that this tendency would not operate *selectively* in his achievement performance, as does n Achievement, to favor intermediate degrees of difficulty. And since n Affiliation and n Achievement are not systematically correlated within college samples (or a national sample, see Veroff et al., 1960), we have previously assumed that the influence of n Affiliation, a constant source of "error" in our data, would be equivalent among groups that did otherwise differ in strength of n Achievement. As our sophistication concerning the effects of situational factors has increased, we have attempted to minimize this "irrelevant" source of positive motivation when the main point of an experiment has been to examine the nature of the relationship between *achievement* motivation and performance. We have proceeded on the following assumption: Total strength of motivation for performance = Strength of resultant achievement motivation + Strength of extrinsic (or irrelevant) motivation (Atkinson and Reitman, 1956; Feather, Chapters 8, 9; Smith, Chapter 18). Ideally, then, we should create conditions in which total strength of motivation equals strength of resultant achievement motivation. Atkinson and Reitman (1956) argue that this state of affairs is probably best approximated by giving S an achievement-oriented instruction and then leaving him alone in a room with the task to be performed. But this approximation to the ideal case imposes too many restrictions on what can be attempted to be generally useful.

The unanticipated result of the present experiment calls into question the simple assumptions we have been making about the influence of affiliative motivation (the need for social approval) and suggests, quite strongly, that *the incentive value of any extrinsic reward that appears to S to be contingent upon the adequacy of his performance when skill and effort is demanded may be proportionate to the apparent difficulty of the task.* Specifically, this hypothesis means that a person in whom the achievement motive is very weak (i.e., a person who produces very little imagery having to do with excellence of performance in thematic apperceptive stories under neutral conditions) might display all of the behavioral symptoms of "an entrepreneurial risk-taker" if some extrinsic reward like love or money, for which he does have a strong motive, were offered as a general inducement for performance.

It is obviously premature to claim that these or any results to date offer very adequate support of the hypothesis. Yet it is impossible to minimize how well the TAT measure of affiliative motive predicts which Ss prefer intermediate difficulty on the decision-making task *and also* show very little persistence at an insoluble puzzle when the stated probability of success is .05 and the S knows he may turn to another puzzle any time he desires. The percentages of Ss scoring High ($N = 11$), Moderate ($N = 12$), and Low ($N = 12$) in n Affiliation who displayed this particular pattern of behavior were, respectively, 64%, 33%, and 8% ($\chi^2 = 8.48$, $df = 2$, $p < .02$).

It is exceedingly difficult to explain why Ss strong in affiliative motive should show this particular pattern of behavior more frequently than Ss weak in affiliative motive, given our general assumption that strength of a goal-directed tendency equals $M_G \times E_{r,g} \times I_g$, without the special assumption that I_{app} (like I_s) must, in this circumstance at least, equal $1 - P_s$.

Further analysis shows that 91% of the Ss highest in n Affiliation ($N = 11$) and only 8% of the Ss lowest in n Affiliation ($N = 12$) were classified above the median on the predicted achievement-oriented response for two or three of the three behavioral measures—risk preference, speed, persistence ($\chi^2 = 11.64$, $df = 2$, $p < .01$).

JOINT EFFECTS OF RESULTANT ACHIEVEMENT MOTIVATION (n ACHIEVEMENT–TEST ANXIETY) AND n AFFILIATiON

Given this evidence of the influence of n Affiliation on "achievement-oriented" performance when tasks are undertaken in the immediate presence of an examiner, we undertook a further analysis of the results. We sought to determine whether or not expected effects of differences in strength of resultant achievement motivation would be more pronounced among those Ss who should be least influenced by the possibility of immediate social approval, namely, those who are relatively weak in n Affiliation. This further analysis of the data is suggested by the assumption advanced in earlier studies that the *total* strength of motivation to perform a task in the usual experimental situation is equal to the strength of resultant achievement motivation plus extrinsic sources of motivation. Atkinson and Reitman (1956) report that the performance of Ss who are low in n Achievement and high in n

Affiliation profits most from the additional incentive of having examiners present as proctors in a group situation as compared with being left alone to work in a small room with only an achievement-oriented instruction to induce motivation for task performance. Their results suggested the possibility of performance decrement among Ss strongly motivated to achieve when additional incentives are introduced to further heighten motivation, a trend also apparent in a similar study by Smith (Chapter 18) but interpreted differently.

The purpose of this further analysis, then, was to determine whether or not resultant achievement motivation is related to the various performance measures, as predicted, when the influence of n Affiliation is relatively weak, and to explore the possibility that the additive combination of strong resultant achievement motivation and motivation for immediate social approval produces a decrement in the expected pattern of achievement-oriented performance. Our supposition was that among Ss who are relatively weak in n Affiliation, the originally predicted relationships between resultant achievement motivation and performance should appear, but that when n Affiliation (the need for social approval) is strong, all Ss may show the achievement-oriented pattern of behavior *or* those who are also high in resultant achievement motivation may actually show the kind of decrement in discriminative performance which Yerkes and Dodson (1908) attributed to greater than optimal intensity of motivation for a given task (see also Courts (1942) and Broadhurst (1957)). In either case, it is quite obvious that the distribution of performance scores for the whole group would be affected in a way which would reduce the overall positive relationship between performance measures and our criterion measure of resultant achievement motivation (n Achievement-Test Anxiety).

METHOD OF ANALYSIS. The following steps were taken: (a) Average deviation scores, which provide the measure of degree of preference for intermediate risk on the Decision-Making Task, were recomputed in terms of the median choices and average deviation of ten Ss *who were low in n Affiliation* (scores of 0, 1, 2) but above the median in resultant achievement motivation. This follows the logic already outlined for estimating the degree of difficulty where probability of success can be assumed near .50 from the choices of those Ss, who, according to theory, should approach that point in their preferences; (b) raw performance scores on each of the tasks undertaken in the presence of the E were converted to standard scores (Z scores) in terms of the mean and standard deviation of the whole group ($N = 35$) to allow summation of the several measures into a single, most-reliable index of the predicted pattern of achievement-oriented performance; *(c)* Ss having scores above the median *n* Affiliation score assigned independently by each of the two coders were classified High ($N = 17$), and the remainder of Ss were classified Low ($N = 18$) in *n* Affiliation; *(d)* the distribution of resultant achievement motivation scores (*n* Achievement-Test Anxiety) for the whole group ($N = 35$) was divided into approximate thirds to yield subgroups within High ($N = 17$) and Low ($N = 18$) *n* Affiliation groups which are comparable in assessed strength of resultant achievement motivation.

The number of cases in various subgroups is very small. Nevertheless the analysis of results which follows is instructive. Table 8 provides

Table 8

Achievement-oriented performance in presence of *E* as a function of resultant achievement motivation (*n* Achievement-Test Anxiety) and *n* Affiliation (per cent above median of whole group ($N = 35$))

When n Affiliation Is Low:

	n Achievement-Test Anxiety		
	Low ($N = 5$)	Mid ($N = 8$)	High ($N = 5$)
Risk preference	20%	50%	60%
Speed	0	63	80
Persistence	20	38	60
*Composite (risk preference + speed + persistence)	0	63	80
Composite (risk preference + speed)	20	63	80

* Low versus High, $U = 2$, $p = .016$ (one tail), Mann-Whitney U test.

When n Affiliation Is High:

	Low ($N = 5$)	Mid ($N = 5$)	High ($N = 7$)
Risk Preference	100%	40%	43%
Speed	60	40	57
Persistence	60	60	71
Composite (risk preference + speed + persistence)	60	40	57
Composite (risk preference + speed)	80	20	43

the best overa summary of the joint effects of resultant achievement motivation ar l *n* Affiliation in the present experiment. In Table 8 the distributions of behavioral scores for the whole group ($N = 35$) have been divided at the common median as in earlier analyses of results. On each single behavioral measure, and on the composite measures, there is an orderly increase in frequency of Ss showing the predicted achievement-oriented tendency as a function of strength of resultant achievement motivation when *n Affiliation is low* and the possible confounding influence of immediate social approval as an incentive is relatively weak. And in every case, Ss who are low (weak) in resultant achievement motivation but high in *n* Affiliation show as strong an achievement-oriented response as Ss who are low in *n* Affiliation but at least moderate (Mid) in resultant achievement motivation. In other words, *n* Affiliation alone was sufficient to produce the predicted achievement-oriented trends in the present experiment. In the case of risk preference and speed, the difference attributable to *n* Affiliation when resultant achievement motivation is weak is fairly substantial. But high *n* Affiliation added to moderate or high resultant achievement motivation apparently produces a performance decrement on these two tasks. The statistical significance of this unanticipated decrement was evaluated using a two-tail Mann-Whitney U test of the difference between High and Low *n* Affiliation groups in which resultant achievement motivation was moderate to high. The composite measure of risk preference and speed obtained by summing the Z scores for these two measures was examined. When resultant achievement motivation was moderate to high and *n* Affiliation was low ($N = 13$), 69% were above the median score implying achievement-oriented performance. However, when resultant achievement motivation was moderate to high and *n* Affiliation was also high ($N = 12$), only 33% were above the median score. The probability of this difference, given the null hypothesis, is .10. There is, in other words, suggestive evidence of a performance decrement among those Ss who were relatively strong in both achievement and affiliative motivation on the tasks which call for rapid discrimination among competing response tendencies. These are the kinds of task which should be sensitive to the decrement in discriminative performance produced by too intense motivation that was first reported by Yerkes and Dodson (1908).

Table 8 also shows that the measure of persistence, not influenced by a demand for rapid discrimination under time pressure, *does not* yield evidence of performance decrement attributable to the summation of resultant achievement motivation and *n* Affiliation. This measure, which appears less sensitive to the moderate difference in strength of motivation defined by a difference in resultant achievement motivation when *n* Affiliation is weak, or by a difference in *n* Affiliation when resultant achievement motivation is weak, gives the clearest evidence of the total effects of the two kinds of motivation. The predicted achievement-oriented response (low persistence) is most evident when both resultant achievement motivation and n Affiliation are strong ($N = 7$): then 71% of Ss fall above the median of achievement-oriented performance. When both kinds of motivation are weak ($N = 5$), only 20% fall above the median. A two-tailed Mann-Whitney U test of this difference yields a $U = 7$ and $P = .106$.

We conclude, from this exploratory analysis of the total pattern of results, that both resultant achievement motivation and n Affiliation contributed to the determination of the predicted achievement-oriented performances. From earlier work, we had expected that n Affiliation and achievement motivation might summate to influence the speed of performance, but we did not anticipate that the incentive value of immediate social approval might be related to the difficulty of a task (P_s) as the incentive value of success is related to difficulty. Thus the unanticipated results are those which suggest that n Affiliation and resultant achievement motivation summate in the determination of preference for intermediate risk and low persistence at a very difficult task when other more moderate risks are available as alternatives.

We also conclude that the measure of persistence is less sensitive to moderate differences in strength of motivation, and, because it does not require discrimination under time pressure, it is also less susceptible to performance decrement when positive motivation is very intense. On the other hand, both the Decision-Making Task, which required a rapid decision concerning level of aspiration on novel tasks, and the substitution task, which was explicitly a measure of speed under changing conditions, are very sensitive to moderate differences in strength of motivation. Both record performance decrement when motivation is very intense.

Performance as a Function of Intensity of Motivation. Although the evidence suggesting performance decrement attributable to greater than optimal intensity of motivation is no more than suggestive, because our sample is very small and the statistical significance borderline, the possibility is of considerable importance. It has been virtually ignored in the program of research on achievement motivation.

We are forced seriously to consider the possibility that some of the reported failures to obtain predicted TAT n Achievement-performance relations in previous research (e.g., Reitman, 1960; Smith, Chapter 18) may be the result of decrements in the performance of Ss classified high in n Achievement when other, uncontrolled and unassessed sources of motivation are also operative. In the past, we have attempted to explain negative results on other grounds (e.g., inadequate control of conditions at the time of assessment of achievement motive; unreliable coding of thematic apperceptive stories; failure to engage achievement motivation at the time of performance, etc.). The present results demand that we examine more fully the implications of the assumption advanced in earlier studies (Atkinson and Reitman, 1956; Atkinson, 1958c; Reitman, 1960; Feather, Chapter 8; Smith, Chapter 18) concerning the composition of the total strength of motivation for task performance in light of the Yerkes-Dodson law, which states that there is an optimal level of motivation for a given level of task complexity. The Yerkes-Dodson argument refers explicitly to the ease or difficulty of discriminating and selecting among competing alternative responses. The possibility of performance decrement should certainly influence the choice of criterion tasks and the design of future experiments that seek to establish the validity of tests of individual differences in the strength of a particular motive by producing a positive correlation between the measure of motive strength and some performance criterion which is a function of the *total strength of motivation*.

A Novel Hypothesis Concerning Test Anxiety. In addition to calling attention to the need for a much more discerning analysis of the requirements of particular tasks employed as performance criteria of strength of motivation, the present analysis has another implication of theoretical interest. It is assumed that Test Anxiety is a measure of a disposition to avoid failure, which, when aroused, opposes or dampens positive motivation to achieve (Chapters 2, 5, 8). The lower level of achievement-oriented performance normally associated with high Test Anxiety is viewed as evidence that resultant achievement motivation is weaker; hence performance level is lower, when Test Anxiety is strong than when Test Anxiety is weak. This interpretation makes very good sense, in light of the present line of argument, as long as positive motivation is not excessive. *But when the intensity of positive motivation is greater than optimal, a strong tendency to avoid failure acting to inhibit, dampen, and effectively weaken the resultant motivation for performance should, paradoxically, enhance performance.* In this circumstance, high Test Anxiety scores would imply lower resultant motivation that is closer to the optimal level for performance than that implied by low Test Anxiety scores. Careful examination of the present results tends to sustain this implication of the assumptions (a) that there is an optimal level of motivation, and (b) that Test Anxiety measures the strength of a disposition which functions to oppose and dampen positive motivation for performance. When n Affiliation is weak, Test Anxiety score is negatively related to achievement-oriented performance (the usual case). However, when n Affiliation is strong, the relationship of Test Anxiety to the performance measures is substantially changed. Subjects having the highest Test Anxiety scores then show the *highest* level of performance on the composite measure of risk preference and speed, the two tasks most sensitive to performance decrement when motivation for performance is too intense. The number of Ss in subgroups is too small to warrant more than this statement of an interesting and nonobvious hypothesis for future research.

Final Word Concerning the Achievement Risk Preference Scale. The ARPS, which was filled out privately and not in the immediate presence of the E, yielded a measure of preference for achievement risk which was positively related to n Achievement-Test Anxiety but not to n Affiliation in the initial analysis of results ($N = 35$). Having unraveled the results of the experiment and discovered that the criterion measure of resultant achievement motivation is positively related to the achievement-oriented performance only when n Affiliation is relatively weak (Table 8), we may again assess the potential validity of ARPS as a substitute for TAT n Achievement-Test Anxiety.

Table 9

Achievement-oriented performance in presence of E related to score on Achievement Risk Preference Scale in Low ($N = 18$) and High ($N = 17$) n Affiliation groups (per cent above median of whole group ($N = 35$))

	Low n Affiliation Group		High n Affiliation Group	
ARPS Score	N	Composite*	N	Composite*
High	7	29%	6	33%
Mid	4	50	4	100
Low	7	71	7	43

* Prefer intermediate risk + fast performance + low persistence when $P_s = .05$.

We must conclude from Table 9 that the Achievement Risk Preference Scale, like other self-report devices that have been presented to assess strength of achievement motivation, presently lacks predictive validity. It obviously does not relate to achievement-oriented performance in the same manner as the criterion measure of resultant achievement motivation (n Achievement-Test Anxiety), although it is positively related to this measure. At present, we can offer no coherent explanation of this result.

SUMMARY

Thirty-five male college students performed a variety of tasks under achievement orientation, which yielded measures of risk preference (level of aspiration), speed of performance, and persistence. Subjects were tested individually by a female experimenter. Hypotheses derived from the theory of achievement motivation were: individuals in whom the motive to achieve success (*n* Achievement) is relatively strong and motive to avoid failure (Test Anxiety) is relatively weak should show greater preference for intermediate risk, perform faster and more efficiently, and show *less* persistence at a very difficult task when other less difficult alternatives are available than do individuals in whom motive to achieve success is relatively weak and motive to avoid failure is relatively strong.

An Achievement Risk Preference Scale filled out privately by each *S* yielded a measure of risk preference confirming the hypothesis that resultant motivation to achieve (*n* Achievement-Test Anxiety) is positively related to preference for intermediate risk. But a performance measure of risk preference, a speed test, and a task yielding the measure of persistence all undertaken in the immediate presence of the *E* yielded unanticipated positive relationships with TAT *n* Affiliation scores. The hypotheses concerning resultant achievement motivation (*n* Achievement-Test Anxiety) were confirmed only among *S*s who were weak in *n* Affiliation.

The results highlight the importance of two problems that have been neglected in earlier research on achievement motivation and performance: *(a)* apparently the incentive value of immediate social approval (the goal of the affiliative motive) is positively related to the difficulty of a task in much the same manner that incentive value of success (the goal of the achievement motive) is related to task difficulty; *(b)* the summative effects of achievement-related motivation and *n* Affiliation can produce decrements in the achievement-oriented performance of *S*s who are high in TAT *n* Achievement and low in Test Anxiety. The implications of these unanticipated results for future research on achievement-related performance are discussed.

20. THE EDITORS

Review and Appraisal

The preceding chapters have presented a variety of studies related to the theory of achievement motivation. In this final chapter we summarize the main ideas of the theory and contributions of these investigations and discuss some implications of this work in relation to problems of assessment and more general theoretical issues. Although the chapter is written as a "summing up," it is certainly not our intention to represent the research as a neatly wrapped package. It is obvious that some of the studies, which are presented in sequence, were actually designed and executed by different persons almost simultaneously, without the opportunity for each investigator to profit by the mistakes and hard-won conclusions of his predecessor. In social psychological research the unavoidable time lag that exists between initial design of a study and the communication of findings to others defines a need for this type of collation of interrelated studies to encourage evaluation of progress and identification of both neglected and critical issues for future work.

THE BASIC CONCEPTS: RESTATEMENT AND IMPLICATIONS

One of the main values of an effort to test the implications of a theory is increased understanding of the essential ideas and implications of the theory itself. It takes a while to become familiar with the fundamental points and to discover the possible pitfalls in communication. Once there is a common understanding of the implications of a theory, there can begin to be agreement about the theoretical implications of particular experimental facts. This is essential for the self-corrective process of science.

We begin this review of the book with a succinct restatement of the theory and its major implications. Having recognized the possibility of misunderstanding engendered by our use of the term *motivation* in a technical sense to refer to an activated goal directed tendency (see

Atkinson, 1964), we have decided to encourage the use of the term *tendency* when referring to the product of *motive, expectancy,* and *incentive.* This product represents, in the theory language, an active impulse to engage or not to engage in a particular action which is expected to have a certain consequence; thus we have substituted the term "tendency" for the term "motivation" in this summary statement of the theory, without implying any change in meaning.

The theory of achievement motivation is one of a class of theories which attribute the strength of a *tendency* to undertake some activity to the cognitive expectation (or belief) that the activity will produce a certain consequence and the attractiveness (or value) of the consequence to the individual. The theory refers, specifically, to a very important but limited domain of behavior, namely, achievement-oriented activity. Achievement-oriented activity is activity undertaken by an individual with the expectation that his performance will be evaluated in terms of some standard of excellence. It is presumed that any situation which presents a challenge to achieve, by arousing an expectancy that action will lead to success, must also pose the threat of failure by arousing an expectancy that action may lead to failure. Thus achievement-oriented activity is always influenced by the resultant of a conflict between two opposed tendencies, the tendency to achieve success and the tendency to avoid failure. Normally, achievement-oriented activities are also influenced by other *extrinsic* motivational tendencies, which are attributable to other kinds of motive and incentive. The theory of achievement motivation focuses primarily upon the resolution of the conflict between the two opposed tendencies that are inherent in any achievement-oriented activity, but it also emphasizes the importance of extrinsic sources of motivation to undertake an activity, particularly when the resultant achievement-oriented tendency is negative.

The Tendency to Achieve Success (T_s). This tendency—to approach a task with interest and the intent of performing well—is considered a multiplicative function of the motive or need to achieve success (M_S), the strength of expectancy (or subjective probability) that success will be the consequence of a particular activity (P_s), and the incentive value of success at that particular activity (I_s). The incentive value of success is assumed to be proportionate to the difficulty of the task (i.e., $I_s = 1 - P_s$). Together, the general motive to achieve (M_S) and the incentive value of success at a particular activity (I_s) determine what Lewinians call the *valence* of success (Va_s) and what decision theorists refer to as the *utility* of success. It is assumed, in other words, that the assertion $T_s = M_S \times P_s \times I_s$ may also be written $T_s =$

$P_s \times (M_S \times I_s)$ and that the product of $M_S \times I_s$ may be conceived as equivalent to the subjective value of success, the utility of success, or the valence of success at a particular activity to a particular person. One important implication of viewing motive to achieve and incentive value of success as the determinants of the attractiveness of success at a particular activity is *the hypothesis that the slope of attractiveness of success plotted in relation to increasing difficulty of task* (i.e., decreasing P_s) *will be steeper, the stronger the motive to achieve*. This hypothesis follows from assumptions that the two variables M_S and I_s combine multiplicatively and $I_s = 1 - P_s$. This idea, developed in Chapters 3, 7, and 11 provides theoretical justification for a new method of assessing the strength of achievement motive undertaken with promising results by Morgan (Chapter 14). Other uses of this method are discussed by McClelland (1961, Chapter 5).

The main implications of the two assumptions $T_s = M_S \times P_s \times I_s$ and $I_s = 1 - P_s$ are shown in Table 1 and Figure 1. They are:

1. The tendency to achieve success should be strongest when a task is one of intermediate difficulty, but the difference in strength of tendency to achieve success that is attributable to a difference in the difficulty of the task (P_s) will be substantial only when M_S is relatively strong.

2. When the difficulty of a task is held constant, the tendency to achieve success is stronger when M_S is strong than when it is weak, but the difference in strength of tendency to achieve success that is attributable to a difference in strength of achievement motive (M_S) will be substantial only when the task is one of intermediate difficulty.

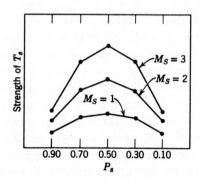

Figure 1   Graphic representation of assuming that $T_s = M_S \times P_s \times I_s$ and that $I_s = 1 - P_s$, when $M_S = 1, 2,$ and 3.

Table 1

Tendency to achieve success (T_s) as a joint function of motive to achieve (M_s), expectancy of success (P_s), and incentive value of success (I_s) for individuals in whom $M_s = 1$, 2, and 3, assuming that $I_s = 1 - P_s$

			$(T_s = M_s \times P_s \times I_s)$		
			When	When	When
Task	P_s	I_s	$M_s = 1$	$M_s = 2$	$M_s = 3$
A	.90	.10	.09	.18	.27
B	.70	.30	.21	.42	.63
C	.50	.50	.25	.50	.75
D	.30	.70	.21	.42	.63
E	.10	.90	.09	.18	.27

These implications of the theory provide the foundation for a hypothesis that has been tested and confirmed in a number of studies: Persons in whom *n* Achievement is relatively strong will show greater preference for intermediate risk (or for setting an intermediate level of aspiration) than persons in whom *n* Achievement is relatively weak. In addition, we also find here the theoretical justification for a hypothesis that persons in whom *n* Achievement is relatively strong should normally show higher level of performance in achievement-oriented activities, and greater persistence in these activities *when faced with the option of engaging in some nonachievement-related activity*, than persons in whom *n* Achievement is relatively weak.

According to the theory (Figure 1), differences in T_s that are attributable to differences in M_s will only be large when P_s is near .50. This implication suggests that failure to find the normally expected superiority in performance of persons high in *n* Achievement may sometimes be attributable to the fact that the task is either very difficult or very easy. If so, the combination of only moderate reliability in assessment of individual differences in *n* Achievement (see Haber and Alpert, 1958), coupled with small expected differences in T_s, would effectively account for what might otherwise appear a disconfirmation of the theory. The theory puts great emphasis on the importance of the apparent difficulty of a task to an individual, or expectancy of success, as a *manipulable* motivational variable. It has been relatively neglected in earlier studies which focus upon level of performance as the dependent variable (e.g., Atkinson, 1958a, Part 3).

The Functional Properties of a Motive. One of the important general implications of the theory can be read from Table 1 and Figure 1. It specifies the functional property of a motive *(M_G)* conceived as a *relatively* general disposition that will influence actions expected to lead to a particular kind of consequence or goal. When an individual confronts a number of alternative opportunities, or paths to achievement, as he does in the typical risk-preference or aspiration experiment, the motive to achieve *(M_S)* is *relatively* nonspecific in its influence. That is, it combines multiplicatively with the product of expectancy of success *(P_s)* and incentive value of success *(I_s)* for each of the separate alternatives or paths that are available. But this nonspecific influence of the motive *(M_S)* is limited to the class of achievement-oriented activities (i.e., to activities that are expected to lead to *success*, but not to activities that are expected to lead to food, affiliation, or some other irrelevant goal). Thus it can be seen that a motive, as here conceived, functions differently than the *completely* nonspecific *drive* of S–R behavior theory. A motive has a nonspecific influence on actions that have the same functional significance. These are actions that represent alternative or substitutable paths to *the same general goal*. But a motive has a selective or directive influence when an individual confronts alternatives which lead to different kinds of goals (e.g., affiliation versus achievement, as in French, 1956). When an individual faces a choice between continuing an achievement-oriented activity (e.g., working on an examination, as in Chapter 5), or undertaking some non-achievement-oriented activity instead, the motive to achieve should selectively enhance the strength of the achievement-oriented tendency. This functional role of a motive as a determinant of persistence in an activity is amplified by Feather (Chapter 4), Atkinson and Cartwright (1964) and Atkinson (1964, Chapter 10).

The Tendency to Avoid Failure (T_{-f}). The theoretical conception of the determinants of the tendency to avoid failure (T_{-f}) is parallel. The motive to avoid failure *(M_{AF})* combines multiplicatively with the expectancy of failure (P_f) and the incentive value of failure (I_f). The special assumption that incentive value of failure is more negative the easier a task, $I_f = -P_s$, together with the assumption that $T_{-f} = M_{AF} \times P_f \times I_f$, produces the general implications shown in Table 2 and Figure 2. They are:

1. The tendency to avoid failure should be strongest when a task is one of intermediate difficulty, but the difference in strength of tendency to avoid failure that is attributable to a difference in the difficulty of the task (P_f) will be substantial only when M_{AF} is relatively strong.

2. When the difficulty of a task is held constant, the tendency to avoid failure is stronger when M_{AF} is strong than when it is weak, but the difference in strength of tendency to avoid failure that is attributable to a difference in motive to avoid failure (M_{AF}) will be substantial only when the task is one of intermediate difficulty.

Table 2

Tendency to avoid failure (T_{-f}) as a joint function of motive to avoid failure (M_{AF}), expectancy of failure (P_f), and negative incentive value of failure (I_f) for individuals in whom $M_{AF} = 1$, 2, and 3. It is assumed that $I_f = -P_s$

| | | | $(T_{-f} = M_{AF} \times P_f \times I_f)$ | | |
| | | | When $M_{AF} = 1$ | When $M_{AF} = 2$ | When $M_{AF} = 3$ |
Task	P_f	I_f			
A	.10	−.90	−.09	−.18	−.27
B	.30	−.70	−.21	−.42	−.63
C	.50	−.50	−.25	−.50	−.75
D	.70	−.30	−.21	−.42	−.63
E	.90	−.10	−.09	−.18	−.27

Since the incentive value of failure is negative, so is the sign of the tendency to avoid failure (T_{-f}) negative. This means that the tendency to avoid failure must function in a way that is just the opposite of the tendency to achieve success, which is positive in sign. If we interpret the positive sign to mean excitement to undertake actions that are expected to produce success, we are compelled by the inherent logic of an

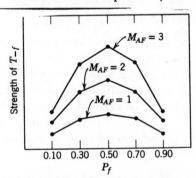

Figure 2 Graphic representation of theoretical implications of assuming that $T_{-f} = M_{AF} \times P_f \times I_f$ and that $I_f = -P_s$, when $M_{AF} = $ 1, 2, and 3.

expectancy $\times$ value formulation to interpret a *negative* tendency as an *inhibitory* tendency (i.e., as a tendency *not* to undertake actions that are expected to lead to failure (Atkinson, 1964, pp. 244–246, 285–292). Literally, the tendency to avoid failure, which refers to a particular activity, is a tendency to resist performance of the activity *because* it is expected to lead to failure. This avoidant tendency does not tell us specifically what acts will be performed, but it does tell us specifically what acts will be resisted. It has been argued elsewhere that the anxiety experienced by an individual in achievement-oriented situations is proportionate to the magnitude of his tendency to avoid failure at the time (Atkinson, 1964, pp. 289–290). This assumption, or one like it, is needed to justify the use of self-report anxiety questionnaires to assess the strength of the motive to avoid failure (M_{AF}).

The Resultant Achievement-Oriented Tendency. Achievement-oriented activities are influenced by the resultant of the conflict between the tendency to approach success (T_s) and the tendency to avoid failure (T_{-f}). By remembering that the sign of the tendency to avoid failure is negative, we may designate the *resultant-oriented tendency* as $T_s + T_{-f}$. The resultant achievement-oriented tendency $(T_s + T_{-f})$ is positive when $M_S > M_{AF}$ and negative when $M_{AF} > M_S$.

The whole theory may be simplified algebraically, as pointed out by Edwards (1962b), to show the basic determinants of the resultant achievement-oriented tendency:

(A) $\quad T_s + T_{-f} = (M_S \times P_s \times I_s) + (M_{AF} \times P_f \times I_f)$

But $I_s = 1 - P_s$, and P_f is also assumed equal to $1 - P_s$, and $I_f = -P_s$. Making these substitutions in (A) we have

(B) $\quad T_s + T_{-f} = [M_S \times P_s \times (1-P_s)] + [M_{AF} \times (1-P_s) \times -P_s]$

(C) $\qquad\qquad = \{M_S \times [P_s \times (1 - P_s)]\} - \{M_{AF} \times [(1 - P_s) \times P_s]\}$

(D) $\qquad\qquad = (M_S - M_{AF}) \times [P_s \times (1 - P_s)]$

This simplification shows quite clearly that the theory of achievement motivation represents a specification of the personality and environmental determinants as well as the nature of the interaction summarized programmatically in Lewin's equation, $B = f(P, E)$, a point given special emphasis by Feather in Chapter 4. When the resultant achievement-oriented tendency $(T_s + T_{-f})$ is negative, there will be no active impulse *to undertake* a particular achievement-oriented activity (T_A) unless some positive extrinsic tendency to perform the activity (T_{ext}) overcomes the resistance of $T_s + T_{-f}$: that is, $T_A = T_s + T_{-f} + T_{ext}$ (see Figure 3).

The logic of *adding* these various components of the total motivation

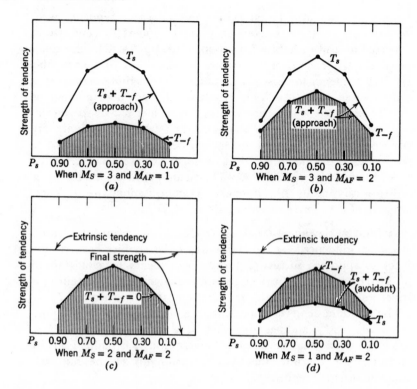

Figure 3   Tendency to achieve success $(T_s = M_s \times P_s \times I_s)$, tendency to avoid failure $(T_{-f} = M_{AF} \times P_f \times I_f)$, and resultant achievement-oriented tendency $(T_s + T_{-f})$ for individuals who differ in strength of M_s and M_{AF}. The assumed effect of extrinsic positive motivation on the *final* strength of tendency to undertake an activity is shown for cases where $T_s + T_{-f}$ is zero or negative (i.e., avoidant). In (c) the final strength of tendency = the strength of extrinsic tendency because $T_s + T_{-f}$ is 0. In (d) the final strength of tendency (not shown) would = the extrinsic tendency — the value of $T_s + T_{-f}$ seen in the shaded portion of the graph. The curve describing final strength of tendency would, in this case, be U-shaped, having its lowest value where $P_s = .50$.

to perform an activity was suggested in experiments testing the influence of several different kinds of motivation on level of performance (see Atkinson and Reitman, 1956, and Smith, Chapter 18) and in the investigation of persistence (see Feather, Chapters 8 and 9). Adding these components is consistent with the logic of contemporary decision theory.

The several assumptions about the determinants of the tendency to avoid failure and its inhibitory function provide the foundation for these hypotheses:

HYPOTHESIS 1. Persons in whom $M_{AF} > M_S$, who therefore have *negative* resultant achievement-oriented tendencies, will avoid intermediate risk when constrained to undertake an achievement-oriented activity by some extrinsic tendency.

HYPOTHESIS 2. The tendency to avoid failure, in resisting and dampening (i.e., subtracting from) the influence of positive tendencies to undertake an activity, will *normally* produce a decrement in achievement-oriented performance.

In the light of results reported in Chapter 19, which suggest that performance decrement may also occur when the final strength of a tendency to undertake a task is very high, we are reminded that the tendency to avoid failure may not *always* produce a decrement in resultant achievement-oriented *performance,* even though it should always produce a decrement in resultant achievement-oriented *tendency.* The interesting and nonobvious hypothesis suggested for future research is the notion that *under conditions of very intense positive motivation, a strong tendency to avoid failure may actually enhance rather than hinder the efficiency of performance.*

The concept of an inhibitory tendency—rather than the notion that anxiety is a source of nonspecific drive that activates competing response tendencies (Taylor, 1956; Spence, 1958) or that it elicits task-irrelevant responses (Mandler and Sarason, 1952)—yields the explanation derived from the theory of achievement motivation of why persons who score high on anxiety questionnaires normally tend to perform more poorly on competitive achievement tests than their less anxious peers.

Determinants of Avoidance Behavior. A second important general implication of the theory is based on this same conception of the tendency to avoid failure. It is the idea that so-called avoidance or defensive behavior may not be caused by "anxiety" and reinforced by "anxiety reduction," as conceived within the framework of S–R behavior theory (Mowrer, 1939; Miller, 1948). In the case of achievement-oriented activity, anxiety about failure is associated with the tendency to inhibit a particular activity. What the individual in whom $M_{AF} > M_S$ does in an achievement-oriented context may be construed as avoidant behavior or defensive behavior. But a closer look at the determinants of either an unrealistically high or low level of aspiration shows that the occurrence of one or the other of these alternatives is explained by the assumed presence of some extrinsic positive tendency to undertake the dreaded achievement-oriented action that is sufficient to overcome resistance (Figure 3). The individual is viewed as acting merely to comply with an authority or to gain approval for doing what is expected. In a very real sense, he is not achievement-oriented at all, but is merely going through the motions of what for others *is* achievement-oriented activity. He does what he does because other alternative activities (those representing intermediate or moderate risk) are inhibited. Consequently, the final strength of the tendency to engage in a very safe or a very speculative venture, although weak, wins out in the competition among action tendencies.

The same sort of thing may happen to produce what is generally called avoidance behavior. Suppose that in a given situation, a number of different positive action tendencies are initially aroused in an individual, among them being one to engage in activity which would take him from the situation. Suppose that this positive tendency "to leave the field," whatever its determinants, stands relatively low in the initial hierarchy of activated tendencies. The individual will perform other activities which keep him in the stimulus situation instead of, or before, he expresses this tendency. If the individual is punished while, or immediately after, performing these other activities, he should later expect that they will lead to punishment. As a result, the activities should begin to suffer resistance. The so-called avoidance activity would then be more likely to occur, because even though nothing has happened to strengthen the tendency to engage in it, a lot has happened to weaken the *resultant* tendencies to engage in other activities. In time, the tendency to undertake the so-called avoidance activity would become *relatively* stronger than the others. In this conception, the so-called avoidance behavior is considered a weakly, but *positively* motivated activity which occurs at all only because each of the tendencies to engage in some other activity is now effectively blocked by an inhibitory tendency resulting from the expectancy of punishment.

This alternative to the anxiety-reduction theory of avoidance behavior is elaborated more fully elsewhere (Atkinson, 1964, Chapter 10). It suggests that "anxiety" be viewed as symptomatic that an individual is engaging in some activity with an expectancy of a negative outcome but not as the *cause* of the so-called avoidance response. Accordingly, there should be little or no anxiety when an individual is performing an activity with little or no expectancy of a negative outcome (i.e., when there is little or no resistance to the activity). As pointed out in the initial statement of the theory (p. 18), the person in whom $M_s > M_{AF}$ should voluntarily place himself in a competitive activity which will *maximize* his anxiety about failure. But the person in whom $M_{AF} > M_s$, when given an opportunity, should voluntarily follow a strategy of *minimizing* his anxiety about failure.

Motivational Consequences of Success and Failure. A third general implication of the theory follows from what it has to say about the changes in motivation (i.e., the changes in strength of tendency) brought about by success and failure. The assumption that success strengthens the expectancy of success and failure weakens the expectancy of success, coupled with the assumption that incentive value of success is dependent upon strength of expectancy of success ($I_s = 1 - P_s$), provides the foundation for hypotheses about the motivational consequences of success and failure. In a conventional level of aspiration or risk-preference experiment, the individual in whom $M_s > M_{AF}$ should initially set a moderately high level of aspiration (i.e., pick a task which represents an intermediate degree of risk). If he succeeds, he should raise his level of aspiration (i.e., pick a somewhat more difficult task). If he fails, he should lower his level of aspiration (i.e., pick a somewhat easier task). These responses have been called the "typical" consequences of success and failure, because they are the frequently observed effects in educated subgroups of societies, in which the achievement motive is relatively strong. The "atypical" (i.e., less frequent) changes have been discussed at length by Moulton in Chapter 10.

The changes in motivation produced by success and failure, which account for the "typical" changes in level of aspiration, are shown in Figures 4 and 5. In the illustration, it is assumed that success produces an increase and failure a decrease of .20 in P_s at the initial task, which is generalized to other similar tasks (i.e., the other levels of difficulty). The result in each case is some loss of interest in the initial activity and a stronger tendency, on a subsequent occasion, to engage in a *different* activity. Following success, the change in strength of achievement-oriented tendencies favors what is traditionally called an increase in level of aspiration—following failure, a decrease in level of aspiration.

Contradiction of Law of Effect. Of substantial general importance is the implication, confirmed in much of the earlier work on level of aspiration (Lewin, Dembo, Festinger, and Sears, 1944) and by Moulton in Chapter 10, that success should often lower rather than heighten the probability of repetition of the same activity among individuals who are relatively strong in motivation to achieve. This contradiction of the Law of Effect in the domain of achievement-oriented activity was noted by Gordon Allport (1943) more than twenty years ago. Success does not

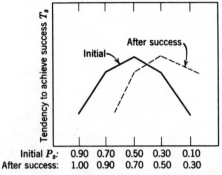

Initial P_s:	0.90	0.70	0.50	0.30	0.10
After success:	1.00	0.90	0.70	0.50	0.30

Figure 4   Change in level of aspiration following success when motive to achieve is dominant (i.e., $M_s > M_{AF}$). Success produces an increase in P_s at the same and similar tasks. Since $I_s = 1 - P_s$, the change in motivation following success favors a change in activity, namely, raising the level of aspiration. (From Atkinson, 1965, with permission of Rand McNally and Company).

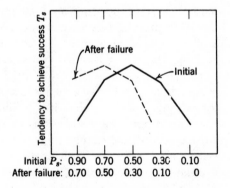

Initial P_s:	0.90	0.70	0.50	0.30	0.10
After failure:	0.70	0.50	0.30	0.10	0

Figure 5   Change in level of aspiration following failure when motive to achieve is dominant (i.e., $M_s > M_{AF}$). Failure produces a decrease in P_s at the same and similar tasks. Since $I_s = 1 - P_s$, the change in motivation following failure favors lowering the level of aspiration. (From Atkinson, 1965, with permission of Rand McNally and Company).

always increase the likelihood of repeating the same activity. Why? Because the increase in strength of expectancy of success, the cognitive change resulting from the experience, affects the subsequent incentive value of success $(I_s = 1 - P_s)$. For the case under discussion, namely, when $M_S > M_{AF}$ and the initial activity occurs where P_s is .50, this means that the tendency to undertake the same activity on a later occasion is weakened rather than strengthened, and the tendency to undertake some other activity is strengthened.

If the incentive value of the consequence of an activity is *constant* (i.e., not affected by the change in expectancy of attaining it), the product of expectancy and incentive value, which determines the strength of tendency to undertake the activity (holding strength of motive constant), will always increase as the expectancy of attaining the consequence increases. This change in motivation produces behavioral consequences that *are* adequately summarized by the Law of Effect (Figure 6).

Thus it can be seen that the kind of theory evolved in the study of achievement-oriented activity, which attributes the strength of tendency to undertake an activity to the strength of expectancy that an activity will produce a given consequence and the incentive value of the consequence (holding strength of motive constant), can account for the increased likelihood of rewarded responses summarized by the Law of Effect and also for the inadequacy of that law in the domain of achievement-oriented activity. From the viewpoint of this kind of theory, the Law of Effect is eschewed as a generally useful guiding principle. It is recovered as a useful memory aid about the behavioral consequences of attaining and not attaining goals when the incentive value of the goal is independent of the strength of expectancy of attaining it (as is presumed to be the case when concrete rewards like money, food, water, etc. are

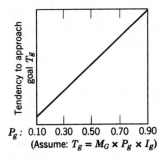

P_g: 0.10 0.30 0.50 0.70 0.90
(Assume: $T_g = M_G \times P_g \times I_g$)

Figure 6 Theoretical effect of increasing the strength of expectancy of attaining a goal (P_g) *when the incentive value of the goal* (I_g) *is constant and not affected by a change in* P_g. From this conception of the effect of "reward" on subsequent expectation concerning the consequence of an act are derived the behavorial phenomena summarized by the Law of Effect. (From Atkinson, 1965, with permission of Rand McNally and Company).

employed). And the law would also be expected to hold in any domain of activity in which the incentive value of the consequence of an activity increases as the expectancy of the consequence increases. But when the incentive value of the consequence of an activity is inversely related to the strength of expectation of bringing it about through performance of the activity, the Law of Effect is a systematically misleading guide.

Some of the studies reported here (Chapters 8, 9, 19) have examined the motivational consequences of success and failure in studies of persistence, and one has focused explicitly on the traditional paradigm for change in level of aspiration—the recent study by Moulton, Chapter 10. Under conditions offering excellent control of subjective probability of success at various tasks, Moulton has shown that individuals in whom *n* Achievement is strong and anxiety weak exhibit the "typical" changes in aspiration—an increase following success and a decrease following failure—while their less positively motivated and more anxious peers show a significantly higher frequency of "atypical" changes as predicted by the theory. Moulton's results extend those of an early unpublished exploratory investigation of this question by Vitz (1957).

So speaks the theory. In Chapter 3 Feather has compared it to four other models involving similar concepts that have emerged from quite different fields of inquiry, namely, the original theory of level of aspiration (Lewin, et al., 1944); principles of performance (Tolman, 1955); social learning theory (Rotter, 1954); and SEU Decision Theory (Edwards, 1954b).

Feather noted that the models differ in that two (level of aspiration theory, the theory of achievement motivation) assume that incentive values and subjective probabilities are inversely related, whereas the other models generally assume independence. It is then argued that one would expect an inverse relationship between attractiveness of success and subjective probability of success in *achievement* situations on the basis of past learning experiences. It is also argued that achievement incentive values should depend upon the nature of the situation (e.g., achievement-oriented versus relaxed, ego-related versus chance-related) as well as upon the subjective probability of success. This assumption is more general than that now made in the theory of achievement motivation, where incentive values for a given task are completely determined by the level of difficulty.

The theory of achievement motivation presented in Chapter 2 and reviewed here may therefore be seen as one of a class of expectancy $\times$ value models that are discussed more fully in Chapter 3 and elsewhere (Atkinson, 1964).

THE STUDIES OF ASPIRATION AND PERSISTENCE

The experimental studies presented in Part II examine the implications of the theory of achievement motivation for choice, performance, and persistence. In an early exploration, Atkinson, Bastian, Earl, and Litwin (1960) showed that men who are high in n Achievement do tend to prefer risks that are intermediate in difficulty in a shuffleboard game. Later, after practice, when they confronted a restricted range of choice with P_s near .50 up close to the target, they then took more shots closer to the target than did men low in n Achievement. This finding reminds us that the theory refers to intermediate degree of difficulty *as defined by the individual,* and not simply by the array of tasks before him. A restriction of the range of available choice might sometimes be responsible for all the relatively more anxious persons selecting either the easiest or most difficult of available tasks.

This study also explored, for the first time, the relationship between n Achievement and gambling preferences in subjects. A more frequent preference for bets representing intermediate (i.e., 4/6, 3/6, or 2/6 chances of winning in an imaginary dice game) than extreme risk (i.e., 5/6 and 1/6) among the High n Achievement group, when compared with the Low n Achievement group, was shown to be the result of avoidance of intermediate probabilities by the Low n Achievement group. The High n Achievement group did not choose the intermediate probabilities in gambling more frequently than would be expected by chance. They were indifferent among the different probabilities, but subjects low in n Achievement did avoid intermediate risk even in a gamble.

The follow-up study by Atkinson and Litwin (Chapter 5) introduces the idea of employing both the projective measure of n Achievement to assess M_S and the Test Anxiety Questionnaire to assess M_{AF}. These two measures are uncorrelated among college men when both are administered under *neutral* conditions. In this book, the following correlations between Test Anxiety and *neutral* n Achievement are reported: — .15 (Chapter 5); — .005 (Chapter 7); .09 (Chapter 12); .05 (Chapter 16); .11 (Chapter 18); and — .12 (Chapter 19).

The results reported by Atkinson and Litwin provide an empirical link between the general program of research on achievement motivation and the current one that studies effects of individual differences in anxiety (Sarason, Davidson, Lightall, Waite, and Ruebush, 1960; Spence, 1958). College men standing high in n Achievement and low in Test Anxiety—about whom it is assumed that M_S greatly exceeds

M_{AF}—more frequently choose intermediate distances for shots in a ring-toss game, spend more time working on a final examination in a college course,[1] and obtain higher grades on the final examination than do men standing low in n Achievement and high in Test Anxiety, about whom it can be assumed either that M_{AF} is dominant or—what is more often likely to be the case—that the superiority of M_S over M_{AF} is very small. This latter group of subjects does not actually avoid intermediate risk in the Ring Toss Game (see p. 89). This fact may mean that when a representative sample of American college students is divided at the median on n Achievement and Test Anxiety, the resultant achievement motivation of most persons in the group, often referred to as $M_{AF} > M_S$ in terms of scores on the two tests, may actually be weak positive rather than avoidant. One can have greater confidence that the achievement-oriented tendency of a subgroup is avoidant when more extreme criteria are employed, as in several of the other studies (e.g., Chapters 6, 8, 10). On the other hand, the absence of avoidance of intermediate risk by those classified as $M_{AF} > M_S$ may also be attributable to a factor ignored until very recently, namely, that unmeasured n Affiliation may function just like n Achievement to overcome resistance to intermediate degree of difficulty under the public, gamelike conditions of the Ring Toss experiment (Chapter 19).

The important point is that the theory does not demand evidence that a group of persons classified below the median in n Achievement and above the median in Test Anxiety actually avoid intermediate risk. It does demand evidence that they show much weaker preference for intermediate risk than persons scoring high in n Achievement and low in Test Anxiety; and that is the character of the evidence presented in Chapter 5.

In a more thorough analysis of gambling preferences, Littig (Chapter 6) examines probability preferences in a game involving poker dice. He finds that subjects in whom (by assumption) $M_{AF} > M_S$ tend to avoid intermediate probabilities of success. This much is consistent with earlier results (Atkinson et al., 1960); so also is the relative indifference among probabilities of those in whom $M_S > M_{AF}$ at the beginning of the experiment. But in time these highly motivated persons develop a pattern of bidding which expresses a preference for higher probabilities of success. This result is consistent with Feather's argument (Chapter 3) that in a *chance-related* situation involving commitment and the con-

---

[1] Smith (1964), using a measure of intelligence to isolate students for whom an exam would be relatively easy or more difficult shows the importance of taking into account the level of difficulty of the exam, a factor ignored in the initial Atkinson-Litwin study but elaborated fully by Feather (Chapter 8).

sequent probability of loss of objective benefits, there may be a greater tendency to choose the more likely alternative. Littig argues that here is a case where the incentive value of success (i.e., winning in a gamble) is not related to probability because there is no differential sense of accomplishment. The subject knows that he is not responsible for the outcome. If I_s is here a constant, those who are strong in M_S still like to win (i.e., $Va_s = M_S \times I_s$). The product of subjective probability of winning and a constant subjective value of winning favors choice of the alternative offering the highest probability (see Figure 6).

Litwin's study (Chapter 7) replicates earlier results concerning risk preference in several different games and also explores the relative sensitivity of different indices of preference for intermediate risk. The expected differences between motivation groups are most pronounced when an index based on the obtained distribution of choices is employed. But, and here we begin to confront the conditions under which predictions from the theory are not sustained, Litwin finds that *the expected difference between motivation groups in risk preference does not occur when subjects are required to estimate their probabilities of success at each task immediately prior to performance.* At present, we do not know what this means.

Other evidence presented by Litwin shows that achievement-oriented subjects state higher estimates of probability of success than do failure-oriented subjects when few cues to define actual probabilities are available. Furthermore, his is the first study to explore directly the hypothesis that $Va_s = M_S \times I_s$. On the assumption that the monetary prize suggested for success at a given task would be proportionate to Va_s (the attractiveness of success at that task to the person), Litwin had subjects assign prizes for hitting the target at various distances in a ring toss game. He found the slope of the curve of attractiveness of success as a function of increasing difficulty to be greatest among those scoring high in n Achievement and low in Test Anxiety. In this study, as in the investigations reported by Atkinson, et al. (1960) and in Chapter 5—which replicate similar exploratory findings by McClelland (1958b) with very young children—there is greater preference for intermediate risk among subjects relatively strong in n Achievement when tasks involving skill are presented in a gamelike atmosphere and performance is public.

A study by Smith (1963) suggests that this motivationally determined risk preference may be a function of the way in which the situation is structured. Again we confront possible limitations on the generality of the theory. When a set of tasks involving different levels of difficulty was presented to subjects under Relaxed conditions (tasks described as of little importance, no need to try hard), Smith found that subjects in whom $M_S > M_{AF}$ show greater preference for tasks of intermediate difficulty. But this did not occur in a neutral condition (no special instructions other than those relevant to the task) or in an extrinsic condition (instructions to work hard in order to finish in time for dinner) of his experiment. A follow-up study by Raynor and Smith (forthcoming) found the predicted relationship between n Achievement and risk preference under both relaxed and achievement-oriented conditions.

The two studies of persistence (Feather, Chapters 8 and 9) investigate the degree to which an individual will keep working at an achievement task in the face of continual failure when similar achievement activities are available as alternatives. The results of the first study agree with predictions that achievement-oriented subjects $(M_S > M_{AF})$ persist longer at the initial task when it is presented to them as easy rather than as very difficult. Failure-oriented subjects $(M_{AF} > M_S)$ do just the reverse; they persist longer at the initial task when it is presented to them as very difficult rather than as easy. The results of the second study are consistent with predictions when subjects' own reported estimates of probability of success at the initial task are taken into account in the analysis of data.

These two studies of persistence dramatize the importance of considering both personality dispositions (motives) and situationally determined factors (expectations and incentive values) in the investigation of persistence. They also imply that, in conceptual analysis of achievement-oriented behavior, it is especially important to specify the components of the total strength of motivation to perform alternatives. Even under laboratory conditions a person is usually confronted with a number of alternative courses of action. The experimenter needs to know what these alternatives are and how to conceptualize their influence on the dependent variable that is being studied. It becomes necessary to make specific assumptions about how different component motivations combine in a task situation and how they might change in the course of task performance. An important characteristic of performance and persistence situations is their *dynamic* quality. Expectations may change as the subject acquires information about his task performance over a period of time (see Diggory, Riley, and Blumenfeld, 1960). Under these conditions, when expectations are modified as the subject obtains feedback about his performance, we expect motivation to vary over time. Such changes in motivation should occur in level-of-aspiration studies when the subject works at the same task for a number of trials. In contrast, a simple choice situation is more *static;* it is compressed into a narrower time interval and motivation is hence less likely to vary (Feather, 1965b).

Moulton's investigation of changes in level of aspiration following success and failure (Chapter 10) produces firm evidence of the non-obvious, "atypical" shifts predicted by the theory for persons in whom $M_{AF} > M_S$: following success they are likely to lower aspiration and following failure to raise it. In contrast, those highly motivated to achieve show the "typical" rise in aspiration following success and decline following failure. These results are consistent with early exploratory findings of Vitz (1957). Of additional importance is the method devised by Moulton to control the P_s of particular individuals. He makes it credible to a particular person that the task before him is one that *he*, in fact, can expect to succeed on .30, .50, or .70 of the time. In a later study, Moulton (personal communication) has shown that ability group norms of the sort described in Chapter 10 produce much more effective control of the P_s of particular persons than age group norms. The latter allow much more biasing of P_s in terms of generalized past experience in competition with others of similar age but dissimilar ability.

APPLICATIONS AND SOCIAL IMPLICATIONS

The studies presented in Part III of this book go beyond observing college students in contrived experimental situations to analysis of problems having more obvious social significance. Atkinson (Chapter 11) presents the argument for wider applications of the theory of achievement motivation. It rests securely on the fact that estimates, by college and high school students, of the percentage of people having sufficient general ability to succeed in various occupations are nearly a perfect, linear, inverse function of the prestige standing of the occupation (i.e., $r = -.85$ and $-.90$). It can be assumed, in other words, that the basic assumption $I_s = 1 - P_s$ holds in reference to the occupational hierarchy that defines success (status) in life.

Mahone (Chapter 12) applies the theory of achievement motivation to the problem of vocational aspiration. He tests the prediction that college students who are relatively high in "fear of failure" will be more likely to have unrealistic vocational aspirations. On each of several criteria, a significantly greater number of failure-oriented men $(M_{AF} > M_S)$ are classified as unrealistic than are achievement-oriented men $(M_S > M_{AF})$. Thus the major hypothesis is clearly supported, and it has also been confirmed among male high school students above median intelligence, by Atkinson and O'Connor (1963).

Crockett (Chapter 13) examines the influence of strength of achievement motive on intergenerational occupational mobility in the United States. He argues that the occupational system is generally perceived by Americans as hierarchically structured in terms of the prestige attached to various occupations, which indicates that the higher prestige occupations are perceived as having greater incentive value and as being more difficult to attain than are the lower prestige occupations. He predicts that, among people sharing equal opportunity, strength of achievement motive will be positively associated with upward occupational mobility and negatively associated with downward occupational mobility. An analysis of survey data from a national sample shows that the expected results are obtained with respect to upward mobility among persons from the lower social strata but not among persons reared in the middle and upper social strata. Among those having a middle-class background, n Affiliation rather than n Achievement is positively related to upward mobility. Here, as in Chapter 19, is a suggestion of the potential, and relatively ignored, importance of the need for affiliation (or social approval) as a determinant of achievement-oriented behavior.

Morgan (Chapter 14) takes up the suggestion that the slope of the curve defining attractiveness of success in relation to increasing difficulty may be used as a measure of the strength of achievement motive. This suggestion is based on earlier results reported by Litwin (Chapter 7) and independently by Strodtbeck, McDonald, and Rosen (1957). Morgan argues that an index of the strength of achievement motive would be provided by the extent to which a person places high value on succeeding in difficult, highly prestigeful occupations and low values on succeeding in easy occupations. He employs the regression of an evaluation index on the occupational prestige score as a measure of the strength of a person's achievement motive, and combines this with information about the person's subjective expectation that hard work pays off, in order to investigate relationships with a variety of economic behaviors. The promise of the validity of this new, theoretically derived measure of achievement motive is enhanced by its relationship to the hourly earnings of an individual and the extent of his planning ahead, as evinced by savings and plans for the education of children. Yet in the light of increasing evidence that n Affiliation also functions to influence achievement-oriented behavior in society (Chapter 13)—perhaps often in exactly the same manner as n Achievement (Chapter 19)—we must suspend judgment about whether Morgan has measured *only* the achievement motive or the joint effect of several different motives that are functionally equivalent in promoting achievement-oriented activities.

Finally, O'Connor, Atkinson, and Horner (Chapter 15) apply the theory of achievement motivation to the problem of ability grouping in schools. They consider an ability-grouped class to be one in which the probabilities of success and failure are nearly equal for most students. Results show that students who are relatively high in n Achievement show greater interest and enhancement in learning when they are grouped by ability than when they are not. Ability grouping does not, however, produce the expected decrement in performance among students who are relatively high in Test Anxiety, although there is evidence of a significant decline of interest in schoolwork when these students are placed in ability-grouped classes. While not in every detail a confirmation of the theory, the results of this study strongly emphasize that *expectancy of success is a manipulable motivational variable,* and demonstrate the motivational significance of intelligence test scores. Earlier, Spielberger (1962) had shown that individual differences in anxiety apparently had very little effect on the grade-point average (academic performance) of college students who scored either very high or very low in scholastic aptitude. Only among those in the intermediate range of ability was there evidence of the expected decrement among the highly anxious subjects. These two studies illustrate the utility of the theory of achievement motivation as a guide for educational research.

SOME CRITICAL PROBLEMS

Part IV of this book contains a set of recent studies that raise issues for future investigation.

Brody (Chapter 16) is concerned with the effects of both n Achievement and Test Anxiety on subjective probability of success (measured in terms of reported confidence) and risk-taking behavior. He studied this in a sequential decision problem where probability of success goes from low to high as the subject is presented with more relevant information, but where the payoff, in terms of points won, becomes less as he delays his decision. Brody's results show that the overall level of subjective probability of success tends to be higher among subjects high in n Achievement than among subjects low in n Achievement. Achievement-oriented subjects ($M_S > M_{AF}$) tend to increase confidence rapidly up to the level of 50% confidence and then to diminish their rate of increase in confidence relative to failure-oriented subjects ($M_{AF} > M_S$). It is interesting to note that achievement-oriented subjects do not tend to make their decisions when reported confidence is .50. However, their decision making more frequently falls in the intermediate quartiles of the distribution of reported confidence at the trial of decision than does that of failure-oriented subjects. This latter finding is consistent with results from those analyses in the Atkinson and Litwin (Chapter 5) and Litwin (Chapter 7) studies where intermediate risks are defined in terms of the median of the frequency distribution of goal-setting behaviors. The fundamental question raised by these and some other results is whether estimates of confidence, in terms of probabilities, should be taken as exactly equivalent to the theoretical concept—subjective probability of success (P_s)—or merely as a crude indication of the relative strength of P_s. To assume that a reported subjective probability of success *equals* the P_s referred to in the theory, is to assume that no other factor influences the verbal report. It seems more consistent with the general theoretical position adopted *to view any self-descriptive verbal report as a complexly determined instrumental act and to undertake the task of explicit conceptual analysis of the determinants of this type of instrumental activity.*

Feather (Chapter 17) investigates the relationship of reported probability of success to n Achievement and Test Anxiety scores in two conditions: in one the task is represented to subjects as moderately difficult, and in the other the task is presented as fairly easy. Reported probabilities obtained prior to task performance are positively related to n Achievement scores in the Moderately Difficult condition but negatively related to these scores in the Easy condition. These initial reported probabilities are negatively related to Test Anxiety scores in both experimental conditions. The predictions of this study are based on the assumption that *in a relatively ambiguous situation* subjects rely on knowledge of their previous performance at similar tasks, performed under conditions similar to those present, to estimate their chances of success. Their present estimates of probability are therefore related to factors that influenced their previous performance. Among these factors are the relatively stable motives to achieve success and to avoid failure. Hence, one would expect probability estimates and measures of these motives to be correlated in situations where the subject falls back upon past performance as a guide to present chances of success. This interpretation, which emphasizes the dominant role of past experience, may be compared with Brody's (Chapter 16) assumption about biasing of subjective probabilities, namely, that achievement-oriented subjects $(M_S > M_{AF})$ tend to state probabilities to maximize positive resultant achievement motivation. A further possible interpretation of results is also indicated in the paper, namely, that a person's probability statements may be influenced by the subjective attractiveness of success and the subjective repulsiveness of failure.

Obviously more work is needed to untangle the alternative explanations of the relationship that is frequently observed between measures of M_S or M_{AF} and measures of P_s. And proposals advanced by Moulton (personal communication) should be central in this work. Moulton, concerned with the same general issue, argues that particular experimental instructions and procedures, (described in Chapter 10) enable an experimenter to minimize the subjective biasing of experimentally defined probabilities, but other procedures (e.g., the use of rather general age-group norms) tend to encourage it. His results show that when the experimentally defined probability of success is relatively more ambiguous, the nature of the subjective bias by achievement-oriented and failure-oriented individuals is apparently opposite in direction. But this, paradoxically, makes their overt, aspirant behavior more similar. Both groups then show greater preference for more difficult tasks. The specific results predicted by the theory are more clearly shown when P_s is credibly defined *with special reference to the particular individual* in each case.

Smith (Chapter 18) is concerned with investigating two premises underlying research on n Achievement: first, that "achievement imagery" in thematic apperception reflects *only* achievement motivation; second, that performance scores of subjects high and low in n Achievement can be compared on the assumption that the two groups are similar, on the average, in all important respects other than achievement motivation. His results show that as the proportion of overall motivation for performance attributable to an achievement incentive increases, the strength of the positive relationship between n Achievement and performance increases. But the magnitude of this positive relationship is sufficiently small to suggest that one or more unmeasured motives that are negatively related to n Achievement may often influence achievement-oriented performance. It is indeed surprising how widespread is the tendency among psychologists to assume *all other things equal* to justify comparisons between two groups or conditions differentiated on one particular variable. Our relative ignorance forces us to this questionable assumption. Recognizing this, we may consider it more likely that two groups of subjects known to be alike in one respect (i.e., all are high in n Achievement) are more likely to be comparable in other respects than two groups of subjects already known to differ in at least one respect (i.e., one group is high and the other is low in n Achievement). This assumption would lead future experimental analysis of determinants of performance level to comparisons between High n Achievement groups *under different conditions* (e.g., Atkinson, 1953) rather than to comparison of the High and Low n Achievement groups within the *same* condition. Such a situation would probably hold true until more is learned about the tenability of the assumption, "all other things equal" when it applies to the various components of motivation to perform a task.

Smith's results also suggest that under some conditions thematic apperceptive *n* Achievement scores may reflect *extrinsic* motivation instead of, or in addition to, achievement motivation. The possibility is sufficiently important to make this one of the most significant problems for future study. If sustained definitively in future studies, this result would raise serious questions about the motivational implications of "achievement imagery" in folktales and other forms of literary expression that are produced under unknown conditions. To date, the appearance of "achievement imagery" in some product of imagination has been viewed as an expression of motivation *to achieve* (McClelland, Atkinson, Clark, and Lowell, 1953; Atkinson, 1958a; McClelland, 1961). The question raised by Smith is just what is needed to redirect attention to the task initially undertaken by McClelland and coworkers (1953), but lately largely ignored, of discovering and refining the definition of the unique symptoms of particular motives in thematic apperception.

Atkinson and O'Connor (Chapter 19) also suggest the importance of considering other types of motivation (particularly social approval) in studying achievement-oriented performance. Their results imply that *under certain conditions the positive incentive value of social approval may be negatively related to subjective probability of success,* and that *different types of motivation may summate to produce a performance decrement,* once total motivation exceeds an optimal point.

Neither of these possibilities is more than suggested by a completely unanticipated pattern of results. Again, it is the potential importance of the ideas, rather than firm factual evidence, which justifies their consideration as primary hypotheses for future work. If the need for affiliation can function just like the need for achievement to generate interest in moderate risks *under certain conditions,* then "entrepreneurial behavior" may be less uniquely related to the achievement motive than we presently suppose. One might, for example, encourage interest in the moderate risk by offering a variety of types of incentive, according to the rule $I_g = 1 - P_g$ (see Atkinson, 1965). It is a possibility that obviously deserves thorough investigation.

On the other hand, if efficiency of performance is decreased after a certain intensity of motivation has been reached, then much of the earlier work in which performance level at particular tasks is the dependent variable must be thoughtfully reexamined. For all of this work, at least within the program on *n* Achievement, has been interpreted on the premise of a positive monotonic relationship between strength of goal-directed tendency and level of performance.

OTHER DIRECTIVES FOR RESEARCH

In the preceding summary of chapters we have noted many suggestions concerning directions for future research. There are some other important issues, both methodological and theoretical, which define future avenues of inquiry, discussed in the following pages.

Assessment of Motives. There has been no advance in technique for assessing individual differences in *n* Achievement since 1949. This discouraging record is not for want of effort (see McClelland, 1958a). For reasons still not completely understood, objective tests that seem as though they should work as measures of M_S (e.g., the Edwards Personal Preference Scale (1954), called *n* Achievement in Chapter 5) or of M_S-M_{AF} (The Achievement Risk Preference Scale in Chapter 19) do not work. The failure of any self-report test to yield anything even approaching consistent evidence of construct validity as a measure of *n* Achievement is all the more bewildering in the light of the obvious utility of self-report tests of anxiety. Certainly an objective test would have the advantage of ease of administration and scoring, whereas the coding of projective protocols of *n* Achievement takes more time and requires more training. The "slope index" suggested by Litwin's results (Chapter 7) and used by Morgan (Chapter 14) is one possible alternative to the projective approach that deserves systematic investigation.

In addition to the development of alternative methods of assessing *n* Achievement, there now exists the possibility of applying the theory to interpret the results of those early studies (see McClelland, et al., 1953; Atkinson, 1958a) that were instrumental in the development of the projective measure of *n* Achievement. It seems likely that the *n* Achievement score derived from thematic apperception protocols for a particular group of subjects is a measure of the *personality component of the resultant achievement-oriented tendency* (namely, $M_S - M_{AF}$) in a situation where these subjects, having worked at a task under the same conditions, now write stories with a minimum of constraint. This resultant achievement-oriented tendency, and not *n* Achievement alone, is elicited by cues in the task situation immediately prior to the administration of the projective test and continues to influence imaginative thought as subjects write their stories to the TAT pictures. The resultant tendency would also be sustained by cues from the pictures themselves. If this interpretation is correct, it would be possible to vary the strength of the resultant achievement-oriented tendency among groups of subjects prior to administration of the projective test and to predict differences in n Achievement scores. The early work of McClelland et al. (1953) may be interpreted in this light, since the resultant achievement-oriented tendency would be more generally and reliably elicited under achievement-oriented conditions of prior task performance than under relaxed conditions, leading to a greater percentage of achievement imagery in the test protocols for the former condition. Now, however, it should be possible to go further and to use the theory in studying the effects on subsequent imagination of varying the probability of success associated with prior task performance. Thus one would predict that subjects who have just worked at an achievement task for which their expectations of success were intermediate should obtain higher n Achievement scores on the thematic apperception test than subjects who worked at the same achievement task with either very high or very low expectations of success. Murstein (1963) and Easter and Murstein (1964) report some positive evidence on this point, while another study by Murstein and Collier (1962) does not. The hypothesis is sufficiently important to deserve considerable systematic study and a definitive conclusion.

This type of interpretation suggests that the measurement of n Achievement under neutral conditions (i.e., where the pictures are simply presented to subjects and no attempt is made to control immediately prior experience) may provide a less valid measure of $M_S - M_{AF}$ since the immediately prior experience could vary among subjects and produce an uncontrolled difference in resultant achievement-oriented tendency. Some subjects, for example, may have come straight from a midsemester examination, others from relaxing over a cup of coffee just prior to taking the projective test. The resultant achievement-oriented tendency reflected in n Achievement scores would then be a function not only of differences in personality dispositions $(M_S - M_{AF})$ but also of differences in immediately prior experience (i.e., a situational effect). There remains a need for systematic methodological research to determine the extent of advantage in attempting to control the nature of the situation just prior to administration of the thematic apperception test. Some studies (e.g., Smith, 1961) have directed attention to these problems but with results that are not completely conclusive.

Although the projective procedure provides an n Achievement score that now seem likely to be a measure of $M_S - M_{AF}$, this measure is only moderately re able (see Haber and Alpert, 1958). Hence prediction is improved by also employing a questionnaire measure of Test Anxiety, which, we assume, independently assesses M_{AF}. Earlier attempts to develop a projective measure of fear of failure did not prove very satisfactory (see Atkinson, 1958a, Part 6 and Chapter 42). New efforts by Heckhausen (1963 and forthcoming) and Birney, Burdick, and Teevan (1964) appear more promising, although it is too early to assert with confidence that the variable being measured corresponds to M_{AF} in its behavioral implications. Our conception of the tendency to avoid failure as inhibitory in character implies that a strong tendency to avoid failure would be expressed in avoidance of achievement-oriented thoughts and activities in imaginative stories (see p. 89). This should be particularly likely since the subject is simply told to use his imagination, and there are virtually no constraints on his choice of topic. He is not, in other words, forced to engage in an achievement-oriented activity when he writes a story. Consequently, the symptoms of fear of failure in thematic apperception are likely to be much less direct and obvious than the symptoms of positive motivation to achieve. Current research takes this difficulty into account.

In summary, the theory suggests that the n Achievement score probably measures $M_S - M_{AF}$, the personality component of the resultant achievement-oriented tendency that is elicited by situational cues prior to administration of the pictures and is sustained by the picture cues. The reliability of this measure of $M_S - M_{AF}$ can be increased by supplementing the projective procedure with an independent measure of M_{AF} by means of questionnaires such as the Test Anxiety Questionnaire (Mandler and Cowen, 1958) or the Debilitating Anxiety Scale from the Achievement Anxiety Test (Alpert and Haber, 1960).

Methods of Varying Expectation of Success. The studies reported in this book have involved a number of different procedures to vary strength of subjective probability of success. Some of these involve structuring the actual task situation so that different levels of difficulty are quite apparent to the subject. Thus, varying the time required to complete a task (Feather, Chapter 3), the number of positive marbles in a "lottery box" (Feather, Chapter 3), the distance from the target in a shuffleboard game (Atkinson, et al., 1960) and a ring toss game (Atkinson and Litwin, Chapter 5), and the apparent complexity and/or length of a task (Litwin, Chapter 7; Smith, 1963) are all examples of experimental procedures presenting subjects with a task involving different levels of difficulty that are easily discernible in terms of available cues. Other methods of varying subjective probability of success present subjects with objective probabilities (Littig, Chapter 6) or reported norms which involve reference to the performance of related groups (Feather, Chapters 8, 9, and 17; Moulton, Chapter 10). Still other procedures rely upon the number of trials taken at the task (Brody, Chapter 16), the actual performance of subjects over trials (Feather, 1963c), or the *E*'s stated conclusions based on the *S*'s past performance on similar tests (Moulton, Chapter 10) to effect differences in subjective probabilities. An indirect procedure for assessing individual differences in P_s holding the task constant, assumes that intermediate subjective probabilities of success are more likely among subjects who are average in intelligence. Subjects who are high or low in intelligence are assumed more likely to begin an achievement task requiring intelligence with high or low P_s, respectively (O'Connor, Atkinson, and Horner, Chapter 15; Smith, 1964).

The direct procedures involved in the present set of studies are all basically concerned with varying the perceived difficulty of the task in terms of the degree to which the subject expects that he can succeed; they appear to have been relatively successful in meeting this aim. It would, however, be of interest to study the relative effectiveness of these methods and to investigate the possibility that these different procedures may have other types of effects apart from influencing subjects' expectations of success. Are subjective probabilities that are based on the structure of the task more sharply defined than those which are based upon reported norms? Are subjects more confident about their chances of success when these probabilities are based upon their own experience at a task than upon knowledge of how others have performed?

To check the effectiveness of these experimental operations we have sometimes asked subjects to rate their own chances of success (e.g., Litwin, Chapter 7; Feather, Chapters 8, 9). In other studies these probability judgments have been related to other variables such as *n* Achievement and Test Anxiety (Brody, Chapter 16; Feather, Chapter 17). We have also investigated the relationship of dependent variables such as persistence (Feather, Chapter 9) and performance (Feather, 1965b) to these ratings. In fact, we have argued that probability estimates obtained just prior to task performance are likely to reflect the influence of experience at related tasks performed in the past (Feather, 1963a; 1965a; 1956b; 1966) and summarize, as it were, the "batting-average" of the subject on tasks similar to the task that is to be performed in the present test. In two recent studies, Feather (1965b; 1966) has discovered that performance scores tend to be related positively to these initial probability estimates in situations where the nature of the task is *truthfully represented to subjects* (i.e., where subjects are not misled by false instructions or by fictitious norms). He argues that this positive relationship may simply reflect a similarity and stability in underlying factors influencing performance. Subjects who have done well at similar tasks in the past begin the present task with high expectations of success. They rate their chances of success as high, and, if the task has been truthfully represented to them, they tend to obtain performance scores which are higher than those of subjects who have been relatively less successful in the past and who begin the present task with lower expectations of success (see Feather, 1966). Such positive relationships between performance scores and initial probability estimates would be upset in situations where the task is misrepresented to subjects, since their expectations would be based on past performance at tasks which *differ* in some way from the actual task at hand.

It would be naïve to suppose that probability estimates obtained from subjects provide completely valid measures of the underlying subjective probabilities. Just how one would develop accurate direct measures of these subjective probabilities is a question which we cannot yet answer. But a subject's *verbal report* of his chances of success is likely to be influenced not only by the subjective probability of success (P_s) but also by other expectations and by certain motives and incentive values. In other words, we should consider the verbal report as another social act, an *instrumental response determined by motives, expectations, and incentive values.* We should begin to conceptualize the determinants of this act in terms of expectancy-value theory. In stating a probability estimate, a subject may be very concerned about how others will react to the estimate he gives and, in particular, he may be inclined to state a probability estimate which would be instrumental in gaining social approval. For example, he may avoid stating a very low estimate of his chances even when this is his considered belief because others might then label him as a "pessimist" and lacking in confidence. Similarly, he may avoid stating a very high estimate of his chances because he might anticipate that others might possibly regard him as unduly "optimistic" or even conceited. Research does show that subjects tend to overestimate low objective probabilities of success and to underestimate high objective probabilities of success (Feather, 1963a). Future research must explore differences in these tendencies in relation to strength of need for social approval and the subject's expectation that particular verbal responses will or will not lead to social approval (see Crowne and Marlowe, 1964).

Finally, it is likely that expectations of success may vary not only in their general level but also in the degree to which they are relatively well defined. A subject may develop an average level of expectation while working at a task, which becomes more sharply defined as he receives more information over trials. One study in this book (Feather, Chapter 9) shows that subjects become more confident about their probability estimates with experience at a task.

Definition of Intermediate Risk. A special case of the problems posed in the preceding section involves the definition of intermediate risk under experimental conditions. A number of procedures have been used to define intermediate risk. Atkinson and Litwin (Chapter 5) consider both intermediate geographic distance from the peg and the middle of the obtained distribution of shots as possible ways of defining intermediate risk in a Ring Toss Game. Litwin (Chapter 7) describes a Deviation Index which involves calculating the deviation of the difficulty level of a subject's choice from the median difficulty level of all choices and dividing by a measure of the dispersion of the difficulty level of the choices. In this procedure, a Deviation Index of zero is taken to define intermediate risk. Feather (1963c) attempts to create a condition of intermediate risk by controlling the proportion of successes over a sequence of trials at a problem-solving task (i.e., 50% success over trials).[2] More recently, reported norms of fictitious peer groups have been used in conjunction with sequences of success and failure to try to create a condition of intermediate risk, and an attempt is made to gauge the effectiveness of this procedure by an analysis of subjects' reported estimates of chances of success (see Feather, 1966). Moulton has recently proposed that the ambiguity inherent in the use of a reference group norm can be removed by having the experimenter consider the actual past performances of the subject and then have him inform the subject, presumably with the authority of an expert, that he has a 50–50 chance of success on a given task (Chapter 10). O'Connor, Atkinson, and Horner (Chapter 15) indicate the possibility of considering subjects with average ability as more likely to be in a situation of intermediate risk when

---

[2] This study (Feather, 1963c) investigated the effects of differential failure on expectations of success, reported anxiety, and response uncertainty. Results indicated that expectations of success (assumed to be reflected in trial-by-trial predictions of success) increased as the actual proportion of successes increased, and there was a general tendency to overpredict. Reported anxiety about failure, time taken to complete the test, and response uncertainty scores all tended to increase with degree of failure. A *fixed-incentive* model was introduced as an alternative to the *variable-incentive* model of the theory of achievement motivation. This fixed-incentive model implies an increase in tendency to avoid failure as P_s decreases with failure at the task, the rate of increase being greater when initial P_s is high and when M_{AF} is strong. The fixed-incentive model of tendency to avoid failure deserves further investigation (see also Feather, 1965b).

confronted with certain competitive academic tasks than are subjects with either very high or very low ability in a traditional heterogeneous class.

Still another possibility is noted by Atkinson and O'Connor (Chapter 19). Their suggested procedure is to define intermediate risk on a given task in terms of the choices of subjects assumed to be relatively strong in the motive to achieve success (i.e., subjects in whom $M_S > M_{AF}$). This experimentally defined level of intermediate risk may then be applied to the analysis of choices made by *other* subjects (e.g., those in whom it is assumed that $M_{AF} > M_S$) to investigate whether *their* choices are consistent with predictions from the theory of achievement motivation.

Accurate specification of intermediate risk is obviously the most important prerequisite for testing some of the basic implications of the theory of achievement motivation. Of the procedures listed above, the one recently evolved by Moulton (Chapter 10) appears most promising. The usual attempt to define intermediate risk only in terms of obviously discriminable differences in task difficulty may often lead to serious error when *the range of difficulty is truncated.* In a Ring Toss Game, for example, the line *nearest* to the peg may produce only intermediate expectations of success, and a definition of intermediate risk in terms of intermediate geographic distance from the peg would then be in serious error, since expectations of success for intermediate distances would be very low (see Chapter 5).

Analysis of Traditional Level of Aspiration Scores. So far, very little has been done to apply the theory of achievement motivation to analysis of the traditional verbally reported level of aspiration. In this situation a subject works for a number of trials at a task that permits different levels of performance (e.g., solving arithmetic problems). He is informed of his performance score for each trial and is required to set a level of aspiration for the succeeding trial. Setting the level of aspiration amounts to a choice by the subject between different levels of possible future performance. The sequence of events in this type of experiment, together with the possible scores which may be abstracted from the data sheet, are described by Lewin, et al. (1944). The score most frequently considered is the *goal discrepancy score,* which is defined as the difference between the level of aspiration for Trial $(n + 1)$ and the performance score of Trial n. It is positive if the level of aspiration for Trial $(n + 1)$ exceeds the performance score for Trial n. Usually goal discrepancy scores are averaged for a subject over trials. A positive average goal discrepancy score would therefore indicate that the subject generally tends to set his aspirations above his immediate past performance. In typical studies of college students, the distribution of goal discrepancy scores runs from small negative to large positive goal discrepancy with the central tendency normally a moderate positive goal discrepancy. The negative goal discrepancy score corresponds to a very low level of aspiration where P_s is very high; the very high positive goal discrepancy score corresponds to an aspiration level where P_s is very low. Somewhere in between, the small to moderate positive goal discrepancy score corresponds to the level at which P_s is .50, particularly if, as is typical, it is a task at which the subject believes he is improving over trials.

Unlike the procedure of a ring toss type of game, where a subject is committed to success or failure at a given level of difficulty, the traditional level of aspiration procedure allows for partial success or a greater success than the individual anticipated in setting his level of aspiration.

A recent study (Feather, 1964) has shown that the size of the mean goal discrepancy score is a function of the *payoff* following success (where success is defined as occurring when the subject attains or exceeds his stated level of aspiration) and the *cost* attendant upon failure (where failure is defined as occurring when the subject fails to attain his stated level of aspiration). In the *usual* level of aspiration experiment the payoff following success tends to be high and the cost of failure tends to be relatively low, since the subject wins points *equal to his actual performance*. If, for example, he sets his level of aspiration at 15, and in fact obtains a performance score of 17 (a success), he is credited with a score of 17. If he sets his level of aspiration at 15, and in fact obtains a performance score of 13 (a failure), he is credited with a score of 13. This combination of high payoff and low cost is generally associated with moderately *positive* goal discrepancy scores. But other types of level of aspiration situation can be defined which correspond to different conditions of payoff and cost. In one condition, for example, the subject may be credited with points *equal to his stated level of aspiration* following a success, but he obtains no extra credit if he exceeds the level of aspiration on a given trial. Should he fail to attain his level of aspiration on a given trial, he would obtain *zero* points. In this condition of low payoff with high cost, goal-setting tends to be more conservative. In fact, goal discrepancy scores tended to be *negative* (see Feather, 1964). This effect is similar to that noted by Feather in Chapter 3, where it was argued that the possibility of loss of objective benefits may determine a tendency to select easy alternatives that virtually guarantee success.

In view of these and other observed effects of differential payoffs and costs on goal-setting behavior, it becomes rather hazardous to apply the theory of achievement motivation to conceptualization of scores such as the goal discrepancy without taking into account the influence of points won and lost on a given trial.

The theory of achievement motivation is more simply applied to choice situations where alternatives vary in difficulty but where success and failure are not associated with gain or loss of points defined by some numerical scale. The Ring Toss Game obviously falls into this category as do many other simple choice situations. What is now needed is a concerted effort to clarify the nature of the combined influence of resultant achievement motivation and extrinsic tendencies (namely, expected value of points or money won or lost) on the traditional, but far from simple, measures of level of aspiration.

Interrelationships of Motive, Expectations, and Incentive Values. There is also some need for further analysis of interrelationships between measures of motives, expectations, and incentive values. Brody (Chapter 16) and Feather (Chapter 17) report studies in which judgments of probability of success are found to be related to measures of the strength of achievement-related motives, and they provide theoretical discussion of these results. A question of vital importance is: To what extent do these results imply complex interactions between the basic terms of the theory such that it becomes difficult or impossible to apply? If these studies necessarily imply both that subjective probabilities can influence incentive values and that incentive values can somehow act back to influence subjective probabilities, it would seem the theory is hopelessly entangled in a complex circuit of mutual influence. Slovic (1964) lists a number of different hypotheses implied by previous research and shows that judged probabilities of events are influenced by their desirability but in very complicated ways. At present we view the basic assumption $I_s = 1 - P_s$ as descriptive of conditions which pertain, for whatever reason, in the domain of achievement-oriented activities; and we (the editors) view relationships between n Achievement scores or Anxiety scores and some measure of P_s as an expression of different past frequency of success among persons who differ in motivation. It is entirely consistent with the logic of all that has been said about the influence of the tendency to achieve success and the tendency to avoid failure on the level of performance to expect that Ss in whom $M_s > M_{AF}$ would bring a greater history of success to most tasks. When there is sufficient ambiguity about the situational cues defining the individual's chances of success, the generalized effect of past history is to be expected. One can apparently minimize the pitfalls of this special problem by use of some procedure for defining an individual's P_s comparable to that recommended by Moulton (Chapter 10).

Situational Effects on Incentive Values. The incentive value of success at a particular task is fixed in the theory of achievement motivation by the subjective probability of success $(I_s = 1 - P_s)$. Hence, once subjective probability of success is known, incentive value of success is also known and vice versa. Measures of attractiveness of success (e.g., Feather, Chapter 3; Litwin, Chapter 7; Atkinson, Chapter 11; Morgan, Chapter 14) are really to be considered measures of "positive valence," which, according to the theory, express the product of motive to achieve success and incentive value of success (i.e., $Va_s = M_S \times I_s$). In the same way, measures of repulsiveness of failure are to be considered measures of "negative valence" which represent the product of motive to avoid failure and incentive value of failure (i.e., $Va_f = M_{AF} \times I_f$).

Future research might, given the cautions already stated concerning complications which arise when using an individual's own reports concerning his beliefs and values, explore such measures of valence and determine the degree to which they vary among situations for a given level of subjective probability of success or failure. There is some evidence already (see Feather, Chapter 3) to suggest that the attractiveness of attaining a goal object may be a function of the type of situation as well as a function of subjective probability of success. In the same way, the negative incentive value of failure may be influenced not only by the subjective probability of failure, as now assumed in the theory of achievement motivation $(I_f = -P_s)$, but also by particular aspects of the situation. For example, given the same subjective probability of failure, it is reasonable to assume that the repulsiveness of failure would be less in a situation where reassurance is provided, and the subject is told not to worry if he does not do well, than in a situation where this reassurance is absent (see Feather, 1965b).

One way of accounting for differences in "valence" between situations is to assume that situations may vary in the degree to which they engage particular motives. The motive to achieve success (M_S) may, for example, be more reliably elicited in a test situation than in a relaxed, game-like situation. Hence, one would expect to find a greater proportion of subjects perceiving success as attractive in a test situation than in a game-like situation, since the valence of success is a function of M_S. One might, however, design a situation so that *all* subjects see success as attractive (i.e., by assumption M_S is elicited in all subjects) and then attempt to increase the test-like character of the situation. Since M_S is assumed to be a relatively stable personality disposition, once elicited it should not vary in strength, and any increase in attractiveness of success under these conditions would suggest a situational effect on the incentive value of success (I_s). To take account of this type of situational effect, it might be necessary to include another weighting factor in the theory of achievement motivation.

An increase in the attractiveness of success due to a situational factor other than level of difficulty would determine an increase in the tendency to approach success. Similarly, when subjective probability of success is constant, we might expect the tendency to avoid failure to be stronger if the subject were explicitly told how bad it would be to fail than if he were informed that there is no cause to worry about failure.

It is quite possible that some situations influence attractiveness of success or repulsiveness of failure, but not both. One might, for example, contrast a test situation where reassurance about failure is provided with the same test situation where there is no such reassurance, and assume that this situational difference would have an effect on repulsiveness of failure but not on attractiveness of success. If subjective probability of success is constant in both situations, the resultant achievement-oriented tendency would be stronger in the first situation because the tendency to avoid failure would be weaker. In a corresponding way one might contrast a test situation where the subject is told that success is something to be prized with a game-like situation where there is no such instruction, and assume that this situational difference would influence the attractiveness of success but not the repulsiveness of failure. If subjective probability of success is constant in both situations, the resultant achievement-oriented tendency would be stronger in the first situation because the tendency to approach success would be stronger. Finally, one could proceed to a comparison of situations where *both* attractiveness of success and repulsiveness of failure are influenced by situational conditions other than level of difficulty. For example, the effects of a test situation with no reassurance could be compared with the effects of a game-like situation with reassurance. One might also try to reduce the strong tendency to avoid failure among subjects in whom $M_{AF} > M_S$ in a situation of intermediate risk by employing reassuring instructions. By such means it might be possible to determine moderate risk-taking among subjects in whom $M_{AF} > M_S$.

There is obviously plenty of scope for future investigation of the effect of situational factors *in addition to* the level of difficulty on attractiveness of success and repulsiveness of failure. Such studies will have important implications for the theory of achievement motivation and perhaps will require the introduction of another weighting factor to take account of differences in "valence" when P_s is constant among situations and when the probability that motives will be elicited in these situations is the same. The major problem in this work is to ascertain that a change in an individual's "concern" over success or failure at a task expresses a change in the intensity of *achievement* motivation and not the addition or subtraction of *some other kind of incentive* from the task, (e.g., social approval, social rejection, etc.). The present theory places increasing emphasis on extrinsic sources of motivation for what appears to be achievement-oriented activity.

The Concept of Availability of Response. Future studies of performance based on the theory of achievement motivation must explore the variable referred to as "task complexity." Behavior theorists in the S-R tradition (e.g., Taylor, 1956) consider this variable using the concept of the dominant response in a hierarchy of responses, a simple task being one where the correct response is dominant and a complex task one where the correct response may be low in the hierarchy. So far, the theory of achievement motivation has not dealt with the problem of *availability* of response. A stimulus situation may elicit not only expectations but also *habits*, some of which are more dominant than others. A more complete statement of the present theory would, perhaps, assume that the tendency to perform a given response in an achievement situation is a function of the availability of the response (strength of habit) as well as a function of the motives, expectations, and incentive values already included in the model (see Atkinson, 1964, p. 279). In the Ring Toss situation, for example, the dominant response is to face the target and throw the ring with an under-arm action. Other responses (e.g., throwing the ring over one's head while standing backward in relation to the target) are less dominant. They are lower in availability (weaker in habit) and the tendency to perform them is correspondingly weaker.

The problem which will require most attention when the theory of achievement motivation is directed to analysis of performance at simple and complex tasks is the probable confounding of variables. The simple task, almost by definition, is one which the subject should consider relatively easy (i.e., he almost always performs the correct response). The complex task, in contrast, is one which by definition should appear relatively difficult to the subject (i.e., less frequently does he perform the correct response). According to theory, achievement-oriented motivation should be more strongly aroused by the complex task if it is moderately difficult (holding instructions and other influences constant), and performance effects attributable to the personality variables M_S and M_{AF} should be most pronounced on the complex task. Considerable attention must be given this problem of separating "task complexity" and "apparent difficulty" to determine whether or not, and if so, how the concept of availability of response or habit should be included in a motive-expectancy-incentive formulation.

Hope, Fear, Disappointment, and Relief. In a recent paper Feather (1963d) has presented an alternative conceptualization to Mowrer's concepts of hope, fear, disappointment, and relief (Mowrer, 1960a, 1960b). The four concepts are not defined as increments or decrements in the fear response (as in Mowrer) but are developed within the framework of expectancy-value theory. *Hope motivation* is defined as motivation to approach a positive incentive or reward and corresponds to what we now call the tendency to perform a response leading to a goal. *Fear motivation* is defined as motivation to avoid a negative incentive or punishment, and corresponds to what we now call the tendency *not* to perform a response leading to punishment. *Motivational disappointment* is defined as the amount of reduction in hope motivation (mediated by a change in expectancy) that occurs following nonconfirmation or only partial confirmation of an expectation of reward (i.e., the reward does not occur or occurs in reduced quantity or quality). *Motivational relief* is defined as the amount of reduction in fear motivation (also mediated by a change in expectation) that occurs following nonconfirmation or partial confirmation of an expectation of punishment (i.e., the punishment does not occur or occurs in reduced quantity of quality). It may be noted that motivational disappointment and motivational relief are *secondary* concepts, as it were, since each is defined in terms of reduction in hope motivation and fear motivation, respectively, following nonconfirmation or partial confirmation of the corresponding expectation of reward or punishment.

The above concepts are discussed for the case where subjective probabilities and incentive values are assumed to be independent, and also in relation to the theory of achievement motivation, where subjective probabilities and incentive values are inversely related. They are not identified as the *emotional* responses of hope, fear, disappointment, and relief, respectively, but as theoretical concepts which may be developed within a class of models involving the concepts of motive, expectation, and incentive value. However, we would expect measures of hope motivation, fear motivation, motivational disappointment, and motivational relief to correlate with measures of the emotional responses of hope, fear, disappointment, and relief, respectively. When the tendency to perform a response leading to a goal ("hope motivation") is strong we would expect the subject to be more "hopeful" than when this tendency is weak. When nonattainment of a goal reduces, by a great amount, the tendency to perform a response leading to a goal, we would expect the subject to be more "disappointed" than when this tendency is reduced by a small amount. When the tendency to avoid performing a response leading to a punishment ("fear motivation") is strong, we would expect the subject to be more "fearful" than when this tendency is weak, provided of course that the subject is in a situation where the response has to be performed. Finally, when nonoccurrence of the punishment reduces, by a great amount, the tendency to avoid making a response leading to the punishment, we would expect the subject to be more "relieved" than when this tendency is reduced by a small amount.

In a study of persistence (Feather, Chapter 9), in which ratings of disappointment about failure were obtained incidentally, it was found that these ratings were positively correlated with subjects' initial estimates of probability of success at the task (i.e., subjects with high initial probability estimates tended to report more disappointment about their performance following successive failures at a task). This positive relationship agrees with prediction, if reported disappointment may be taken as a measure of motivational disappointment (Feather, 1963d). In a subsequent study (Feather, 1965b), where subjects could obtain some success at the task (solving a list of anagrams), ratings of disappointment were negatively correlated with number of anagrams solved (i.e., the more successful the subject, the less disappointment he reported). These studies suggest that where performance level is allowed to vary among subjects, it may become the dominant factor influencing reported disappointment. Where, however, performance level is constant among subjects (and particularly where there is uniform failure), reported disappointment will tend to be a positive function of initial expectation of success. There is plenty of scope for further investigation in this area.

The Concept of Inertial Tendency. In recent discussions of the effects of success and failure it is argued that an additional motivational effect must be taken into account (namely, the persistence of the unsatisfied tendency when the goal is not attained). As stated in this book, the theory of achievement motivation emphasizes the change in cognitive expectations produced by success and failure and consequently the effect on the strength of resultant achievement-oriented tendency on some later trial or occasion. Atkinson and Cartwright (1964) and Atkinson (1964, Chapter 10) now propose the assumption that a goal-directed tendency, once aroused, persists until it is satisfied. This would mean that following failure at some task there should be, in addition to a change in motivation mediated by a change in expectancy of success, a persisting tendency, that would also influence any subsequent achievement-oriented performance. The *inertial tendency* is designated T_{G_i} to convey the idea that once the tendency to attain some particular goal *(g)* is aroused and thwarted what persists is a general tendency toward that class of goal *(G)*. Thus, in the case of achievement-oriented activity, there should be a general inertial tendency to achieve success (T_{Si}) that persists following a failure, to influence the strength of any subsequently aroused tendency to achieve success—whether at the same or some different task. The final strength of some newly aroused tendency to achieve success (T_{S_f}) should equal $(M_S \times P_s \times I_s)$ $+ T_{S_i}$, where T_{S_i} represents the persistent unfulfilled wish to achieve that is carried over from the past. It is assumed that a goal-directed tendency is reduced when a goal is attained. Consequently, there should always be a greater inertial tendency to achieve following failure than there is following success.

This variable for some time was implicitly assumed in the unformalized discussions of achievement motivation to explain the effect of experimentally induced motivation on thematic apperception—particularly the higher TAT *n* Achievement scores that were obtained following failure rather than success (McClelland, et al., 1953, p. 184) and is also suggested in Feather's discussion of an effect that is similar to a Zeigarnik Effect (p. 129), which appeared to be operating in his initial study of persistence. The inertial tendency, conceived as a general tendency toward a particular class of goal, should influence persistence in achievement-oriented activity, particularly *when the alternative is to engage in some other class of activity* (for example, in Chapter 5 when subjects left the examination room to do something else when they terminated work at the exam). A general inertial tendency to achieve success (T_{S_i}) would be expected to have no differential effect—or at least *less* differential effect—on persistence at some task when the alternative is also an achievement-oriented activity as in Feather's studies (Chapters 8 and 9). In this case, the inertial tendency would equally enhance the tendency to continue the initial task and the tendency to undertake an alternative path toward success. It is conceivable, however, that such an inertial tendency might have an influence on verbal reports concerning expectations of success following failure, or on verbal reports descriptive of various emotional states (e.g., anxiety, disappointment, etc.). Thus this factor should be given serious consideration in future research.

Presently, too little is known about the way in which the persistence of previously aroused motivation influences subsequent choice, performance, and persistence to enable us to spell out, with any degree of confidence, what reinterpretations of results reported here may be required by the new concept. The preceding general discussions provide the guiding hypotheses for future work.

The first application of these ideas to achievement-oriented activity is reported by Weiner (1963). He studied the effect of continued success on persistence when initial P_s is .70, versus continued failure when initial P_s is .30, and the alternative to which the subject may turn is *not* an achievement-oriented activity. According to the theory of achievement motivation as stated in this book, persons in whom $M_S > M_{AF}$ should lose interest in the initial task after about the same number of trials in the two conditions, assuming that P_s increases, following success, at about the same rate that it decreases, following failure. But if there is an inertial tendency following failure—to enhance the strength of the subsequent tendency to perform the initial task, even though P_s has changed to lower motivation—there should be greater persistence following failure.

Weiner's initial results on this problem, while not definitive, are more consistent with the assumption of an inertial tendency. The trend of measures of both persistence and level of performance for subjects scoring high in *n* Achievement and low in Test Anxiety support the assumption of an inertial tendency following failure. There is, in addition, some suggestive evidence of an inertial avoidance tendency among subjects scoring high in Test Anxiety and low in *n* Achievement.

Given these results, studies of effects of success and failure that are aimed at isolating and measuring motivational effects that are mediated by changes in expectancy of success (P_s) and immediate inertial motivational effects (T_{S_i}) become of paramount importance. The concept of inertial tendency formally begins to take into account the influence on present motivation of previous deprivation, a factor long emphasized by psychoanalytically oriented writers such as Lazarus (1961) in discussions of the need for achievement. At present, it appears that *the concept of inertial tendency defines an important direction of future evolution of the theory of achievement motivation.*

THE STUDY OF PERSONALITY AND PROCESS

Perhaps of more lasting significance than any of the general implications of the theory or any of the hypotheses leading to specific "next steps" in research—since many or all of them may prove to be incorrect —is the model that is provided by the theory and the research concerning implementation of conceptual integration of the study of personality and the study of basic behavioral processes. Psychology has a split tradition. Concern with description of how people differ has been isolated from concern with analysis of the fundamental processes of behavior (in the present case, the process of motivation). Cronbach (1957) has spelled out the problem in his analysis of "the two disciplines of scientific psychology." We have constantly been mindful of the issues he raised.

In specifying the nature of the interaction between attributes of personality and immediate environmental influences that produce achievement motivation, the theory encourages a research strategy which employs both techniques of assessment—evolved in descriptive differential psychology—and techniques of control and manipulation of environmental factors—evolved within experimental psychology. The theory and the results of research influenced by it suggest that neither of the traditional approaches, in isolation from the other, will ever produce a very useful conception of human motivation, because, each alone, tends to ignore half the relevant antecedents of the behavior under scrutiny.

The research reviewed in this book has tended to emphasize the process orientation. We have focused on the joint influence of personality and environment under particular conditions (i.e., particular situations). There have been no case studies. But the theory does not ignore the individual personality. To illustrate how easily and effectively one may shift within the framework of the theory from the process orientation to the personality orientation, which emphasizes the characteristics of particular persons (but without ignoring the determinative role of the changing environment), let us consider the image the theory projects of an *achievement-oriented personality* and of the other fellow who is dominated by a dread of failure, a *failure-threatened personality*. From the continuum of quantitative differences—between strength of motive to achieve and motive to avoid failure—that the theory has conditioned us to think about, we select for special attention the extreme cases. First, what pattern of behavior might we expect most consistently from an individual in whom the motive to achieve greatly exceeds the motive to avoid failure?

The Achievement-Oriented Personality. The achievement-oriented person is generally attracted to activities which require the successful exercise of skill. He is not particularly interested in gambling, where the outcome depends upon chance. Among activities that pit his skill against some standard or the skill of others he is more challenged by the task of intermediate difficulty, the 50–50 risk, than easier and safer ventures or much more difficult and speculative ones. If he is successful, he will raise his sights; if he is unsuccessful, he will lower them accordingly. He is realistic. Although less interested in easy or very difficult tasks, he is more likely than others to undertake even these when they are the only available opportunities. He does this because he likes the challenge and the sense of having done something well a good deal more than others do, and probably a good deal more than he likes other potentially gratifying activities. Whatever the level of the challenge to achieve, he will strive more persistently than others when confronted with an opportunity to quit and undertake some different kind of activity instead. But within the context of his effort to achieve, he does not waste time in pursuit of the impossible nor rest content with continual mastery of old familiar tasks when there are new, realistic possibilities of accomplishment open to him. In contrast to those who are not really much involved in the effort to achieve, he will not stick doggedly at a highly improbable venture when there is a more moderate risk available to him. Although he does not exhaust himself in the pursuit of illusory goals, he does believe that substantially greater prizes (whatever form they may take) should be awarded to persons who perform very difficult feats rather than easier ones. This is an expression of his pride in accomplishment and the extent to which he, more than others, sensitively appraises differences in merit. When he approaches a task in which there is considerable ambiguity about the possibility of success, he will be more confident than others. Why? This is probably because his realistic approach to challenges in the past, his enthusiasm, and persistence have made him more successful than others. He extrapolates this higher "batting average" (i.e., more frequent success) to the new venture when little concrete information about his chances is available. Consequently, many tasks which appear very difficult to others are likely to be viewed as realistic or calculated risks by the achievement-oriented personality. He is so often surrounded by ambiguous possibilities that he can construct for himself a world of interesting challenges. This he does in imagination, providing the most generally useful measure of the strength of his motive to achieve.

The Failure-Threatened Personality. In contrast, we have the individual in whom the motive to avoid failure greatly exceeds the motive to achieve. He is dominated by the threat of failure, and so resists activities in which his competence might be evaluated against a standard or the competence of others. Were he not surrounded by social constraints (i.e., spurred by a need to be approved for doing what is generally expected by his peers) he would never voluntarily undertake an activity requiring skill when there is any uncertainty about the outcome. When forced into achievement-oriented activities, he is most threatened by what the other fellow considers the greatest challenge. Constrained, but given a choice, he will defend himself by undertaking activities in which success is virtually assured or activities which offer so little real chance of success that the appearance of trying to do a very difficult thing (which society usually applauds) more than compensates for repeated and minimally embarrassing failures. Given an opportunity to quit an activity that entails evaluation of his performance for some other kind of activity, he is quick to take it. Often constrained by social pressures and minimally involved, not really achievement-oriented at all, he will display what might be taken for dogged determination in the pursuit of the highly improbable goal. But he will be quickly frightened away by failure at some activity that seemed to him to guarantee success at the outset. The dogged persistence is really rigid, apathetic compliance, as is his tolerance for continual routine success at tasks offering virtually no possibility of failure. This fellow's general resistance to achievement-oriented activity opposes any and all sources of positive motivation to undertake the customary competitive activities of life. Thus he suffers a chronic decrement in achievement tests. His long history of relative failure means he will view his chances in new ventures more pessimistically than others unless there is specific information to contradict a simple generalization from past experience. Most startling, perhaps, are the erratic changes in his level of aspiration, which take place when the least likely outcome occurs. Should this fellow fail at a task he undertook as a reasonably safe venture, he might respond with a startling increase in his level of aspiration instead of persistence at the initial activity. Should he begin to succeed at a task initially conceived as very difficult, he might then exhibit a dramatic decrease in his level of aspiration, a retreat to the safest of ventures. These apparently irrational moves—like his inability to move away from continual failure when the probability of success is remote—are to be understood as aspects of a defensive strategy, the avoidance of an intermediate degree of risk, the peak of competitive activity, where his anxiety reaches an intolerable level.

The level of anxiety is symptomatic of the degree of resistance to an activity. When it is strong we know that the individual has been constrained to overcome great resistance. When it is weak the resistance to that activity must be weak. Because the level of experienced anxiety is symptomatic of the strength of resistance (i.e., the tendency to avoid failure) we are able to assess the strength of this man's motive to avoid failure from self-report questionnaires concerning the great amount of anxiety he has experienced in the nonvoluntary achievement tests endured in schooling. In the strange pattern of defensive behavior expressed by the person who is dominated by dread of failure, we confront pathology in the domain of achievement-oriented activity.

While no doubt wrong in some or even many particulars, these images of two distinctively different types of men have the scientific virtue of being derived from the inexorable logic of an explicitly stated theory. It is a theory which gives equal emphasis to the role of enduring properties of personality and to transient features of the immediate environment in its analysis of the process of motivation. A scientific theory is not a settled creed but a policy, a guide for future experiments (Conant, 1952). We are confident that future experiments will correct the inadequacies in this, our current conception of achievement motivation.

References

Alexander, W. P. (1935). Intelligence, concrete and abstract. *Brit. J. Psychol. monogr. Supple.,* No. 19.

Allport, G. W. (1943). The ego in contemporary psychology. *Psychol. Rev.,* 50, 451–478.

Alpert, R. (1957). Anxiety in academic achievement situations: Its measurement and relation to aptitude. Unpublished doctoral dissertation, Stanford University.

Alpert, R. and Haber, R. N. (1960). Anxiety in academic achievement situations. *J. abnorm. soc. Psychol.,* 61, 207–215.

Atkinson, J. W. (1950). Studies in projective measurement of achievement motivation. Unpublished doctoral dissertation, University of Michigan.

Atkinson, J. W. (1953). The achievement motive and recall of interrupted and completed tasks. *J. exp. Psychol.,* 46, 381–390.

Atkinson, J. W. (1954). Explorations using imaginative thought to assess the strength of human motives. In M.R. Jones (Ed.), *Nebraska symposium on motivation.* Lincoln: University of Nebraska Press, pp. 56–112.

Atkinson, J. W. (1955). The achievement motive and recall of interrupted and completed tasks. In D. C. McClelland (Ed.), *Studies in motivation.* New York: Appleton-Century-Crofts, pp. 494–506.

Atkinson, J. W. (1957). Motivational determinants of risk-taking behavior. *Psychol. Rev.,* 64, 359–372.

Atkinson, J. W. (Ed.) (1958a). *Motives in fantasy, action, and society.* Princeton: Van Nostrand.

Atkinson, J. W. (1958b). Toward experimental analysis of human motivation in terms of motives, expectancies, and incentives. In J. W. Atkinson (Ed.), *Mo-tives in fantasy, action, and society.* Princeton: Van Nostrand, pp. 288–305.

Atkinson, J. W. (1958c). Thematic apperceptive measurement of motives within the context of a theory of motivation. In J. W. Atkinson (Ed.), *Motives in fantasy, action, and society.* Princeton: Van Nostrand, pp. 596–616.

Atkinson, J. W. (1959). Notes concerning the generality of the motive $\times$ expectancy $\times$ incentive formulation of achievement motivation and motivation to avoid failure. Unpublished manuscript.

Atkinson, J. W. (1960). Personality dynamics. *Annu. Rev. Psychol.,* 11, 255–290.

Atkinson, J. W. (1964). *An introduction to motivation.* Princeton: Van Nostrand.

Atkinson, J. W. (1965). The mainsprings of achievement-oriented activity. In J. Krumboltz (Ed.), *Learning and the educational process.* Chicago: Rand-McNally.

Atkinson, J. W. and Raphelson, A. C. (1956). Individual differences in motivation and behavior in particular situations. *J. Pers.,* 24, 349–363.

Atkinson, J. W. and Reitman, W. R. (1956). Performance as a function of motive strength and expectancy of goal attainment. *J. abnorm. soc. Psychol.,* 53, 361–366.

Atkinson, J. W., Bastian, J. R., Earl, R. W., and Litwin, G. H. (1960). The achievement motive, goal-setting, and probability preferences. *J. abnorm. soc. Psychol.,* 60, 27–36.

Atkinson, J. W. and Litwin, G. H. (1960). Achievement motive and test anxiety conceived as motive to approach success and motive to avoid failure. *J. abnorm. soc. Psychol.,* 60, 52–63.

Atkinson, J. W. and O'Connor, Patricia

(1963). Effects of ability grouping in schools related to individual differences in achievement-related motivation. Project 1283 of Cooperative Research Program of the Office of Education, United States Department of Health, Education, and Welfare. Microfilm copies available for $2.25 from Photoduplication Center, Library of Congress, Washington, D. C.

Atkinson, J. W. and Cartwright, D. (1964). Some neglected variables in contemporary conceptions of decision and performance. *Psychol. Reports*, **14**, 575–590. Monograph Supplement 5–V14.

Barber, B. (1957). *Social Stratification*. New York: Harcourt-Brace.

Bendix, R. and Lipset, S. M. (Eds.) (1953). *Class, status, and power*. Glencoe, Illinois: Free Press.

Bindra, D. (1959). *Motivation: A systematic reinterpretation*. New York: Ronald.

Birney, R. C. (1958). The achievement motive and task performance: A replication. *J. abnorm. soc. Psychol.*, **56**, 133–135.

Birney, R. C., Burdick, H., and Teevan, R. C. (1964). Fear of failure and the achievement situation. Technical Report No. 1, Contract NONR 3591(01), NR 171-803 (Richard C. Teevan, Bucknell University, Principal Investigator).

Bitterman, M. E., Federson, W. E., and Tyler, D. W. (1953). Secondary reinforcement and the discrimination hypothesis. *Amer. J. Psychol.*, **66**, 456–464.

Boulding, K. (1964). *The meaning of the 20th century*. New York: Harper and Row.

Broadhurst, P. L. (1957). Emotionality and the Yerkes-Dodson law. *J. exp. Psychol.*, **54**, 345–352.

Brody, N. (1963). *N* achievement, test anxiety, and subjective probability of success in risk taking behavior. *J. abnorm. soc. Psychol.*, **66**, 413–418.

Brown, J. S. (1953). Problems presented by the concept of acquired drives. In *Nebraska symposium on motivation*. Lincoln: University of Nebraska Press, pp. 1–21.

Brown, J. S. (1961). *The motivation of behavior*. New York: McGraw-Hill.

Brown, J. S. and Farber, I. E. (1951). Emotions conceptualized as intervening variables—with suggestions toward a theory of frustration. *Psychol. Bull.*, **48**, 465–495.

Brown, M. C. (1955). The status of jobs and occupations as evaluated by an urban Negro sample. *Amer. Sociol. Rev.*, **20**, 561–566.

Brown, R. (1953). A determinant of the relationship between rigidity and authoritarianism. *J. abnorm. soc. Psychol.*, **48**, 469–476.

Bush, R. R. and Mosteller, F. (1955). *Stochastic models for learning*. New York: John Wiley.

Cartwright, D. and Festinger, L. (1943). A quantitative theory of decision. *Psychol. Rev.*, **50**, 595–622.

Centers, R. C. (1941). *The psychology of social classes*. Princeton: Princeton University Press.

Centers, R. C. (1953). Social class, occupation, and imputed belief. *Amer. J. Sociol.*, **58**, 543–555.

Clark, R. A., Teevan, R., and Ricciuti, H. N. (1956). Hope of success and fear of failure as aspects of need for achievement. *J. abnorm. soc. Psychol.*, **53**, 182–186.

Cochran, W. G. and Cox, G. (1957). Experimental designs. New York: *John Wiley*.

Cohen, J. (1960). *Chance, skill, and luck*. Baltimore: Penguin Books.

Conant, J. B. (1952). Modern science and modern man. New York: Columbia University Press.

Coombs, C. H. and Beardslee, D. (1954). On decision-making under uncertainty. In R. M. Thrall, C. H. Coombs, and R. L. Davis (Eds.), *Decision processes*. New York: John Wiley, pp. 255–285.

Coombs, C. H. and Pruitt, D. G. (1960). Components of risk in decision making: Probability and variance preferences. *J. exp. Psychol.*, 265–277.

Corah, N. L., Feldman, M. J., Cohen, I. S., Gruen, W., Meadow, A., and Ringwall, E. A. (1958). Social desirability as a variable in the Edwards Personal Preference Schedule. *J. consult. Psychol.,* **22,** 70–72.

Counts, G. S. (1925). The social status of occupations. *School Rev.,* **33,** 16–27.

Courts, F. A. (1942). Relationships between muscular tension and performance. *Psychol. Bull.,* **39,** 347–367.

Crandall, V. J., Solomon, D., and Kellaway, R. (1955). Expectancy statements and decision times as functions of objective probabilities and reinforcement values. *J. Pers.,* **24,** 192–203.

Crockett, H. J., Jr. (1960). Achievement motivation and occupational mobility in the United States. Unpublished doctoral dissertation, University of Michigan.

Crockett, H. J., Jr. (1962). The achievement motive and differential occupational mobility in the United States. *Amer. Sociol. Rev.,* **27,** 191–204.

Crockett, H. J., Jr. (1964). Social class, education, and motive to achieve in differential occupational mobility. *The Sociol. Quart.,* **5,** 231–242.

Cronbach, L. J. (1957). The two disciplines of scientific psychology. *Amer. Psychol.,* **12,** 671–684.

Cronbach, L. J. and Meehl, P. E. (1955). Construct validity in psychological tests. *Psychol. Bull.,* **52,** 281–302.

Crowne, D. P. and Marlowe, D. (1964). *The approval motive.* New York: John Wiley.

Crutcher, R. (1934). An experimental study of persistence. *J. Appl. Psychol.,* **18,** 409–417.

Darley, J. G. (1941). *Clinical aspects and interpretation of the Strong Vocational Interest Blank.* New York: The Psychological Corporation.

Davis, Allison, Gardner, B. B., and Gardner, Mary R. (1941). *Deep south.* Chicago: University of Chicago Press.

de Charms, R., Morrison, H. W., Reitman, W., and McClelland, D. C. (1955). Behavioral correlates of directly and indirectly measured achievement motivation. In D. C. McClelland (Ed.), *Studies in motivation.* New York: Appleton-Century-Crofts, pp. 414–423.

Deeg, Martha E. and Paterson, D. G. (1947). Changes in social status of occupations. *Occupations,* **25,** 205–208.

Diggory, J. C., Riley, E. J., and Blumenfeld, R. (1960). Estimated probability of success for a fixed goal. *Amer. J. of Psychol.,* **73,** 41–55.

Dollard, J. and Miller, N. E. (1950). *Personality and psychotherapy: An analysis in terms of learning, thinking, and culture.* New York: McGraw-Hill.

Douvan, Elizabeth M. (1956). Social status and success strivings. *J. abnorm. soc. Psychol.,* **52,** 219–223.

Douvan, Elizabeth M. and Adelson, J. B. (1958). The psychodynamics of social mobility in adolescent boys. *J. abnorm. soc. Psychol.,* **56,** 31–44.

Drake, St. Clair and Cayton, H. M. (1945). *Black metropolis.* New York: Harcourt, Brace and World.

Drèze, J. H. (1958). Individual decision making under partially controllable uncertainty. Unpublished doctoral dissertation, Columbia University.

Dunnett, C. W. (1955). A multiple comparison procedure for comparing several treatments with a control. *J. Amer. statist. Ass.,* **50,** 1096–1121.

Dynes, R. R., Clarke, A. C., and Dinitz, S. (1956). Levels of occupational aspiration: some aspects of family experience as a variable. *Amer. Sociol. Rev.,* **21,** 212–215.

Easter, L. V. and Murstein, B. I. (1964). Achievement fantasy as a function of probability of success. *J. consult. Psychol.,* **28,** 154–159.

Edwards, A. L. (1954). *Edwards Personal Preference Schedule.* Manual. New York: Psychological Corporation.

Edwards, A. L. (1957). *The social desirability variable in personality assessment and research.* New York: Dryden.

Edwards, W. (1953). Probability preferences in gambling. *Amer. J. Psychol.,* **66,** 349–364.

Edwards, W. (1954a). The reliability of probability-preferences. *Amer. J. Psychol.,* **67,** 68–95.

Edwards, W. (1954b). The theory of decision making. *Psychol. Bull.*, **51**, 380–417.

Edwards, W. (1955). The prediction of decisions among bets. *J. exp. Psychol.*, **50**, 201–214.

Edwards, W. (1962). Utility, subjective probability, their interaction, and variance preferences. *J. Conflict Resolution*, **6**, 42–51.

Ellis, Evelyn (1952). Social psychological correlates of upward social mobility among unmarried career women. *Amer. Sociol. Rev.*, **17**, 558–563.

Empey, L. T. (1956). Social class and occupational aspiration: A comparison of absolute and relative measurement. *Amer. Sociol. Rev.*, **21**, 703–709.

Escalona, Sybille K. (1940). The effect of success and failure upon the level of aspiration and behavior in manic-depressive psychoses. *Univer. Ia. Stud. Child Welf.*, **16**, 199–302.

Eysenck, H. J. (1947). *Dimensions of personality*. London: Routledge and Kegan Paul.

Eysenck, H. J. (1952). *The scientific study of personality*. New York: Macmillan.

Eysenck, H. J. (1953). *The structure of human personality*. London: Methuen.

Eysenck, H. J. (1955). A dynamic theory of anxiety and hysteria. *J. ment. Sci.*, **101**, 28–51.

Eysenck, H. J. (1957). *The dynamics of anxiety and hysteria*. London: Routledge and Kegan Paul.

Eysenck, H. J. and Himmelweit, Hilde T. (1946). An experimental study of the reactions of neurotics to experiences of success and failure. *J. gen. Psychol.*, **35**, 59–75.

Farber, I. E. (1954). Anxiety as a drive state. In M. R. Jones (Ed.), *Nebraska symposium on motivation*. Lincoln: University of Nebraska Press, pp. 1–46.

Feather, N. T. (1959a). Subjective probability and decision under uncertainty. *Psychol. Rev.*, **66**, 150–164.

Feather, N. T. (1959b). Success probability and choice behavior. *J. exp. Psychol.*, **58**, 257–266.

Feather, N. T. (1960). Persistence in rela-

tion to achievement motivation, anxiety about failure, and task difficulty. Unpublished doctoral dissertation, University of Michigan.

Feather, N. T. (1961). The relationship of persistence at a task to expectation of success and achievement related motives. *J. abnorm. soc. Psychol.*, **63**, 552–561.

Feather, N. T. (1962). The study of persistence. *Psychol. Bull.*, **59**, 94–115.

Feather, N. T. (1963a). The relationship of expectation of success to reported probability, task structure, and achievement-related motivation. *J. abnorm. soc. Psychol.*, **66**, 231–238.

Feather, N. T. (1963b). Persistence at a difficult task with alternative task of intermediate difficulty. *J. abnorm. soc. Psychol.*, **66**, 604–609.

Feather, N. T. (1963c). The effect of differential failure on expectation of success, reported anxiety, and response uncertainty. *J. Pers.*, **31**, 289–312.

Feather, N. T. (1963d). Mowrer's revised two-factor theory and the motive-expectancy-value model. *Psychol. Rev.*, **70**, 500–515.

Feather, N. T. (1964). Level of aspiration behavior in relation to payoffs and costs following success and failure. *Australian J. Psychol.*, **16**, 175–184.

Feather, N. T. (1965a). The relationship of expectation of success to need achievement and test anxiety. *J. pers. soc. Psychol* **1**, 118–126.

Feather, N. T. (1965b). Performance at a difficult task in relation to initial expectation of success, test anxiety, and need achievement. *J. Pers.*, **33**, 200–217.

Feather, N. T. (1966). Effects of prior success and failure on expectations of success and subsequent performance. *J. pers. soc. Psychol.*, forthcoming.

Feld, Sheila (1959). Studies in the origins of achievement strivings. Unpublished doctoral dissertation, University of Michigan.

Festinger, L. (1942a). Wish, expectation, and group standards as factors influencing the level of aspiration. *J. abnorm. soc. Psychol.*, **37**, 184–200.

Festinger, L. (1942b). A theoretical interpretation of shifts in level of aspiration. *Psychol. Rev.*, **49**, 235–250.

Festinger, L. (1954). A theory of social comparison processes. *Hum. Relat.*, **7**, 117–140.

Festinger, L. (1957). *A theory of cognitive dissonance.* New York: Harper and Row.

Field, W. F. (1951). The effects on thematic apperception of certain experimentally aroused needs. Unpublished doctoral dissertation, University of Maryland.

Filer, R. J. (1952). Frustration, satisfaction, and other factors affecting the attractiveness of goal objects. *J. abnorm. soc. Psychol.*, **47**, 203–212.

French, Elizabeth G. (1955). Some characteristics of achievement motivation. *J. exp. Psychol.*, **50**, 232–236.

French, Elizabeth G. (1956). Motivation as a variable in workpartner selection. *J. abnorm. soc. Psychol.*, **53**, 96–99.

French, Elizabeth G. (1958). Development of a measure of complex motivation. In J. W. Atkinson (Ed.), *Motives in fantasy, action, and society.* Princeton: Van Nostrand, pp. 242–248.

French, Elizabeth G. and Thomas, F. H. (1958). The relation of achievement motivation to problem-solving effectiveness. *J. abnorm. soc. Psychol.*, **56**, 46–48.

French, Elizabeth G. and Lesser, G. S. (1964). Some characteristics of the achievement motive in woman. *J. abnorm. soc. Psychol.*, **68**, 119–128.

Glick, P. C. (1954). Educational attainment and occupational advancement. In *Transactions of the second world congress of sociology.* London: International Sociological Association, pp. 183–193.

Goodnow, Jacqueline J. (1955). Determinants of choice-distribution in two choice situations. *Amer. J. Psychol.*, **68**, 106–117.

Gurin, G., Veroff, J., and Feld, Sheila C. (1960). *Americans view their mental health.* New York: Basic Books.

Haber, R. N. and Alpert, R. (1958). The role of situation and picture cues in projective measurement of the achievement motive. In J. W. Atkinson (Ed.), *Motives in fantasy, action, and society.* Princeton: Van Nostrand, pp. 644–663.

Hartshorne, M., May, M. A., and Maller, J. B. (1929). *Studies in the nature of character: II. Studies in service and self-control.* New York: Macmillan.

Hebb, D. O. (1949). *The organization of behavior.* New York: John Wiley.

Heckhausen, H. (1963). *Hoffnung und Furcht in der Leistungsmotivation.* Verlag Anton Hain: Meisenheim am Glan.

Heckhausen, H. Anatomy of achievement motivation. In B. A. Maher (ed.), *Progress in experimental personality research. Vol. 3.* New York: Academic Press (in press).

Henle, Mary (1944). The influence of valence on substitution. *J. Psychol.*, **17**, 11–19.

Himmelweit, Hilde T. (1947). A comparative study of the level of aspiration of normal and neurotic persons. *Brit. J. Psychol.*, **37**, 41–59.

Hollingshead, A. B. (1949). *Elmtown's youth.* New York: John Wiley.

Hull, C. L. (1943). *Principles of behavior.* New York: Appleton-Century-Crofts.

Humphreys, L. G. (1939a). Acquisition and extinction of verbal expectations in a situation analogous to conditioning. *J. exp. Psychol.*, **25**, 294–301.

Humphreys, L. G. (1939b). The effect of random alternation of reinforcement on the acquisition and extinction of conditioned eyelid reactions. *J. exp. Psychol.*, **25**, 141–158.

Hyman, H. H. (1953). The value systems of different classes: A social psychological contribution to the analysis of stratification. In R. Bendix and S. M. Lipset (Eds.), *Class, status, and power.* New York: The Free Press of Glencoe.

Inkeles, A. (1960). Industrial man: The relation of status to experience, perception, and value. *Amer. J. Sociol.*, **66**, 1–31.

Inkeles, A. and Rossi, P. H. (1956). National comparisons of occupational prestige. *Amer. J. Sociol.*, **61**, 329–339.

Irwin, F. W. (1953). Stated expectations as functions of probability and desirability of outcomes. *J. Pers.*, **21**, 329–334.

Irwin, F. W., and Mintzer, M. G. (1942). Effects of differences in instruction and motivation upon measures of the level of aspiration. *Amer. J. Psychol.*, **55**, 400–406.

Irwin, F. W., Armitt, F. M., and Simon, C. W. (1943). Studies in object-preferences: I. The effect of temporal proximity. *J. exp. Psychol.*, **33**, 64–72.

James, W. H. and Rotter, J. B. (1958). Partial and 100% reinforcement under chance and skill conditions. *J. exp. Psychol.*, **55**, 397–403.

Jarvik, M. E. (1951). Probability learning and a negative recency effect in the serial anticipation of alternative symbols. *J. exp. Psychol.*, **41**, 291–297.

Jenkins, W. O. and Stanley, J. C. (1950). Partial reinforcement: A review and critique. *Psychol. Bull.*, **47**, 193–234.

Kagan, J. and Moss, H. A. (1959). The stability and validity of achievement fantasy. *J. abnorm. soc. Psychol.*, **58**, 357–364.

Kagan, J. and Moss, H. A. (1962). *Birth to maturity: A study in psychological development.* New York: John Wiley.

Kasl, S. V. (1962). Some effects of occupational status on physical and mental health. Unpublished doctoral dissertation, University of Michigan.

Katona, G. (1960). *The powerful consumer.* New York: McGraw-Hill.

Kish, L. (1957). Confidence intervals for clustered samples. *Amer. Sociol. Rev.*, **22**, 154–165.

Kish, L. and Hess, Irene (1959). On variances of ratios and their differences in multi-stage samples. *J. Amer. statist. Ass.*, **54**, 416–446.

Knapp, R. H. (1958). N achievement and aesthetic preference. In J. W. Atkinson (Ed.), *Motives in fantasy, action, and society*. Princeton: Van Nostrand, pp. 367–372.

Kornhauser, A. M. (1939). Analysis of "class structure" of contemporary American society—Psychological bases of class divisions. In G. W. Hartmann and T. M. Newcomb (Eds.), *Industrial conflict.* New York: Dryden.

Kremer, A. H. (1942). The nature of persistence. *Stud. Psychiat. Cath. U. Amer.*, **5**, 1–40.

Lazarus, R. (1961). A substitutive-defensive conception of apperceptive fantasy. In J. Kagan and G. S. Lesser (Eds.), *Contemporary issues in thematic apperceptive methods.* Springfield, Illinois: Charles C. Thomas.

Lenski, G. E. (1954). Status crystallization: A non-vertical dimension of social status. *Amer. Sociol. Rev.*, **19**, 405–413.

Lenski, G. E. (1958). Trends in inter-generational occupational mobility in the United States. *Amer. Sociol. Rev.*, **23**, 514–523.

Lesser, G. S., Krawitz, Rhoda N., and Packard, Rita (1963). Experimental arousal of achievement motivation in adolescent girls. *J. abnorm. soc. Psychol.*, **66**, 59–66.

Lewin, K. (1935). *Dynamic theory of personality.* New York: McGraw-Hill.

Lewin, K. (1943). Defining the "field at a given time." *Psychol. Rev.*, **50**, 292–310.

Lewin, K. (1946). Behavior and development as a function of the total situation. In L. Carmichael (Ed.), *Manual of child psychology.* New York: John Wiley, 1946, pp 791–844.

Lewin, K. (1951). *Field theory in social science.* New York: Harper.

Lewin, K., Dembo, Tamara, Festinger, L., and Sears, Pauline S. (1944). Level of aspiration. In J. McV. Hunt (Ed.), *Personality and the behavior disorders.* New York: Ronald, pp. 333–378.

Lewis, D. J. (1960). Partial reinforcement: A selective review of literature since 1950. *Psychol. Bull.*, **57**, 1–28.

Lewis, D. J. and Duncan, C. P. (1957). Expectation and resistance to extinction of a lever-pulling response as a function of reinforcement and amount of reward. *J. exp. Psychol.*, **54**, 115–120.

Lewis, D. J. and Duncan, C. P. (1958). Expectation and resistance to extinction of a lever-pulling response as a function of percentage of reinforcement and number of acquisition trials. *J. exp. Psychol.*, **55**, 121–128.

Lindquist, E. F. (1953). *Design and analysis of experiments in psychology and education.* Boston: Houghton Mifflin.

Lipset, S. M. and Zetterberg, H. L. (1954). A theory of social mobility. In *Transactions of the second world congress of sociology.* London: International Sociological Association, pp. 155–157.

Lipset, S. M. and Bendix, R. (1959). *Social mobility in industrial society.* Berkeley: University of California Press.

Littig, L. W. (1959). The effect of motivation on probability preferences and subjective probability. Unpublished doctoral dissertation, University of Michigan.

Litwin, G. H. (1958). Motives and expectancy as determinants of preference for degrees of risk. Unpublished honors thesis, University of Michigan.

Lowell, E. L. (1950). A methodological study of projectively measured achievement motivation. Unpublished masters' thesis, Wesleyan University.

MacArthur, R. S. (1955). An experimental investigation of persistence in secondary school boys. *Canad. J. Psychol.*, **9**, 42–54.

MacKinnon, D. W. (1944). The structure of personality. In J. McV. Hunt (Ed.), *Personality and the behavior disorders.* New York: Ronald, pp. 3–48.

McClelland, D. C. (1951). *Personality.* New York: Dryden.

McClelland, D. C. (1955). Some social consequences of achievement motivation. In M. R. Jones (Ed.), *Nebraska symposium on motivation.* Lincoln: University of Nebraska Press, pp. 41–69.

McClelland, D. C. (1958a). Methods of measuring human motivation. In J. W. Atkinson (Ed.), *Motives in fantasy, action, and society.* Princeton: Van Nostrand, pp. 7–42.

McClelland, D. C. (1958b). Risk-taking in children with high and low need for achievement. In J. W. Atkinson (Ed.), *Motives in fantasy, action, and society.* Princeton: Van Nostrand, pp. 306–321.

McClelland, D. C. (1958c). The importance of early learning in the formation of motives. In J. W. Atkinson (Ed.), *Motives in fantasy, action, and society.* Princeton: Van Nostrand, pp. 437–452.

McClelland, D. C. (1958d). The use of measures of human motivation in the study of society. In J. W. Atkinson (Ed.), *Motives in fantasy, action, and society.* Princeton: Van Nostrand, pp. 518–552.

McClelland, D. C. (1961). *The achieving society.* Princeton: Van Nostrand.

McClelland, D. C. and Atkinson, J. W. (1948). The projective expression of needs. I. The effect of different intensities of the hunger drive on perception. *J. Psychol.*, **25**, 205–232.

McClelland, D. C. and Liberman, A. M. (1949). The effect of need for achievement on recognition of need-related words. *J. Pers.*, **18**, 236–251.

McClelland, D. C., Atkinson, J. W., Clark, R. A., and Lowell, E. L. (1953). *The achievement motive.* New York: Appleton-Century-Crofts.

MacCorquodale, K., and Meehl, P. E. (1953). Preliminary suggestions as to formalization of expectancy theory. *Psychol. Rev.*, 1953, **60**, 55–63.

McDougall, W. (1908). *An introduction to social psychology.* London: Methuen.

MacLeod, Catherine M. (1961). The relationship of persistence to motivational and situational factors. Unpublished honors thesis, University of New England.

Mahone, C. H. (1958). Fear of failure and unrealistic vocational aspiration. Unpublished doctoral dissertation, University of Michigan.

Mahone, C. H. (1960). Fear of failure and unrealistic vocational aspiration. *J. abnorm. soc. Psychol.*, **60**, 253–261.

Mandler, G. and Sarason, S. B. (1952). A study of anxiety and learning. *J. abnorm. soc. Psychol.*, **47**, 166–173.

Mandler, G. and Cowen, Judith E. (1958). Test anxiety questionnaires. *J. consult. Psychol.*, **22**, 228–229.

Marks, Rose W. (1951). The effect of probability, desirability, and "privilege" on the stated expectations of children. *J. Pers.*, **19**, 332–351.

Marlowe, D. (1959). Relationships among direct and indirect measures of the achievement motive and overt behavior. *J. consult. Psychol.*, **23**, 329–332.

Martire, J. G. (1956). Relationships between the self concept and differences in strength and generality of achievement motive. *J. Pers.*, **24**, 364–375.

Merbaum, Ann (1960). Need for achievement in Negro and white children. Unpublished masters' dissertation, University of North Carolina.

Merbaum, Ann (1961). Need for achievement in Negro and white children. Unpublished doctoral dissertation, University of North Carolina.

Miller, D. R. (1951). Responses of psychiatric patients to threat of failure. *J. abnorm. soc. Psychol.*, **46**, 378–387.

Miller, D. R. and Swanson, G. E. (1958). *The changing American parent*. New York: John Wiley.

Miller, N. E. (1948). Studies in fear as an acquirable drive. I. Fear as motivation and fear-reduction as reinforcement in the learning of new responses. *J. exp. Psychol.*, **38**, 89–101.

Milstein, Freda A. (1956). Ambition and defense against threat of failure. Unpublished doctoral dissertation, University of Michigan.

Morgan, J. N., Snider, M., and Sobol, Marion (1959). *Redemption settlements and rehabilitation*. Ann Arbor: Institute for Social Research.

Morgan, J. N., David, M. H., Cohen, W. J., and Brazer, H. E. (1962). *Income and welfare in the United States*. New York: McGraw-Hill.

Morgan, J. N. and Sonquist, L. (1963a). Problems in the analysis of survey data—and a proposal. *J. Amer. statist. Ass.*, **58**, 415–434.

Morgan, J. N. and Sonquist, L. (1963b). Some results from a non-symmetrical branching process that looks for interaction effects. *Proceedings of the social statistics section of the American Statistical Association*, 40–53.

Moss, H. A. and Kagan, J. (1961). Stability of achievement and recognition seeking behavior from early childhood through adulthood. *J. abnorm. soc. Psychol.*, **52**, 504–513.

Mosteller, F. and Nogee, P. (1951). An experimental measurement of utility. *J. pol. Econ.*, **54**, 371–404.

Moulton, R. W., Raphelson, A. C., Kristofferson, A. B., and Atkinson, J. W. (1958). The achievement motive and perceptual sensitivity under two conditions of motive arousal. In J. W. Atkinson (Ed.), *Motives in fantasy, action, and society*. Princeton: Van Nostrand, pp. 350–359.

Mowrer, O. H. (1939). A stimulus-response analysis of anxiety and its role as a reinforcing agent. *Psychol. Rev.*, **46**, 553–565.

Mowrer, O. H. (1960a). *Learning theory and behavior*. New York: John Wiley.

Mowrer, O. H. (1960b). *Learning theory and the symbolic processes*. New York: John Wiley.

Murstein, B. I. (1963). The relationships of expectancy of reward to achievement performance on an arithmetic and thematic test. *J. consult. Psychol.*, **27**, 394–399.

Murstein, B. I. and Collier, H. L. (1962). The role of the TAT in the measurement of achievement motivation as a function of expectancy. *J. Project. Techn.*, **26**, 96–101.

Murray, H. A., et al. (1938). *Explorations in personality*. New York: Oxford University Press.

O'Connor, Patricia A. C. (1960). The representation of the motive to avoid failure in thematic apperception. Unpublished doctoral dissertation, University of Michigan.

O'Connor, Patricia A. and Atkinson, John W. (1962). An achievement risk preference scale: A preliminary report. *Amer. Psychol.*, **17**, p. 317 (abstract).

Pavlov, I. P. (1927). *Conditioned reflexes*. London: Oxford University Press.

Peak, Helen (1955). Attitude and motivation. In M. R. Jones (Ed.), *Nebraska symposium on motivation*. Lincoln: University of Nebraska Press, pp. 149–188.

Phares, E. J. (1957). Expectancy changes in skill and chance situations. *J. abnorm. soc. Psychol.*, **54**, 339–342.

Pottharst, Barbara C. (1955). The achievement motive and level of aspiration after experimentally induced success and failure. Unpublished doctoral dissertation, University of Michigan.

Preston, M. G. and Baratta, P. (1948). An experimental study of the auction-value of an uncertain outcome. *Amer. J. Psychol.*, **61**, 183–193.

Ramsey, F. P. (1931). Truth and probability. In F. P. Ramsey, *The foundations of mathematics and other logical essays*. New York: Harcourt, Brace and World.

Raphelson, A. (1956). Imaginative and direct verbal measures of anxiety related to physiological reactions in the competitive achievement situation. Unpublished doctoral dissertation, University of Michigan.

Raphelson, A. (1957). The relationship between imaginative, direct verbal, and physiological measures of anxiety in an achievement situation. *J. abnorm. soc. Psychol.*, **54**, 13–18.

Raynor, J. O. and Smith, C. P. Achievement-related motives and risk taking in games of skill and chance. *J. Pers.*, (forthcoming).

Reitman, W. R. (1957). Motivational induction and the behavioral correlates of the achievement and affiliation motives. Unpublished doctoral dissertation, University of Michigan.

Reitman, W. R. (1960). Motivational induction and the behavior correlates of the achievement and affiliation motives. *J. abnorm. soc. Psychol.* **60**, 8–13.

Rethlingschafer, D. (1942). The relationship of tests of persistence to other measures of continuance of activities. *J. abnorm. soc. psychol.*, **37**, 71–82.

Riesman, D., with Glazer, N. and Denny, R. (1950). *The lonely crowd*. New Haven: Yale University Press.

Ritchie, B. F. (1954). Comments on Professor Atkinson's paper. In M. R. Jones (Ed.), *Nebraska symposium on motivation*. Lincoln: University of Nebraska Press, pp. 116–120.

Rosen, B. C. (1956). The achievement syndrome. *Amer. Sociol. Rev.*, **21**, 203–211.

Rosen, B. C. (1958). The achievement syndrome: A psychocultural dimension of social stratification. In J. W. Atkinson (Ed.), *Motives in fantasy, action, and society*. Princeton: Van Nostrand, pp. 495–508.

Rosen, B. C. (1959). Race, ethnicity, and the achievement syndrome. *Amer. Sociol. Rev.*, **24**, 47–60.

Rotter, J. B. (1954). *Social learning and clinical psychology*. New York: Prentice-Hall.

Rotter, J. B., Fitzgerald, B. J., and Joyce, J. N. (1954). A comparison of some objective measures of expectancy. *J. abnorm. soc. Psychol.*, **49**, 111–114.

Ryans, D. G. (1938). An experimental attempt to analyze persistent behavior: II. Measuring traits presumed to involve persistence. *J. gen. Psychol.*, **19**, 333–353.

Ryans, D. G. (1939). The measurement of persistence: An historical review. *Psychol. Bull.*, **36**, 715–739.

Sarason, I. G. (1961). The effects of anxiety and threat on the solution of a difficult task. *J. abnorm. soc. Psychol.*, **62**, 165–168.

Sarason, I. G. (1963). Test anxiety and intellectual performance. *J. abnorm. soc. Psychol.*, **66**, 73–75.

Sarason, S. B. and Mandler, G. (1952). Some correlates of test anxiety. *J. abnorm. soc. Psychol.*, **47**, 810–817.

Sarason, S. B., Mandler, G., and Craighill, P. G. (1952). The effect of differential instructions on anxiety and learning. *J. abnorm. soc. Psychol.*, **47**, 561–565.

Sarason, S. B., Davidson, K. S., Lightall, F. F., Waite, R. R., and Ruebush, B. K. (1960). *Anxiety in elementary school children*. New York: John Wiley.

Savage, L. J. (1954). *The foundations of statistics*. New York: John Wiley.

Scott, W. A. (1956). The avoidance of threatening material in imaginative behavior. *J. abnorm. soc. Psychol.*, **52**, 338–346.

Sears, Pauline S. (1940). Level of aspiration in academically successful and unsuccessful children. *J. abnorm. soc. Psychol.*, 35, 498–536.

Seeman, M. (1958). Social mobility and administrative behavior. *Amer. Sociol. Rev.*, 23, 633–642.

Siegel, S. (1956). *Nonparametric statistics for the behavioral sciences.* New York: McGraw-Hill.

Siegel, S. (1957). Level of aspiration and decision making. *Psychol. Rev.*, 64, 253–262.

Simpson, R. L. and Simpson, Ida H. (1960). Correlates and estimation of occupational prestige. *Amer. J. Sociol.*, 66, 135–140.

Slovic, P. (1964). Value as a determiner of subjective probability. Unpublished doctoral dissertation, University of Michigan.

Smith, C. P. (1961). Situational determinants of the expression of achievement motivation in thematic apperception. Unpublished doctoral dissertation, University of Michigan.

Smith, C. P. (1963). Achievement-related motives and goal setting under different conditions. *J. Pers.*, 31, 124–140.

Smith, C. P. (1964). Relationships between achievement-related motives and intelligence, performance level, and persistence. *J. abnorm. soc. Psychol.*, 68, 523–532.

Smith, C. P. and Feld, Sheila C. (1958). How to learn the method of content analysis for *n* Achievement, *n* Affiliation, and *n* Power. In J. W. Atkinson (Ed.), *Motives in fantasy, action, and society.* Princeton: Van Nostrand, pp. 685–735.

Smith, M. (1943). An empirical scale of prestige of occupation. *Amer. Sociol. Rev.*, 8, 185–192.

Spence, K. W. (1958). A theory of emotionally based drive (*D*) and its relation to performance in simple learning situations. *Amer. Psychologist*, 13, 131–141.

Spielberger, C. D. (1962). The effects of manifest anxiety on the academic achievement of college students. *Mental Hygiene*, 46, 420–426.

Strodtbeck, F. L. (1958). Family interaction, values, and achievement. In D. C. McClelland (Ed.), *Talent and society.*

Princeton: Van Nostrand, pp. 135–194.

Strodtbeck, F. L., McDonald, Margaret R., and Rosen, B. C. (1957). Evaluation of occupations: A reflection of Jewish and Italian mobility differences. *Amer. Sociol. Rev.*, 22, 546-553.

Sutcliffe, J. P. (1957). A general method of analysis of frequency data for multiple classification designs. *Psychol. Bull.*, 54, 134–137.

Taylor, Janet A. (1956). Drive theory and manifest anxiety. *Psychol. Bull.*, 53, 303–320.

Thomas, F. H. (1956). Visualization, experience, and motivation as related to feedback in problem solving. *Amer. Psychol.*, 11, 444 (abstract).

Thornton, G. R. (1939). A factor analysis of tests designed to measure persistence. *Psychol. Monogr.*, 51 (3 Whole No. 229)

Tolman, E. C. (1932). *Purposive behavior in animals and men.* New York: Appleton-Century-Crofts.

Tolman, E. C. (1955). Principles of performance. *Psychol. Rev.*, 62, 315–326.

Tolman, E. C. and Postman, L. (1954). Learning. *Ann. Rev. Psychol.*, 5, 27–56.

Veroff, J., Atkinson, J. W., Feld, Sheila C., and Gurin, G. (1960). The use of thematic apperception to assess motivation in a nationwide interview study. *Psychol. Monogr.*, 74, 1–32.

Veroff, J., Feld, Sheila, and Gurin, G. (1962). Achievement motivation and religious background. *Amer. Sociol. Rev.*, 27, 205–217.

Vitz, P. (1957). The relation of aspiration to need achievement, fear of failure, incentives, and expectancies. Unpublished honors thesis, University of Michigan.

Von Neuman, J., and Morgenstern, O. (1944). *Theory of games and economic behavior.* Princeton: Princeton University Press.

Warner, W. L. and Lunt, P. S. (1942). *The social life of a modern community.* New Haven: Yale University Press.

Warner, W. L. and Abegglen, J. C. (1955). *Big business leaders in America.* New York: Harper.

Webb, E. (1915). Character and intelligence. *Brit. J. Psychol. Monogr. Suppl.*, No. 3.

Weiner, B. (1963). Effects of unsatisfied achievement-related motivation on persistence and subsequent performance. Unpublished doctoral dissertation, University of Michigan.

Wendt, H. W. (1955). Motivation, effort, and performance. In D. C. McClelland (Ed.), *Studies in Motivation*. New York.

West, J. (1945). *Plainville, U.S.A.* New York: Columbia University Press.

White, R. K. (1951). *Value-analysis: the nature and use of the method*. New York: Society for the Psychological Study of Social Issues.

Whyte, W. H. (1956). *The organization man*. New York: Simon and Schuster.

Winterbottom, Marian R. (1953). The relation of childhood training in independence to achievement motivation. Unpublished doctoral dissertation, University of Michigan.

Winterbottom, Marian R. (1958). The relation of need for achievement to learning experiences in independence and mastery. In J. W. Atkinson (Ed.), *Motives in fantasy, action, and society*. Princeton: Van Nostrand, pp. 453–478.

Wolf, T. H. (1938). The effect of praise and competition on the persistent behavior of kindergarten children. *Inst. Child. Welf. Monogr., U. Minn.*, No. 15.

Worell, L. (1956). The effect of goal value upon expectancy. *J. abnorm. soc. Psychol.*, **53**, 48–53.

Wright, H. F. (1937). The influence of barriers upon strength of motivation. *Duke Univ. Series, Contr. to Psychol. Theory*, **1**, No. 3.

Yerkes, R. M. and Dodson, J. D. (1908). The relation of strength of stimulus to rapidity of habit-formation. *J. comp. and Neurol. Psychol.*, **18**, 459–482.

Zweibelson, I. (1956). Test anxiety and intelligence test performance. *J. consult. Psychol.*, **20**, 479–481.

Name Index

Abegglen, J. C., 186
Adelson, J. B., 186
Alexander, W. P., 53
Allport, G. W., 337
Alpert, R., 169, 172, 182, 261–262, 288, 303, 330, 352–353
Armitt, F. M., 37
Atkinson, J. W., 3–4, 6–8, 11–14, 20, 24, 28, 31, 35–36, 38–39, 45–47, 50–51, 60, 62–65, 69, 71, 75–76, 78, 80, 87, 90, 93–94, 100–101, 103–104, 110, 115, 118–119, 123, 131–132, 137, 143, 145, 147–152, 157, 159, 163, 169–170, 172, 178, 186–187, 189, 194, 199, 202, 206–209, 225, 231–232, 236, 251–253, 255, 258–259, 261–263, 272–273, 275, 277, 279–281, 283, 289, 291, 293–296, 299–300, 302–304, 309–310, 315, 317–318, 323, 327–328, 330–331, 333–334, 336, 338–343, 345, 347–354, 356–357, 360, 362, 365

Baratta, P., 94, 142
Barber, B., 210
Bastian, J. R., 7, 28, 80, 90, 93–94, 115, 148–150, 259, 303, 310, 341–343
Beardslee, D., 34–36, 38, 45
Bendix, R., 185, 187–188, 190–191, 193, 202
Bindra, D., 50
Birch, J. D., 261
Birney, R. C., 77, 278, 353
Bitterman, M. E., 57
Blumenfeld, R., 344
Boulding, K., 6
Brazer, H. E., 213
Broadhurst, P. L., 319

Brody, N., 8, 251, 272–273, 347–348, 354, 359
Brown, J. S., 12, 277
Brown, M. C., 187–188
Brown, R., 75
Burdick, H., 353
Bush, R. R., 39

Campbell, A., 185
Cartwright, D., 32, 145, 331, 365
Cayton, H. M., 185
Centers, R. C., 185, 187, 195
Clark, R. A., 3, 11, 13, 22–24, 38, 63–64, 75–76, 94, 104, 115, 123, 137, 152, 169–170, 172, 186, 208, 232, 236, 252, 263, 277, 279, 283, 293, 299, 303, 309, 350–352, 365
Clarke, A. C., 186
Cochran, W. G., 110, 112
Cohen, I., 88
Cohen, J., 142
Cohen, W. J., 213
Collier, H. L., 352
Conant, J. B., 370
Coombs, C. H., 34–36, 38, 45, 93, 102
Corah, N. L., 88
Counts, G. S., 187
Courts, F. A., 319
Cowen, Judith E., 75, 78, 104, 152, 281, 353
Cox, G., 110, 112
Craighill, P. G., 75–76, 85, 87, 236, 303
Crandall, V. J., 46
Crockett, H. J., 8, 185, 188, 196, 200, 209, 302, 345
Cronbach, L. J., 5, 77, 367
Crowne, D. P., 355
Crutcher, R., 53

Darley, J. G., 179
David, M. H., 213
Davidson, K. S., 232, 236, 341
Davis, Allison, 185
DeCharms, R., 77, 88, 208
Deeg, Martha E., 187
Dembo, Tamara, 4, 6, 15–16, 20, 28, 31–32, 35–39, 45–47, 147, 170, 337, 340, 357
Diggory, J. C., 344
Dinitz, S., 186
Dodson, J. D., 319, 321
Dollard, J., 50
Douvan, Elizabeth M., 165, 186, 209, 278
Drake, St. Clair, 185
Drèze, J. H., 45
Duncan, C. P., 57, 59
Dunnett, C. W., 287, 289
Dynes, R. R., 186

Earl, R. W., 7, 28, 80, 90, 93–94, 115, 148–150, 259, 303, 310, 341–343
Easter, L. V., 352
Edwards, A. L., 77–78
Edwards, W. L., 6, 28, 31, 34, 36, 38, 45, 47, 93, 304, 340
Ellis, Evelyn, 186
Empey, L. T., 190
Escalona, Sybille K., 4, 15–16, 31
Eysenck, H. J., 28, 53–54, 90

Fajans, Sara, 61
Farber, I. E., 277–278
Feather, N. T., 3–4, 6–8, 31–32, 37, 40, 43, 49, 58, 62, 64–65, 68, 71, 117, 131, 135, 137–138, 141–142, 144, 148, 150, 253, 261–263, 267–269, 273, 304, 307, 317, 323, 327, 331, 333–334, 340, 342, 344, 348, 353–356, 358–360, 363–365
Federson, W. E., 57
Feld, Sheila, 8, 94, 167–168, 172, 187, 189, 199, 206, 208–209, 216, 293
Feldman, M. J., 88
Ferguson, L. L., 299
Festinger, L., 4, 6, 15–16, 20, 28, 31–32, 35–39, 45–47, 147, 170, 232, 255, 337, 340, 357
Field, W. F., 278
Filer, R. J., 37–38

Fitzgerald, B. J., 34
French, Elizabeth G., 21, 62–63, 65, 76, 78, 87, 115, 118–119, 131–132, 277–278, 293, 303–304, 315, 331

Gardner, B. B., 185
Gardner, Mary R., 185
Glick, P. C., 195
Goodnow, Jacqueline J., 47
Gruen, W., 88
Gurin, G., 8, 172, 185, 187, 189, 199, 206, 208–209, 216, 293, 317

Haber, R. N., 169, 172, 182, 261–262, 288, 303, 330, 352–353
Halford, G. S., 263
Harberg, E., 191
Hartshorne, M., 51–52
Hebb, D. O., 50
Heckhausen, H., 353
Herdrickson, Lois, 78
Henle, Mary, 62
Hess, Irene, 192
Himmelweit, Hilde T., 28, 90
Hollingshead, A. B., 185
Horner, Matina, 8, 231, 347, 354, 356
Hull, C. L., 50
Humphreys, L. G., 56, 59
Hyman, H. H., 29, 185–186

Inkeles, A., 163, 209
Irwin, F. W., 37, 46
Isaacson, R. L., 302

Jackson, E. F., 191
James, W. H., 58–59, 68, 120, 130
Jarvik, M. E., 252
Jenkins, W. O., 56
Joyce, J. N., 34

Kagan, J., 214
Karabenick, S., 309
Kasl, S., 302
Katona, G., 205
Kellaway, R., 46
Kish, L., 191–192
Knapp, R. H., 283
Kornhauser, A. M., 185

Krawitz, Rhoda N., 21
Kremer, A. H., 53
Kristofferson, A. B., 75

Larkin, W., 123
Lazarus, R., 366
Lenski, G. E., 190–191, 195
Lesser, G. S., 21
Lewin, K., 4, 6, 15–16, 20, 28, 31–33, 35–39, 45–47, 50, 61, 114, 145, 147, 170, 333, 337, 340, 357
Lewis, D. J., 56–57, 59
Liberman, A. M., 169
Lighthall, F. F., 232, 236, 341
Lindquist, E. F., 107–108
Lipset, S. M., 185, 187–188, 190–191, 193, 202
Lissner, Kate, 145
Littig, L. W., 7, 58, 78, 93, 342–343, 353
Litwin, C. Ann, 104
Litwin, G. H., 7, 28, 62, 65, 69, 75, 80, 82, 87, 90, 93–94, 103, 115, 118, 131–132, 143, 148–150, 163, 170, 178, 208, 253, 258–259, 279, 289, 302–305, 309–310, 341–343, 346, 348, 351, 353–354, 356, 360
Lowell, E. L., 3, 11, 13, 24, 38, 63–64, 75–76, 94, 104, 115, 123, 137, 152, 169, 172, 186, 208, 232, 236, 252, 263, 277, 279, 283, 293, 299, 309, 350–352, 365
Lunt, P. S., 185

MacArthur, R. S., 53–54
McClelland, D. C., 3, 5, 11, 13, 22–24, 38, 63–64, 75–78, 81, 88, 94, 104, 115, 123, 137, 148, 152, 169–170, 172, 186, 206, 208, 220, 228, 232, 236, 252, 262–263, 272, 277, 279–280, 283, 288, 293–295, 299, 303, 309, 329, 343, 350–352, 365
MacCorquodale, K., 64
McDonald, Margaret R., 164–165, 187, 209, 346
McDougall, W., 49
MacKinnon, D. W., 50–51
MacLeod, Catherine M., 137
Mahone, C. H., 7, 148, 169, 188, 303, 345

Maller, J. B., 51–52
Mandler, G., 18, 65, 75–76, 78, 85, 87, 94, 104, 152, 169, 182, 236, 262–263, 281, 303, 309, 335, 353
Marks, Rose W., 46
Marlowe, D., 77, 355
Martire, J. G., 89
May, M. A., 51–52
Meadow, A., 88
Meehl, P. E., 64, 77
Merbaum, Ann, 217
Meyer, H., 299
Miller, D. R., 28, 90, 200
Miller, N. E., 50, 335
Milstein, Freda A., 165, 209
Mintzer, M. G., 46
Morgan, J. N., 5, 8, 205, 208, 213, 230, 302, 329, 346, 351, 360
Morgenstern, O., 34
Morrison, H. W., 77, 88, 208
Moss, H. A., 214
Mosteller, F., 39, 93
Moulton, R. W., 5, 7, 75, 147, 337, 340, 345, 349, 354, 356–357
Mowrer, O. H., 335, 363
Murray, H. A., 282
Murstein, B. I., 352

Nogee, P., 93

O'Connor, Patricia, 8, 209, 231, 296, 299–300, 302, 345, 347, 350, 354, 356–357
Ovsiankina, Maria, 145

Packard, Rita, 21
Paterson, D. G., 187
Pavlov, I. P., 54
Peak, Helen, 50
Phares, E. J., 38, 46, 58
Postman, L., 64
Pottharst, Barbara C., 24, 259
Preston, M. G., 94, 142
Pruitt, D. G., 93, 102

Ramsey, F. P., 34
Raphelson, A. C., 23, 75, 89, 119, 279–280, 303, 315
Raynor, J. O., 344

Reitman, W. R., 8, 12, 14, 77, 87–88, 119, 208, 277, 279–280, 283, 295–296, 303, 315, 317–318, 322–323, 334

Rethlingschafer, Dorothy, 53

Ricciuti, H. N., 22–23, 170, 303

Riesman, D., 200

Riley, E. J., 344

Ringwall, E. A., 88

Ritchie, B. F., 277

Rosen, B. C., 164–165, 186–187, 208–209, 216, 225, 346

Rossi, P. H., 163

Rotter, J. B., 6, 12, 28, 31, 33–36, 38, 45, 47, 58–59, 68, 120, 130, 340

Ruebush, B. K., 232, 236, 341

Ryans, D. G., 52–53

Sarason, I. G., 261–264, 271

Sarason, S. B., 18, 65, 75–76, 78, 85, 87, 94, 152, 169, 182, 232, 236, 262–263, 281, 303, 309, 335, 341

Savage, L. J., 34

Scott, W. A., 89

Sears, Pauline S., 4, 6, 15–16, 20, 28, 31–32, 35–39, 45–47, 147, 170, 337, 340, 357

Seashore, C., 88

Seeman, M., 186, 202

Siegel, S., 31

Simon, C. W., 37

Simpson, Ida H., 188

Simpson, R. L., 185, 188–189

Slovic, P., 359

Smith, C. P., 8–9, 94, 123, 277, 282, 289, 303, 315, 317, 319, 322–323, 334, 342–344, 349–350, 352–354

Smith, M., 187

Snider, M., 208

Sobol, Marion, 208

Solomon, D., 46

Sonquist, L., 230

Spence, K. W., 335

Spielberger, C. D., 347

Stanley, J. C., 56

Strodtbeck, F. L., 164–165, 186–187, 209, 346

Sutcliffe, J. P., 42, 127, 140

Swanson, G. E., 200

Taylor, Janet A., 335, 362

Teevan, R. C., 22–23, 170, 303, 353

Thomas, F. H., 62–64, 76, 87, 118, 131–132, 304

Thorton, G. R., 53

Tolman, E. C., 6, 12–13, 31, 33, 36, 38, 47, 49, 64, 340

Tyler, D. W., 57

Veroff, J., 8, 78, 172, 187, 189, 199, 206, 208–209, 216, 293, 317

Vitz, P., 87, 340, 345

Von Neuman, J., 34

Waite, R. R., 232, 236, 341

Warner, W. L., 185–186

Webb, E., 52

Weiner, B., 366

Wendt, H. W., 303

West, J., 185

West, R., 231

White, R. K., 282

Whyte, W. H., 200

Winterbottom, Marian R., 13, 62–63, 164, 167, 214, 225, 236

Wolf, T. H., 61

Worell, L., 46

Wright, H. F., 37

Yerkes, R. M., 319, 321

Zeigarnik, Bluma, 151, 365

Zetterberg, H. L., 190

Zweibelson, I., 182

Subject Index

Ability, and Debilitating Anxiety, 181–182
and Test Anxiety, 271
and vocational aspiration, 169–183
influence on expectation of success, 270–271, 347
influence on performance, 85, 182–183, 270–271
Ability grouping in schools, and expectation of success, 231–232
and reported interest in schoolwork, 244–247, 347
and scholastic performance, 239–244, 347
and theory of achievement motivation, 231–248, 347
Achievement Anxiety Test (AAT), 169, 171–172, 261
Achievement imagery, in different situations, 278, 287–289, 293–294, 350
Achievement motivation, *see* Theory of achievement motivation
Achievement motive (*n* Achievement), 12, 76, 87, 120, 147, 168, 207, 279, 328, 331
and ability grouping in schools, 231–248
and estimated subjective probability of success, 254–259, 261–263, 264–274, 348
and occupational mobility, 192–194, 197–203, 207
and parental background, 23, 164–168, 213–216
and performance, 14, 75, 77, 82–83, 87, 239–244, 262, 272, 279–281, 289–297, 311–313, 320–322, 330, 342, 349

Achievement motive (*n* Achievement), and persistence, 63–64, 77, 82–83, 87, 127, 139–141, 311–313, 320–322, 330, 342
and probability preferences in gambling, 100–102, 341
and reported interest in schoolwork, 244–247
and risk-preference, 22, 77, 82–83, 311–313, 320–322, 330, 341–343
and vocational aspiration, 174–181, 345
assessed by slope index, 114, 166, 208–213, 329, 346
assessed by Test of Insight, 63, 65, 76, 78, 86, 115
assessed by Thematic Apperception Test, 21, 63, 94, 104, 123, 133, 137, 152, 171–172, 189, 208, 252, 263, 277–297, 301, 304, 309, 351–353
assessed by verbal cues, 234–236
assessed in national survey, 189, 199, 202, 208, 213, 317
in females, 21–22
projective versus direct methods of assessment, 77, 86, 88, 208, 324–325, 351
Achievement-oriented personality, 368
Achievement-related situation, definition of ideal situation, 5, 14, 101, 279, 317, 328
Achievement Risk Preference Scale (ARPS), 300–303, 308, 310, 351
and *n* Achievement, 302, 311
and *n* Affiliation, 315–318
and performance, persistence, risk-preference, 313–315, 324
and Test Anxiety, 302, 311

Achievement values (*see also* Incentive values), 38–40, 44–48, 279

Anxiety about failure, conceived as a symptom, 336
 conceived as source of inhibition, 6, 19–20, 333, 335–336

Approach-avoidance conflict, in achievement situations, 328

Assessment of motives, theoretical considerations, 351–353

Attainment attractiveness, 37–38

Attitude towards hard work, 220–230, 346

"Atypical" changes in aspiration, 26–27, 147–159, 337, 340, 345

Autistic biassing of probability estimates, 274

Availability of response, 362–363

Avoidance behavior, in achievement-oriented context, 335–337

Behavior potential, concepts equivalent to, 36

California Achievement Test, 238–239, 241–242

California Test of Mental Maturity, 234, 238

Choice, expressed as a wish, 38, 42, 44, 46–47
 involving commitment, 39–40, 44, 46–47, 273, 342–343

Choice potential, 37, 39, 46

Choice situation, compared with performance and persistence situation, 344

Cluster sampling technique, 191–192

Cognitive dissonance, 255

Confidence ratings, 126, 138, 144–145, 253–259, 347

Conflict in achievement situation, 14–16, 328

Constraining effect, of success probability, 39, 44

Construct validity, 77, 87–88

Debilitating Anxiety, and estimated subjective probability of success, 261
 and vocational aspiration, 174–181

Debilitating Anxiety Scale, 172

Decision-making Test, 303, 305–306, 309, 311–313, 316, 319, 322

Decision theory, 34–36

Defensive biassing of probability estimates, 274

Deviation index, of intermediate risk, 82, 108, 309–310, 356

Difficulty of task (*see also* Expectation of success), and task complexity, 362–363

Disappointment about failure (*see also* Motivational disappointment), 364

Drive, contrasted with motive, 12, 331

Dynamic character of persistence and performance situations, 344

Economic behavior, and theory of achievement motivation, 205–230

Edwards' Personal Preference Schedule (EPPS), 77–78, 85–87, 351

Edwards' SEU model, 34–35

Entrepreneurial behavior, 350

Expectancy, *see* Expectation

"Expectancy × Value" theory, 6, 32–37, 328, 340

Expectation, 12, 147

Expectation of success (P_f) (*see also* Subjective probability of failure), 15–16, 35, 331–333

Expectation of success (P_s) (*see also* Subjective probability of success), 15–16, 35, 328–330
 and ability-grouped classes, 232–233
 and performance level, 20–21, 269, 354–355
 and persistence, 49, 117–133, 135–146
 and task complexity, 362–363
 and verbal ability, 270–271
 concepts equivalent to, 36
 estimated by subjects, 90–91, 106–108, 126, 138, 142, 154, 253, 261, 264, 343, 354–356
 gradient of valence of success, 114, 163–164, 166, 208–213, 328–329
 influenced by motives, 23–24, 46, 103, 112–113, 150, 159, 251–259, 261–275, 345, 347–349, 359–360
 influenced by value of outcome, 46, 273–275, 348

Expectation of success (P_s), methods of varying, 20–22, 41, 78–79, 95, 105–106, 125, 138, 153, 232–233, 263–264, 305–306, 347, 353–356

modified by success and failure, 25–27, 67–68, 120, 129, 142, 144–145, 148–149, 154, 262–263, 269–271, 337, 344, 348, 354, 359–360

Extraversion-introversion, and level of aspiration, 28

Extrinsic incentives, effect on imagery and performance, 278–297

Extrinsic motivation, 27, 66–67, 70, 76, 118–122, 137, 295–297, 315–317, 328, 334–336, 350, 362

Failure, motivational effects of, 25–28, 69, 120–123, 135–137, 148–151, 337

Failure-threatened personality, 369–370

Fear motivation, 363–364

Fixed-incentive model, 356

Gambler's fallacy, 58

Goal-discrepancy score, and vocational aspiration, 176–179

traditional level of aspiration measure, 357–359

Habit, 362, *see* Availability of response

Hierarchy of response tendencies, in avoidance training, 336

Homogeneous versus heterogeneous ability grouping, 231–247

Hope motivation, 363–364

Incentive, 12

Incentive value, of failure (I_f), and expectation of failure (P_f), 15, 16, 148, 316, 331–333

of social approval, and expectation of success, (P_s), 316–318, 342, 350

of success (I_s), and expectation of success (P_s), 15, 16, 102, 147, 316, 328–330, 339

Incentive values, modified by situation (*see also* Achievement values), 360–362

Independence of incentive values and expectations, 32, 36–37, 45–46, 69, 131, 339–340

Independence training, and motive development, 165–168

Inertial tendency (T_{Gi}), 364–366

Interaction of personality and environment, in study of persistence, 62, 65–66, 117, 130, 344

Intermediate risk, definition of, 356–357

Interrelations of performance, persistence, risk-preference, 87, 312

Law of effect, contradiction of, 337–340

Level of aspiration (*see also* Risk-preference), atypical changes in, 26–27, 147–159, 337, 340, 345

change when achievement motive is dominant, 25–26, 148–149

change when anxiety is dominant, 26–27, 148–149

definition of traditional situation, 357

in relation to payoffs and costs, 358–359

realistic and unrealistic, 170 ff.

resultant valence theory, 4, 15–16, 32–33, 147

typical changes in, 25–26, 148–149

Lewinian field theory, 60–62

Motivation, definition of problem of, 11

components of total motivation, 66, 118, 317, 334

conceived as product of motive, expectation, incentive value, 13–14, 279

determined by personality and situation, 4–5, 7, 51, 60, 65, 247, 367

to achieve success, *see* Theory of achievement motivation

to avoid failure, *see* Theory of achievement motivation

Motivational disappointment, 363–364

Motivational relief, 363–364

Motive, 12–13, 279

and early childhood experience, 13, 165–168

as a capacity for satisfaction, 13, 167–168, 279

Motive, as one factor influencing motivation, 64, 118
  contrasted with non-specific drive, 12, 331
  functional properties of, 331
Motive to achieve success, (M_S), *see* Achievement motive
Motive to avoid failure, (M_{AF}), 14–20, 120, 147, 166–168, 331–332, *see also* Test Anxiety
  and child training, 166–168
  and probability preferences, 100
  and slope index, 166

n Achievement, *see also* Achievement motive
  and different testing conditions, 277–297, 350
  correlation with Debilitating Anxiety, 172–173
  correlation with *n* Affiliation, 309, 317
  correlation with Test Anxiety, 86, 89–90, 105, 253, 289, 309, 341
n Affiliation, and *Achievement Risk Preference Scale*, 315–318
  and level of aspiration, 28
  and occupational mobility, 194–195, 200–202, 207, 346
  and performance, 119, 315–324
  and persistence, 315–318, 320–322
  and risk-preference, 315–318, 320–322
  as an extrinsic influence, 314–317
  correlation with *n* Affiliation, 309, 317
  correlation with Test Anxiety, 309
Neuroticism, as autonomic sensitivity, 28
n Power, and occupational mobility, 195–196, 207

Occupational hierarchy, 163, 187–191, 209–213, 345–346
Occupational mobility, 29, 163, 185–203, 346
  and *n* Achievement, 192–194, 197–203, 207
  and *n* Affiliation, 194–195, 200–202, 207, 346
  and *n* Power, 195–196, 207

Occupational mobility, and occupational prestige of fathers, 192–203

Perceptual Reasoning Test, to measure persistence, 123–125, 131, 137–138, 307, 311
Performance, and ability, 85, 182–183, 271
  and expectation of success, 20–21, 269, 354–355
  and intensity of motivation, 322–324, 335, 350–351
  and *n* Achievement, 14, 75, 77, 82–84, 87, 239–244, 262, 279–281, 289–297, 311–313, 320–322, 330, 342, 349
  and *n* Affiliation, 119, 315–324
  and persistence, 87, 344
  and risk-preference, 87, 312
  and Test Anxiety, 75, 77, 83–84, 87, 239–244, 262, 311–313, 320–324, 342
  and theory of achievement motivation, 16–20, 77–87, 233–234, 303, 342
Persistence, and expectation of success, 49, 118, 127–128, 139–141, 269
  and extrinsic motivation, 119–120
  and *n* Achievement, 63–64, 77, 82–84, 87, 127–128, 139–141, 311–313, 320–322, 330, 342
  and *n* Affiliation, 315–318, 320–322
  and risk-preference, 87, 312
  and Test Anxiety, 77, 83–84, 87, 127–128, 139–141, 311–313, 320–322, 342
  and theory of achievement motivation, 66–67, 77–87, 117–133, 135–146, 344
  as a complex problem in decision, 68
  as a distinguishing characteristic of motivated behavior, 49–50
  conceived as a motivational phenomenon, 60–71
  conceived as a trait, 51–55, 70, 130
  conceived as resistance to extinction, 55–60, 71, 130
  effect on later choice, 145
Persistence of unsatisfied tendency, 145, *see also* Inertial tendency
Persistence situation, 49, 117, 130, 135
  different types of, 69–70, 130–132

Prestige hierarchy of occupations, 187–191, 209–213, 345–346

Probability preferences, and *n* Achievement and Test Anxiety, 28–29, 93–102, 341–343

Reinforcement value, concepts equivalent to, 36

Resultant achievement motivation, $(T_s + T_{-f})$, 16–20, 35, 118–119, 304, 333–334, 351
in College and University students, 89–90, 143–144, 342
joint effects with *n* Affiliation, 318–322, 324
modified by success and failure, 25–28, 69, 76, 121–123, 135–137, 147–149, 337

Resultant achievement-oriented tendency $(T_s + T_{-f})$, *see* Resultant achievement motivation

Resultant valence theory of level of aspiration, 4, 15–16, 32–33, 147

Risk-preference (*see also* Level of aspiration), and *n* Achievement, 77, 82–84, 311–313, 320–322, 330, 341–343
and *n* Affiliation, 315–318, 320–322
and performance, 87, 312
and persistence, 87, 312
and Test Anxiety, 77, 83–84, 87, 311–313, 320–322, 342–343
measures of, 79–85, 108–110, 303 ff., 356–357

Risk-taking behavior, *see* Risk-preference

Rotter's social learning theory, 33–34

Salience of achievement incentives, index of, 284–286, 293–294

Selection, effects on resultant achievement motivation, 89–90, 143–144, 342

Skill and chance situations, 29, 38–47, 58–59, 68, 101, 120, 340

Slope index of achievement motive, (M_N), 114, 166, 208–213, 329, 346
and economic behavior, 217–230, 346
and parental background, 213–216
and TAT *n* achievement, 213
related to other factors, 216–217

Slope index of motive to avoid failure (M_{AF}), 166

Social comparison theory, 232

Social desirability, 150, 158–159

Social mobility, *see* Occupational mobility

Strong Vocational Interest Blank (SVIB), 171, 179

Subjective probability of failure (P_f), *see* Expectation of failure

Subjective probability of success, (P_s). *see* Expectation of success

Subjectively expected utility (SEU), concepts equivalent to, 36

Success, motivational effects of, 25–28, 148–151, 337

Success probability, 37, 39, 44

Tendency, definition of, 328
resultant achievement-oriented, *see* Resultant achievement motivation

Tendency to achieve success (T_s), 328–330

Tendency to avoid failure (T_f), 331–333
conceived as a source of inhibition, 6, 19–20, 333, 335–336

Test AL, 271

Test Anxiety, and ability grouping in schools, 231–248
and estimated subjective probability of success, 254–259, 261–263, 264–269, 270, 272, 275, 348
and performance, 75, 77, 83–85, 87, 239–244, 262, 311–313, 320–322, 342
and persistence, 77, 83–84, 87, 127–128, 139–141, 311–313, 320–322, 342
and psychogalvanic index, 23
and reported interest in schoolwork, 244–247
and risk-preference, 77, 83–84, 87, 311–313, 320–322, 343
and verbal ability, 271
and vocational aspiration, 174–181, *see* Debilitating Anxiety
correlation with *n* Achievement, 86, 89–90, 105, 253, 289, 309, 341

Test Anxiety, correlation with *n* Affiliation, 309
  possible paradoxical effect on performance, 323–324, 335
Test Anxiety Questionnaire (TAQ), 7, 18, 23, 65, 75–76, 78, 83, 94, 104, 123, 133, 137, 152, 169, 172, 236, 252, 262–263, 281, 301, 304, 309
Test of Insight, 63, 65, 76–78, 86, 115
Theory of achievement motivation, 5, 14–16, 35–36, 64–65, 76, 118–119, 136, 147–148, 327–341
  and ability grouping in schools, 231–248, 347
  and availability of response, 362–363
  and economic behavior, 205–230, 346
  and estimated subjective probability of success, 251–259, 261–275
  and hope motivation, fear motivation, motivational relief, motivational disappointment, 363–364
  and inertial tendency, (T_{G_i}), 364–366
  and occupational mobility, 29, 163, 185–203, 345–346
  and performance, 16–20, 77–87, 233–234, 303, 342
  and persistence, 66–67, 77–87, 117–133, 135–146, 303–304, 342, 344
  and probability preferences, 28–29, 93–102, 342–343
  and projective assessment of motives, 351–353
  and risk-preference, 16–20, 25–28, 77–87, 103, 108–110, 113–115, 147–159, 303, 342–344
  and sequential decision-making, 251–259, 347–348
  and situational effects on incentive values, 360–362

Theory of achievement motivation, and traditional level of aspiration situation, 357–360
  and vocational aspiration, 169–183, 345
  as a conflict theory, 328
  compared with other "expectancy $\times$ value" theories, 36
Tolman's principles of performance, 13, 33
Typical changes in aspiration, 25–26, 148–149

Unrealistic vocational choice, *see* Vocational aspiration
Utility, 34–35, 328; *see also* Valence
  concepts equivalent to, 36

v Achievement, 88
Valence, as a function of motive and incentive value, 35, 114, 163–164, 208, 273, 328–329, 343, 360
  of success estimated by subjects, 106, 110–112
Variable-incentive model, 356
Variance, and probability, 95, 98–100
Variance preferences, 102
Verbal report, considered as an instrumental act, 348, 355
Vocational aspiration, and *n* Achievement, 174–181, 345
  and Debilitating Anxiety, 174–181
  and theory of achievement motivation, 169–183, 345
  with respect to ability, 173–179
  with respect to interest, 179–180

Yerkes-Dodson Law, 319, 321, 323

Zeigarnik effect, 151, 365